Assessment of Problem Solving Using Simulations

Assessment of Problem Solving Using Simulations

Edited by

Eva Baker
Jan Dickieson
Wallace Wulfeck
Harold F. O'Neil

Lawrence Erlbaum Associates
Taylor & Francis Group

New York   London

Lawrence Erlbaum Associates
Taylor & Francis Group
270 Madison Avenue
New York, NY 10016

Lawrence Erlbaum Associates
Taylor & Francis Group
2 Park Square
Milton Park, Abingdon
Oxon OX14 4RN

© 2008 by Taylor & Francis Group, LLC
Lawrence Erlbaum Associates is an imprint of Taylor & Francis Group, an Informa business

Printed in the United States of America on acid-free paper
10 9 8 7 6 5 4 3 2 1

International Standard Book Number-13: 978-0-8058-6293-5 (Hardcover)

Library of Congress Cataloging-in-Publication Data

Assessment of problem solving using simulations / Eva Baker, Jan Dickieson, Wallace Wulfeck, editors.
   p. cm.
   Includes bibliographical references and index.
   ISBN-13: 978-0-8058-6293-5 (alk. paper)
   ISBN-10: 0-8058-6293-5 (alk. paper)
   1. Educational technology--Evaluation. 2. Computer-assisted
instruction--Evaluation. 3. Problem-solving--Simulation methods. I. Baker, Eva L. II. Dickieson, Jan. III. Wulfeck, Wallace.

LB1028.3.A769 2007
371.26--dc22   2007016038

Visit the Taylor & Francis Web site at
http://www.taylorandfrancis.com

Contents

Preface[*]

If we were asked to predict the future of training and education, we would argue that learning must be complex, instruction should approximate the reality of application, and that effectiveness of the instructional and learning settings must require seamless measurement and adaptation to assure efficiency and ultimate effectiveness in achieving learning goals. In our analysis, our view of the R&D needed for dramatically more effective and economical training and education is supported by three legs: problem-solving tasks expected of the learner, simulation as a major form of instruction and assessment, and assessment of science and technology that will lead to intuitive understanding of learning progress and instructional adaptation. Each of these three design arenas brings a different history. They vary in their research warrants, short-term utility, and seemingly intractable issues. Problem solving is as old as using flint to make tools, and both formal and informal problem solving involve us in workplace, education, and leisure. The conceptions of problem solving have ranged from general critical thinking, to procedural use of the "scientific method" of hypothesis formulation and empirical testing, to newer approaches that model how actual experts approach difficult, multistep, ambiguously constrained

[*] The work reported herein was supported in part by the Office of Naval Research, under Award No. N00014-04-1-0209, Award No. N00014-02-1-0179, and Award No. N00014-06-1-0711, and in part under the Educational Research and Development Centers Program, PR/Award Number Award Number R305A050004, as administered by the Institute of Education Sciences, U.S. Department of Education. The opinions, findings, and conclusions or recommendations expressed in this material are those of the author(s) and do not reflect the views of the Office of Naval Research, or the positions or policies of the National Center for Education Research, the Institute of Education Sciences, or the U.S. Department of Education.

tasks. Simulation connotes task(s) behaviors displayed under realistic conditions. One might think of a dress rehearsal for a drama or even two children playing school or Star Wars for commonplace examples. In training and education, the design of simulation-based problem solving can attempt near-perfect to grossly approximate fidelity.

The authors of this volume focus on problem solving and assessment in technology-based simulations, a heretofore arcane environment, save the relatively recent explosion of myriad environments available on personal computers or game platforms. Now child and adult users of game or practice environments on the Web, and most professionals in education and training, can easily understand the importance of advances in this linked field. In this volume, we blend modern conceptions of complex problem solving, computer-supported simulations, and ways to detect their quality, either through experimental or conceptual analyses.

To develop a balanced approach to the book, as editors, we have assembled a stellar array of research and development professionals who either have specialized in simulation, problem solving, or assessment, or have integrated two or all of the areas in their programs of work. We have also attempted to represent an expanded frame for interpreting the chapters. We have some authors whose use of simulation is experimental and whose main focus is on learning, in contrast to others who address their topics from the real time urgency of practical training to meet particular goals with limited resources.

Underlying the set of chapters are a number of important questions that are partly answered. How should simulations be designed to accomplish different tasks? Are there lessons learned that can be applied to simulation design from experiences in different areas? What are the boundaries of any generalization of design of assessment or simulations? Do the topic, task, trainee, or cognitive explanations of the implementation limit them? Are there general principles that can be inferred from reading these contributions that will help increase the effectiveness or reduce the costs of other instructional interventions? And finally, in what ways do we know simulation-based training of problem solving works against criteria of task performance and considered against competing instructional environments? We believe that the reader will confront alternative views and be able to draw conclusions relevant to instructional settings of particular interest. We also expect more questions to be raised than answered.

This edited book is divided into four major sections. The first is a context that provides the reader background in assessment, problem solving, and simulation. This is followed by two sections on the stakes regarding the assessment of problem solving—low-stakes assessments, where the consequences to the learner are minimal, and high-stakes assessments, where the consequences to the individual are serious and potentially life-threatening. The final section consists of authoring options with software tools to make the creation of simulations and assessments for problem solving either more efficient or more effective, or both.

This book could not have come into existence without the help and encouragement of many people. Our thanks to our LEA editors, Lane Akers and Lori Kelly, for their support and guidance in the publication process. We thank Katharine Fry and Rob Sitter for their excellent assistance in preparing the manuscript.

—Eva L. Baker
CRESST/UCLA
Los Angeles, California

—Jan Dickieson
Naval Health Research Center
San Diego, California

—Wallace H. Wulfeck
Space and Naval Warfare Systems Center
San Diego, California
Office of Naval Research
Arlington, Virginia

—Harold F. O'Neil
University of Southern California/CRESST
Los Angeles, California

1

Simulations and the Transfer of Problem-Solving Knowledge and Skills

EVA L. BAKER, DAVID NIEMI, AND GREGORY K. W. K. CHUNG

CRESST/UCLA

Introduction

It is a general precept of learning theory that knowledge and skills learned in school should apply to new situations in school, everyday life, and specific technical domains. Our focus in this chapter is on the assessment of a set of problem-solving knowledge and skills typically addressed in simulations or other technologically enhanced task settings, and the principal question considered is which conditions enable simulations to be used as a direct measure and as a measure of transfer of problem-solving knowledge and skills. Because the concept of transfer implies that some knowledge has domain-independent properties, we consider several influential perspectives on transfer and what they imply or explicitly state about the domain dependence or independence of knowledge.

Although it is common in the literature on transfer of problem-solving skills to discuss domain-dependent (the target of learning sequences) and domain-independent (the generalization of learning) skills and knowledge as if they were mutually exclusive, in this chapter we consider a more nuanced conceptual continuum intended to inform simulation design for instructional and assessment purposes. After defining problem solving, we review some of the major points along the continuum of positions on transfer and problem solving, from unfettered generalization to highly specific and limited learning, from Thorndike's theories to those of contemporary cognitive scientists. We demonstrate how the design of simulations to assess problem solving can be influenced by these theoretical positions and give examples of the ways assessment design and validation strategies are determined by theoretical commitments made regarding the transfer, generalizability, and domain specificity or independence of knowledge. The chapter concludes with recommendations for simulation design strategies derived from a synthetic view of problem-solving knowledge and transfer.

Review of Transfer of Problem-Solving Knowledge and Skills

We adopt Mayer and Wittrock's definition of problem solving as "cognitive processing directed at achieving a goal when no solution method is obvious to the problem solver" (1996, p. 47); this definition is consistent with many others dating at least to Newell and Simon's seminal work (1972). A useful framework to understand the components of problem solving was specified by O'Neil (1999), who outlined problem solving as composed of domain knowledge, domain-specific problem-solving strategies, and self-regulation. Self-regulation is composed of metacognition (planning and self-checking) and motivation (effort and self-efficacy). A successful problem solver possesses knowledge of the domain, the strategies to manipulate the knowledge, the capability to plan and monitor one's progress toward the solution, and willingness to carry out the actions (effort and self-efficacy). Although O'Neil's framework captures the dimensions of knowledge and cognitive processes involved in problem solving, the conditions that lead to the transfer of such knowledge and cognitive processes from one condition to another condition are not specified.

Although *transfer* is defined somewhat differently by different theorists ranging to Thorndike in the early 1900s, it is commonly understood as the application of knowledge learned in one context to other contexts and tasks. Research over many decades has demonstrated that teaching for transfer, as opposed to training specific skills in specific contexts, leads to greater mastery of larger areas of knowledge and far greater ability to apply knowledge in disparate situations (Bransford & Stein, 1993; Judd, 1908, 1936; National Research Council, 1999). For this reason, transfer is commonly held to be a major goal of education: Students should know how to apply what they learn to a variety of situations in and out of school. As Bruner put it many years ago, "The first object of any act of learning, over and beyond the pleasure it may give, is that it should serve us in the future.

Learning should not only take us somewhere, it should allow us later to go further more easily" (1960, p. 17). "Going further," going beyond the specific information, skills, and contexts that one has learned, is precisely what is involved in transfer.

The question of what kind of knowledge transfers, and under what conditions, is a complex question without a single definitive answer. There are strong advocates for various positions, and researchers have accumulated evidence suggesting that different types of knowledge and skill transfer differently. The major positions on transfer may be seen as running along a continuum from the extreme views that (a) no knowledge can transfer to other situations, to (b) all knowledge can transfer to other situations. We are not aware of any advocates of the first position because learning would not be possible under that view. As individuals move through time and space, they never encounter situations that are identical in every respect to previous situations, so knowledge and skills could not persist in time unless they could be transferred to *some* new and different situations. As Mayer and Wittrock (1996) wrote, "Transfer is a pervasive characteristic of human cognition: New learning always depends on previous learning, new problem solving is always influenced by prior problem solutions" (p. 49). Likewise, there are few, if any, known advocates of the second position because experiments have shown that many kinds of knowledge do not seem to transfer beyond the specific types of problems, situations, or domains in which they were learned. Some theorists have in fact concluded that only domain-specific knowledge can transfer, and then only within the original domain. To evaluate this claim, it will be necessary to arrive at a precise understanding of *domain* because that term has carried disparate meanings for different theorists. Our first step, however, is to review some of the best-known and most influential views on transfer and the domain independence of knowledge; in the course of this discussion, we review the assumptions about the domain independence of knowledge that are implicit in each. Subsequently, we describe types of simulations that exemplify different positions taken with respect to the transfer and domain independence or specificity of knowledge and examine how simulations can be developed to assess various kinds of transfer.

The three major positions on transfer that we examine are general transfer of general skills across subject areas, domain-dependent transfer, and transfer of domain-independent principles and strategies within subject areas. One of the most interesting points that emerges from a review of these "landmark" views of transfer is that they actually deal with different kinds of knowledge and in some cases imply divergent and radically incompatible views of what knowledge is.

General Transfer Across Subject Areas

In the early 1900s educators and others believed that certain so-called formal disciplines, such as Latin and geometry, could strengthen general mental faculties. The idea has certain natural logic to it, based on an analogy between mental and physical development: If one builds larger muscles, then those muscles can be helpful in a large range of tasks. Researchers have found it difficult, however, to demonstrate that formal disciplines have this kind of effect. In fact, Thorndike (1906; Thorndike & Woodworth, 1901) undertook a series of studies to show that they did not, finding, for example, that studying Latin and geometry had little effect on general intellectual abilities that might apply in other subject areas. Mastery of one subject seemed to affect performance in another subject only when the two were similar, as in the case of arithmetic and book-keeping. Latin proficiency, however, does not improve bookkeeping. The effects of studying formal disciplines or other courses were not, according to Thorndike, a function of the intellectual "muscles" they developed, but "the special information, habits, interests, attitudes, and ideals which they demonstrably produce" (1924, p. 98).

Thorndike's studies of formal disciplines have been taken by some as the death knell for general transfer, but his outcomes were limited to those claimed by the advocates of formal disciplines, and the fact that these claims did not hold up cannot be taken as definitive evidence that knowledge and skills cannot transfer across problem-solving domains or even across subject areas. Russian psychologists, for example, studied the general effects of schooling on intellectual development and proposed that formal schooling mediated the development of logical reasoning capabilities that transferred across logical problem-solving tasks and domains (cf. Van der Veer & Valsiner, 1993; Vygotsky, 1962).

Domain-Specific Transfer

According to Mayer (2003), "Specific transfer means that elements in A are identical to B" (p. 20), where A and B are problems or tasks. This view is often associated with Thorndike, who came to believe that transfer across task domains would only occur if there were elements in common between the two domains. Anticipating cognitive scientists such as Minsky (1986), Thorndike wrote that "The mind is a host of highly particularized and independent abilities" (1906, p. 39), and, "One mental function or activity improves others in so far as and because they are in part identical with it, because it contains elements common to them" (1906, p. 243).

Thorndike's views, however, raise the question of what it means to say that problem elements are identical. What is an element, for one thing?

Is an element a feature of the physical representation of a problem, such as the kind of words or graphics used to exhibit the problem? Or, is it some kind of mental state that is evoked by a problem? For Thorndike, it is clear, elements of problem solving were purely behavioral, and he conducted a series of studies demonstrating that minute learned behaviors, such as typing a particular letter on a typewriter, do not transfer to other problem or task domains that do not require the same behaviors (Thorndike & Woodworth, 1901).

Thorndike and Woodworth (1901) further showed that learning to estimate short lengths did not improve the ability to estimate longer lengths, and it could then be inferred, after the fact, that these tasks do not have any common elements. They also found that training on estimating rectangles could improve the ability to estimate the areas of other rectangles, circles, and triangles, but the improvement was less for the nonrectangular figures. In this case, they hypothesized that the nonrectangular figures had some common and some dissimilar elements.

The research literature in educational psychology beginning with Thorndike offers many examples not only of specific transfer but also of a related kind of transfer, *vertical transfer*, which refers to the transfer of simple skills, such as single-digit addition, to more complex skills, such as multidigit addition. The idea of vertical transfer underlies the behavioral objectives approach to curriculum development (e.g., Popham & Husek, 1969) and the decomposition of skills in behavioral task analysis (Jonassen, Tessmer, & Hannum, 1999). Domain-specific theories of knowledge also motivate the analyses of knowledge domains into highly specified task types for assessment purposes, as in the work of Hively, Patterson, and Page (1968), discussed further in the section on models of test design and use.

Transfer of Principles and Strategies

As Mayer argued, if Thorndike's views are rigorously applied to education, then "the only way to teach for transfer is to know in advance every transfer problem the student would encounter and to teach the behaviors needed to solve those problems. In short, if all transfer is specific, then preparing students for completely novel problems is impossible" (2003, p. 22). In the long run, students will need to be able to solve problems that have not been posed to them by their teachers. If teachers only teach the behaviors needed to solve known problems, then this hardly qualifies as teaching for transfer to novel problems in the future. It is now well established, however, that concepts, principles, and strategies can be transferred to novel problems if instruction follows certain research-based guidelines. As Mayer (2004) and many others have observed, efforts to teach general problem-solving skills have been less than successful, and in fact people often find it difficult to retrieve any relevant prior knowledge in problem-solving situations (Bransford, Vye, Kinzer, & Risco, 1990). But, under the right conditions, concepts, principles, and problem strategies can transfer across problem types, and this fact is critical in understanding the development of domain expertise.

Historically, education researchers such as Brownell (1945) and Judd (1908), and Gestalt psychologists including Katona (1940) and Wertheimer (1959) were among the first to show that students can learn to understand principles and strategies that can then be applied to a variety of novel problems and situations. Singley and Anderson (1989) later developed a theory of skills overlap in transfer based on studies such as one of secretaries who were skilled typists learning three different text-editing programs. Their theory is reminiscent of Thorndike's "identical elements" theory, except that for Thorndike an element is an observable behavior such as stating or writing an addition fact or finding words with the letters "a" and "e" in a text passage, whereas for Singley and Anderson the relevant elements of problem solving are cognitive, such as representing goals and subgoals.

There are many other examples, collected over decades, of the transfer of abstract principles across task domains and of the value of instruction in improving the transfer of abstract concepts and principles (e.g., Kornilaki & Nunes, 2005; Mayer, 2003; National Research Council, 1999). It has been found, for example, that learning and problem-solving strategies can be successfully transferred if students are taught to focus on self-evaluation or metacognition (Koriat & Bork, 2006; Moreno & Mayer, 2005; Palincsar & Brown, 1984; Pressley & Brainerd; 1985), the conditions for applying strategies (Gick & Holyoak, 1983; Judd, 1908, 1936; Kilpatrick, 1992), or building principled representations of problem situations (Fuchs, Fuchs, Finelli, Courey, & Hamlett, 2004; Kilpatrick, Swafford, & Findell, 2001). Another powerful strategy for transfer is studying worked-out examples as a way to build problem schemas (Chi & Bassok, 1989; Pawley, Ayres, Cooper, & Sweller, 2005).

An additional form of evidence confirming the transfer of general principles in problem-solving situations derives from studies conducted under the expert-novice paradigm. What these studies make clear is that, for experts, conceptual understanding drives problem solving (e.g., Chi, Glaser, & Rees, 1982; Mayer, 2003; National Research Council, 1999). In the search phase of problem solving (as originally defined by Newell and Simon in 1972), when the problem solver is trying to activate knowledge that might apply or transfer to the problem at hand, experts typically develop representations of problems based on abstract concepts or principles, and these representations then activate domain-specific problem-solving procedures and strategies. Novices, on the other hand, typically represent problems in terms of immediate "surface" features (e.g., there is an inclined plane in the problem) and have difficulty finding valid solution strategies based on these representations. As a result of their ability to activate general principles across a broad range of problems, experts' problem solving is far more powerful and accurate than that of novices.

Summary

In this section, we reviewed major views on what transfers and the conditions under which transfer occurs. The literature suggests that the transfer of general problem-solving processes in the context of a particular domain is the most robust finding. In the next section, we use this finding as a point of departure to describe how simulations can be used to assess problem solving.

Using Simulations to Assess Transfer of Problem-Solving Skills

Simulations

As an assessment platform, simulations are attractive because they can provide the technical means to (a) create a range of task scenarios for students, from well-defined problems with one correct answer to open-ended problems with multiple solutions, all within the same setting; (b) require students to reason while demonstrating their understanding of the content; and (c) respond dynamically to students' interactions with the simulation (Baker & O'Neil, 2002). In addition, computer-based tasks have the capability to embed behavioral measures of students' interactions with the simulator, presumably indexed to the learner's cognitive processing. How students learn about and interact with the simulated system — the information students use, decisions they make, parameters they vary — serve as indicators of students' use of learning and problem-solving strategies.

The assumption that transfer of problem-solving processes is most likely to occur in the context of a particular domain poses a challenge for the design of simulations. On the one hand, a highly domain-independent approach (in its extreme case) is virtually context free, such as many critical thinking tasks that encourage the user to apply general precepts of logic. The abstractness of the task does not bind it to a particular context or require particular content knowledge. On the other hand, a highly domain-specific design can result in tasks that are highly contextualized, accurate, and of high fidelity. The task is tuned for a specific purpose and use but is unlikely to be reusable for other purposes. The challenge for simulation design is how to design tasks that can tap students' use of known cognitive processes that have some generalization potential while also making the task highly relevant to a particular domain. The synthetic view of transfer, which we adopt, bridges domain-independent and domain-dependent designs by first identifying the characteristics that are more generalizable or domain independent underlying successful problem solving and then instantiating these characteristics and processes in the context of a particular domain. In assessment design, the challenging step is embedding general principles and cognitive processes into actual simulation tasks, activities, and conditions.

Examples of Using Simulations to Measure Problem Solving

In this section, we provide concrete examples of how processes, driven in the ideal case by domain-independent principles and strategies, could be incorporated into assessments of content and measured in a subject matter context. We draw from our existing work, in which strong process-tracing methods were used and linked to outcome performance. Table 1.1 presents an abstraction of task properties and cognitive processes across the exemplar studies. We specify five variables that we believe modulate the complexity of task: type of simulation (dynamic or static); whether the simulation has an ill-defined or well-defined solution; the degree of relevant prior knowledge the learner has at the start of the task; the degree of domain-specific information sources in the task that would help the learner solve the task; and the degree to which the problem is identified.

Table 1.1 Sample of Task and Cognitive Processing Variables

Sample of simulation task features
- Simulation type
- Solution type
- Learner's domain-specific knowledge
- Amount of domain-specific information sources available in the task that would help identify or solve the problem
- Degree of explicitness about what the problem is

Sample of domain-independent cognitive processes related to simulation task features
- Accurately discriminate between more and less important variables and information sources in the simulation
- Draw accurate inferences about the variable states and relations among variables in the simulation
- Learn and comprehend specialized information that directly bears on understanding the variables and relations in the simulation
- Accurately evaluate solution adequacy against specified criteria or actual solution criteria
- Monitor progress to solution

The task properties were adopted from the work of Baker and O'Neil (2002), and a more detailed description can be found in the work of Chung et al. (in press). Table 1.1 also lists the types of cognitive processes that underlie many problem-solving situations. For example, an important cognitive process that differentiates high from low problem-solving performance is the differentiation between more and less important information. The processes in Table 1.1 are consistent with O'Neil's (1999) framework but narrower in scope.

In the following section, we examine three studies that have available process and outcome data. The domains of all studies were different, but the task designs were similar in type of simulation (all static), and all studies were explicit about what the problem was. Our analyses suggest that features of the tasks are related to particular cognitive demands, and these processes can be identified and measured. Further, the task structure—the type of problem participants are expected to solve, the type and amount of information about the state of the simulation, and the availability of domain-specific (instructional) information during the task—appears to influence the cognitive demands of participants. These assertions need to be verified empirically; if borne out, then the linkage between particular cognitive demands and task features can be encoded in an ontology.

In the first study, Chung, de Vries, Cheak, Stevens, and Bewley (2002) investigated the cognitive processes underlying a task in which participants were given an online task for which the problem was to help a fictitious friend determine who her "true" parents were from a list of five sets of parents. Participants could request various medical tests (e.g., blood type) that would eliminate one or more sets of parents. A library was available that described each test and how to interpret the results. Distracter information in the form of "expert" opinions was provided. Participants' think-aloud data were yoked to their clickstream data; thus, rich process data were available to complement performance data.

Regarding task features, the task used in the Chung et al. (2002) study had a well-defined solution (a single correct answer), used students with low prior knowledge of the domain, and provided students access to domain-specific content such that students could learn about the domain as part of using the simulation. With respect to cognitive processes, successful participants (a) focused on the results of the simulation test results rather than the nondata opinions and hearsay available in the expert distracters; (b) drew accurate inferences about the meaning of the test results (which parents the test result eliminated); (c) accessed the library to learn about unfamiliar medical tests; and (d) kept track of which parents were eliminated, which parents were untested, and which tests led to ambiguous results.

In the second study, Chung and Baker (2003) investigated whether the "generate-and-test" problem-solving strategy could be modeled from participants' interaction with a novel user interface. Participants were required to modify a bicycle pump design to meet certain performance constraints and had available to them information about the various states of variables (e.g., volume under the cylinder). Simulation information available to the participant were values of the various pump variables.

As for task features, the task used in the Chung and Baker (2003) study had a well-defined solution (a single correct answer) and used students with low prior knowledge of the domain but did not provide students with supplementary domain-specific content. Thus, students did not have access to content that they could use to learn about bicycle pumps. With respect to cognitive processes, successful participants (a) tended to access only the information needed to solve the problem rather than view all information for all pump parameters and (b) converged to a solution (i.e., specified valid values for the pump parameters) faster than less-successful participants. In addition, participants could in general access the values of the pump parameters to judge when the solution was adequate, and participants received feedback on whether their attempted solution was correct. After incorrect solution attempts, participants tended to examine pump parameters and adjust their pump design, suggesting they were reevaluating the adequacy of their design. Finally, participants' clickstreams suggested they used the generate-and-test strategy, implying monitoring and consideration of solution results to revise their solution.

In the third study, by Schacter, Herl, Chung, Dennis, and O'Neil (1999), participants were required to construct a knowledge map on environmental science. Participants had available (a) feedback on the quality of their maps in the form of concepts needing improvement and (b) a simulated Web site that they could search or browse for more information about the different concepts. Participants' search and browsing behaviors, use of feedback, and knowledge map scores were recorded.

With respect to task features, the task used in the Schacter et al. (1999) study had an ill-defined solution (multiple correct answers), used students with a range of prior knowledge of the domain, and provided students with material that they could use to learn about the domain. Thus, students could learn about environmental science concepts as they engaged in the simulation. As for cognitive processes, successful participants (a) engaged in browsing Web pages that were highly relevant to the concepts students were concept mapping; (b) engaged in browsing and key word searching of Web pages that were relevant to the concepts they were expected to map; (c) presumably browsed and searched as a result of their access to the feedback about the quality of their maps; and (d) requested feedback about the quality of their maps.

Toward the Assessment of Problem-Solving Transfer Using Simulations

Models of Test Design and Use

We showed how problem solving could be measured and how domain-independent processes could be used to describe simulation tasks. In this section, we first describe important assessment considerations and then describe potential ways of measuring problem-solving transfer.

An important point is the relation of the assessment design to its purpose and actual use. Much of psychometrics has been developed using the mechanics associated with the normal distribution, with the explicit goal of comparing individuals to one another. This approach is best considered for purposes of selection for which the construct measured (e.g., ability) is thought to be stable, and the task of interest is choosing the best or highest-ranking individuals. The norm-referenced approach has been contrasted with criterion-referenced assessment, an approach that focuses on getting students to reach a target that presumably represents a known level of proficiency within a domain of interest. In criterion-referenced assessment, the implication is that instruction as well as student background variables have an impact on test scores. The assessments are designed to detect the effects of instruction. That is, there should be clear differences among groups of different ability levels when instruction is provided. One theoretical implication of criterion-referenced testing is that the trainee group could move from positions of nonproficiency (assuming a random distribution) to a position at which all students met the proficiency standard.

An additional assumption of criterion- or domain-referenced assessment is that the set of tasks represents a stratified sample of important attributes desired in the posttraining or on-the-job context (Hively et al., 1968). Thus, the problem of task comparability must be addressed, both by qualitative analysis of task and content attributes (and required prior knowledge) and by empirical item characteristics.

Finally, a related topic of importance is the way criterion levels of proficiency are commonly set. It is our position that obtaining opinions of skilled persons, using a procedure such as the modified Angoff approach (Angoff, 1971; Brandon, 2004), is only the beginning. We also argue from a validity perspective that expert performance on the task should be used to set progressive criterion points.

Assessment of Transfer

A synthetic view of transfer assumes that transfer of general principles and problem-solving strategies best occurs in the context of a specific domain. Thus, developing assessments of problem-solving transfer would involve first specifying the domain-independent cognitive processing of interest and then creating tasks in the context of the domain of interest that evoke the domain-independent processes in a particular situation. Presumably, domain-independent processes are generally robust and invariant. If the assessment tasks are designed to evoke invariant processes from participants, then performance on one task should generalize to performance on other tasks that evoke the same processes.

The utility of simulations for the assessment of problem-solving transfer is that simulations can be used to create a test bed to assess performance across a variety of tasks that require the same problem-solving processes for success while differing on other variables. Simulations could be designed to target specific cognitive demands by constraining or expanding the simulation tasks, and transfer could be tested by varying the domain. In a sense, this has already been done for the system described by Chung et al. (2002). Stevens and colleagues have developed many simulations with similar task features, such as requiring the use of an elimination strategy (e.g., Stevens & Casillas, 2006; Vendlinski & Stevens, 2002). This situation also reflects the Web-based searching system described by Schacter et al. (1999). Subsequent work has used the same basic shell but varied type of feedback and added a collaborative dimension to the work (Chuang & O'Neil, 2006; Hsieh & O'Neil, 2002).

Computational Supports for the Design of Assessment of Problem-Solving Transfer

To support the efficient generation of assessment tasks, it is important to conduct an analysis of the relations among the cognitive demands of the task, simulation properties, and how these variables affect each other. Such an analysis would be guided by empirical evidence (e.g., prior research), expert judgment (e.g., experienced subject matter expert) or logical analyses (e.g., hypothesized influences). In effect, this analysis lays out the domain-independent relations of the problem-solving task (Baker, Chung, & Delacruz, in press) in the context of a specific domain.

As a practical matter, it is advantageous to capture the result of this analysis into a representation that is capable of encoding the richness of the structure such as an ontology (Chandrasekaran, Josephson, & Benjamins, 1999; Gruber, 1995; McGuinness, 2003). Such a representation could serve as a design model (e.g., Baker, 1997, 2002; Baker, Aschbacher, Niemi, & Sato, 2005; Mislevy & Riconscente, 2006). In this approach, domain-specific tasks are designed as an instantiation of the domain-independent relations represented in the ontology. For example, if the purpose of the assessment is to gather information on participants' competency at evaluating and monitoring their progress toward the solution, then the simulation would have a solution that is open ended. Similarly, if the purpose of the assessment is to gather information on participants' reasoning processes, then the simulation would make available to participants information of various quality that the participant needs to solve the problem.

Summary and Discussion

We reviewed major views of transfer and described how transfer of problem solving could be assessed with simulations. Based on the literature describing conditions for the transfer of general principles and strategies, an important assessment implication is that the identification of the general principles and strategies is foundational. These abstractions drive the design of the particular problems, situations, and activities that are embedded in the simulation.

It is important to note that the design features not only serve as technical requirements for simulation design but also serve to encapsulate the empirical base of what is known about learning and problem solving. The choice of which set of cognitive processes, skills, and other domain-independent variables to include in the simulation is guided in part by requirements specific to an application and in part by scientific base. The benefit of this design approach is that tasks embed features that are likely to evoke from respondents the critical processes of interest and the processes likely to be sensitive to different levels of knowledge, skill, and expertise while also omitting less-important and irrelevant features. As illustrated by the examples from our prior work, even simple simulations can deliver tasks with high cognitive fidelity.

A second important point is that the approach we have outlined directly attends to the structure of the domain itself, inclusive of content and performance, and in doing so highlights the opportunities for transfer. The explicit specification in an ontology of the important concepts and their relations to content, performance, and task features provides a principled referent structure. The ontology provides a road map that can be used to specify the content and performance boundaries of the assessment design. In the context of simulations, the existence of a machine-readable referent structure suggests the tantalizing possibility of delivering simulation tasks that can be easily modulated based on principled design.

As we move toward developing simulation-based assessments of problem-solving transfer, an important first step is to identify the capabilities of simulations that can be leveraged to advance assessment capabilities. We have argued that one of the most compelling aspects of simulation-based assessments is its potential to establish direct links among task features, to-be-learned content, problem-solving processes, and performance. Future work should be directed at empirically validating our approach.

Acknowledgment

The work reported here was supported under Office of Naval Research Award N00014-02-1-0179, as administered by the Office of Naval Research, and under the Educational Research and Development Centers Program, PR/Award R305B960002, as administered by the Office of Educational Research and Improvement, U.S. Department of Education. The findings and opinions expressed in this report do not necessarily reflect the positions or policies of the Office of Naval Research or the U.S. Department of Education. We would also like to thank Joanne Michiuye of UCLA/ CRESST for review and editorial help with the manuscript.

References

Angoff, W. H. (1971). Scales, norms, and equivalent scores. In R. L. Thorndike (Ed.), *Educational measurement* (2nd ed., pp. 508–600). Washington, DC: American Council on Education.

Baker, E. L. (1997). Model-based performance assessment. *Theory Into Practice, 36*, 247–254.

Baker, E. L. (2002). Design of automated authoring systems for tests. In National Research Council, Board on Testing and Assessment, Center for Education, Division of Behavioral and Social Sciences and Education (Eds.), *Technology and assessment: Thinking ahead: Proceedings from a workshop* (pp. 79–89). Washington, DC: National Academy Press.

Baker, E. L., Aschbacher, P. R., Niemi, D., & Sato, E. (2005). *CRESST performance assessment models: Assessing content area explanation* (CSE Tech. Rep. No. 652). Los Angeles: University of California, National Center for Research on Evaluation, Standards, and Student Testing (CRESST).

Baker, E. L., Chung, G. K. W. K., & Delacruz, G. C. (in press). Design and validation of technology-based performance assessments. In J. M. Spector, M. D. Merrill, J. J. G. van Merriënboer, & M. P. Driscoll (Eds.), *Handbook of research on educational communications and technology* (3rd ed.). Mahwah, NJ: Erlbaum.

Baker, E. L., & O'Neil, H. F. (2002). Measuring problem solving in computer environments: Current and future states. *Computers in Human Behavior, 18*, 609–622.

Brandon, P. R. (2004). Conclusions about frequently studied modified Angoff standard-setting topics. *Applied Measurement in Education, 71*, 59–88.

Bransford, J. D., & Stein, B. S. (1993). *The ideal problem solver* (2nd ed.). New York: Freeman.

Bransford J. D., Vye, N., Kinzer, C., & Risco, V. (1990). Teaching thinking and content knowledge: Toward an integrated approach. In B. F. Jones & L. Idol (Eds.), *Dimensions of thinking and cognitive instruction* (pp. 381–413). Hillsdale, NJ: Erlbaum.

Brownell, W. A. (1945). When is arithmetic meaningful? *Journal of Educational Research, 23,* 481–498.

Bruner, J. (1960). *The process of education.* Cambridge, MA: Harvard University Press.

Chandrasekaran, R., Josephson, J. R., & Benjamins, V. R. (1999). What are ontologies, and why do we need them? *IEEE Intelligent Systems, 14,* 20–26.

Chi, M. T. H., & Bassok, M. (1989). Learning from examples via self-explanations. In L. B. Resnick (Ed.), *Knowing, learning, and instruction* (pp. 251–282). Hillsdale, NJ: Erlbaum.

Chi, M. T. H., Glaser, R., & Rees, E. (1982). Expertise in problem solving. In R. Sternberg (Ed.), *Advances in the psychology of human intelligence* (Vol. 1, pp. 7–75). Hillsdale, NJ: Erlbaum.

Chuang, S.-H., & O'Neil, H. F. (2006). *Role of task-specific adapted feedback on a computer-based collaborative problem-solving task* (CSE Tech. Rep. No. 684). Los Angeles: University of California, National Center for Research on Evaluation, Standards, and Student Testing (CRESST).

Chung, G. K. W. K., & Baker, E. L. (2003). An exploratory study to examine the feasibility of measuring problem-solving processes using a click-through interface. *Journal of Technology, Learning, and Assessment, 2*(2). Retrieved July 5, 2005 from http://jtla.org

Chung, G. K. W. K., Baker, E. L., Delacruz, G. C., Bewley, W. L., Elmore, J., & Seely, B. (2008). A computational approach to authoring problem-solving assessments. In E. L. Baker, J. Dickieson, W. Wulfeck, & H. F. O'Neil (Eds.), *Assessment of problem solving using simulations* (pp. 289–307). Mahwah, NJ: Erlbaum.

Chung, G. K. W. K., de Vries, L. F., Cheak, A. M., Stevens, R. H., & Bewley, W. L. (2002). Cognitive process validation of an online problem solving assessment. *Computers in Human Behavior, 18,* 669–684.

Fuchs, L. S., Fuchs, D., Finelli, R., Courey, S. J., & Hamlett, C. L. (2004). Expanding schema-based transfer instruction to help third-graders solve real-life mathematical problems. *American Educational Research Journal, 41,* 419–445.

Gick, M. L., & Holyoak, K. J. (1983). Schema induction and analogical transfer. *Cognitive Psychology, 15,* 1–38.

Gruber, T. R. (1995). Toward principles for the design of ontologies used for knowledge sharing. *International Journal of Human-Computer Studies, 43,* 907–928.

Hively, W., Patterson, H. L., & Page, S. H. (1968). A "universe defined" system of arithmetic achievement tests. *Journal of Educational Measurement, 5,* 275–290.

Hsieh, I. G., & O'Neil, H. F. (2002). Types of feedback in a computer-based collaborative problem-solving task. *Computers in Human Behavior, 18,* 699–715.

Jonassen, D. H., Tessmer, M., & Hannum, W. H. (Eds.). (1999). *Task analysis methods for instructional design.* Mahwah, NJ: Erlbaum.

Judd, C. H. (1908). The relation of special training to general intelligence. *Educational Review, 38,* 28–42.

Judd, C. H. (1936). *Education as the cultivation of higher mental processes.* New York: McMillan.

Katona, G. (1940). *Organizing and memorizing.* New York: Columbia University Press.

Kilpatrick, J. (1992). A history of research in mathematics education. In D. A. Grouws (Ed.), *Handbook of research in mathematics education* (pp. 3–38). New York: Macmillan.

Kilpatrick, J., Swafford, J., & Findell, B. (2001). *Adding it up: Helping children learn mathematics.* Washington, DC: National Academy Press.

Koriat, A., & Bork, R. A. (2006). Mending metacognitive illusions: A comparison of mnemonic-based and theory-based procedures. *Journal of Experimental Psychology: Learning, Memory, and Cognition, 32,* 1133–1145.

Kornilaki, E., & Nunes, T. (2005). Generalising principles in spite of procedural differences: Children's understanding of division. *Cognitive Development, 20,* 388–406.

Mayer, R. E. (2003). *Learning and instruction.* Upper Saddle River, NJ: Merrill Prentice-Hall.

Mayer, R. E. (2004). Teaching of subject matter. *Annual Review of Psychology, 55,* 715–744.

Mayer, R. E., & Wittrock, M. C. (1996). Problem-solving transfer. In D. C. Berliner, & R. C. Calfee (Eds.), *Handbook of educational psychology* (pp. 47–62). New York: Simon and Schuster Macmillan.

McGuinness, D. L. (2003). Ontologies come of age. In D. Fensel, J. Hendler, H. Lieberman, & W. Wahlster (Eds.), *The semantic web: Why, what, and how* (pp. 171–191). Cambridge, MA: MIT Press.

Minsky, M. (1986). *The society of mind.* New York: Simon and Schuster.

Mislevy, R. J., & Riconscente, M. M. (2006). Evidence-centered assessment design: Layers, concepts, and terminology. In S. Downing & T. Haladyna (Eds.), *Handbook of test development* (pp. 61–90). Mahwah, NJ: Erlbaum.

Moreno, R., & Mayer, R. E. (2005). Role of reflection, guidance, and interactivity in an agent-based multimedia game. *Journal of Educational Psychology, 97,* 117–128.

National Research Council. (1999). *How people learn.* Washington, DC: National Academy Press.

Newell, A., & Simon, H. A. (1972). *Human problem solving.* Englewood Cliffs, NJ: Prentice-Hall.

O'Neil, H. F. (1999). Perspectives on computer-based performance assessment of problem solving. *Computers in Human Behavior, 15,* 255–268.

Palincsar, A. S., & Brown, A. L. (1984). Reciprocal teaching of comprehension-fostering and comprehension-monitoring activities. *Cognition and Instruction, 1,* 117–175.

Pawley, D., Ayres, P., Cooper, M., & Sweller, J. (2005). Translating words into equations: A cognitive load theory approach. *Educational Psychology, 25,* 75–97.

Popham, W. J., & Husek, T. R. (1969). Implications for criterion-referenced measurement. *Journal of Educational Measurement, 6,* 1–9.

Pressley, M., & Brainerd, C. J. (Eds.). (1985). *Cognitive learning and memory in children: Progress in cognitive development research.* New York: Springer-Verlag.

Schacter, J., Herl, H. E., Chung, G. K. W. K., Dennis, R. A., & O'Neil, H. F., Jr. (1999). Computer-based performance assessments: A solution to the narrow measurement and reporting of problem-solving. *Computers in Human Behavior, 15,* 403–418.

Singley, M. K., & Anderson, J. R. (1989). *Transfer of cognitive skill.* Cambridge, MA: Harvard University Press.

Stevens, R. H., & Casillas, A. (2006). Artificial neural networks. In D. M. Williamson, I. I. Behar, & R. J. Mislevy (Eds.), *Automated scoring of complex tasks in computer-based testing* (pp. 259–312). Mahwah, NJ: Erlbaum.

Thorndike, E. L. (1906). *The principles of teaching based on psychology.* Syracuse, NY: Mason-Henry Press.

Thorndike, E. L., & Woodworth, R. S. (1901). The influence of improvement in one mental function upon the efficiency of other functions. *Psychological Review, 8,* 247–261.

Thorndike, E. L. (1924). *Educational psychology: Briefer course.* New York: Teachers College, Columbia University.

Van der Veer, R., & Valsiner, J. (1993). *Understanding Vygotsky: A quest for synthesis.* Cambridge, MA: Blackwell.

Vendlinski, T., & Stevens, R. (2002). Assessing student problem-solving skills with complex computer-based tasks. *Journal of Technology, Learning, and Assessment, 1*(3). Retrieved on July 5, 2005 from http://www.jtla.org

Vygotsky, L. S. (1962). *Thought and language.* Cambridge, MA: MIT Press.

Wertheimer, M. (1959). *Productive thinking* (enlarged ed.). New York: Harper & Row.

2

Assessment to Steer the Course of Learning

Dither in Testing

ALAN LESGOLD

University of Pittsburgh

This chapter focuses on measuring a specific problem-solving capability: the ability to solve novel or emergent problems in a domain for which one has acquired expertise. This capability is especially important in the information age because routine problem solving increasingly can be done by computer systems, leaving dealing with the novel and the emergent as a special province of human capability. As is discussed here, measuring the ability to stretch one's knowledge to handle the novel is a task that has not received sufficient attention in the past. Indeed, a broad concern for fairness in schooling and school-related testing often has made tasks featuring novelty problematic because no single task is exactly as novel for every possible student who might be tested: One person's novelty is the next person's routine.

The approach I suggest is one that focuses more on assessing performance over a wide range of problems rather than selecting problems because they have specific characteristics. Indeed, I suggest that variance in problem characteristics, even uncontrolled variance, may be part of a successful strategy for measuring the ability to solve emergent and novel problems. In taking this approach, I appeal to a physical engineering approach called dither.

Many physical systems, especially control systems, benefit from the introduction of a small amount of noise, called *dither*, into feedback signals. This noise overcomes resting inertia and can decrease certain kinds of distortion. Below, I suggest that "quick-and-dirty" use of microassessment opportunities embedded in instruction can be much more effective in guiding the course of learning than increased use of standardized tests. The noise inherent in imperfect reliability of such microtesting, rather than appearing as a problem for assessment, may turn out to be a benefit for the guiding of effective learning and training. If the goal is usable, rather than inert, knowledge, then this dither may remove the distortion created when only "school stuff" is tested. Further, there are at least a few approaches to assessment emerging that may make it possible to induce accountability data from such microtesting, thus eliminating some of the need for stressful "high-stakes" testing. A dithering approach would be possible if cooperative item banks for teachers became available and contained appropriate indexing by curricular goal and by experiential background for each item.

Introduction

A jokester once remarked that if President Kennedy had dealt with going to the moon the way we deal with education, then he would have called for the building of a giant telescope so that if anyone got to the moon, we would know about it immediately; landings on the far side would, of course, be disclaimed because they could not be seen through the telescope. In many respects, our national policy on education — and much of training policy — has been focused on instructional telescopy rather than learning progress. We invest heavily in developing high-stakes tests that are fair, reliable, and valid.

Students and their teachers undergo great stress when they take these tests, and because the number of stakeholders who can insist on accountability is large, stressful high-stakes testing is consuming a progressively greater part of the total available learning time. Further, evidence is emerging that the impact of test-related stresses is not uniform, that minority students are differentially affected (cf. Steele, & Aronson, 1995). It is not clear either that the focus on high-stakes testing once a year (or less) is a good strategy for educational improvement or that our current approaches to fairness and reliability are achieving their goals. In this chapter, I suggest a possible alternative approach.

Quite a while ago (Lesgold, 1987), I suggested that the course of instruction, like the steering of a car, is best shaped by regular feedback in small amounts, and that the individual instances of this feedback need not be individually perfect to be effective. I compared the guiding of instruction to the steering of a car and noted that we do not wait to have a perfect sense of the car's heading and speed before we move the steering wheel to keep the car on the road. In this chapter, I develop this idea further, note that the imperfections in microtesting data may be a virtue rather than a problem, and suggest that we may be able to develop schemes for using the patterning of microtests as an alternative for some of our high-stakes testing. If this were possible, then I suggest that it also would produce more valid assessments, in some important respects, as well as more effective steering of the course of instruction.

Dither in Physical Control Systems

To make this case, it is necessary first to consider the positive role of noise in physical control systems and other physical situations. When engineers began to develop systems to facilitate and later to guide the control of moving devices, they discovered the importance of dither, the introduction of a small amount of noise to a feedback or control signal. Initially, this dither was introduced to overcome the effects of static versus moving friction. Objects like the rudder on a ship tend to "stick" in their current position. A small amount of continual movement prevents that sticking and thus makes steering more responsive. Today, dither is routinely engineered into steering systems, especially when those systems are operated by autopilot devices. Further, even when steering a car, movement is smoother when there is a little bit of continual motion of the steering wheel, which is a normal characteristic of steering by humans, who are neither perfect in their perception nor perfectly and continually attentive. Compare expert driving to the behavior of novice drivers, and one important difference is that novices' steering motions are less frequent but more extreme, resulting in more erratic vehicle movement. In short, reacting more regularly to less-precise guiding data results in more efficient progress.

The concept of dither arises also in the design of audio systems (cf. Gammaitoni, 1995; Vanderkooy & Lipshitz, 1987), for which, paradoxically, adding dither decreases distortion. This seems strange, but the idea is readily demonstrated. Hold a hand in an open position with fingers spread apart in front of your face. You will be able to see parts of the scene beyond your hand but parts will be obscured by the structural interference of your fingers. On the other hand, if you move your hand back and forth an inch or so, you actually increase your ability to see clearly what is beyond, even though parts of the image that were clear before now are sometimes obscured. In audio systems, structural interference from such sources as digitization is attenuated by random noise.

Another example is an antilock braking system. Many people, when they use the brakes on a car, press at maximal strength. So, their signal to the brake system has only two levels: on or off. But, the brakes work best when an intermediate amount of pressure — just short of what would lock the brakes — is applied. This can be approximated by having an automatic system turn the brakes on and off at high speed when the brakes are applied and they are locking. The noise from the antilocking braking system has the effect of making the signal from the driver more precise.

We can take these metaphors and use them to reconsider the nature of assessment in the course of instruction. The first order of business in doing this is to consider how distortion creeps into tests.

Distortion in Testing

There are several sources of distortion in testing (cf. American Educational Research Association, American Psychological Association, National Council on Measurement in Education, 1999). First, there are language style differences between the test writer and the test taker. These differences can result in the test underestimating student competence. In the worst case, for example, a student who speaks only Spanish will underperform on a mathematics test that is given in English even if he knows the relevant mathematics. Although this case seems extreme, a famous court case considered situations like this, involving both language and culture differences between test developers and test takers that led to understatement of the competence of the test takers and their inappropriate classification as mentally impaired (*Larry P. v. Riles*, 1984).

In fact, it is this second source of distortion, cultural differences, that is one primary concern. If two students have identical competence in, say, mathematics but come from different experiential backgrounds, it is quite possible still for one to perform better on a test of mathematics than the other simply by having problems on the test that refer to situations that are familiar to one student but not the other. Because test makers desire that their tests be fair, there is a natural tendency for tests to limit problems to a modest set of situations that are likely to be familiar to all students. On the surface, this seems like a reasonable approach.

However, consider the distortion that such an approach can generate. Rather than measuring the ability to use mathematical knowledge in everyday life, tests that are rendered fair by this "lowest common denominator" become tests only of "school math" because school situations are the one kind that are common to all students in our increasingly multicultural society. Put slightly differently, the attempt to be fair can turn a test of mathematical knowledge into a test of that part of mathematical knowledge most likely to be "inert" by Whitehead's (1929) estimation.

Cultural bias often is hard to spot because anyone looking for such bias will himself be immersed more in some cultures than others. For this reason, such bias is checked for statistically using a technique called differential item function analysis (cf. Cole, 1993; Zenisky, Hambleton, & Robin, 2003). Differential item function analyses look for the possibility that a test item that is highly correlated with overall performance for one group of test takers might be uncorrelated or even negatively correlated with overall scores for another group. Another way of thinking about this approach to fairness is that we traditionally call a test culturally fair if the relative order of difficulty of its items is the same for any two cultural groups who may take the test.

Although this approach is defensible, the practical consequences of such analyses is to limit the range of situations about which test items will be posed, especially in high-stakes general tests of subject matter achievement. The problem is less likely to arise when developing a test of mathematics for carpenters, for example. For that test, it makes perfect sense to design all items to require that the student apply mathematics to situations that arise in the practice of carpentry. One could have some items test applications to simple situations and other items requiring a further stretch to situations that are complex but still within the scope of carpentry; all items would be appropriate and fair for students immersed in carpentry.

When the same approach is taken in school mathematics, though, the situation is more difficult. With almost no experiences outside school itself that are common across all the cultures that make up the modern American student body, the natural tendency is to have all problems refer to school situations. But, this is exactly the path that leads to knowledge inertness. In any given area of familiarity, we acquire competences that are a mixture of fundamental, transferable knowledge and "tricks of the trade" that capture the special characteristics of the familiar domain. So, for example, Carraher, Carraher, and Schliemann (1985) noted that children who work in the streets as numbers runners (practitioners of lotteries that are not government sanctioned) can do the arithmetic needed to calculate the payoffs on complex bets but cannot do the same arithmetic when it is posed in school problems because they spend most of their time on the street and not much in school. For these children, the artifacts of the numbers business provide scaffolding just as fingers do in the initial development of counting skill. In contrast, we would expect a suburban child in this country to be able to do some mathematics in school settings that the child cannot apply to the numbers racket.

In fact, the world of school knowledge is just another culture, distinguished by its commonality to most children and distinctly different from everyday life. School math, for example, has tricks of the trade that afford the opportunity to perform better than one's broadly usable mathematical knowledge might permit. Every child knows — often from being told this by a teacher — that in math word problems, you should consider adding two numbers given in the problem if the word *altogether* appears as part of the problem text (e.g., "Mary has two apples, and John has four. How many do they have altogether?"). With such knowledge, a word problem meant to measure the ability to apply addition simply becomes a standard addition problem, with the word *altogether* replacing the plus (+) sign.

Restricting test items to the domain of school activity, then, is a distortion. It selectively filters out information about the ability to transfer or apply school-taught knowledge to everyday life. Of course, a culturally unfair test also has distortions to the extent that a test taker cannot understand the statement of problems because of cultural deprivation. So, for example, it would be unfair to load a test with items requiring the application of mathematics to rituals of the Catholic church if some but not all of the test takers are Catholic or to load a test with vocabulary only heard in specific African American subcultures if some test takers have neither heard those words before nor had the experiences to which they refer. The standard approach to test bias, then, removes distortions caused by cultural difference and adds distortions that mask the ability to apply school knowledge outside school.

This may be one source of a commonly seen phenomenon in which a school system shows strong performance of its students on mathematics tests in early grades and then lower performance in higher grades (cf. National Center for Educational Statistics, 1999). Conceivably, what is filtered out by the testing strategy is information about the ability to build on the simpler skills taught in the early grades. If overlearning school skills is all that is needed to be able to progress in the curriculum, then there should be no problem. On the other hand, the ability to see mathematical relationships in less-familiar situations may be a separate component of mathematics learning ability, one selectively distorted and undermeasured by current approaches to fair testing. Robust ability to use simple mathematics may be the foundation for learning more complex mathematics.

A similar situation may arise in industrial and military settings in which highly focused mastery tests are given. Mastery curricula, when they involve small units of instruction that are immediately tested but not tested further as the curriculum progresses, easily can create the impression that students have learned more transferable skills than actually is the case. My own experience in working with electronics technicians in the military, for example, showed that students who had demonstrated "perfect mastery" of curriculum on how individual electronic components function often were completely unable to understand the role of those components in even relatively simple circuits. This was contrary to training doctrine but real in terms of working competence. For example, technicians who had passed mastery tests on components such as diodes could not explain what those diodes might be doing in a circuit (some thought they were fuses because circuits failed when diodes burned out). All they really had mastered was a verbal definition and perhaps a simplistic scenario to which the verbiage applied (Gott, Lesgold, & Kane, 1997).

The distortions that are engineered into current tests by the approaches now taken to fairness seem, then, to produce predictable biases. Specifically, they overestimate the ability to use the knowledge tested in new situations, and they may underestimate the ability to use the knowledge tested in familiar situations that effectively scaffold that knowledge. We next consider the potential use of dither in testing to overcome these distortions.

Dither for Steering the Course of Learning

Standardized tests are designed to minimize noise, that is, to maximize reliability. One way this is done is to eliminate the noise that comes from imperfect scoring. Prior to the rise of psychometrics, testing tended to involve students writing essay responses to open-ended questions. In knowledge domains involving formalisms, test responses might also include diagrams, equations, and mathematical derivations. Homework still operates this way to some extent, and the dictum "show your work" remains in the arsenal of many a good teacher.

To a traditional psychometrician this creates potential unreliability. Different teachers may interpret the imperfect writings of students differently, and particularly divergent thinking may be over- or underappreciated. But, if one could identify an explicit "answer" that is undeniably the correct one, then a test in which students have to pick the correct answer from among alternatives will no longer have the unreliability that comes from open-ended responses and human judgment. Thus, the multiple-choice test has become a mainstay of testing, especially high-stakes testing.

A related issue here is cost. The more reliable one wants human judgment of open-ended responses to be, the more expensive the scoring process becomes. Judges must be trained, tight evaluation rubrics must be developed, and continual checking is required to ensure that judges adhere to standard scoring procedures. Comparing tests such as Advanced Placement and a few professional licensing examinations to mass-administered standardized tests, one sees an order of magnitude difference in the cost of high reliability in constructed-response testing.

Most efforts to improve the validity of testing have focused on reducing the costs associated with the scoring of constructed responses because it often appears that constructing a response exercises somewhat different knowledge than picking a correct answer to a question. Choosing among stated answers seems to involve more recognition and intuitive levels of analysis, and constructed responses can directly exhibit the quality and completeness of reasoning. We have made considerable progress in developing more efficient constructed-response testing, as is illustrated by a number of the chapters in this volume. However, it just may be possible that preserving a bit of the noise in constructed response testing could actually be a positive achievement.

To examine this possibility, we need to consider the different sources of noise. First, there is scoring noise. This comes from imperfections in student communication of what they are thinking, from miscomprehension by the scorer of student responses, and from inattentiveness by the scorer. Another source of noise arises in item construction. Because free-response items need not be as precise, instructors may occasionally ask questions that require more knowledge than is within the scope of a course. Often, the culprit is the knowledge that mediates between a socially shared body of situational knowledge and the specific course content. Or, there may be an inference to be drawn between two knowledge elements that are in the curriculum, in which the inference is not explicitly within the curriculum. We need to consider each of these possibilities.

Student Communication Failures

Is it sufficient to know things but not to be able to talk clearly about them? Generally, it is not. Consequently, when a student receives a lower score because of the inability to talk about something that the student learned, this may actually be revealing an incompleteness in student knowledge. A multiple-choice test might allow such a student to demonstrate general understanding of the knowledge element in question, but such knowledge may well remain "inert" (Whitehead, 1929). In contrast, when a student can successfully convey knowledge through a constructed response, it is more likely that the student can use the knowledge, at least in the domain in which that knowledge must be applied for the item in question.

The problem then is scoring reliability. Increasingly, scoring rubrics have been used in ways that substantially reduce scoring reliability problems. Moreover, as long as a number of different scorers are involved in scoring the various items administered to a given student, reliability issues should be reasonably well controlled. If scoring reliability is the primary barrier to using more open-ended responses, then a combination of multiple scorers, different forms of scoring rubrics, and some use of intelligent machine scoring of constructed responses should eliminate reliability problems.

Transfer Failures

The more significant problems — and the more interesting opportunities — involve issues of transfer from the limited domain of the classroom to the various situations of real life. Again, if the intent is to measure whether a body of knowledge has been acquired, independent of whether it is inert, then traditional approaches to fairness and validity are fine, although they may overestimate learning because many traditional items afford the possibility that everyday school knowledge may scaffold performance, as when the word *altogether* signals addition.

If we want to know whether knowledge has been acquired that is not inert, then we face a more complex problem. In the modern classroom, one may find almost as many patterns of experiential difference as there are students. Thus, it will not be easy to assess which contexts for applying knowledge represent greater or lesser transfer challenges for which students. There are two basic ways to deal with this uncertainty. For many purposes, the simpler approach, randomly choosing contexts of application from a pool, can work very well. This is the case especially when overall accountability of a school or classroom is the issue. The alternative approach, which may be possible given improved cognitive modeling tools, is to assess the relative familiarity of each of a collection of domains to a given student and then systematically to build test items for domains selected to present varying levels of transfer challenge for that student. I consider each of these two alternatives in turn.

For both approaches, I must make an assumption that the realization of the scheme I propose would require the existence of a domain generalization utility, a centralized source of domain content for test items for key components generally found in the curricula of school systems. Such a utility might be maintained by a state, by a school district, by the federal government, or by multiple private agencies. As long as testing within a district used the same utility consistently from year to year, progress in school improvement should be easy to detect. Current programs such as the National Assessment of Educational Progress (NAEP) could establish the likely validity of whichever utility a given state chose to use. Individual district choices would require expansion of NAEP to include individual school — or at least district — performance indicators in its reports. The processes that might be followed in using such a utility are discussed in more detail next.

The *random selection option* assumes a significant number of test items administered over the course of a year. What would be needed is a large pool of experiential domains, each represented with some degree of fullness. Test items would then be generated by randomly selecting a domain and then building a test item anchored in that domain. For some subjects, such as basic mathematics, it should be possible to do this relatively automatically because both the mathematical knowledge to be tested and the domain representations can be formalized reasonably well.

For other subjects, this will be much more complex. One possibility is slowly to accumulate a pool of items for each domain over time. In this scheme, whenever a test item was requested from a domain generalization utility, if an appropriate item were available, then it would be provided. If not, then the requester would be given detailed instructions on how to develop an appropriate item, and that item would then be uploaded into the utility for use by others. If requesters were permitted also to rate items they used, then this scheme would automatically accumulate a socially moderated set of items for each of the experiential domains it covered.

Part of any item in this scheme would need to be a scoring protocol. In some cases, this could be simple. In most cases, however, a scoring protocol would need to include some sort of rubric for evaluating the open-ended response of the test taker. Rubrics can range from specific properties that should be present in a response to the item to comparison templates for analogue schemes such as latent semantic analysis, which is a process for comparing the relative proximity of different terms in one written document to those in a standard document. Latent semantic analysis has proven its validity as an approach to machine scoring of essays (Landauer, Foltz, & Laham, 1998). Now that the major testing services have substantial experience with use of rubrics by large groups of scorers on tests such as the College Board Advanced Placement program, it should be quite manageable to handle scoring this way.

One likely requirement of this bootstrapping approach to randomized choices of experiential domains as test item backgrounds will be some sort of moderation of the developing item bank. Not every teacher will be able to produce uniformly reliable scoring rubrics for items, and indeed not every teacher will be able to generate items that have the properties attributed to them. A professional moderation team would prove useful both in culling inadequate items from the accumulating pool and in adding items when teachers seem to be having trouble generating appropriate items and scoring rubrics.

Given sufficient use of a pool of items across a wide-ranging pool of test-taker backgrounds, it should be possible to validate experiential domains using scaling approaches: Items referring to a particular range of life experiences should cluster if scaled according to the extent to which they are consistently given correctly or incorrectly by a given pool of students. That is, two items can be considered empirically from the same domain if the same students get the two items correct. Further, once a set of items has been validated both through sociological analysis and through this empirical approach, then differential item function analysis (Cole, 1993; Zenisky et al., 2003) can be used to determine whether a given item in the set really "fits."

An alternative possibility, although one not yet easy to realize, would be to develop *screening approaches* that establish the range of domains with which a given student is familiar. The idea would be to screen students for their experiences in a number of different domains. This could be done using a combination of self-assessment and testing approaches. Students might be asked to rate their familiarity with each of a variety of experiential domains. Assuming that they know what they have experienced, this should give pretty reasonable results. Moreover, it should not be difficult to conduct sociogrammetric studies to validate students' selections. For example, if two students select the same domains as part of their experiences, then they should share a number of common friends who also have experience in those domains; it is difficult to befriend someone with whom one shares no experiences.

This alternative approach of basing item selection on some level of screening of the test taker's experiential background may be a bit difficult to develop, but there are no apparent barriers to building such a system, although it is not obvious that such screening would be preferable to self-assessment as discussed above. In a screening approach, an accumulating library of defined experiential domains might include, for each domain, a screening test to provide information about the test taker's familiarity with the domain.

Given some sort of self-assessment or other screening, there should be, for each student tested, a list of experiential domains on which some sort of triage has been applied to sort the domains into the completely unfamiliar, the mostly unfamiliar, the partly familiar, and the familiar (to that student). A test could then be constructed by randomly choosing some number of domains from each triage group and using each as the background for a test item. This would produce information relevant to the issue of how robust the knowledge tested is in terms of its utility to the student in domains of varying levels of familiarity.

The Basic Microtesting Scheme

Given these ideas, we can now consider how an overall testing system might work. In such a system, rather than having a simple yes/no answer to whether a student has mastered a particular curricular goal, there would be something more like a zone of mastery defined by performance on items involving demonstrating the target knowledge in domains of varying degrees of familiarity. This zone of mastery might be treated more or less like Vygotsky's (1930, 1933, 1935/1978) zone of proximal development. A student who could demonstrate the target knowledge only in the domain of school stuff would be characterized as having fragile command of the knowledge; a student who could demonstrate the target knowledge in both familiar and unfamiliar domains would be characterized as having robust command. For at least some key curricular goals that are foundation components for later learning, robust command would be the ultimate target.

This is an interesting variation on the original uses of Vygotsky's ideas. Vygotsky wanted to establish that some students could learn well, but only if they were not stretched too far beyond what they already knew. Indeed, the zone of proximal development can be seen as an alternative way of defining intelligence. On the other hand, the present proposal is to use a similar approach to assess the zone of proximal development but to think of it as an index of learnable knowledge robustness rather than enduring aptitude. Some of the work done on dynamic testing (Elliott, 2003; Sternberg, 2005) comes close to this in spirit, and it is likely that the dither strategy, if it proves useful, will come to incorporate ideas from dynamic testing.

Teachers administering test items developed to assess the scope of mastery using a dynamic strategy would be guided by small quizzes from day to day. From those quizzes, they could accumulate a picture of the student's competence and metacompetence. Some students, for example, might be behind in acquiring content even at the traditional school stuff level. They would need extra assistance in catching up with their peers. Other students might be on track as far as school stuff goes but not readily able to apply what they learn to outside situations. These students might be candidates for metacognitive training focused specifically on how to apply school knowledge in novel situations.

Although it has yet to be tested, there is an obvious prediction from this kind of scheme. Students who demonstrate mastery at the school stuff level but who do not show the ability to apply what has been learned to novel situations are likely candidates for exhibiting a drop in performance in later grades. This is because the knowledge they already have acquired may not be robust enough to anchor additional learning. On the other hand, students who are only a little bit behind normative curricular goals but who display robust learning of what they have learned should be more likely to stay on track as they move on to later grades.

Validity and the View From the Teacher Level

For this kind of scheme to work for both the steering of instruction and accountability, there will be a need for some calibration of teacher-selected and teacher-produced items against some sort of normative scale. As we know, it is not easy to make such calibrations if they are to meet all of the usual psychometric requirements (cf. Feuer, Holland, Green, Bertenthal, & Hemphill, 1999). On the other hand, if tests are systematically forcing instruction to focus only on school stuff and school systems are finding repeatedly that although they look okay in earlier grades they fail to achieve curricular goals in later grades, then they lack a certain form of validity ipso facto. This suggests that we might usefully explore ways of partly calibrating the microtests given by individual teachers, even if this calibration never can be done perfectly.

There are two basic approaches that can be taken. The easier would be to continue administering the annual high-stakes tests and then to provide feedback to teachers about the agreement between the high-stakes results and what would be predicted for each child given the microtests administered throughout the year. This would be possible only if test items were in fact developed through and stored in a test item utility as suggested in this chapter. Although such a scheme would be new for teachers, it could be made worthwhile if enough service were provided along with it.

For example, the utility might offer the teacher a flexible grade book that allowed both performance on the individual microtest items to be recorded as well as other grades. Grades might even be averaged automatically as a service for the teacher. And, of course, the utility would be a helpful source of test items in the first place. In an ideal world, textbook manufacturers might offer these test item utilities just as they already offer homework environments for individual students and already accumulate records of students' homework performance.[1]

Especially important would be the analyses that are possible when both the microtest and the accountability test results are simultaneously available. Consider the possibilities. In an ideal situation, students' microtest scores would predict their accountability test scores. But, there is much to be learned from the other possible outcomes. For example, if school domain mastery on the microtests is highly related to accountability test results but robustness data do not account for any additional accountability test variance, then we might worry that the accountability test is not assessing knowledge robustness.

If a class's microtest results correlate well with the accountability results but an individual child does poorly on the accountability test but decently on the microtests, then perhaps we can make some hypotheses about that child. If the child showed robustness in learning from day to day, then the low accountability test performance might be because of test anxiety or "test-taking skill" problems. On the other hand, if the child scored well on direct school stuff measures during the year but did not demonstrate

---

[1] Currently, homework utilities are widely used at the college level. Their usage at the pre-college level is limited by the lack of universal computer and networking support for teachers, but that shortfall is beginning to disappear.

knowledge robustness, then the need might be for stronger metacognitive skill development. Overall, for the teacher, the microtests would guide day-to-day instruction, and the accountability test would provide broader guidance on general issues in the child's learning and performance.

The View from the Accountability Level

From the accountability level, microtesting data should, over time, become a primary management tool. As items become better calibrated, there should be fewer surprises on accountability tests given the overall data that can be summarized from microtests. Indeed, it may become possible to audit microtesting data through less-frequent use of current accountability tests, thus eliminating the need for high-stakes testing as a regular annual occurrence. This can occur once there is a track record of microtesting data, in aggregate, revealing the same information as the standardized formats. Moreover, microtest data, available at regular intervals throughout the school year, can help school leaders coach teachers whose students are not showing strong learning progress.

There are other side benefits that might be achieved. Microtests, focusing on current instructional goals, can be useful ways to exchange information with parents and with afterschool programs. Just as teachers can generate microtests for their students, they can also generate example tests for parents and for other people who might be working with students who need extra help. This may help improve the outside assistance in learning that students receive.

For example, some tutors fall prey to focusing too tightly on school stuff, offering hints that only work when knowledge is tested in school contexts (such as using the words *altogether* and *left over* as cues to add or subtract, respectively, on word problems). Students with inadequate study skills also tend to focus on simple and predictable school stuff content when studying. Having relevant microtests readily available will permit tutors to understand better both their tutees' level of learning and the depth of content that should be their aim.

The Catch

There is, of course, a catch to this entire argument. For the whole scheme to work well, we will need a technology for mapping experiential domains. This will facilitate more computational assistance in test item generation and will permit another form of validation of the distance between a given child's experiences and a particular domain that might be used as a background for test items. Indeed, existing work on ontology engineering (Mizoguchi & Ikeda, 1996) and on structure mapping (Falkenhainer, Forbus, & Gentner, 1989; Gentner & Kurtz, 2006; Markman & Genter, 2000) suggests a possible direction this computational assistance might follow.

Work in artificial intelligence on translation, instruction, and machine assistance to thinking has led to the realization that understanding a phenomenon requires understanding the fundamental ontology for the domain of that phenomenon. By *ontology* is meant the core concepts — and the experiences that anchor those concepts — that guide the community of people who think about the phenomenon in question. Similarly, to translate a sentence, one must understand the ontology underpinning the meaning of that sentence to its speaker and then be able to project that meaning onto the ontology of the intended listener. Instruction, from this viewpoint, also involves bridging between the ontology of the community that understands a concept and the ontology underpinning the student's current thinking.

Posing a test item that is anchored in a particular experiential domain, then, can be seen as mapping the content to be tested into the ontology of people who have shared in the domain's core experiences. Once the ontologies for the various relevant domains are specified, then it is possible to analyze the "distance" between what was taught in school and what the student's experience includes, on the one hand, and between the student's understanding of a new concept and how that concept is represented within the ontology of a new domain on the other hand (approaches such as structure mapping are extremely promising for this; Falkenhainer et al., 1989).

My assignment in writing this chapter was to reflect on what new science of assessment would be helpful for training and instruction. The discussion here leads me to assert that key components of a new science, perhaps technology, of assessment will be work done on ontology engineering, approaches such as structure mapping that can help specify the distance between one set of experience-based knowledge and another, and a platform to support the easy generation and management of microtest elements that are mapped onto the same curricular goal structure (sometimes called standards) as accountability tests. I believe that the needed work will be challenging but is possible and certainly is worthy of the investment of time and resources.

Acknowledgment

This work benefited from comments by Harry O'Neil and Irene Conrad on an earlier draft.

References

American Educational Research Association, American Psychological Association, and National Council on Measurement in Education. (1999). *Standards for educational and psychological testing*. Washington, DC: Author.

Carraher, T. N., Carraher, D. W., & Schliemann, A. D. (1985). Mathematics in the streets and in schools. *British Journal of Developmental Psychology, 3*, 21–29.

Cole, N. S. (1993). History and development of DIF. In P. W. Holland and H. Wainer (Eds.), *Differential item functioning* (pp. 25–29). Hillsdale, NJ: Erlbaum.

Elliott, J. (2003). Dynamic assessment in educational settings: Realising potential. *Educational Review, 55,* 15–32.

Falkenhainer, B., Forbus, K. D., & Gentner, D. (1989). The structure-mapping engine: algorithm and examples. *Artificial Intelligence, 41,* 1–63.

Feuer, M. J., Holland, P. W., Green, B. F., Bertenthal, M. W., & Hemphill, F. C. (1999). *Uncommon measures: equivalence and linkage among educational tests* (Report of the National Research Council Committee on Equivalency and Linkage of Educational Tests). Washington, DC: National Academy Press.

Gammaitoni, L. (1995). Stochastic resonance and the dithering effect in threshold physical systems. *Physical Review E, 52,* 4691–4698.

Gentner, D., & Kurtz, K. J. (2006). Relations, objects, and the composition of analogies. *Cognitive Science, 30,* 1–34.

Gott, S. P., Lesgold, A. M., & Kane, R. S. (1997). Promoting the transfer of technical competency. In S. Dijkstra, F. Schott, N. Seel, & R. D. Tennyson (Eds.), *Instructional design: International perspectives* (Vol. 2). Hillsdale, NJ: Erlbaum.

Landauer, T. K., Foltz, P. W., & Laham, D. (1998). An introduction to latent semantic analysis. *Discourse Processes, 25,* 259–284.

Larry P. v. Riles, 495 F. Supp. 926 (9th Cir. 1984).

Lesgold, A. (1987). The integration of instruction and assessment in technical jobs. In *Assessment in the Service of Learning. Proceedings of the 1987 ETS Invitational Conference.* Princeton, NJ: Educational Testing Service.

Markman, A. B., & Gentner, D. (2000). Structure mapping in the comparison process. *The American Journal of Psychology, 113,* 501–538.

Mizoguchi, R., & Ikeda, M. (1996). Ontology engineering—towards the basic theory and technology for content-oriented research. *Journal of the Japanese Society for Artificial Intelligence, 4,* 559–569. English version retrieved on May 9, 2007 from http://www.ei.sanken.osaka-u.ac.jp/pub/miz/miz-onteng.pdf

National Center for Educational Statistics. (1999). *Highlights from TIMMS: Overview and key findings across grade levels* (Report No. NCES 1999-081). Washington, DC: Author.

Steele, C. M., & Aronson, J. (1995). Stereotype threat and the intellectual test performance of African Americans. *Journal of Personality & Social Psychology, 69,* 797–811.

Sternberg, R. J. (2005). WICS: A model of positive educational leadership comprising wisdom, intelligence, and creativity synthesized. *Educational Psychology Review, 17,* 191–262.

Vanderkooy, J., & Lipshitz, S. P. (1987). Resolution below the least significant bit in digital systems with dither. *Journal of the Audio Engineering Society, 35,* 966–975.

Vygotsky, L. S. (1978). *Mind and society: The development of higher mental processes.* Cambridge, MA: Harvard University Press. (Original work published 1930, 1933, 1935)

Whitehead, A. N. (1929). *The aims of education and other essays.* New York: Macmillan.

Zenisky, A. L., Hambleton, R. K., & Robin, F. (2003). Detection of differential item functioning in large-scale state assessments: A study evaluating a two-stage approach. *Educational and Psychological Measurement, 63,* 51–64.

3

Studying Situated Learning in a Multiuser Virtual Environment

DIANE JASS KETELHUT, CHRIS DEDE, JODY CLARKE,
BRIAN NELSON, AND CASSIE BOWMAN
Harvard Graduate School of Education

Multiuser virtual environments (MUVEs) enable multiple simultaneous participants to access virtual contexts (such as graphically represented buildings), interact with digital artifacts and tools (such as digitized images and virtual microscopes), represent themselves through *avatars* (graphical representations of participants), communicate with other participants and with *agents* (personalities simulated by a computer), and enact collaborative learning activities of various types (Dede, Clarke, Ketelhut, Nelson, & Bowman, 2005). Most students now using MUVEs do so in the context of online gaming (Dede, 2005) through commercial products such as the Sims™ (various lifestyles), Everquest™ (swords and sorcery), Grand Theft Auto™ (crime), or Halo™ (war). Our research group is studying the motivational power of MUVEs and the sophisticated learning processes they enable to increase educational outcomes for deep academic knowledge and higher order thinking skills, as opposed to the largely useless fantasy content and skills participants gain from these entertainment products. This chapter describes multiple ways in which the detailed record of student actions and utterances automatically collected in MUVEs offers great potential for assessment, both from a research perspective and in terms of formative, diagnostic information that could help tailor instruction to individual needs.

Overview of River City Learning Environment

Using an MUVE as a pedagogical vehicle, our research team is exploring how a technology-intensive learning experience that immerses participants in a virtual "world" with residents who face chronic illnesses can help middle school students learn both deep inquiry skills (scientific processes) and science knowledge. In particular, we are working to dramatically improve the educational outcomes of students performing in the bottom third of their class, pupils who — even by middle school — frequently have given up on themselves as learners. These students are disengaged from schooling and typically are difficult to motivate, even by good teachers using best-practice, inquiry-based pedagogies. We are investigating whether the use of educational MUVEs, which resemble the entertainment and communication media kids use outside school, can both reengage these students in learning and aid them in mastering higher order thinking processes as well as standards-based content in biology and ecology (National Research Council [NRC], 1996). This focus of our MUVE, River City, grew out of conversations with science teachers about the subject areas they had the most difficulty teaching: problem finding, hypothesis formation, and experimental design.

The virtual world of River City consists of a city, set in the late 1800s, with a river running through it, different forms of terrain that influence water runoff, and various neighborhoods, industries, and institutions, such as a hospital and a university. On entering the city, the students' avatars can interact with each other, computer-based agents, digital artifacts, and the avatars of instructors (Figure 3.1). In exploring, students also encounter various visual and auditory stimuli that provide tacit clues regarding possible causes of illness. Content in the right-hand interface window shifts based on what the participant encounters or activates in the virtual world, such as a digital, interactive microscope that allows students to examine samples of water (Figure 3.2).

In River City, students work in teams to develop hypotheses regarding one of three strands of illness in the town (waterborne, airborne, and insect borne). These three disease strands are integrated with historical, social, and geographical content, allowing students to experience the inquiry skills involved in disentangling multicausal problems embedded within a complex environment. At the end of the curriculum, student teams compare their research findings with those from other groups of students in their class to delineate some of the many potential hypotheses and causal relationships embedded in the virtual world.

In 2002, we conducted our pilot implementations of River City and a matched control curriculum in four public school classrooms in a large

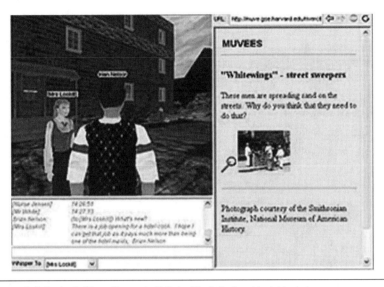

Figure 3.1 Avatar talking with agent; digital artifact displayed in right window.

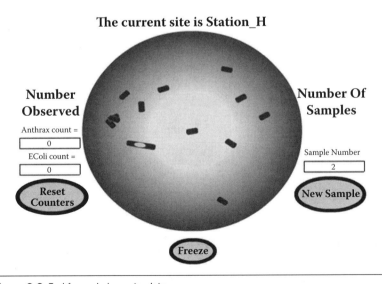

Figure 3.2 Tool for analyzing water data.

urban area in Massachusetts with high percentages of English language learners and students receiving free or reduced lunch. We examined usability, student motivation, student learning, and classroom implementation issues (Dede & Ketelhut, 2003; Dede, Ketelhut, & Reuss, 2002). Whole classes were assigned to the treatment (using River City) or to the control. The control condition utilized a curriculum in which the same content and skills were taught in equivalent time to comparable students via a guided social constructivist (GSC)-based pedagogy (Vygotsky, 1978) but in a paper-based format without the use of computers. Activities were matched closely between the two curricula. This type of control curriculum enables us to focus on the strengths and limits of MUVEs, as well as the types of pedagogy best supported by this medium, as compared to best-case science teaching far superior to the typical content and pedagogy in our implementation sites.

Our results from the pilot study indicated this first-generation MUVE was motivating for all students, including lower-ability students typically uninterested in classroom activities. The River City group, on average, had more positive changes in motivation than did the control group. Subscale averages for students' perceptions of global science self-efficacy also showed significant differences between the two groups ($t = 3.36$, $p < .05$), with the River City group showing an increase of one point out of five on average as opposed to the control group's decrease of .31 (Dede & Ketelhut, 2003).

We also found that students discovered multiple intriguing situations in the MUVE to investigate. In one classroom, five different hypotheses about the illnesses emerged, with posited causes ranging from population density to immigration to water pollution. Another finding is that the MUVE seemed to have the most positive effects for students with high perceptions of their own thoughtfulness of inquiry. These students, on average, scored the highest on the postcontent test, controlling for socioeconomic status, science grade point average, ethnicity, and content pretest score (Dede & Ketelhut, 2003). Also, the data showed no differences between English language learning (ELL) and non-ELL students in performance, despite the reliance in this medium on reading and writing, indicating the success of our design strategy, which ensured each team of students included someone who could read English.

Based on this pilot work, in our current research we have developed multiple second-generation variations of the River City curriculum leading to three treatments along with a control. One variant centers on a GSC model of learning by doing, in which inquiry experiences in the MUVE are supported by both virtual and physical lab notebooks and complemented by in-class interpretive sessions led by the teacher. Another variant shifts the learning experience to a situated pedagogy based on expert modeling and coaching (EMC), as described by Brown, Collins, and Duguid (1989), in which students interact with expert avatars (played by college science majors) and computer-based agents embedded in the MUVE. The third variant, legitimate peripheral participation (LPP), is based on Lave and Wenger's (1991) concept of a community of practice; students move from simple peripheral roles to more complex tasks through tacit forms of learning, such as internships, that are supported by a computer-based agent and the lab notebook.

Through a series of implementations from 2003 to 2005, these River City variants were compared to a control condition similar to that in our pilot research. Based on studies of these variants, a best-of-the-best version of the River City curriculum has been developed to include the most successful features of each variant as well as an individualized, computer-based guidance system (Nelson, 2005). We implemented this version in a variety of classrooms during May–October 2005 and are just beginning our analysis of it.

In 2003–2004, to assess the effectiveness and value of the River City MUVE curriculum, we conducted four large-scale implementations involving more than 2,500 students in major urban areas in New England, the Midwest, California, and the Southeast, in schools with high proportions of English language learners and students receiving free or reduced lunch. Depending on the implementation, different computer-based variants were randomly assigned to students within each classroom, with teachers instructed to minimize cross contamination of treatments. The paper-based control treatment was randomly assigned to whole classes, with each teacher offering both the computer-based treatments and the control. After 2 weeks of designing and conducting their experiments, students in both the control and River City treatments were asked to write letters to the mayor of River City to discuss their hypothesis, experimental design, findings, and recommendations for solving the city's health problem. More detailed information about the River City curriculum and our research findings is available at http://muve.gse.harvard.edu/rivercity/.

River City as a Database

From a technical standpoint, MUVEs are unique in their ability to keep minutely detailed records of the moment-by-moment movements, actions, and utterances of each participant in the environment. As part of the River City project, Active Worlds Corporation (www.activeworlds.com) has developed a customized plug-in server that provides additional functionality to the River City MUVE environment. The features most relevant to our research are the data-tracking system and log files. With the data-tracking system, we are able to collect, store, and retrieve information on the activities of each student as the student explores the MUVE. These data form the basis of a personal MUVE history of each student that follows the student from session to session; the data are in the form of extensive log files, a feature impossible to replicate in a classroom-based experience. The level of detail in these records is extensive: The logs indicate exactly where students went, with whom they communicated, what they said in these interactions, what virtual artifacts they activated, and how long each of these activities took.

To create these personalized histories for each student in River City, all the items with which students could interact were programmatically tagged with identification codes. Every time a student clicks on an object or "speaks" to a River City resident (a computer-based agent) or other avatars, a record of the event is stored in a server-side database. A wide array of objects with which students can interact is available in River City, and consequently a richly varied store of data exists from which to build a sophisticated analysis of student participation in the MUVE.

A more detailed description of River City will serve to illustrate the complexity of potential student actions. River City features a river running through the town (Figure 3.3) and is divided into several geographic zones. The river begins in the mountainous upper elevations of town, where the wealthy residents live and the university is housed. It then travels down past the middle-class homes, curving around south of the downtown shopping district and slowly flowing through the tenement district along the dump.

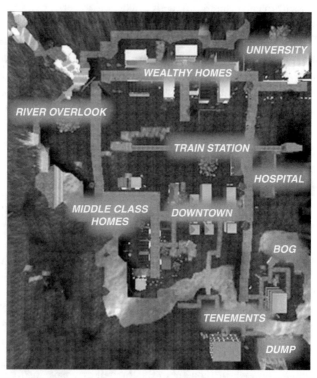

Figure 3.3 The River City layout.

In addition to the river, there is a bog in which tenement residents often swim, bathe, and even wash their clothes. A centrally located train station is a beehive of activity, with new residents arriving daily; nearby, River City's hospital cares for the town's sick.

Within each area of town, there are a number of items with which students can interact to gain information about the illnesses in *River City*. These items include

- *Historical photos and accompanying text:* Buildings throughout town contain digitized historical images. Clicking on an in-world image causes a Web page to appear in the right-hand screen; the page contains information about the town, its people, environmental factors, and other clues about the illnesses in town.
- *Books and charts:* Scattered throughout the world are digital signs and books that link to Web pages containing additional information. For example, the hospital has an admissions chart containing a list of newly admitted patients and their ages, addresses, and symptoms. The town library has virtual books that link to online dictionaries and encyclopedias.
- *Data stations:* Data collection stations appear in some sessions of the world. Clicking on these stations opens a virtual tool that provides a microscopic view of the water in a specific place, allowing students to collect and analyze samples.

In addition, students can use the chat system in the MUVE to ask a limited range of questions addressed to the River City residents. There are 32 residents (computer-based agents) scattered throughout town. These residents offer short sets of information about happenings in town and the illnesses. As an illustration, the agents can respond with a short answer to the question, "What's new?" Asking this question of Nurse Patterson in the River City hospital, for example, elicits a clue about the recurring stomach illness in River City: "We have a couple of new patients with that stomach upset we saw last summer. I hope this isn't becoming an epidemic again! Most of them seem to be from the tenement homes."

Through collecting data about how students interact with the various types of artifacts described, we can analyze student movement through the world, looking at patterns of movement, interactions, chat, and questioning of River City residents. Combining these data with basic student-level predictors (demographic characteristics such as gender, socioeconomic status, age, and ethnicity; pre- and posttest scores on quantitative measures of scientific knowledge; judgments along multiple dimensions about the quality of their "summative performance" letter to the mayor; and, for some students, in-class observations and pre-/postinterviews) allows for sophisticated analysis of how participant characteristics interact with in-world activity over time and how these interactions may influence student learning.

Analysis of the River City Database Information

Analysis of this extensive River City database is in its early stages, so the following findings represent some preliminary trends in the data. Sample sizes are noted. As we discussed in the preceding section, essentially all student interactions are recorded in this database, offering an opportunity to see variations in patterns of student behavior nearly impossible to detect in any other type of learning context.

The early analysis of student-to-River City resident conversation for four classes having the same teacher $(n = 96)$ illustrates this potential power for detailed student assessment (Crusoe, 2005). In an attempt to provide a virtual world comfortable for girls, we intentionally created more female residents (21) than male (13) in River City. Also, to supply role models in science for girls, 4 of the 5 resident (computer-based) experts are female. Therefore, one research question we are interested in exploring is whether students discriminate between the residents to whom they talk based on the gender of the resident.

The students in these four classes logged in over 3,000 conversational gambits to various River City residents during the 2-week implementation. Of the conversations that boys had with River City residents, 40% were directed toward male figures; similarly, 39% of the conversations that girls had with residents were directed toward male residents. These numbers roughly reflect the percentage of male residents of River City. From this evidence, it does not appear as if gender of the residents is affecting conversational choices. However, on further investigation, we discovered that although boys constitute 46% of the students in this sample, they only account for 31% of these conversational entries. We are now conducting additional analyses of data to determine if boys differentially preferred other methods of gaining information (e.g., exploring, interacting with artifacts) rather than conversation with residents.

In addition, there is a difference in what students said to residents. Although the residents of River City can understand and respond to "hello," "thank you," "where am I," and "good-bye," "what's new" is the only phrase that will elicit a clue about the problems in River City. For the students in this subsample, "what's new" constituted 35% of the girls' comments to residents, and this phase was uttered 48% of the time for boys. So, although boys talk less frequently than girls, their conversation is relatively more task oriented; in contrast, girls' interactions with residents frequently first attempt to establish a social relationship. It is too early for us in this analysis to make claims or offer explanations for these trends, but we offer them here instead as an example of the power of MUVEs to help illuminate students' learning patterns.

River City Individualized Guidance System

As another example of the rich analytic power possible through the use of MUVE log files, our project is the first to create and investigate the use of an embedded individualized guidance system (IGS) with an educational MUVE. The guidance system utilizes personalized interaction histories collected on each student's activities to offer real-time, customized support. The IGS offers reflective prompts about each student's learning in the world, with the content of the messages based on in-world events and basic event histories of that individual. To create the IGS, all the items with which students could interact were programmatically tagged with identification codes. Every time a particular student clicked on an object or "spoke" to a River City resident, a record of the event was stored in a server-side database. The cumulative record of events resulted in a personalized history for each student.

A guidance model, operated by a back-end software agent, was triggered after each student interaction event in the MUVE. A subset of events was associated with guidance scripts, and the guidance model used these scripts to offer a specific selection of messages to each student. As a default, three links to guidance messages related to the current world object are displayed. The default messages are designed to help students process information on the content or attributes of the object itself. For example, there are many clickable pictures hanging on walls around River City. When students click on these, a Web page appears showing a brief paragraph providing information about the picture or the illnesses in the city. If a given picture includes guidance hints, then the default hints will present students with guiding questions about the text associated with the picture.

In addition to the default messages, each tagged object could display up to three customized guidance messages. These customized messages were displayed when a predefined set of prerequisite objects or interactions existed within a given student's personal history. For example, a clickable admissions chart is located in the River City hospital. When a student clicked on this chart, the guidance model read a script to see if the given student had previously clicked on objects defined as prerequisites for showing customized messages. Up to three sets of prerequisite interactions could exist in the rules script for any tagged object (one set for each customized guidance message). In the example case of clicking on the admissions chart, a predefined rule stated that if the student had previously visited the tenement district and talked to a resident there, then a customized guidance message would be shown reminding the student that he or she had previously visited the tenement district and asking the student how many patients listed on the chart came from that part of town.

Multilevel multiple regression analysis findings show that use of this guidance system with our MUVE-based curriculum has a statistically significant, positive impact ($p < .05$) on student learning for both girls and boys (Nelson, 2005). This fitted relationship is plotted for both boys and girls in Figure 3.4. Students who viewed more guidance earned higher GAIN scores than those who viewed fewer messages, and the benefit of guidance system use varied by gender, with boys doing worse, on average, at each level of guidance viewing. We are currently studying possible explanations for these outcomes.

In addition to using the log files to personalize the guidance provided to each student, we are able to make use of these data to conduct sophisticated analyses of guidance use. We know when and if students first choose to use the guidance system, which messages they view, where they are in the virtual world when they view them, and which actions they take subsequent to viewing a given guidance message. This provides diagnostic information that potentially teachers could access to gain formative assessment insights to guide their daily instruction.

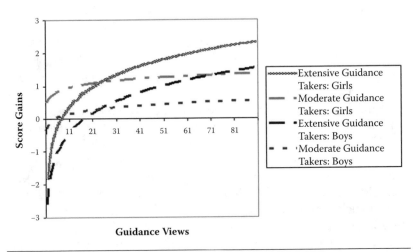

Figure 3.4 The fitted relationship between content test score gains and levels of guidance system use by students exposed to extensive or moderate levels of guidance who chose to "take up" the guidance at least one time in a MUVE-based curriculum, by gender ($n = 272$).

Case Studies

The log files of student experiences also enable another type of assessment: tracking the learning trajectory of individual students to see which aspects of River City engaged them and were helpful in their learning. An example of this can be seen in the transformation of Kimmie (a pseudonym) to Shorty (Kimmie's River City persona) as she gains critical thinking skills (Partnership for 21st Century Skills, 2003) in the course of her longitudinal experiences in River City. Based on log file analysis and interview transcripts, we can see Shorty move from the periphery of the decision-making process of her team to a more central role in her team's experimenting (Clarke, 2005).

Kimmie is a 12-year-old female in the seventh grade. She does not think she is good at science and claims, "It's boring when he [her teacher] talks a lot." Kimmie appears to view science differently from science class. As a preassessment, we ask each student to draw a self-portrait doing science in science class. Kimmie drew herself in a science laboratory doing an experiment and explained it as, "Once we did an experiment with a ruler to see if you could … catch it fast." However, when asked if the picture captures how she usually feels in science class, she replied, "Sometimes he just teaches us like the things about like about science and then we study and we have tests on it."

Kimmie further describes her science class as, "We write notes and sometimes we do experiments. … Well, when he usually just talks a lot, like I remember one day, we didn't do nothing except for write notes, and he talked a lot." Not surprisingly, on a scale of 1 to 5, with 5 her most favorite, she rated her science class as 2. If given a choice, then, Kimmy would not take science classes in high school "because … I am not really interested in science."

Both Kimmie and her teacher describe her stance in class as a follower rather than a leader. In the beginning of the project, as Shorty, she relies on her teammates, hype69 and rhia, to tell her what to do:

Shorty: hype69 rhia what do we have to do
Shorty: what d we do
Rhia: Doctor Paterson Said they cant find a cure yet for the new problem.
Shorty: what page is it on
Rhia: 17
Shorty: what else do we do

As the project progresses, Shorty makes observations and inferences about her discoveries and shares them with her teammates. However, initially her low *self-efficacy* in science (belief that one can succeed in learning a particular subject) still causes her to defer to rhia's discovery over her own observations:

Shorty: miss howell said that there is a bad stomach problem at the tenements
Hype69:   wathank you
Rhia: Mrs Lopas saiys that the sewage runs into the stream where the people get water
Shorty: is that the problem
Shorty: because if it is do we tell the teacher
Rhia: yes

Even though Shorty observed the trash in the water near the tenements and found information from Miss Howell, she refrains from pushing her point: We wanted to move the sewage pipe. I mean, I thought it was the dump but I think it was both so sewage was going down near the tenements but the dump was right there.

At this point, we see that Shorty is beginning to move from the periphery of the team toward the center in terms of leadership because she has begun to espouse her own theory without need for direction. However, at this stage of the River City experience, she still yields to her other teammates' ideas. Further log file analysis indicates that, by the end of the project, Shorty is no longer asking her teammates what she should do but has begun to tell them what to do. As one illustration, she takes the lead on sampling the water and tells rhia to go to the hospital:

Shorty: i'm goin to da water samplin sation in the wealthy homes
Shorty: rhia do da hospital im takin wata samples

This shift indicates Shorty's growing engagement and self-efficacy.

Students collect data first in a control world and then in an experimental world. To compare their data, they need to conduct observations and tests in the same places in both worlds. We can see from the log files that Shorty understands this and is directing her teammates to ensure that this is accomplished successfully:

Hype69:   what do we do
Shorty: do the same thing u did on friday ask the same people and write down what the said this time

This represents an important change for Shorty as she moves from the role of a novice to a stance more closely resembling that of an expert (Brown et al., 1989; Lave & Wenger, 1991).

In follow-up interviews, Shorty confirms what we are seeing in the log files and helps us make sense of why this shift happened for her. She tells us that she felt like a scientist "because we had to figure out things and ask questions and use our brains and really think hard." Actively solving the problem made it easier to "understand" and helped her comprehend concepts such as *hypothesis* and *procedure*:

> It helped me understand hypothesis and procedure better. ... I knew what they were but then this project it was easy to write a hypothesis and procedure for. Ummm because there was more data than sometimes you don't have a lot data and there was a lot because you could ask a lot of people and talk to a lot of people.

Shorty had learned about these concepts before, but solving a problem by visually seeing tacit information helped make abstract concepts like hypothesis and procedure more concrete:

> We actually got to see where everything is, where the dump is and the tenements and the scenic lookout where the pipe, the sewage pipe was going to the water. Yeah, because you got to do more and get more information and actually see the thing instead of just imagining it. You get to actually see it. It helps because we can ask people questions and they can tell us. Like they can talk to us and we got to walk around and see what the city looks like if it is dirty in some spots and really clean in other spots.

Shorty learned immersively by walking around, talking to residents, and noting tacit visual and auditory clues, yet we would not have known this solely through examination of the summative affective and content measures. Examining the log files and talking to Shorty about her experience enables understanding the processes that led to her engagement and learning.

Contrasting Conventional versus Performance-Based Methods of Assessing Learning

Up to this point, we have discussed the power of MUVEs for tracking students' learning trajectories to a degree not possible with other techniques. What are the difficulties in using these methods to measure the complex learning that happens in MUVEs, both for research purposes and for formative, diagnostic assessment to aid instruction?

Our students complete two pre-/postmeasures. The first is an affective measure adapted from three different surveys, Self-Efficacy in Technology and Science (Ketelhut, 2005), Patterns for Adaptive Learning Survey (Midgley et al., 2000), and the Test of Science Related Attitudes (Fraser, 1981).

This modified measure has scales to evaluate students' efficacy of technology use (videogame, computer, chat, etc.); science efficacy; thoughtfulness of inquiry; science enjoyment; and career interest in science. Its individual subscales have reasonable internal consistency reliability estimates (ranging from .8 to .93), as well as validity evidence from prior research (Ketelhut, 2005).

Our second survey assesses understanding and content knowledge, such as science inquiry skills, science process skills, and biology. Previously published and validated instruments for assessing science process skills are available (Dillashaw & Okey, 1980); however, these are not appropriate for the student developmental level and curricular units in our project. Therefore, we have developed our own measures to assess student learning of content and scientific problem-solving skills. Internal consistency reliability was estimated using Cronbach's alpha and principal components analysis, indicating a reliability of .86. Content validity was established through analysis by a team of experts.

We are still in the early stages of analyzing data from these instruments, but interesting patterns are emerging about which students do best under our various pedagogical treatments. Results of a randomly chosen representative subgroup of students from 4 of the 11 teachers in the first implementation ($n = 330$) were analyzed via multilevel modeling using students' class assignment as the grouping variable. The examination of the results indicates that, on average, students in the GSC experimental group achieved 16% higher scores on the posttest in biology than students learning with the control curriculum.

Similar results were seen from the affective measures. In the initial pilot implementation ($n = 81$), over the course of the study experimental students raised their average score in *thoughtfulness of inquiry*, a measure of metacognition, significantly more than control students. This initial result was confirmed in the later implementation. Student scores for thoughtfulness of inquiry on the postsurvey were significantly higher ($p < .01$) on average for two of the experimental groups in comparison to the scores for students in the control group. For example, students scoring an average of 1 (strongly disagree) on the scale of 1–5 for the pretest were associated with scores of 1.8 on the posttest for GSC and 1.9 for EMC, nearly double their starting average score (as a result of a curricular intervention of approximately 10 hours). Students in the control group also improved, on average, but only to 1.3.

However, when we looked for evidence of improved inquiry skills using our content survey questions, we found equivocal results. Improvements were seen across the board for knowledge and application of scientific processes, but there were no significant differences between treatments. This result was replicated in all of our implementations to date for nearly 2,000 students.

Is this because our project does not affect student learning in this area, or because inquiry is difficult to assess with close-ended survey questions? This is an issue that has been in the forefront of assessment research for decades, even more so now that standardized national and state testing have taken such a prominent role in accountability sanctions. Possibly as a reaction to the concerns voiced in *A Nation at Risk,* interest in assessing student learning for accountability purposes grew in the 1980s (Kane, Khattri, Reeve, & Adamson, 1997). The current trend toward high-stakes standardized testing has its roots in this decade.

In reaction to the emphasis on high-stakes tests and based on influential reports calling for the inclusion of more inquiry in science curricula (American Association for the Advancement of Science, 1990; NRC, 1996), the 1990s saw increased interest in alternative assessments, such as performance-based assessments in which a student's process in analyzing a problem was revealed (Baxter & Shavelson, 1994; Klein et al., 1997; Stecher & Klein, 1997). Published reviews are available that detail the debate between the proponents of each of these styles of assessments (Kane et al., 1997; Mehrens, 1998; Moore, 2003). To summarize, proponents of alternative assessments view them as capturing student understanding better than standardized tests, which they feel measure decontextualized knowledge. Opponents argue that performance-based assessments are not cost-effective, cannot be compared from teacher to teacher because of individual grading differences, and are inconclusive about what the tasks are actually measuring (Stecher & Klein, 1997).

Multiuser Virtual Environments as a Means of Integrating Conventional and Performance-Based Assessments

This debate informs the assessment methods in our project. We have designed River City to see if MUVEs enable students to engage in scientific inquiry and make sense of complex data. The NRC defines *science inquiry* as a multifaceted activity that involves students actively making observations, posing questions, planning and conducting experiments, and communicating results (NRC, 1996). This view of inquiry as an ongoing process involves higher order skills that are not easily measured by multiple-choice tests (Resnick & Resnick, 1992). We want to establish what type of assessments will allow us to infer that students have learned how to engage in inquiry, particularly at the "front end" of using inquiry processes to make sense of complexity: problem finding, hypothesis formation, and experimental design.

Because we are still in the early stages of establishing how MUVEs can aid assessment, we are interested in comparing (a) what we learn from traditional assessments, such as pre- and postmeasures with (b) what we see in our log file database and with (c) how students perform on performance-based assessments, such as the letters to the mayor.

To date, we have analyzed a random subsample of students' letters to the mayor in both the treatment and control groups ($n = 224$) for evidence of inquiry. In particular, we look for the following:

- Problem identification
- A testable hypothesis based on observations
- An experimental design appropriate to test the hypothesis
- Conclusions based on collected data
- Recommendations

Our scoring rubric based on these items evolved throughout our project, and the current version reflects input from the research team as well as from science teachers. To control for coding differences, the team coded the first letters separately and discovered an 80% agreement rate. Coding differences were discussed to improve accuracy.

Our preliminary results suggest students are developing an understanding of the process of inquiry that is not well captured in traditional pre-/posttest measures (Ketelhut et al., 2005). Overall, students in the River City treatments as a group earned "letter-evaluation" scores more than double that of their paper-based control peers ($p < .01$), a surprising result given the roughly equivalent score for these groups in inquiry gains on the pre-/postmeasures. Further, although we found no differences by type of pedagogical treatment on the inquiry section of our pre-/postmeasures, when we analyzed the letters to the mayor data using multilevel modeling, we discovered interesting differences by treatment.

Table 3.1 summarizes the results of that analysis. The leftmost column of this table lists the letter-evaluation categories that showed differences across the treatments. The treatments with significantly higher scores for that category are denoted with a ‡ in the other four columns; treatments that had worse scores are denoted with an − in those same columns.

As can be seen in Table 3.1, students in the GSC treatment had higher scores in nearly every category, whereas students in the control treatment did not do significantly better on any aspect of the letters to the mayor than did the River City treatment students. In addition, the letters written by students in the control curriculum often were much shorter in length, did not demonstrate motivation or engagement, did not mention the experiment, and did not explicitly recognize the interconnectedness of the chosen problem with other possible causes of the larger problem.

Our point here is not to expound on the differences we found because of our treatments but to show the richness of learning that is difficult to uncover with multiple choice tests. For example, students who scored low on the science inquiry posttest wrote letters that were of similar quality to

Table 3.1 Coded Sections of the Letters to the Mayor That Showed Significant Differences ($p < .05$) by Treatment in Student Scores Relative to One or More of the Other Treatments ($n = 173$) With ‡ Indicating the Treatment That Had the Highest Scores

Areas that differed significantly by treatment ($p < .05$)	GSC	EMC	LPP	Control
Overall quality	‡	–	X	–
Summarizing the problem	X	X	‡	–
Awareness that different symptoms were related to different diseases	‡	–	‡	–
Stating a testable hypothesis	‡	–	‡	X
Collecting evidence to test hypothesis	‡	–	–	–
Understanding the vector of disease transmission	‡	‡	–	X
Stating a conclusion	‡	X	X	–

EMC, expert modeling and coaching treatment;
GSC, guided social constructivist treatment;
LPP, legitimate peripheral participation treatment.
‡, treatment that on average had highest scores in this category.
–, treatments that on average had worse scores in this category relative to ‡ treatments.
X, treatments that on average were not significantly different from the others in this category.

those written by students who scored higher on the posttest. As one illustration, in their letters low-performing-content students matched the high-performing-content students around criteria of stating an opinion regarding the cause of the problem or the outcome of the experiment. Interestingly, more of the lower-performing test students met the criteria of providing potential interventions or suggesting further research than did students who scored higher on the inquiry test pre-/postmeasures. This suggests that the complexity of the MUVE treatment creates intricate patterns of learning more appropriately measured with a performance-based activity, such as writing an experimental report.

These results, however, are still open to the criticisms levied against performance-based assessments stated: potential lack of standardization of grading and questionable validity of the task. To address those concerns, we need to connect a student's letter to the mayor to other data that also show evidence of the process of inquiry, such as that in our MUVE database. As we have seen with the case study of Kimmie, MUVE technologies capture and document students' strategies and allow us to gather a series of observations that sheds light on multiple aspects of a student's knowledge and higher order thinking skills.

Developing Learning Trajectories for Complex Reasoning Processes

To understand our students' learning processes more fully, we are combining evidence from the log files that traces students' movements in the world and matching this evidence to data from our pre-and postmeasures and from the letters to the mayor. By connecting and triangulating these sources of data, we can create rich cases of students' learning and produce evidence of validity. For example, the case of Audrey/Princess illustrates the process of a student engaging in learning about inquiry. Audrey (a pseudonym) is a 12-year-old female in the seventh grade whose teacher has below-average expectations of her ability to master science content. (Interestingly, this teacher has higher expectations for some boys in her class with worse academic histories.) In her preinterview, Audrey indicated that she has low feelings of self-efficacy in science, and before the intervention she scored slightly below average for this sample on the self-efficacy in scientific inquiry subscale. She is reading below grade level and scored at the 10% level on the content presurvey.

Yet, when Audrey enters River City, she transforms, taking on the avatar identity of Princess and leaving Audrey's damaged sense of self-efficacy behind. She starts out slowly, mostly engaged in organizational issues and exploring the world:

princess: whose on my team
princess: james i have found alot steve u guys go to the wealthy homes me me there ok

However, as Princess, she quickly becomes engaged in discovering "what is the problem." She wants to figure out why people are getting sick:

princess: well at the hospital the doors are open and its right near the dump and there are a lot of people in the tentements and they really are sick so yea I think it is the mosiqutos cause they can carry things from the dump

Audrey works at trying to make sense of the complex data in River City, using multiple sources of information:

princess: It could be the horse poop … welll when the miosqutos are attrected to it the smeell so when the get so of it like taste it or somethinf like that they carry it to the tenements

princess: andrea wiggs said (simce they drained the bog, they havent seen any new cases of fever, just like in the winter!
princess: I am at the library to see if I can get any information

On the last day in the world while collecting data about their experiment, one of her teammates thought their hypothesis was wrong based on an interaction with one of the River City residents. Princess quickly investigated the matter by talking to one of the resident (avatar) scientists in the world, Dr. Richards, before drawing the correct conclusion:

slikyste: whats causing it is that the pipe has lead and if the pipe has lead people would be drinking water and theyd get sick thats what i found out
princess: well i dont think that it is the water it was just a hypopthesis its just saying if the pipe was made of of lead. she just said if it was made out of lead she is just teaching her class?
princess: so ...... we still could be right
slikyste: you just heard what he said you
jwrb27:   yeah shes just showing how to do an experiment

As can be seen here, the data from the log files shows Princess engaging in inquiry and growing throughout the project. Does this match with her survey gain scores and her letter to the mayor? According to the content postsurvey, Audrey improved her disease knowledge by 20% and her inquiry skills by 10%. This supports to some degree what we are seeing in the log files but nonetheless is less impressive than her log files, especially given her very low starting score. However, when we coded her letter to the mayor (blindly, as all letters were coded without identification), we discovered that Princess had received the second highest score for her letter to the mayor, clearly reinforcing the evidence in the log files.

The Challenge of Automating Data Collection from Log Files

MUVEs provide an emerging, exciting method for studying sophisticated types of learning and instruction under controlled conditions that in real-world situations are clouded by the many confounds that inexorably occur in complex, authentic settings. However, this potential power is mitigated by the enormous amounts of data about student performance collected in an MUVE. To conduct the research described in this chapter, extensive analysis "by hand" of student log files was required, a laborious and time-consuming process. Thus, achieving the potential of MUVEs for assessment is dependent to some degree on the extent to which one can automate the collection of particular types of data from log files, reducing the analytic burden and also enabling real-time feedback for instructional purposes.

Experimenting with this type of automated collection is high on our list of priorities. Some types of log file data appear relatively easy to aggregate. For example, with well-structured log file formats, writing a computer program to count the number of times a student talks to a computer-based agent during a particular MUVE session is not difficult. Determining what type of talk is occurring (e.g., "what's new?" "hello") is also quite feasible. Because of the conversational limits of the agents, this is a far simpler task than the challenges of automated analysis of person-to-person online dialogues (such as verbal interactions among teammates).

Other types of automated data collection from log files are more complex (Baker, Corbett, & Koedinger, 2004; Levy & Wilensky, 2005). For example, is the pattern of a student engaging in increasingly complex forms of inquiry over the time she spends in the MUVE amenable to collection by a computer program? Although we have not yet attempted this task, this may require sophisticated human judgments beyond what a computer program can accomplish. However, automation might accomplish partial tasks within this overall effort, such as collecting student utterances that include words suggestive about various stages of inquiry (e.g., *hypothesis* and *because* as a possible example of causal inference).

Beyond conversational analysis, understanding how students move in the world is another form of log file analysis. We can imagine creating an automated system that produces a map of each student's trajectory while exploring River City. Time spent in each location would be indicated by the width of the path. Because one of the advantages of using a graphical MUVE over other forms of technology is that students can actively explore the world, this map would allow us to evaluate the impact of this on student learning and engagement. Overall, the degree to which automated data collection could simplify log file analysis in MUVEs is uncertain, but we believe further research on this topic may result in substantial progress.

Conclusion

This analysis sketches multiple ways in which the detailed record of student activities and utterances automatically collected in MUVEs offers great potential for student assessment, both from a research perspective and in terms of formative, diagnostic information that could help to tailor instruction to individual needs. Although not discussed extensively in this chapter, MUVEs are also a powerful test bed for theories of learning and teaching because the designer can shape every aspect of the participant's immersive experience, altering specific variables to conduct research experiments. Although realizing this full potential is not an easy task, MUVEs are likely to add a valuable resource to the spectrum of tools and methods available for assessing student learning.

Acknowledgments

This material is based on work supported by the National Science Foundation under grant 0310188. Any opinions, findings, and conclusions or recommendations expressed in this material are those of the authors and do not necessarily reflect the views of the National Science Foundation.

References

American Association for the Advancement of Science. (1990). *Science for all Americans*. New York: Oxford University Press.

Baker, R. S., Corbett, A. T., & Koedinger, K. R. (2004). Detecting student misuse of intelligent tutoring systems. *Proceedings of the Seventh International Conference on Intelligent Tutoring Systems, 531–540.*

Baxter, G. P., & Shavelson, R. J. (1994). Science performance assessments: Benchmarks and surrogates. *International Journal of Educational Research, 21,* 279–297.

Brown, J. S., Collins, A., & Duguid, P. (1989). Situated cognition and the culture of learning. *Education Researcher, 18,* 32–42.

Clarke, J. (2005). *Making learning meaningful: An exploratory pilot study of using multi user virtual environments in middle school science.* Unpublished qualifying paper, Harvard University Graduate School of Education, Cambridge, MA.

Crusoe, D. (2005). *Citizens' interaction in River City: Possible gender effects within citizen-construct and citizen-citizen conversation data.* Unpublished independent study paper, Harvard University Graduate School of Education, Cambridge, MA.

Dede, C. (2005). Planning for "neomillennial" learning styles: Implications for investments in technology and faculty. In J. Oblinger and D. Oblinger (Eds.), *Educating the net generation* (pp. 226–247). Boulder, CO: EDUCAUSE Publishers. Retrieved on May 17, 2007 from http://www.educause.edu/educatingthenetgen/

Dede, C., Clarke, J., Ketelhut, D., Nelson, B., & Bowman, C. (2005). *Fostering motivation, learning, and transfer in multi-user virtual environments.* Paper presented at the American Educational Research Association Conference, Montreal, April.

Dede, C., & Ketelhut, D. (2003, April). *Designing for motivation and usability in a museum-based multi-user virtual environment.* Paper presented at the American Educational Research Association Conference, Chicago.

Dede, C., Ketelhut, D., & Ruess, K. (2002). Motivation, usability, and learning outcomes in a prototype museum-based multi-user virtual environment. In P. Bell, R. Stevens, & T. Satwicz (Eds.), *Keeping learning complex: The proceedings of the Fifth International Conference of the Learning Sciences (ICLS)* (pp. 530–531). Mahwah, NJ: Erlbaum.

Dillashaw, F. G., & Okey, J. R. (1980). Test of integrated process skills for secondary science students. *Science Education, 64,* 601–608.

Fraser, B. (1981). *TOSRA: Test of Science Related Attitudes*. Hawthorne, VIC: Australian Council for Educational Research.

Kane, M., Khattri, N., Reeve, A., & Adamson, R. (1997). *Studies of education reform: Assessment of student performance*. Washington, DC: U.S. Education Department's Office of Educational Research and Improvement.

Ketelhut, D. (2005, April 4–8). *Assessing science self-efficacy in a virtual environment: A measurement pilot*. Paper presented at the National Association of Research in Science Teaching Conference, Dallas.

Ketelhut, D. J., Clarke, J., Dede, C., Nelson, B., & Bowman, C. (2005, April 4–8). *Inquiry teaching for depth and coverage via multi-user virtual environments*. Paper presented at the National Association for Research in Science Teaching, Dallas.

Klein, S. P., Jovanovic, J., Stecher, B. M., McCaffrey, D., Shavelson, R. J., Haertel, E., et al., &. (1997). Gender and racial/ethnic differences on performance assessments in science. *Educational Evaluation and Policy Analysis, 19*, 83–97.

Lave, J., & Wenger, E. (1991). *Situated learning: Legitimate peripheral participation*. New York: Cambridge University Press.

Levy, S., & Wilensky, U. (2005). *An analysis of patterns of exploration found in logs of students' work with NetLogo models embedded in the Connected Chemistry environment*. Paper presented at the American Educational Research Association Conference, Montreal, April.

Mehrens, W. (1998). *Consequences of assessment: What is the evidence?* Education Policy Analysis Archives, 6(13). Retrieved on May 2, 2005 from http://epaa.asu.edu/epaa/v6n13.html

Midgley, C., Maehr, M. L., Hruda, L. Z., Anderman, E., Anderman, L., Freeman, K. E., et al., (2000). *Manual for the Patterns of Adaptive Learning Scales (PALS)*. Ann Arbor: University of Michigan.

Moore, Wayne. (2003). *Facts and assumptions of assessment: technology, the missing link*. THE Journal, 30(6), 20–26.

National Research Council. (1996). *National science education standards*. Washington, DC: National Academy Press.

Nelson, B. (2005). *Investigating the impact of individualized, reflective guidance on student learning in an educational multi-user virtual environment*. Unpublished dissertation, Harvard University, Cambridge, MA.

Partnership for 21st Century Skills. (2003). *Learning for the 21st century*. Washington, DC: Author. Retrieved on May 4, 2005 from http://www.21stcenturyskills.org

Resnick, L. B., & Resnick, D. P. (1992). Assessing the thinking curriculum: New tools for educational reform. In B. Gifford & M. O'Connor (Eds.), *Changing assessments: Alternative views of aptitude, achievement, and instruction* (pp. 37–75). Norwell, MA: Kluwer Academic.

Stecher, B. M., & Klein, S. P. (1997). The cost of science performance assessments in large-scale testing programs. *Educational Evaluation and Policy Analysis, 19*, 1–14.

Vygotsky, L. (1978). *Mind in society*. London: Harvard University Press.

4

Structural, Functional, and Semiotic Symmetries in Simulation-Based Games and Assessments

JOHN T. BEHRENS AND DENNIS FREZZO

Cisco Systems Inc.

ROBERT MISLEVY, MARC KROOPNICK, AND DAISY WISE

University of Maryland

Introduction

Question 1: For each of the activities listed below, categorize them exclusively as either a test or a game:

> *Who Wants to Be a Millionaire?*
> Brain Quest
> The Scholastic Aptitude Test (SAT)
> Your life
> This question

Despite the structural appearance of a test (albeit in a single question), we hope that some readers take sufficient pleasure in the question to consider it a game. As illustrated in the example, the thesis of this chapter is that in many structural, functional, and semiotic ways there exist important parallels between the goals, requirements, artifacts, and systems of games and those of educational assessments. We argue for this view in the following sections. First, we discuss functional and semiotic parallels between games and assessments. Second, we discuss valued structural characteristics of assessments and follow with a section addressing valuable features of simulation-based games. The fourth section presents an example of a simulation-based educational game under construction in the Cisco Networking Academy Program (Behrens, Collison, & DeMark, 2005) and analyzes it in terms of the categories provided in the previous sections. The chapter closes with a summary and discussion. For the purposes of this discussion, we focus on the relationship between games and assessments that involve delivery and simulation of activities with real-world representations and references. For example, although tic-tac-toe could likely provide assessors valuable information about cognitive development, strategy, and process, we do not consider the task a real-world task because it has no parallel activity to which it is referring. On the other hand, a game that simulates the building of medieval empires (e.g., Microsoft's 1999 Age of Empires) is specifically designed to simulate economic, political, and social realities as they once existed in the world.

Functional Parallels

In this section, we discuss what we call functional similarities between games and assessments. By *functional*, we mean aspects of these systems that are related to purpose and use.

After a broad overview of multiple theoretical views, examples, and definitions, Salen and Zimmerman (2004), in their book *Rules of Play*, defined *games* as follows: "A *game* is a system in which players engage in an artificial conflict, defined by rules, that results in a quantifiable outcome" (p. 80). This definition is game-centric rather than play-centric insofar as it omits design-free, purely "play" activities such as 3-year-old dress up and pretend "games" for which there are likely to be rules but unlikely to be quantifiable outcomes. However, from a game-centric perspective, this definition encompasses numerous systems for play, from complex video games to tic-tac-toe on a napkin. If the purpose of a game is to promote play, then a game is a system that promotes play with quantifiable outcomes (use of points, etc.). This provides a parallel understanding with assessment that has the purpose of describing knowledge skills and abilities in a quantifiable manner as well. Mislevy (2003) defined (educational) *assessment* as reasoning from observations of what students do or make in a handful of particular circumstances, to what they know or can do more broadly. In the same way that play is promoted through the artifacts of games, assessment is typically promoted through the artifacts of tests. Consider what we lose if we replace the word *game* with the word *test* in the definition: "A *test* is a system in which examinees (*players*) engage in an artificial task (conflict), defined by rules, that results in a quantifiable outcome."

A test is a system insofar as it consists of the integration of numerous representations, social customs, rules, and interpretive systems. Some of the aspects of the system are highly structured, such as the format for presenting the question and legal parameters around the use of assessment results, but other aspects may be informal, such as the seriousness with which one approaches the SAT.

Although the language of games emphasizes conflict and the language of assessment emphasizes tasks, both aspects are present in both settings. The conflict of a game is induced by the requirement to complete specific tasks (e.g., putting three X's in a row). Likewise, conflict is added to assessments by variation in task characteristics. Typically, the conflict is heightened by restricting the set of possible answers or increasing task difficulty. For example, in the sample question presented in the Introduction, the first draft failed to include the word *exclusively*, so that multiple interpretations could have been made for each part of the question without the conflict or cognitive impasse (VanLehn, 1990) desired for the activity. Indeed, a sense of failure to reach an appropriate level of test conflict leads to the characterization that "the test was too easy." This contrasts with games in which conflict is added in random amounts by the use of dice or other probabilistic devices.

Rules are common to games and tests. In tests, rules define what information is available and what is not, how much time is allowed to complete the activities, which formats the tasks should be completed in, and so on. Scoring rules for individual tasks and rules for summarizing results across tasks using psychometric models are ubiquitous in assessment design. The quantification of outcome is a common goal for which the assessment community has a long history of refinement and improvement.

Although a full account cannot be given here, we would be remiss if we failed to note the importance of semiotic aspects of the interpretation of activities as games or tests. Following from the fundamental work of Peirce (e.g., 1868; cf. Hoopes, 1991) and its application to understanding games from Gee (2003), we refer to *semiotic* as the semantic or meaning-centric analysis that comes from a recognition that different signs take on different meanings in different situations (p. 45). In some semantic environments, tests are seen as "real" and associated with work and consequences; games are associated with leisure and the play of children. These interpretations are not universal. Some individuals "see" the challenge in tests and may approach even high-stakes exams, for which the results have important consequences for examinees (Zieky, 2001), as challenges to be mastered. Likewise, products such as *Brain Quest* flash cards provide a test-based game of knowledge, as do game shows such as *Jeopardy* and *Who Wants to Be a Millionaire?* Indeed, as suggested in the opening question, some worldviews see life itself as a test that ends in an ultimate categorization, and others see life as a low-conflict game that should be played happily (Huff, 1982). Clearly, functional analyses are insufficient to understand fully the relationships between games and tests.

Privileged Attributes of Assessments and Their Relationship to Simulation-Based Games

To achieve the functional commonalities discussed, these systems are likely to have underlying structural commonalities. We discuss these commonalities by describing the structure of assessment as suggested in the evidence-centered design (ECD) framework.

ECD is useful for such broad discussions because it concerns building assessment arguments at a level of generality such that it applies to arguments cast under different psychological perspectives and to data of any kind.

Evidence-Centered Assessment Design

ECD (Mislevy & Riconscente, 2006; Mislevy, Steinberg, & Almond, 2003) offers a principled framework for designing, producing, and delivering assessments, which proves particularly useful when one incorporates developments from fields such as cognitive science, technology, evidentiary reasoning, and statistical modeling in new and often more complex assessments. ECD explicates the connections among assessment designs, inferences regarding students, and the processes needed to create and deliver these assessments.

ECD provides a formal, multiple-layer framework for designing assessments in line with Messick's (1994) guiding questions:

What complex of knowledge, skills, or other attributes should be assessed? What behaviors or performances should reveal those constructs? What tasks or situations should elicit those behaviors?

Figure 4.1 (Mislevy, Steinberg, & Almond, 1994) sketches the main phases of the design process.

The first stage, domain analysis, encourages the designers to consider the domain from a number of perspectives, including cognitive research, curricula, expert input, and constraints to which the assessment may be subject. During this stage, the knowledge (including declarative, procedural, strategic, and sociocultural knowledge, abbreviated KSAs for knowledge, skills, and abilities) involved in the domain is gathered (Mislevy & Riconscente, 2006), as well as the ways and the situations in which people use this knowledge and the things they say or do that reveal it. When games or assessments are based on real-world simulations, similar analysis is required in each case to ensure the sense of realism expected in the end use.

The domain-modeling phase requires the designers to refine and organize this information into assessment arguments, along the lines of Messick's

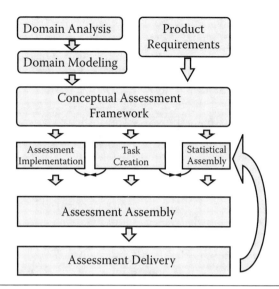

Figure 4.1 Schematic of design and implementation attributes for evidence-centered design.

questions. In line with a conception of the nature of the KSAs, one organizes coherent arguments around the features of situations in which people might act, and the aspects of their work, that will provide evidence about those KSAs. These arguments lay out, often in narrative form, the argument that the more familiar "pieces of machinery" of assessments will need to embody. Like storyboarding for films or games, this phase makes it possible for specialists from different domains to coordinate their work in complex assessments.

The conceptual assessment framework further defines and makes explicit the developing design concepts and assessment argument in terms of the more technical components of an assessment, namely, the structures and variables in the task, evidence, and student models. In traditional assessments, these correspond to item types, item scoring rules, and total scores. In a complex task such as a simulation-based troubleshooting problem or a multiperson game, these notions are inadequate and must be generalized.

A task model now describes the environment in which the student will act and the work products that will serve as evidence. *Task model variables* are features of the environment that are important for interpreting students' actions. Some will be predetermined, such as the components, speed, and affordances in a particular level of a game. Others need to be tracked dynamically in response to the unfolding actions of the students, such as changes they make to a computer network or the resources they have expended thus far. The *work products* are not discrete item responses, but artifacts that hold the potential for gleaning evidence about KSAs — as varied as the state of the network at the end of the problem, the trace of actions the student has taken, rationales provided for actions, or the time and resources expended.

The student model addresses Messick's first question, which asks what complex of knowledge, skills, or other attributes should be assessed. *Student model variables* approximate the KSAs determined in the domain analysis, at a grain size that suits the context of the assessment. These variables are not observed directly, yet it is in their terms that decisions and high-level feedback are determined. It is thus necessary to use what students say or do in various situations as evidence about student model variables. They are not scores in the traditional sense, but rather variables that character-ize aspects of skill or knowledge needed to carry out performances. In our earlier work on performance-based network troubleshooting assessment using a tool called NetPASS (Behrens, Mislevy, Bauer, Williamson, & Levy, 2004; Williamson et al., 2004), for example, one student model variable concerns declarative knowledge in the domain, and another concerns troubleshooting skills; both are required to solve problems, although in different mixes, at different levels of difficulty, in different tasks. Updating belief about a student's values on these variables requires synthesizing the information in patterns of actions across several tasks.

It is the evidence model that bridges between the students' actions in the task and the assessor's belief about the student. It lays out an argument about why and how the observations in a given task situation constitute evidence about student model variables. There are two parts to the evi-dence model: evaluation rules for identifying and evaluating the salient aspects of work products and the measurement model for synthesizing their import in terms of updated belief about student model variables. Human judgment or automated evaluation rules are possible, and they may be carried out at the end of an episode or identify salient events as action progresses. They produce values of *observable variables*. The mea-surement component describes, in terms of a probabilistic (psychometric) model, how the observable variables depend on student model variables. It is used to update belief about them by means of Bayes theorem or other probabilistic model. Of particular importance in simulations and games are the dependencies among observations caused by the impact of past actions on a present situation and the identification of multiple aspects of the same complex performance.

Interestingly, the development of psychometric models to describe task difficulty, learner ability, and the interaction of these elements has been a central focus of the psychometric community for the last 100 years. Meth-ods exist to create detailed probabilistic models of the interrelationship between tasks, dependencies among tasks, and conditional estimates of the probability of task completion by individuals. Both the computational and conceptual frameworks developed here may be of value to the game development community as they seek to quantify performance outcomes on scales that are more abstract than counts or times (Almond, 1995; Gelman, Carlin, Stern, & Rubin, 1995; Mislevy & Gitomer, 1996; Mislevy, Almond, Yan, & Steinberg, 1999; Pearl, 1988).

ECD describes assessment delivery as a cyclical process of activity selection (deciding which activity to present to the examinee next), presentation (interacting with the examinee and collecting a work product), response processing (task-level scoring or pattern recognition on the work product), and evidence accumulation (statistical summarization). In the simplest fixed-form, multiple-choice case, this might look like "choose the next randomly ordered task (activity selection), show it to the examinee and collect an answer (presentation), compare the answer with the key (response processing), and adjust the overall score as appropriate (evidence accumulation)."

In a more complex case such as NetPASS, the cycle works as follows:

Activity Selection: Determine which task (hard, medium, easy) to give based on user desire.

Presentation: Describe the problems and connect them to a simulated computer network. Collect all the commands they typed as well as information on all relevant aspects of the network and its function to comprise the work product.

Response Processing: Apply pattern recognition rules to the work product to create measures describing performance on the tasks.

Evidence Accumulation: Combine the new task-level scores with existing data to update the overall proficiency description using evidence weights via a Bayesian inference network.

Repeat the cycle.

This cycle of choose and present task followed by score work and summarize results can be considered not only a model of assessment, but also ongoing performance management and ongoing game behavior. For example, many multilevel games work as follows:

Task Selection: Determine the level the user is in based on previous performance.

Presentation: Give them more tasks at that level.

Response Processing: Score tasks to see how correct, fast, or the like.

Evidence Accumulation: Summarize score, update estimate of level, pass information to activity selection algorithm.

In complex games with complex underlying simulations, many processes may be going on at once. For example, in the game Age of Empires (Microsoft, 1999), players are immersed in a simulation of empire building. Each activity is calculated to have an impact on a number of variables that can be used as feedback to the player and quantitative measures of outcome. For example, if a player converts villagers to soldiers, the food and wood inventories are likely to decline, although the defenses are improved. This is registered because the changing of roles comprises the player's work, and the record of that change is a work product that is passed to a scoring routine that updates "civilization model" variables regarding wood, food, and other measures related to the villager role. Insofar as the civilization model variables represent actions taken by the players, they are player model variables or, in the language of educational assessment, student model variables as well.

It is important to note that, in these types of situations, the assessment cycle continues in very small loops that provide immediate, detailed, and unobtrusive formative feedback. In this way, the assessment structure is ubiquitously embedded in the system, and the examinee/player does not experience interruptions to instruction for separate assessment activities.

Privileged Attributes of Simulation-Based Games and Their Relationship to Assessment

Whereas in the preceding section we stressed assessment features that can be used to conceptualize game features, in this section we examine privileged features of simulation-based games that should be leveraged toward assessment. Central to this view are conclusions from research about expertise as reflective practice with feedback from the environment. Simulations do this in ways that static tests cannot because the kinds of feedback you get working with the actual entities in the world can be mimicked (Ericsson, 1996, 2004).

Authenticity

A common complaint regarding the validity of assessments is that they may not look like the thing that they are assessing: It is hard to write a multiple-choice question about changing a car tire to make it actually feel like changing a car tire. Advances in rich media add increasing possibilities for this improvement with visual detail, three-dimensional rendering, access to remote data sets, and the like. It is especially intriguing that as we continue to move toward functioning with digital artifacts (computers, spreadsheets, word processors), assessment for tasks on these media may not have to be simulated but may use the original digital expression itself. For example, in computer networking assessment, examinees are sometimes linked remotely to live networks to perform their assessment tasks. Likewise, assessment activities around spreadsheets can sometimes be accomplished right in the spreadsheets with automated scoring.

Knowledge Representations

Key to the use experience of authenticity, the judgment of face validity, and the alignment of desired and appropriate evidence is the use of appropriate knowledge representations (KRs). KRs are used in creating the contexts in which students work, provide the means by which they express their actions, and constitute essential aspects of knowledge in any semantically rich learning domain (Markman, 1999; Mislevy & Levy, 2005). Because memory and performance are largely situation and stimulus specific, with specific procedures associated with specific representations, representational alignment is important for valid assessment inferences. Here also digital media and simulation allow the transmission of representations that are otherwise difficult to capture and transfer. For example, a common representation of computer networks is a topology diagram that illustrates the existence and interconnection of devices on a network. These images are easy to construct, and software has been developed to score diagrams drawn to particular specifications for assessment purposes. Such rich representations and the corresponding scoring machinery can be built into larger contexts of simulation and activity.

Complexity

Although numerous advances in assessment have focused on the decomposition of component skills and the collection of modular information, assessment models that present and integrate complex and broad-based tasks have been less frequent. This represents a divide between simulation-based games and assessment that should be addressed. The world is complex and evolves over time. Likewise, tasks assessing performance in complex and evolving situations should allow both for the evolution of those tasks through complex scenarios and for computational models of performance that integrate those pieces. This represents a challenge to current assessment models.

Simulation, defined by Salen and Zimmerman (2004) as a procedural representation of aspects of "reality," by its nature is incomplete, so the features of the simulation should be developed in a way that aligns with the focus of the learning or assessment experience. Things only need to be simulated if they are cognitively relevant to the learning or assessment. Many attributes of daily experience are overlooked or incidental to task completion and should be omitted or only partially simulated. The point is to determine just which aspects of the real-world environment are essential for eliciting the targeted knowledge and skills and which might add authenticity at the expense of requiring irrelevant knowledge and skills (Messick, 1994).

Expert performance in real-world domains is by its nature interaction with complex environments. But, environments in their full complexity are not necessarily the best situations for learning: Situations with "fewer moving parts," slower or simplified actions and players, and fewer choices may support novices best. Under such conditions, complexities can be introduced only as learners acquire competencies and strategies. Simulations are particularly well suited to helping students learn in this way: We can use simulations to present optimized sequence of "fish tanks," simplified systems that stress a few key variables and their interactions, for students to learn in and to be assessed (Gee, 2003). In particular, we can express implications of curricular sequence in terms of task model variables that describe, and help task designers create, tasks in this manner. Therefore, we can keep increasing complexity gradually, keeping the learner in the Vygotskian zone of proximal development (Vygotsky, 1978).

As well as optimizing learning, the same sequence has important implications for motivation. Video games, to succeed in the market, must allow a player to get started learning and doing something interesting from the beginning without becoming overwhelmed and gradually (usually as the player moves to a next level in a game) take the skills learned so far and extend them in the next more complex simulated world. In computer network design, these factors include the devices in the system, the degree of interconnectivity, the languages and protocols involved, and the complexity of constraints the network must satisfy.

Network City Example

In an effort to provide motivationally and instructionally rich environments for teaching students in the Cisco Networking Academy Program (Behrens et al., 2005; Murnane, Sharkey, & Levy, 2004), we have built a prototype of a game that illustrates many of the principles discussed in this chapter. The game is called Network City (2005). Network City is an immersive comprehensive simulation that presents students with a complex city that requires knowledge of computer networks to keep it running. A facsimile of the overview screen for this world is presented in Figure 4.2.

This environment is a multiplayer, strategic simulation prototype built around an already-existing highly interactive simulation, animation, and visualization environment called Packet Tracer (2004). In the Packet Tracer simulation environment, network topologies may be created (see Figure 4.3) and networking devices be configured via a command line interface (see Figure 4.4), which simulates the computer environment networking professionals use to configure and troubleshoot computer networks. Target audiences for the game include high school and college students in the

Figure 4.2 City view in Network City educational game prototype.

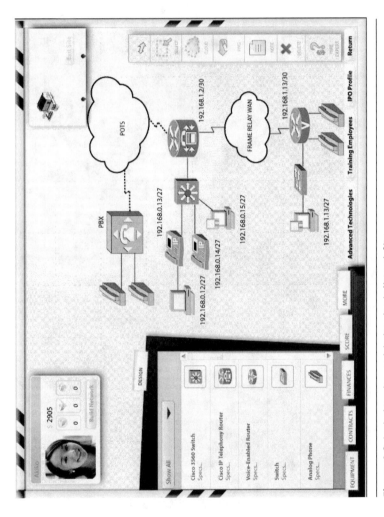

Figure 4.3 Logical topology and design view in Network City.

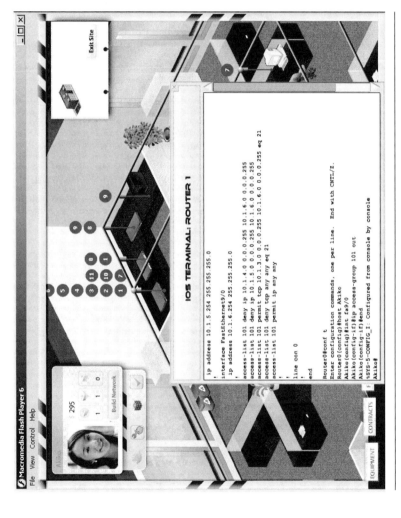

Figure 4.4 View for configuring networking devices via simulated command line interface in Network City.

Cisco Networking Academy Program and Cisco System Inc. employees who are novices in the field of computer networking. Network City uses business scaffolding to help teach technical content. In the following section, we apply the elements discussed as a framework for understanding the design of this educational game.

Authenticity

Network City achieves authenticity via four categories of KRs: scenarios, contracts, views, and underlying domain KRs. *Scenarios* are the high-level winning conditions or outcome rules that drive game play. *Contracts* are the lower level, networking-oriented tasks that learner-players must complete to earn money, future contracts, and market share in the game. *Views* include the various geographic (maps), spatial (offices), financial (equipment lists, see Figure 4.5; balance sheets, see Figure 4.6), and interpersonal (player avatars and skilled virtual employees, see Figure 4.7) "screens" presented to the learner-players. At certain points within the game, the learner-players must use the core domain KRs of computer networking (logical topology, physical topology, internetwork operating system, command line interface, OSI model, and others) to complete the contracts.

Complexity

The key point in our decision to pursue the Network City game prototype was the achievement of an adequately complex simulation environment, Packet Tracer. *Adequate* here refers to sufficiency for use in instruction for a wide range of design, installation, and troubleshooting tasks for novice and apprentice-level computer network technicians and engineers. The underlying simulation environment was deliberately designed with affordances that support a novice-to-expert progression. By using the

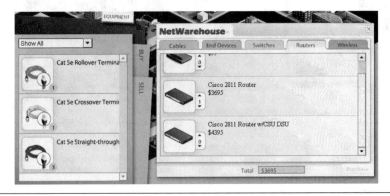

Figure 4.5 Screen shot of environment for making decisions regarding choice of equipment.

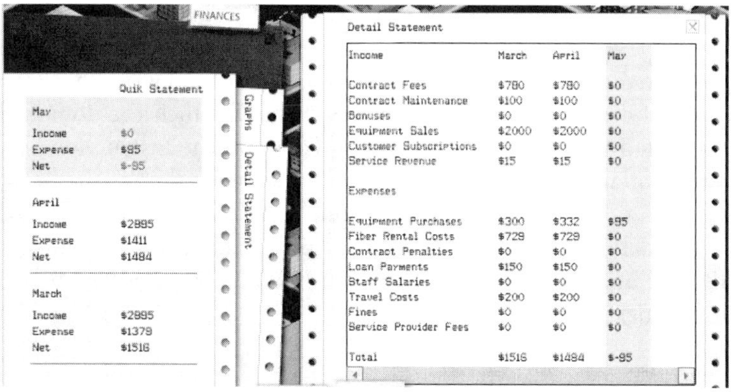

Figure 4.6 Screen shot of balance sheets that provide feedback regarding purchase decisions and performance during game play.

principles of level design of games, a series of scenarios and contracts can be authored, customized to the intended learners' zone of proximal development. The key here is that a finely adjustable level of difficulty can be achieved in both the underlying simulation and the game-oriented learning tasks presented to the student.

Knowledge Representations

We conceptualize the Network City use of KRs as occurring in layers. At the basic layer, there are the underlying domain KRs (logical topology, physical topology, internetwork operating system, command line interface,

Figure 4.7 Screen shot of personnel view providing assessment information regarding players or avatars (computer agents).

OSI model theoretical model of network theory, and others) and the various geographic, spatial, financial, and interpersonal views that characterize the domain of computer networking. At the second layer, there are the designed affordances of game software, through which the domain KRs are presented to the student. At a third layer are the instructional interactions built around the software, which take advantage of the designed affordances to create fun and educational classroom interactions. All of these interactions are occurring in a learning community, which hopes to acculturate and apprentice the learner in the business and technology of running a networking company.

Motivation

The original pedagogical challenge leading to Network City was the difficulty in teaching highly technical content to novices. We wanted to address curriculum, instruction, and assessment in an integrated manner, and research indicated a game was worthy of consideration. Building on our observations of classroom and student use of the existing Packet Tracer simulation environment (e.g., small timed competitions regarding who could build the best network); widespread interest in strategic simulation games (the proliferation games like of SIM City [Maxis, 1989] and Railroad Tycoon [MicroProse, 1990]); and the already multiplayer nature of classroom networking competitions (where instructors pit student teams against each other in hacking competitions), we believed that multiplayer strategic simulation may have potential for increasing student motivation, retention, and recruitment. Achieving "balanced game play" is the key to fun, with *fun* defined simply as pleasurable gaming experience (Salen & Zimmerman, 2004). The affordances of the underlying Packet Tracer simulation for novice to expert progressions is critical in building scenarios and contracts that allow people to learn while experiencing the essence of balanced game play.

Presentation

Both the underlying Packet Tracer simulation, animation, and visualization environment and the Network City business and technical game prototype rely heavily on dynamic, user-driven, interacting KRs. In the Network City prototype, the learner is first presented with an overall scenario in which various networking problems, represented as contracts, are available for bid. Once a contract is awarded, various KRs are presented to the learner. These include, for example, textual or topological descriptions of the problems to be solved. The learner's response (e.g., dragging and dropping networking devices and interconnections or gaining access to a simulated command line interface for programming the networking devices) is captured by the Network City software for processing.

Response Processing

The underlying simulation engine for Network City, Packet Tracer, has an Activity Wizard for authoring predetermined, simply scored activities. This basic capability is exploited by Network City, which adds state-of-the-city-and-company business variables to the underlying state-of-the network variables. Network City is written in terms of scenarios — high-level feedback (see Figure 4.8) in the form of high-level business rules for success, for example, make the most money or serve the most of the city's businesses — and contracts, low-level feedback that requires combinations of networking technical skill and business acumen (see Figure 4.9). The key links between the Network City game and theoretical assessment processes are through these scenarios, which are the means of giving high-level performance and proficiency feedback, and contracts, which are written in the explicit language of claims, component skills, evidence models, and task selection of ECD.

Evidence Accumulation

Because (a) the underlying technical simulation environment is already built in terms of network state variables and (b) the added business layer has business and state-of-game variables, the derivation, via rubrics and then automated scoring rules, of learner proficiency models is a matter of computing from already-existing quantities. Although the static state variables are ultimately limited, they can provide a large amount of feedback to the learner. Pathways through problem solving (Mayer & Whittrock, 1996) consider problem solving as the "cognitive processing directed at achieving a goal when no solution is obvious to the problem solver" (see also O'Neil, 1999, p. 47). Work products relevant to the understanding and analysis of these paths can be captured via log files. Log files could be used in real time to provide diagnostic feedback and hints to the game players. Different levels of the game, the so-called level design issue in game design, can be directly related to determination of different levels of proficiency.

Task Selection

The idea of design patterns around clusters of relevant task characteristics found in ECD (e.g., clusters of troubleshooting tasks) can directly facilitate the construction of the scenarios and contracts of Network City. Crucial to the success of the game will be the development of authoring environments that facilitate the creation of scenarios and contracts, by instructional designers, domain

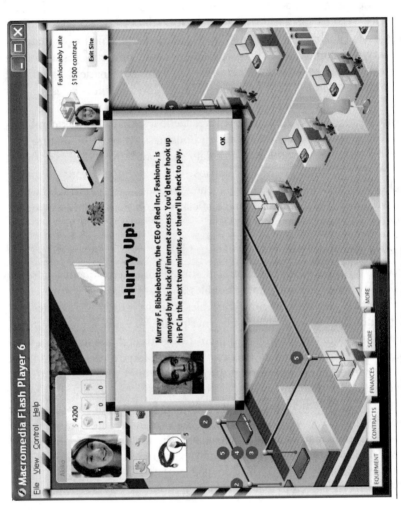

Figure 4.8 Example high-level feedback from Network City.

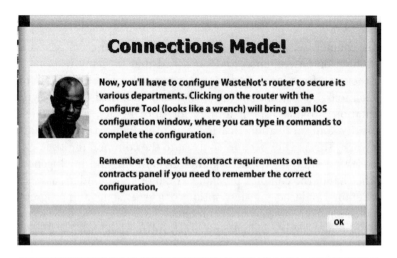

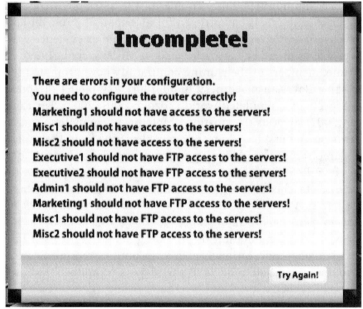

Figure 4.9 Detailed feedback provided by Network City program.

experts, instructors, or learners themselves. The problem of task selection may in some instances be compared to the process of level design familiar to game developers. In the Network City prototype development, the all-important goal of engaging, immersive game play was closely related to the systematic structuring of tasks, contracts, and scenarios.

Summary and Conclusion

In this chapter, we discussed the privileged properties of assessments and simulation-based games and suggested that in many respects there are structural, functional, and semiotic parallels as well as complimentary technologies. On the gaming side, interactive, realistic, and dynamic presentation provides opportunities for authenticity, appropriate KR, complexity, and motivation that is frequently underestimated in assessment work. This may be seen in contrast to the common multiple-choice, text-based question for its face validity, dynamism, and intelligence. On the other hand, the complex psychometric models of modern assessment allow detailed and tractable descriptions of learner states and progressions often missing from gaming environments.

The complimentary values and separate focuses can be illustrated by noting the use of common technologies in both the gaming and the assessment communities. For example, in the assessment community, a number of individuals have argued for an expanding role for application of Bayesian inference networks to solve complex evidence accumulation problems (e.g., Levy & Mislevy, 2004; Mislevy, et al., 1999). At the same time, members of the gaming community have promoted the use of the same Bayesian machinery to appropriately model the presentational aspects of a simulated world (Tozour, 2001, 2002). For example, Tozour (2002) suggests the creation of intelligent computer agents (such as guards or soldiers) based on the agents learning from the experience of the game rather than having privileged knowledge because of their digital basis. Referring to the computer's observation of players, Tozour sounds like a teacher observing an examinee: "We can *estimate the accuracy of our surveillance of a given player* and *determine which opposing players require more surveillance*" (p. 354). This is identical in goal and possibly the computation of providing adaptively chosen tasks to improve student model estimation. Clearly, both communities are motivated to create accurate models of the player's (examinee's) knowledge states and likely behavior.

Although we believe the intersection of the work of these communities and their technologies will be fruitful, it is important to remember that authenticity, KR, motivation, and complexity are only valuable in the context of the specific construct measured. Depending on the claims made, increases in complexity of presentation may lead to tasks that drift from the most informative states and introduce construct-irrelevant variance. Just because a simulation looks cool does not mean it will be effective in meeting its psychometric goals or obligations.

Acknowledgments

We would like to thank our colleagues, whose collaboration has greatly influenced the work described here; especially, we thank Mark Chen, Vanessa Vogel, and Larry Schnicker. Any errors or omissions are our sole responsibility.

References

Almond, R. G. (1995). *Graphical belief modeling.* New York: Chapman and Hall.

Behrens, J. T., Collison, T. A., & DeMark, S. F. (2005). The seven Cs of comprehensive assessment: Lessons learned from 40 million classroom exams in the Cisco Networking Academy Program. In S. Howell and M. Hricko (Eds.), *Online assessment and measurement: Case studies in higher education, K-12 and corporate* (pp 229–245). Hershey, PA: Information Science Publishing.

Behrens, J. T., Mislevy, R. J., Bauer, M., Williamson, D. M., & Levy R. (2004). Introduction to evidence centered design and lessons learned from its application in a global e-learning program. *The International Journal of Testing, 4,* 295–301.

Ericsson, K. A. (Ed.), (1996). *The road to excellence: The acquisition of expert performance in the arts and sciences, sports, and games.* Mahwah, NJ: Erlbaum.

Ericsson, K. A. (2004). Deliberate practice and the acquisition and maintenance of expert performance in medicine and related domains. *Academic Medicine, 10,* S1–S12.

Gee, J. P. (2003). *What video games have to teach us about learning and literacy.* New York: Palgrave Macmillan.

Gelman, A., Carlin, J. B., Stern, H. S., & Rubin, D. B. (1995). *Bayesian data analysis.* London: Chapman and Hall.

Hoopes, J. (1991). *Peirce on signs. Writings on semiotic by Charles Sanders Peirce.* Chapel Hill: University of North Carolina Free Press.

Huff, B. (1982). *The tao of Pooh.* New York: Penguin.

Markman, A. B. (1999). *Knowledge representation.* Mahwah, NJ: Erlbaum.

Mayer, R. E., & Wittrock, M. C. (1996). Problem-solving transfer. In D. C. Berliner, & R. C. Calfee (Eds.), *Handbook of educational psychology* (pp. 47–62). New York: Simon & Simon Schuster Macmillan.

Microsoft Corporation. (1999). Age of Empires II: Age of Conquest [Computer software]. Retrieved in June 2006 from www.microsoft.com/games/empires

Messick, S. (1994). The interplay of evidence and consequences in the validation of performance assessments. *Educational Researcher, 23*(2), 13–23.

Mislevy, R. J. (2003). Substance and structure in assessment arguments. Law, Probability, and Risk, 2, 237–258.

Mislevy, R. J., Almond, R. G., Yan, D., & Steinberg, L. S. (1999). Bayes nets in educational assessment: Where do the numbers come from? In K. B. Laskey & H. Prade (Eds.), *Proceedings of the Fifteenth Conference on Uncertainty in Artificial Intelligence* (pp. 437–446). San Francisco: Morgan Kaufmann.

Mislevy, R. J., & Gitomer, D. H. (1996). The role of probability based inference in an intelligent tutoring system. *User-Modeling and User-Adapted Interaction, 5*, 253–282.

Mislevy, R. J., & Levy, R. (2005, April). *Knowledge representations overview.* Paper presented at the annual meeting of the American Educational Research Association, Montreal.

Mislevy, R. J., & Riconscente, M. M. (2006). Evidence-centered assessment design: Layers, concepts, and terminology. In S. Downing & T. Haladyna (Eds.), *Handbook of test development* (pp. 61–90). Mahwah, NJ: Erlbaum.

Mislevy, R. J., Steinberg, L. S., & Almond, R. G. (1994). Evidence-centered assessment design. Retrieved in June 2006 from the University of Maryland EDMS website:http://www.education.umd.edu/EDMS/mislevy/papers/ECD_ overview.html.

Murnane, R. J., Sharkey, N. S., & Levy, F. (2004). A role for the Internet in American education? Lessons from the Cisco Networking Academies. In P. A. Graham & N. G. Stacey (Eds.), *The knowledge economy and postsecondary education: Report of a workshop* (pp. 127–158). Committee on the Impact of the Changing Economy on the Education System, National Research Council. Washington, DC: National Academies Press.

Network City [Prototype computer software]. (2005). San Jose, CA: Cisco Systems Inc.

Packet Tracer (Version 3.2) [Computer software]. (2004). San Jose, CA: Cisco Systems Inc.

Pearl, J. (1988). *Probabilistic reasoning in intelligent systems: Networks of plausible inference.* San Mateo, CA: Morgan Kaufman.

Peirce, C. S. (1868). Questions concerning certain faculties claimed for man. *Journal of Speculative Philosophy, 2*, 103–114.

Salen, K., & Zimmerman, E. (2004). *Rules of play: Game design fundamentals.* Cambridge, MA: MIT Press.

Tozour, P. (2001). Strategic assessment techniques. In M. DeLoura (Ed.), *Game programming gems 2* (pp. 298–306). Hingham, MA: Charles River Media.

Tozour, P. (2002). Introduction to Bayesian networks and reasoning under uncertainty. In S. Rabin (Ed.), *AI game programming wisdom* (pp. 345–357). Hingham, MA: Charles River Media.

VanLehn, K. (1990). *Mind bugs.* Cambridge, MA: MIT Press.

Vygotsky. (1978). *Mind in society: The development of higher psychological processes.* Cambridge, MA: Harvard University Press.

Williamson, D. M., Bauer, M., Steinberg, L. S., Mislevy, R. J., Behrens, J. T., & Demark, S. (2004). Design rationale for a complex performance assessment. *International Journal of Measurement, 4*, 333–369.

Zieky, M. J. (2001). So much has changed: How the setting of cutscores has evolved since the 1980s. In G. Cizek (Ed.), *Setting performance standards: Concepts, methods, and perspectives* (pp. 19–51). Mahwah, NJ: Erlbaum.

5

Training Evaluation
of Virtual Environments

JOSEPH V. COHN

Naval Research Laboratory

KAY M. STANNEY, LAURA M. MILHAM,
DAVID L. JONES, AND KELLY S. HALE

Design Interactive, Inc.

RUDOLPH P. DARKEN AND JOE A. SULLIVAN

Naval Postgraduate School

Motorola calculates that for every $1 spent on training, there is a $30 productivity gain within three years.

Ronald Henkoff (1993)

Introduction

Henkoff's (1993) claim certainly depends on the effectiveness of the training provided. Tremendous investment and time are dedicated to the development and use of training systems each year, often without thorough evaluation of the compatibility, understandability, and effectiveness of resulting training solutions. It is important to determine if a given solution meets a critical training need, is targeted to a specific training community, is appropriately designed to meet the need, is inserted into existing curricula in the most effective manner, is cost-effective, and has validated techniques for assessing training outcome to ensure the solution

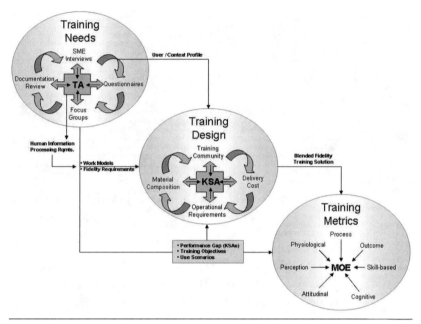

Figure 5.1 Training *Evaluation Process.* KSA, knowledge, skills, and attitudes; MOE, measure of effectiveness; TA, task analysis.

did indeed meet the identified training need. Thus, it is essential to link training needs to training design to training metrics to ensure the effectiveness of a given training solution (see Figure 5.1). This chapter reviews each of these subcomponents of the training evaluation process.

Training Needs Analysis

Training programs are often not directly tied to job performance requirements as comprehensive needs analyses are rarely done (Tannenbaum & Yukl, 1991). Before designing and evaluating a training solution, it is essential to conduct a training needs analysis (TNA). TNA is a process of gathering and interpreting data from the target training community and operational environment in an effort to identify performance gaps and formulate training solutions (Gupta, 1998; Rossett, 1987, 1995, 1999). TNA focuses on providing data concerning current versus desired performance and knowledge in an identified gap area, attitudes toward the targeted performance gap, causes of or contributing factors toward the performance gap, and potential solutions (Rossett, 1987). A comprehensive TNA provides the basis from which to design training solutions that realize substantial improvements in human performance by closing the identified performance gap in a manner that is compatible with current training practices. It is essential not to mistake the word *comprehensive* to mean significant impact on user's time. We have found that when provided with access to current and past training curricula and to subject matter experts (SMEs) to fill in any unresolved questions prior to conducting the TNA, comprehensive TNAs can be accomplished with just a few 1- to 3-day trips to the field. This approach — essentially doing one's homework prior to engaging the customers — removes one of the biggest obstacles to working in an operational setting, namely, the perception that time spent by the customers developing a TNA is an unwanted and time-consuming affair.

Because part of a TNA involves the development of measures to assess expertise, one might assume that identifying the experts to create these metrics would lead to a chicken-and-egg conundrum: How can one define expertise by identifying experts without first having the definition? We have found a good solution to be to take advantage of instructors or of those individuals who are considered, through informal discussions with the unit, company, squadron, or the like, to be "shining stars." Again, this approach does requires that the TNA development team do their homework in advance of starting work, conducting short, informal interviews with senior staff to better identify who these individuals are. In addition, it is beneficial to interview two to three SMEs (whether instructor or otherwise) as each informant's perception of training needs may differ slightly, and thus the core needs can be identified by cross-referencing across multiple SMEs. Often, these interviews can be conducted over the phone, although face-to-face discussions are always preferable.

Methods of Training Needs Analysis

There are several methods for conducting a TNA. Taken together, these methods aim to define what is to be accomplished with the envisioned training solution, expressed in terms of desired performance outcomes. The methods include:

- *Background Information*: Obtain and review background information (e.g., doctrine, field manuals, flow charts, training materials) related to the tasks to be trained to gain familiarity with practices and terminology (Stanney, Smith, Carayon, & Salvendy, 2001). This review provides a foundation of knowledge from which to reason about the tasks and processes to be analyzed, which allows analysts to conduct credible interviews, task analyses, and focus groups.
- *SME Interviews*: Open-ended questions are asked to SMEs in a semi-structured interview format to characterize their understanding of task flows and knowledge, skills, and abilities (KSAs) (Gagne, 1962) associated with targeted task performance, as well as communicate existing performance gaps (Lambe, 2005).

- *Task Analysis* (TA): TA involves identifying specific tasks to be trained combined with a detailed analysis of each of those tasks. Information derived through a TA forms the basis for developing training goals and objectives, choosing the appropriate training methodologies, developing training technologies, and assessing training effectiveness. Although there are many types of TA, three in particular are often encountered when developing training tools: cognitive, job oriented, and worker oriented.
  - Although there are many types of cognitive task analysis (CTA), a common theme running through all is the notion that performance of complex tasks depends on the ability to access knowledge (i.e., declarative, procedural, and strategic) and to make (often, novel) decisions (Hackos & Redish, 1998; Kirwan & Ainsworth, 1992). An additional challenge for those simulations that bring together multiple users is the emphasis on teamwork and the identification of those elements that support training a particular skill. CTA for teams (team task analysis) is a relatively new field, with even less history attached to it than more traditional CTA (Blickensderfer, Cannon-Bowers, Salas, & Baker, 2000).
  - Job-oriented TA involves systematically collecting information about highly specific and distinct tasks required in the conduct of a particular job: what workers do, how they do it, and the results they achieve (Jonassen, Tessmer, & Hannum, 1999). This approach generally involves informants (i.e., workers or supervisors) communicating step by step the sequence of job tasks involved in a target activity.
  - Worker-oriented TA, also known as contextual task analysis (CoTA), characterizes the observable and measurable behaviors associated with performing a given task in terms of their flow, timing, frequency, importance, and current difficulties (Jeffries, 1997; Kirwan & Ainsworth, 1992; Mayhew, 1997; Stanney et al., 2001). The resulting work models and associated use scenarios can then help guide the design of training systems. During CoTA, use of a standardized observation sheet across observers is recommended.
- *Questionnaires*: Questionnaires can be designed (Sudman & Bradbum, 1982) to gather data regarding the performance gap to pursue user profiles and task information (cf. McCormick, Mecham, & Jeanneret, 1989).
- *Focus Groups*: Focus groups can be used to obtain feedback from the target training community to gauge perceptions regarding the performance

Table 5.1 Elements of a User Profile

Demographics

Age (mean, standard deviation) and gender split

Physical characteristics of interest (e.g., color blind)

Language and culture

Education

Knowledge, skill levels

Experience in present or related jobs

Present knowledge and skill levels on job

Perception of current performance on tasks targeted for training

Attitudes

Perception of current work and training culture

Motivation

Attitudes toward past training solutions

Any preconceived interests or biases

---

gap, current issues leading to the gap, and potential solutions, as well as reactions to envisioned solutions (Krueger & Casey, 2000).

A combination of these methods should be used and organized into an overall approach, such as discussed next (see Figure 5.1).

Step 1. Characterize Target Users and Target Environment

- *Objective*: Obtain information that can be used to ensure the training solution is designed to be compatible with the target training community, environment, and culture.
  - Use SME interviews and questionnaires to develop user profiles that characterize the following (see Table 5.1):
    - the targeted training community (i.e., both trainee and instructor/trainer; "know thy user"), capturing their demographics, knowledge/skills, and attitudes toward training and the identified performance gap
    - the target training environment (i.e., context and culture) into which the envisioned training solution is to be inserted
- *Outcome*: User profile and cultural/context profile.

Step 2. Identify Critical Performance Gap

- *Objective*: Identify the optimal problem (see Table 5.2) to address, engage the target training community in the training development effort, and allow the target community to assist in formulating the training solution, thereby developing a sense of ownership.

Table 5.2 Questions to Address With SME During Training Needs Analysis to Identify Performance Gaps

---

Some questions that might be asked to determine training needs are:

Cast a broad net:

○ Which specific skills and abilities do your personnel need or need to improve on?

○ If you could change one thing in the manner in which your personnel currently perform their tasks, what would it be?

○ What knowledge, skills, and attitudes would you most like for your personnel to be trained on?

Narrow down:

○ Which tasks are currently not performed at ideal performance levels?
  • Of these, which are the four most important tasks?
      ○ What currently prevents personnel from performing these tasks at ideal performance levels?
      ○ What are the ideal performance levels for these tasks?
          ▪ How are these levels currently assessed (i.e., what are the current performance metrics)?

○ Are there activities your personnel are supporting that they should not be doing?
  • If so, why are they supporting these activities?
  • What alternatives are currently available?

Discuss potential solutions:

• What new technology would most benefit you in supporting your personnel's training needs?

○ If you are developing a new training technology solution, explain the technology to the SME and then ask: How could this new technology potentially support your personnel in supporting their training needs?

Formalize and prioritize gaps:

○ Based on everything discussed above, which are the most critical performance gaps to address?
  • Which of these training gaps are suitable to address with the envisioned training technology solution?
  • Of the training gaps that are suitable to address with the envisioned training solution, which is the most critical gap to address?
      ▪ Where should the envisioned training solution be inserted into the existing curriculum to address this critical training gap such that it is compatible with current training practices?

- Use semistructured SME interviews to identify the target performance gap, point of insertion, current versus desired performance and knowledge in the identified gap area, attitudes toward the targeted performance gap, causes of or contributing factors toward the performance gap, and potential solutions.
- Use questionnaires to determine if there is consensus in the target training community with the position identified via SME interviews and to characterize attitudes toward the targeted performance gap and potential solutions.
- Use focus groups to drive consensus if dissension is identified in questionnaire responses (cf. Cornwell, 2004, who found a lack of convergence in questionnaire responses during a TNA).
- *Outcome*: Identification of target performance gap and training and performance objectives for the envisioned training solution that will close the gap.

Step 3. Collect Operational Data

- *Objective*: Gather information to support data-driven design decisions.
  - Review documentation to gain familiarity with practices and procedures.
  - Conduct CoTA to identify task flows (see Table 5.3) and leverage SME interviews to characterize declarative, procedural, and strategic knowledge (Anderson, 1995) associated with task performance (see Table 5.4). The TA should identify trainee information-processing requirements, including precise characterization of the inputs (e.g., system and environmental cues and feedback) a trainee must receive and outputs (e.g., actions, responses, communication) the trainee must convey, which provide a basis from which to derive fidelity requirements (Hays & Singer, 1988).
- *Outcome*: Raw data via which to build metrics, models, fidelity requirements, and scenarios.

Step 4. Develop Models, Metrics, Fidelity Requirements, and Scenarios

- *Objective*: Formulate data so that it supports design and evaluation of the envisioned training solution.
  - Develop work models (i.e., use workflow diagrams, use sequences, use hierarchy diagrams, use flow diagrams) (Hackos & Redish, 1998).
  - Characterize specific KSAs associated with target tasks and procedures and the performance metrics currently used to assess these KSAs (Gagne, 1962); these KSAs should be linked to the human information-processing requirements (Hays & Singer, 1988) that

Table 5.3 Data to Gather During Contextual Task Analysis

- Task descriptions, derived from observational analysis and associated documentation (e.g., doctrine, field manuals, flow charts, training materials), provide a user-centered model of tasks as they are currently performed. The data to focus on include
  - ○ What is the general flow of task activity?
  - ○ What is the timing of each task step?
  - ○ How frequently is the task performed?
  - ○ How difficult or complex is the task?
  - ○ How important is the task to overall human-system performance?
    - ▪ What are the consequences of task errors or omission of the task?
  - ○ What are the physical system displays and controls that are needed to support the task?
  - ○ What are the environmental cues that are essential to support the task?
  - ○ What are the information sources (i.e., both documentation and online) that support the task?
  - ○ What are the artifacts (i.e., equipment, tools) that support the task?
  - ○ With which technologies or systems does the task currently interface?
  - ○ Is the task performed individually or as part of collective set of tasks, or does it require coordination with other personnel?
    - ▪ If part of a collective set, what are the interrelationships between the set of tasks?
    - ▪ If coordination is required, what are the roles and responsibilities of each individual in accomplishing the task?
  - ○ Which KSAs are used in the performance of the task?
  - ○ How are these KSAs currently assessed by instructors/trainers (i.e., what are the current performance metrics)?
    - ▪ Which behaviors distinguish good versus poor KSAs?
  - ○ What are the current versus desired performance level on these KSAs?
  - ○ How can the procedures that characterize utilization of these KSAs be formulated into use scenarios?
  - ○ How should a training solution be designed to best support development of these KSAs?

support their development and together are used to formulate the learning objectives and content of the training solution.

- To define the fidelity requirements for a given training solution, characterize the dependency relationships between human information-processing requirements and their associated controls,

Table 5.4 Guidelines for Characterizing Task Knowledge via SME Interviews

When using SME interviews to characterize task knowledge, SMEs (2–3 are generally sufficient) are asked to verbalize their strategies, rationale, and knowledge used to accomplish task goals and subgoals (Ericsson & Simon, 1980).

- To characterize declarative knowledge (i.e., facts, principles, rules, concepts), use a combination of task diagramming (i.e., SME breaks task into 3–6 subtasks, indicating sequencing and cognitive skill needed for each subtask); knowledge audits (i.e., SME identifies knowledge categories [e.g., human information processing abilities, situational awareness, metacognition, diagnosis] associated with a given task by probing concrete scenarios); and card sorting (i.e., SME sorts concepts related to job/task into functional groups based on relatedness and then builds a hierarchy of the related concepts) (Clark & Chopeta, 2004; McDonald, Dearholt, Paap, & Schvaneveldt, 1986; Shadbolt & Wielinga, 1990; Woodward, 1990).

- To characterize procedural knowledge (i.e., how to perform a given task, discrete steps or actions required to accomplish task, alternatives), use a combination of backward thinking (i.e., work backward through task); concept mapping; task action mapping; teach-back (i.e., SME describes procedure to analyst); and reflection (i.e., show SME photographs depicting system state and probe) (Converse & Kahler, 1992; McNeese & Zaff, 1991; Woodward, 1990).

- To characterize strategic knowledge (i.e., action plans to meet specific goals and adjust if information is missing or errors/mishaps occur; context-related knowledge), use a combination of critical decision mapping (i.e., identify perceptual cues, judgment details, decision strategies during routine and nonroutine activities); decision process diagramming; goals-means network analysis (i.e., mapping functional interrelationships); and information weighting (i.e., derive relative weights, functional forms, strategy for combining information sources) (Coury, Motte, & Seiford, 1991; Crandall & Klein, 1990; Hammond, Mumpower, & Smith, 1977; Thordsen, 1991; Woods & Hollnagel, 1987).

displays, and devices (George, Reese, Durham, & Knight, 2000). This analysis identifies the appropriate level of fidelity required for each system component (see Table 5.5).

- Develop a matrix that links KSAs to human information-processing requirements to fidelity requirements to current performance metrics (see Table 5.6).

- Develop use scenarios that characterize work models and procedures associated with utilization of target KSAs, include supporting information sources, artifacts, and interfacing technologies or systems.

Table 5.5 Fidelity Requirement Ratings

Human information processing requirement	Associated controls, displays, and devices	Impact on training	Fidelity requirement
Identify human information-processing requirements (e.g., sensory cues, system feedback) that support development of KSAs	Identify associated controls, displays, and devices that support human information-processing requirements	Rate impact on training of physical, functional, and environmental fidelity from low (little impact on training KSAs) to medium (some replication required to support training) to high (exact replication essential to training)	Rate fidelity requirement from 1 (low fidelity) to 3 (high fidelity)

Note. Adapted from Good Practice in Training: A Guide to the Analysis, Design, Delivery and Management of Training, B. Alston, 2002, Railway Safety, London, http://www.rgsonline.co.uk/docushare/dsweb/Get/Rail-5181/220.pdfAlston.

- *Outcome*: Work models, performance metrics, fidelity requirements, and use scenarios.

In summary, TNA determines the *who* (i.e., target training community), *what* (i.e., target training tasks), *when* (i.e., point of insertion), and *where* (i.e., context of insertion) of the envisioned training solution (Broadbent & Froidevaux, 1998). TNA does not address the *how*, that is, specifically how to design the training solution; however, it provides the basis from which to make data-driven design decisions (Rossett, 1999). It does not address the *how effective*, that is, evaluation of the resulting training solution; however, it provides the metrics from which to base such an evaluation. The how and the how effective are addressed in the next two sections.

Table 5.6 Training Needs Analysis Matrix

Training objectiveve	learning objectiveses	Human information processing requirementsts	Fidelity requirementsts	Performance metricscs	Evaluationon
Reduce/close identified performance gapap	Desired gains in KSAs to be targeted via envisioned training solution to close the performance gapap	Identify human information-processing requirements (e.g., sensory cues, system feedback) that support development of KSAsAs	Characterize relationships between human information-processing requirements and associated controls, displays, and devices, thereby identifying appropriate level of fidelity required for each componentnt	Identify performance metrics that gauge KSAsAs	Determine if learning objectives are met with envisioned training solution (i.e., performance gap closed)

Training Design

Based on the results of the TNA, a mixed or "blended" fidelity training solution can be designed that identifies how best to meet learning objectives that will close the target performance gap. The solution should integrate the optimal mix of classroom instruction training technologies and live events throughout a given course of training to ensure a desired level of readiness is achieved (Carter & Trollip, 1980). The composition of the material to be trained, characteristics of the target training community, cost of delivery, and operational requirements all contribute to the determination of the optimal blend of training delivery methods.

Composition of Material to Be Trained

In terms of the composition of the material to be trained, declarative, procedural, strategic, and cognitive/psychomotor skills, as well as attitudes, can all be developed, honed, and rehearsed, but the effectiveness of a given training solution for addressing each of these KSAs depends on the fidelity of the training solution. In general, van Merriënboer and Kester (2005) recommended following the *fidelity principle*, by which learning is supported via a gradual increase in the fidelity of the training environment (cf. McLaughlin, Doezema, & Sklar, 2002):

- During initial acquisition of declarative knowledge (i.e., general facts, principles, rules, and concepts) and basic skills, it is most effective to use classroom lectures and low-fidelity training solutions (e.g., schematics, mock-ups), the latter of which can be used to allow for short practice sessions of learned knowledge and skills (Kelley, Orgel, & Baer, 1985; Rouse, 1982). High-fidelity simulators are generally less effective for such initial training as they can be overly complex and confusing (Andrews, 1988; Boreham, 1985; Jones, 1990).
- Basic procedural knowledge and problem-solving skills and practice of such skills to mastery are thought to be most effectively trained via medium-fidelity training solutions (Pappo, 1998; Patrick, 1992).
- For consolidation of learned declarative knowledge and basic skills and procedures, practice of acquired knowledge and skills (e.g., mission rehearsal), as well as development of more advanced strategic knowledge and tactical skills, high-fidelity training solutions are recommended (Forrest, Taylor, Postlethwaite, & Aspinall, 2002; Maran & Glavin, 2003; Takayesu et al., 2002; Vozenilek, Huff, Reznek, & Gordon, 2004).
- After knowledge and skills have been well trained without stressors, behavioral conditioning can then be addressed (i.e., initially train without stressors, then add stressors so trainees learn to assess and

manage them). Attitudes and behaviors are likely most appropriately trained in high-fidelity training solutions, which have the authenticity to generate realistic responses from trainees; yet, there is limited research on this topic.

Simulations are useful for training procedures under the stresses associated with group, time, and sensory overload stresses; however, simulations are not able to train the emotional conditioning necessary to operate with the stress of physical, emotional, and legal threats. However, we found little research that directly addresses this issue. Given the expense of training simulators and live training, we believe that the Department of Navy (DoN) should pursue research articulating what skills and behaviors simulators can, and cannot, train. (Smith et al., 2002, pp. 23–24)

High-fidelity simulators can add stressors, such as intense multimodal sensory loading, high task demands, and above-real-time events (i.e., when simulator events are run faster than they would unfold in real-time; see Stanney & Guckenberger, 1995) to condition emotional responses (Smith et al., 2002). Live training (e.g., live fires and maneuvers, live patient, flight time, nautical mileage) is likely necessary for training performance under physical, emotional, and mortal threats; yet, the potential of adding such stressors to high-fidelity training simulators via "story" or other strategies that promote engagement should be explored.

Thus, the most effective training solutions generally rely on leveraging a mix of delivery methods. Such blended fidelity training is based on the premise that the appropriate level of fidelity for a given training solution should be based on the target KSAs that are to be trained, with the objective to formulate a multiplatform training solution, with each platform providing a representation of the training context and associated behaviors that is sufficiently detailed to support effective training while avoiding any unnecessary costly features (Rouse, 1982; Salas, Bowers, & Rhodenizer, 1999).

Blended learning systems employ a wide array of mainstream training and information technologies to support [an] overarching knowledge management methodology and ensure the effective and efficient delivery of training content to users and students anyplace, anytime. (Kucinski, 2005)

When adhering to these guidelines, it is essential to understand that learning is context specific (Anderson, Greeno, Reder, & Simon, 2000). Thus, although learners do adapt knowledge developed in one context to another, such transfer tends to occur only under limited conditions.

This may be because learners tend to oversimplify new concepts, especially those gleaned in dynamic, highly interactive environments; this is known as the *reductive tendency* (Feltovich, Hoffman, & Eccles, 2004). To address such issues and overcome the knowledge shields erected to confirm simplified beliefs and understandings, it is essential to engage principles of cognitive flexibility theory and present materials in multiple contexts and from multiple points of view.

Characteristics of Target Training Community

Training strategies should vary based on the expertise of trainees (Patrick, 1992). The continuum from novice to expert has been characterized by several theories (cf. Dreyfus & Dreyfus, 1986; Ericsson & Smith, 1991). Dreyfus and Dreyfus (1986) proposed a comprehensive five-stage model of this progression in terms of skill acquisition. This sequence was suggested to begin as a novice seeks to establish a foundational understanding of KSAs associated with the target task. This stage is best supported by classroom instruction and context-free practice of learned facts, principles, rules, and concepts; the last should allow for analytical reasoning about what has been learned to foster the early development of mental models. "The proper organization of declarative knowledge into schemata or mental models is the first step on the road to expertise" (Taylor, 1998). Although context free at the novice stage, training curricula at every stage should be directly linked to the KSAs identified as essential during the TNA (Goldstein, 1991; Witkin & Alschuld, 1995).

According to Dreyfus and Dreyfus (1986), supplementing context-free practice with situational practice (e.g., via low-fidelity training solutions such as mock-ups) allows a novice to transform to an advanced beginner, at which stage the trainee begins to generate a set of tentative situational rules that link declarative knowledge to context-specific scenarios.

During the next stage, a competent trainee develops a more sophisticated procedural understanding and becomes more involved in choosing the strategy via which to accomplish a task; however, the competent trainee's growing yet fragile understanding can be overwhelming as clear priorities between action plans and specific context have yet to be established. Thus, at this stage, the training solution should incrementally introduce more situational factors to avoid overwhelming the trainee.

In the next stage, the trainee becomes a proficient performer who engages in problem solving at an intuitive level (e.g., can leverage salient features of a high-fidelity training solution to support spontaneous problem solving) as well as by reflecting on previous courses of action and running speculative if-then mental scenarios to select action plans (Schon, 1983). Thus, at this stage the benefits of fidelity may be harnessed as trainees are equipped to leverage multisensory cues and ecologically valid features. It is important to leverage constructivist theories at this and the subsequent stage, which characterize how best to situate learning in authentic context (Lave & Wenger, 1991).

Dreyfus and Dreyfus's (1986) final expert stage is associated with mature and practiced understanding of a given domain, which leads to intuitive action plan generation (Chi, Glaser, & Rees 1982). Experts often have the sense of existence "in a zone" (Csikszentmihalyi, 1990), in which their experiences and KSAs are effortlessly elicited by a target context to achieve an optimal solution.

Taken together, differences in the novice-to-expert continuum suggest that one should strive for a training strategy that initially focuses on aiding novice trainees in developing knowledge of essential KSAs in a context-free platform (e.g., classroom instruction) using a low-fidelity training solution, then introduces medium-fidelity situational factors that allow for generation of mental models of the target domain without overwhelming the trainee, and gradually introduces more situational practice opportunities of increasing complexity using high-fidelity tools (Taylor, 1998). The bottom line is that trainee expertise is a mediating factor that should be used to guide how to define training content, apply training strategies, and derive blended fidelity requirements.

Cost of Delivery

For any training program, it is essential to ensure that the most cost-effective training solution is achieved, in terms of both economic impact and impact on training effectiveness and ultimately operational readiness. Although live, real-world training will likely remain the basis via which to gauge proficiency/mastery of KSAs and train emotional responses (i.e., behavioral and attitudes), a blended fidelity solution is often necessitated by cost, availability, and environmental concerns. Indeed, as Roscoe (1982) suggested, there are theoretical points within a training curriculum when it may be preferable to use training technologies to enhance the effectiveness of exposure to real-world conditions. Roof (1996) suggested that significant financial savings can be realized by using a blended fidelity training solution with little to no loss in training effectiveness. High-fidelity training solutions, such as live training or full-fidelity simulators, generally are limited by their run-time cost and scheduling constraints. Such training solutions generally require costly ordnance (for live) or bespoke hardware located at a designated training site (for high fidelity), which have limited access because of cost and safety concerns. Medium- and low-fidelity solutions are generally portable, cost-effective, and at least for the low fidelity, widely available. Such training solutions can be used to reduce the risk and cost associated with live or high-fidelity training, particularly during initial knowledge and skill acquisition stages. The aim should be to develop a mix of training delivery methods that effectively trains KSAs while simultaneously compressing the length and minimizing the cost of the training life cycle. Konstantinow (2005) focused on developing cost models that evaluate how to optimize resource allocation across blended training delivery methods.

Operational Requirements

For many training domains (e.g., military, business), the operational environment can be volatile, dynamic, and often unpredictable. Yet, there is a need to identify the training solution that best meets training objectives for the targeted operational context. The effectiveness of any training solution should thus be assessed by establishing a relationship between training objectives and operational requirements (i.e., combat capability, operational readiness, business competitiveness) as derived by well-defined measures of effectiveness (MOEs) and measures of performance (MOPs) (Gentner, Cunningham, & Bennett, 1998). MOEs have been defined as "standards against which the capability of a solution to meet the needs of a problem may be judged. ... MOEs are independent of any solution and do not specify performance criteria" (Sproles, 2001, p. 146). MOPs, on the other hand, assess the inherent performance of a system and are related to specific system parameters (e.g., human, physical, structural) (Sproles, 2000). Sproles suggested that "MOEs relate to how well any from a range of solutions may meet a need; MOPs are concerned with what a particular solution does regardless of its intended purpose" (p. 57). Essentially, MOEs are overall measures of system fitness, and MOPs are the underlying variables associated with each fitness category. Sproles offered a process via which to formulate MOEs targeted at ensuring operational requirements are met.

Training Metrics

> Today, [training system] effectiveness measures must be linked with war-fighting capability measures.
>
> **Gentner et al. (1998)**

When developing a training solution, it is essential to develop training metrics that link training objectives to operational requirements. This linkage can be constructed in the form of a human-system MOE/MOP taxonomy (Gentner et al., 1998). The taxonomy is initially constructed based on the outcome of the documentation review (e.g., military standards, instruction and training manuals, universal task lists) and CoTA conducted during the TNA and then refined, structured, and prioritized via interviews with SMEs and trainers. The interviews should focus on capturing exactly how lower level operational metrics (i.e., MOPs) relate to higher level MOEs (Gentner, Tiller, Cunningham, & Bennett, 1999; Sproles, 2000, 2001, 2002). For example, a high-level MOE may have physiological compatibility between system and user, and a related MOP may be the level of fatigue/stress induced by a training system. The MOPs and MOEs must be prioritized and structured (e.g., into functional groupings) in a flexible manner so that they can be readily used and adapted to the dynamic needs of trainers. Resulting training metrics should be directly related to operational effectiveness; be qualitatively or quantitatively defined to allow for measurement and evaluation; have associated targeted performance levels, allowing for gradations (e.g., trained, partially trained, untrained); and have relative weights associated with impact on operational readiness. The objective is to achieve a set of precisely defined training metrics that enable trainers to predict how effective a given training solution can be in achieving the highest levels of operational readiness and mission effective performance.

To ensure successful training outcomes, it is essential to specify fully the performance measurement requirements for the target tasks to be trained. The TNA provides a characterization of the specific KSAs associated with target tasks and procedures and the performance metrics currently used to assess these KSAs. Based on these data, a set of metrics should be identified that are both sensitive in detecting learning gains and diagnostic in identifying trainee deficiencies (Cuevas, Fiore, Bowers, & Salas, 2004; Cuevas, Fiore, & Oser, 2002; Fiore, Cuevas, & Oser, 2003; Fiore, Cuevas, Scielzo, & Salas, 2002). To achieve such diagnostic ability, the set of metrics should capture all aspects of training effectiveness, not just performance outcome.

Kraiger, Ford, and Salas (1993) delineated a number of training outcomes related to the development of specific KSAs that can be used to structure an overall assessment of training effectiveness. In general, these outcomes can be categorized into either process or outcome measures. *Process measures* examine the manner in which a task is accomplished (Cannon-Bowers & Salas, 1997; Salas, Milham, & Bowers, 2003), whereas *outcome measures* focus on how well a trainee accomplishes the overall task mission. Taken together, performance and outcome measures can be useful diagnostic tools in that they provide information about what happened and why (Fowlkes, Dwyer, Milham, Burns, & Pierce, 1999).

Within both categories of measures, there are a number of specific outcomes related to the KSAs targeted for a given domain. *Skill-based outcomes* assess how well skills associated with a given task or process (e.g., perceptual, response selection, motor, and problem-solving skills) have been developed and capture proficiency in domain-specific procedural knowledge (Kraiger et al., 1993; Proctor & Dutta, 1995). *Cognitive outcomes* involve the development of declarative, procedural, and strategic knowledge, that last of which supports distinguishing between optimal and nonoptimal task strategies, as well as mental models, situation awareness, and self-regulation. *Attitudinal outcomes* describe how attitudes are changed through training. These measures should assess such factors as affective behaviors that are critical to task persistence when faced with difficult operational objectives (e.g., motivation, self-efficacy, goal commitment; Kraiger et al., 1993). *Physiological outcomes* involve conditioning of automatic responses (e.g., stress) associated with task demands. Targeted emotional responses (e.g., remaining calm under pressure) may be achieved when trainees are given the opportunity to practice in affectively valid (i.e., authentic emotional engagement; see Grigorovici, 2000) environments.

A multifaceted approach to performance measurement, capturing each of these training metrics, is critical if training effectiveness is to be successfully interpreted. Specifically, competent performance in complex operational environments requires not only the basic knowledge of how to perform various tasks but also a higher level conceptual and strategic understanding of how this knowledge is applied to optimally select the appropriate strategies and actions to meet task objectives (Fiore et al., 2002; Smith, Ford, & Kozlowski, 1997). Moreover, it is also critical that trainees possess both well-defined, highly organized knowledge structures and the necessary self-regulatory skills to monitor their learning process (Mayer, 1999). Thus, a means of integrating each of the aforementioned measures is needed.

Taken together, training metrics should be used to gauge how effective a given training solution is, expressed in terms of desired performance outcomes. Figure 5.2 shows an approach that can be used to capture overall training effectiveness. The TNA should provide desired performance levels for each metric. Thus, metrics can be normalized against desired levels and plotted on a star chart. The chart will readily determine in which areas a given training solution is training effectively and where performance gaps still exist. In the example in Figure 5.2, skill-based measures are on target; cognitive, attitudinal, and physiological measures are well below target levels, and process and outcome measures are approaching target levels. These data can then be used diagnostically; for example, Figure 5.2 may suggest that improvements in cognitive and physiological measures must be realized prior to meeting process and outcome goals, and attitudinal concerns (e.g., motivation to learn, self-efficacy) are in need of attention to enhance the effectiveness of training.

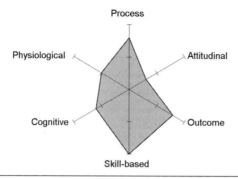

Figure 5.2 Overall training effectiveness

Conclusions

This chapter presented a three-phase training evaluation process (see Figure 5.1) that leverages TNA to develop user profiles (see Table 5.1) and identify target performance gaps (Table 5.2), associated learning objectives, and human information-processing requirements and combines this information to (a) identify fidelity requirements to drive training system design (see Table 5.5) and (b) performance metrics to drive training effectiveness evaluation (see Table 5.6 and Figure 5.2). This process begins with a comprehensive front-end TNA, which is followed by a design phase that identifies a blended fidelity training solution, and concludes with the identification of performance metrics for gauging if learning objectives are effectively met. The TNA phase aims to identify how best to deliver training that supports development of all critical KSAs via the most effective training technique for each learning objective. The training design phase aims to formulate a multiplatform training solution that is sufficiently detailed to support effective training while avoiding any unnecessary costly features. The training metrics phase aims to achieve a set of precisely defined training metrics that predict how effective a given training solution can be in achieving the highest levels of operational readiness and mission-effective performance. Successful completion of each phase should lead to a training solution that meets targeted training objectives in the intended operational environment.

References

Alston, B. (2002). *Good practice in training: A guide to the analysis, design, delivery and management of training*. London: Railway Safety. Retrieved May 14, 2007 from http://www.rgsonline.co.uk/docushare/dsweb/Get/Rail-35406/220.pdf

Anderson, J. R. (1995). *Cognitive psychology and its implications* (4th ed.). New York: Freeman.

Anderson, J. R., Greeno, J. G., Reder, L. M., & Simon, H. A. (2000). Perspectives on learning, thinking, and activity. *Educational Researcher, 29*(4), 11–13.

Andrews, D. H. (1988, January). Relationships among simulators, training devices, and learning: A behavioral view. *Educational Technology*, pp. 48–54.

Blickensderfer, E., Cannon-Bowers, J. A., Salas, E., & Baker, D. P. (2000). Analyzing knowledge requirements in team tasks. In J. Maarten Schraagen, S. F. Chipman, & V. L. Shalin (Eds.), *Cognitive task analysis* (pp. 431–447). Mahwah, NJ: Erlbaum.

Boreham, N. C. (1985). Transfer of training in the generation of diagnostic hypotheses: The effect of lowering fidelity of simulation. *British Journal of Educational Psychology, 55*, 213–223.

Broadbent, B., & Froidevaux, L. (1998). Training needs analysis: A broad view. In *Training Analysis* (pp.251–264). San Francisco, CA: Jossey-Bass/Pfeiffer.

Cannon-Bowers, J. A., & Salas, E. (1997). A framework for developing team performance measures in training. In M. T Brannick, E. Salas, & C. Prince (Eds.), *Team performance assessment and measurement: Theory, methods, and applications. Series in applied psychology* (pp. 45–62). Mahwah, NJ: Erlbaum.

Carter, G., & Trollip, S. R. (1980). A constrained maximization extension to incremental transfer effectiveness, or, how to mix your training technologies. *Human Factors, 22*, 141–152.

Chi, M. T. H., Glaser, R., & Rees, E. (1982). Expertise in problem solving. In R. J. Sternberg (Ed.), *Advances in the psychology of human intelligence* (pp. 7–75). Hillsdale, NJ: Erlbaum.

Clark, R., & Chopeta, L. (2004). *Graphics for learning: Proven guidelines for planning, designing, and evaluating visuals in training materials.* San Francisco: Jossey-Bass/Pfeiffer.

Converse, S. A., & Kahler, S. E. (1992). *Knowledge acquisition and the measurement of shared mental models* (Contract No. DAAL03–86-D-0001). Orlando, FL: Naval Air Warfare Center Training Systems Division.

Cornwell Management Consultants. (2004). *Digital preservation coalition: Training Needs Analysis Final Report.* A Study Funded by the Joint Information Systems Committee, Home Barn Court, The Street, Effingham, Surrey, UK. Retrieved May 23, 2005, from http://www.jisc.ac.uk/uploaded_documents/finalReport.pdf

Coury, B. G., Motte, S., & Seiford, L. M. (1991). Capturing and representing decision processes in the design of an information system. In *Proceedings of the Human Factors Society 35th Annual Meeting* (pp. 1223–1227). Santa Monica, CA: Human Factors Society.

Crandall, B. W., & Klein, G. (1990). The role of knowledge engineering in technology transfer. *Proceedings of the IEEE 1990 National Aerospace and Electronics Conference, 2*, 878–880.

Csikszentmihalyi, M. (1990). *Flow: The psychology of optimal experience.* New York: Harper and Row.

Cuevas, H. M., Fiore, S. M., Bowers, C. A., & Salas, E. (2004). Fostering construc- tive cognitive and metacognitive activity in computer-based complex task training environments [Invited paper for special issue on human-computer interaction]. *Computers in Human Behavior, 20,* 225–241.

Cuevas, H. M., Fiore, S. M., & Oser, R. L. (2002). Scaffolding cognitive and meta- cognitive processes in low verbal ability learners: Use of diagrams in computer- based training environments. *Instructional Science, 30,* 433–464.

Dreyfus, H. L., & Dreyfus, S. E. (1986). *Mind over machine.* New York: Free Press.

Ericsson, K. A., & Simon, H. A. (1980). Verbal reports as data. *Psychological Review, 87,* 215–251.

Ericsson, K. E., & Smith, J. (Eds.). (1991). *Towards a general theory of expertise: Prospects and limits.* Cambridge, UK: Cambridge University Press.

Feltovich, P. J., Eccles, D. W., & Hoffman, R. R. (2004). *Implications of the reductive ten- dency for the re-design of complex cognitive systems.* Report, Institute for Human and Machine Cognition, Pensacola, FL to the Advanced Decision Architectures Collaborative Alliance, sponsored by the U.S. Army Research Laboratory under cooperative agreement DAAD19-01-2-0009. Adelphi, MD: U.S. Army Research Laboratory.

Fiore, S. M., Cuevas, H. M., & Oser, R. L. (2003). A picture is worth a thousand connections: The facilitative effects of diagrams on task performance and mental model development. *Computers in Human Behavior, 19,* 185–199.

Fiore, S. M., Cuevas, H. M., Scielzo, S., & Salas, E. (2002). Training individuals for distributed teams: Problem solving assessment for distributed mission research. *Computers in Human Behavior, 18,* 729–744.

Forrest, F. C., Taylor, M. C., Postlethwaite, K. C., & Aspinall, R. (2002). Use of a high fidelity simulator to develop testing of the technical performance of novice anaesthetists. *British Journal of Anaesthesia, 88,* 338–344.

Fowlkes, J. E., Dwyer, D. J., Milham, L. M., Burns, J. J., & Pierce, L. G. (1999). Team skills assessment: A test and evaluation component for emerging weapons systems. In *Proceedings of the 1999 Interservice/Industry Training, Simula- tion, and Education Conference* (pp. 994–1004). Arlington, VA: National Training Systems Association.

Gagne, R. M. (1962). (Ed.). *Psychological principles in system development.* New York: Holt, Rinehart, & Winston.

Gentner, F. C., Cunningham, P. H., & Bennett, W. (1998). Integrated taxonomy to assess warfighting effectiveness and human performance readiness. In *Proceedings of International Military Testing Association (IMTA) 1998* (AB-40). Pensacola, FL. Retrieved June 13, 2005, from http://www.internationalmta.org/1998/1998.htm

Gentner, F. C., Tiller, T. C., Cunningham, P. H., & Bennett, W. Jr. (1999, Dec). Using mission essential MOEs/MOPs for evaluating effectiveness of dis- tributed mission training. In *Proceedings of 1999 Interservice/Industry Training, Simulation and Education Conference.* Arlington, VA: National Security Industrial Association.

George, G. R., Reese, W. C., Durham, W. H., & Knight, S. (2000). The Army aviation collective training solution: AVCATT-A. Paper presented at Interservice/ Industry Training, Simulation and Education Conference (I/ITSEC) 2000, Orlando, FL, November 27–30.

Goldstein, I. R. (1991). Training in work organizations. In M. Dunnette & L. Hough (Eds.), *Handbook of industrial and organizational psychology* (2nd ed., pp. 507–619). Palo Alto, CA: Consulting Psychologists Press.

Grigorovici, D. (2001). Affectively engaged: affect and arousal routes of entertainment virtual reality. *Proceedings of the 7th International Conference on Virtual Systems and Multimedia* (VSSMM'01) (pp. 634–643). Washington, DC: IEEE Computer Society.

Gupta, K. (1998). *A practical guide to needs assessment.* San Francisco: Jossey-Bass Pfeiffer.

Hackos, J. T., & Redish, J. C. (1998). *User and task analysis for interface design.* New York: Wiley.

Hammond, K. R., Mumpower, J. L., & Smith, T. H. (1977). Linking environmental models with models of human judgment: A symmetrical decision aid. *IEEE Transactions on Systems, Man, and Cybernetics, 7,* 358–367.

Hays, R. T., & Singer, M. J. (1988). *Simulation fidelity in training system design: Bridging the gap between reality and training.* New York: Springer-Verlag.

Henkoff, R. (1993, March 22). Companies that train best. *Fortune Magazine,* pp. 62–70.

Jeffries, R. (1997). The role of task analysis in design of software. In M. Helander, T. K. Landauer, & P. V. Prabhu (Eds.), *Handbook of human-computer interaction* (2nd ed., pp. 347–359). Amsterdam: North-Holland.

Jonassen, D. H., Tessmer, M., & Hannum, W. H. (1999). *Task analysis methods for instructional design.* Mahwah, NJ: Erlbaum.

Jones, K. (1990). General activity for management education — a deliberate ambivalence. *Simulation/Games for Learning, 20,* 142–151.

Kelley, A. I., Orgel, R. F., & Baer, D. M. (1985). Seven strategies that guarantee training transfer. *Training and Development Journal, 39*(11), 78–82

Kirwan, B., & Ainsworth, L. K. (Eds.). (1992). *A guide to task analysis.* London: Taylor & Francis.

Konstantinow, G. (2005). *Optimizing instructor resources for blended training in Navy integrated learning environments.* Paper presented at the 5th annual Navy Workforce Research and Analysis Conference. Retrieved May 14, 2007 from http://www.sm.nps.navy.mil/nwc/05/

Kraiger, K., Ford, J. K., & Salas, E. (1993). Application of cognitive, skill-based, and affective theories of learning outcomes to new methods of training evaluation. *Journal of Applied Psychology, 78,* 311–328.

Krueger, R. A., & Casey, M. A. (2000). *Focus groups: A practical guide for applied research* (3rd ed.). Thousand Oaks, CA: Sage.

Kucinski, C. E. (2005). Technology powers distributed learning. In *Military information technology* [Electronic version], 9(3). Retrieved May 14, 2007 from http://www.military-information-technology.com/article.cfm?DocID=502

Lambe, J. (2005). Conducting successful SME interviews. *Usability Interface, The UUX Community Newsletter, 11* (4), 16–18. Retrived May 14, 2007 from http:// www. stcsig.org/usability/newsletter/0505-sme.html.

Lave, J., & Wenger, E. (1991). *Situated learning: Legitimate peripheral participation.* Cambridge, UK: Cambridge University Press.

Maran, N. J., & Glavin, R. J. (2003). Low- to high- fidelity simulation–a continuum of medical education? *Medical Education, 37*(S1), 22–28.

Mayer, R. E. (1999). Instructional technology. In F. T. Durso, R. S. Nickerson, R. W. Schvaneveldt, S. T. Dumais, D. S. Lindsay, & M. T. H. Chi (Eds.), *Handbook of applied cognition* (pp. 551–569). Chichester, UK: Wiley.

Mayhew, D. J. (1997). *Principles and guidelines in software user interface design.* Englewood Cliffs, NJ: Prentice-Hall.

McCormick, E. J., Mecham, R. C., & Jeanneret, P. R. (1989). *Technical manual for the Position Analysis Questionnaire* (PAQ; 2nd ed.). Logan, UT: PAQ Services. Palo Alto, CA: Consulting Psychologists Press.

McDonald, J., Dearholt, D., Paap, K., & Schvaneveldt, R. (1986). A formal interface design methodology based on user knowledge. In M. Mantei & P. Orbeton (Eds.), *CHI'86 Proceedings* (pp. 285–290). New York: ACM Press.

McLaughlin, S. A., Doezema, D., & Sklar, D. P. (2002). Human simulation in emergency medicine training: A model curriculum. *Academic Emergency Medicine, 9,* 1310–1318.

McNeese, M. D., & Zaff, B. S. (1991). Knowledge as design: A methodology for overcoming knowledge acquisition bottlenecks in intelligent interface design. In *Proceedings of the Human Factors Society 35th Annual Meeting* (pp. 1181–1185). Santa Monica, CA: Human Factors Society.

Pappo, H. A. (1998). *Simulations for skills training.* Englewood Cliffs, NJ: Educational Technology Publications.

Patrick, J. (1992). *Training: Research and practice.* San Diego, CA: Academic Press.

Proctor, R. W., & Dutta, A. (1995). *Skill acquisition and human performance.* London: Sage.

Roof, R. S. (1996). *Naval aviation's use of simulators in the operational training environment: A cost analysis perspective.* Unpublished master's thesis, Naval Postgraduate School, Monterey, CA.

Roscoe, S. N. (1982). *Aviation Psychology.* Ames, IA: Iowa State University Press.

Rossett, A. (1987). *Training needs assessment.* Englewood Cliffs, NJ: Educational Technology Publications.

Rossett, A. (1995). Needs assessment. In G. J. Anglin (Ed.), *Instructional technology: Past, present, future* (2nd ed., pp. 183–196). Englewood, CO: Libraries Unlimited.

Rossett, A. (1999). Knowledge management meets analysis. *Training and Development, 53,* 62–68.

Rouse, W. B. (1982). A mixed-fidelity approach to technical training. *Journal of Educational Technology Systems, 11,* 103–115.

Salas, E., Bowers, C. A., & Rhodenizer, L. (1999). It is not how much you have but how you use it: Toward a rationale use of simulation to support aviation training. *The International Journal of Aviation Psychology, 8*, 197–208.

Salas, E., Milham, L., & Bowers, C. (2003). Training evaluation in the military: misconceptions, opportunities, and challenges. *Military Psychology, 15*(1), 3–16.

Schon, D. (1983). *The reflective practitioner.* New York: Basic Books.

Shadbolt, N., & Wielinga, B. (1990). Knowledge based knowledge acquisition: The next generation of support tools. In B. Wielinga, J. Boose, B. Gaines, G. Schreiber, & M. van Someren (Eds.), *Current trends in knowledge acquisition* (pp. 313–355). Amsterdam: IOS Press.

Smith, E. M., Ford, J. K., & Kozlowski, S. W. J. (1997). Building adaptive expertise: Implications for training design strategies. In M. A. Quinones & A. Ehrenstein (Eds.), *Training for a rapidly changing workplace: Applications of psychological research* (pp. 89–118). Washington, DC: American Psychological Association.

Smith L., Wilhelm, C., Coyle, P., Hawley, R., Hearney, R., Goodman, S., et al. (2002). *Future naval training environments* (Report No. CNR D00068280. A4/2REV). Alexandria, VA: CNA Corporation. Retrieved from http://www.cna.org/documents/D0006280.A4.pdf

Sproles, N. (2000). Coming to grips with measures of effectiveness. *System Engineering, 3*, 50–58.

Sproles, N. (2001). The difficult problem of establishing measures of effectiveness for command and control: A systems engineering perspective. *System Engineering, 4*, 145–155.

Sproles, N. (2002). Formulating measures of effectiveness. *System Engineering, 5*, 253–263.

Stanney, K. M., & Guckenberger, D. (1995). Enhancing the fidelity of virtual environments through the manipulation of virtual time. *Proceedings of the 6th International Conference on Human–Computer Interaction* (July 9–14, Tokyo, Japan), Amsterdam, The Netherlands: Elsevier Science Publishers.

Stanney, K. M., Smith, M. J., Carayon, P., & Salvendy, G. (2001). Human-computer interaction. In G. Salvendy (Ed.), *Handbook of industrial engineering* (3rd ed., pp. 1192–1236). New York: Wiley.

Sudman, M., & Bradbum. A. (1982). *Asking questions: A practical guide to questionnaire design.* San Francisco: Jossey-Bass.

Takayesu, J. K., Gordon, J. A., Farrell, S. E., Evans, A. E., Sullivan, J. E., & Pawlowski, J. (2002). Learning emergency and critical care medicine: What does high-fidelity patient simulation teach? *Academic Emergency Medicine, 9*, 476–477.

Tannenbaum, S., & Yukl, G. (1991). Training and development in work organizations. *Annual Review of Psychology, 41*, 399–441.

Taylor, D. W. (1998). *Aviation maintenance training curriculum evaluation: A case study.* Unpublished doctoral dissertation (E6-A), University of Washington, Seattle, WA. Retrieved June 14, 2005, from http://www.hitl.washington.edu/publications/r-98-2/index.html

Thordsen, M. L. (1991). A comparison of two tools for cognitive task analysis: Concept mapping and the critical decision method. In *Proceedings of the Human Factors Society 35th Annual Meeting* (pp. 283–285). Santa Monica, CA: Human Factors Society.

van Merriënboer, J. J. G., & Kester, L. (2005). Four-component instructional design model: Multimedia principles in environments for complex learning. In R. E. Mayer (Ed.), *The Cambridge Handbook of Multimedia Learning* (pp. 71–96). New York: Cambridge University Press. Retrieved May 14, 2007 from http://www.open.ou.nl/vor/Themaconferenties/VORthemaconferentie2004_Multimediabook2.pdf

Vozenilek, J., Huff, J. S., Reznek, M., & Gordon, J. A. (2004). See one, do one, teach one: Advanced technology in medical education. *Academic Emergency Medicine, 11*, 1149–1154.

Witkin, R. W., & Alschuld, J. W. (1995). *Planning and conducting needs assessments.* Thousand Oaks, CA: Sage.

Woods, D. D., & Hollnagel, E. (1987). Mapping cognitive demands in complex problem-solving worlds. *International Journal of Man-Machine Studies, 26*, 257–275.

Woodward, B. (1990). Knowledge acquisition at the front end: Defining the domain. *Knowledge Acquisition, 2*, 73–94.

6
Representing Cognition in Games and Simulations

J. D. FLETCHER AND JOHN E. MORRISON

Institute for Defense Analyses

Developers of games and simulations are striving to increase realism in both the appearance and the behavior of their computer-generated characters. The physical appearance of characters in games and simulations enhances participants' sense of presence and immersion, but the way the characters behave may matter more (Bailenson et al., 2005; Garau, Slater, Bee, & Sasse, 2001). Interest in imbuing computer-generated characters with human-like behavior is present and growing.

This interest approaches an imperative when it comes to generating friendly, opposition, and neutral characters for simulations used in military training. One side will implement a tactic that the other side will successfully counter, requiring the first side to adjust their tactics, which will affect what the other side does next, and so on. This process creates immersing, problem-solving, decision-making environments that can test the limits of both human and machine cognition. It mimics the poorly structured, rapidly shifting, ill-defined, and time-constrained environments that are typical of real-world problem solving and decision making (Cannon-Bowers, Salas, & Pruitt, 1996). Interest in cognitively realistic characters may be equally imperative in simulating environments for nonmilitary applications, such as those developed for problem solving and decision making in urban planning, economic management, and of course, multiuser fantasy games.

This chapter reviews models that are available for representing human cognitive behavior in games and simulations. It identifies and briefly discusses those models that seem particularly appropriate for representing and assessing human problem-solving capabilities.

Games and Simulations

Computer-based simulations appeared with the first computers that could support them and, for that matter, were a prime motivator for their development (Goldstine, 1972). Simulations intended for education and training appeared almost as soon. Perhaps the first example of computer-based simulation training grew out of the Air Force SAGE (Semi-Automatic Ground Environment) system (Rowell & Streich, 1964). The early 1950s Whirlwind I project demonstrated that computers using radar data to track aircraft could serve as an early warning air defense system for the entire North American continent. Based on this evidence and motivated by the perceived exigencies of the Cold War, the Air Force quickly responded by building SAGE, a system of 20 computer-based, linked direction centers for tracking aircraft and controlling aircraft interceptions.

On the human factors side, SAGE was a large, geographically dispersed system requiring intense human-computer interactions, complex and frequent decision making, and close cooperation among many operators working in relative psychological isolation (Rowell & Streich, 1964). A training system, which the Air Force imaginatively called STP (System Training Program), was embedded in SAGE to train its operators in the mid-1950s. STP included simulated radar inputs, nonradar track inputs, an authoring system for simulation scenarios, a recording capability, and a data reduction feedback feature used for after-action reviews.

STP was a multiplayer training simulation. It served as a prototype and progenitor for a host of military and civilian computer-based simulation systems, as S. R. Mayer (1970), Olsen and Bass (1982), and even Fletcher and Rockway (1986) have suggested. It was the precursor of today's networks of military simulators that engage each other on electronic battlefields (Alluisi, 1991).

Whether STP was a multiplayer game as well as a simulation may depend on the perceptions of its users. Distinctions between games and simulations are varied and a matter for continuing discussion. For the purposes of this chapter, games are considered to be simulations that emphasize engaging, immersing entertainment, often at the expense of realism, in contrast to other simulations, which emphasize realism often at the expense of entertainment. Both games and simulations may involve competition, but that seems more central to games than to simulations.

Multiplayer games have been available for some time, certainly since the advent of multiuser time-sharing systems in the 1960s. Games such as Moonwar[1] and Dogfight hosted on the University of Illinois PLATO system evolved into role-playing games such as Dungeon, which appeared in 1975 and was hosted on time-sharing operating systems supported by PDP-10 mainframes. In about 1978, Dungeon was modified at Essex University in the United Kingdom to support a variety of users playing different roles and was renamed Multi-User Dungeon or MUD (Bartle, 1990). It was immediately and extensively popular.

Personal computing, the Internet, and the World Wide Web have intensified the evolution of games. Even though Dungeon used text commands to control game action, it included line-of-sight displays to simulate what players in different roles might see. Graphics displays in games and simulations continued to evolve with the development of computer display technology. The development of modern graphics-based, role-playing, multiplayer games have been with us since the mid-1990s, when Electronic Arts released Ultima Online. Sony Online's Everquest, released in 1999, may have been the first major hit for multiplayer games, with more than 400,000 subscribers by the end of the year paying $10 per month to play. It was soon followed by Ultima Online, Dark Age of Camelot, Star Wars Galaxies, World of Warcraft, and so on (Robar, 2004). The market for these games continues to grow. By 2005, World of Warcraft had over 1 million players in North America and more than 5 million players worldwide.

Many games and simulations include characters depicted in the action but operating independently under computer control. The quality of the game or simulation depends to a substantial extent on the cognitive behavior and responses of these automated characters. Even when characters operate under some combination of human-computer control, there may be significant cognitive components under computer control, especially when the human operator is managing groups or teams of individual characters. In all cases, the underlying computer capabilities for representing cognition are essential in providing characters that display credible behavior. Many games and simulations include them either implicitly or explicitly.

Games and simulations, multiplayer and otherwise, have significant advantages over other means (e.g., explicit paper-and-pencil testing) for assessing cognitive capabilities (Bennett, Jenkins, Persky, & Weiss, 2003; Drasgow & Mattern, 2005; Fletcher, 2002; Garmine & Pearson, 2006). They employ rich and immersing environments that can take full advantage of the timing, multimedia display, multimodal command, and

---

[1] Moonwar was lesson 0moon on the PLATO system according to one expert, who claims not have spent any time playing it.

instant scoring capabilities of computer-assisted assessment. They can do so continuously and unobtrusively, and they can yield more detailed and complete representation of what users know and, especially, can do than more traditional assessment methods. They may well take us to a future in which explicit testing is minimized while the extent and depth of assessment is significantly enhanced.

Games, Simulation, and Cognition

Empirical research is investigating the ability of computer games to increase cognitive capabilities (Green & Bavelier, 2003; Hayes, 2005; O'Neil, Wainess, & Baker, 2005; Tobias & Fletcher, in press). Some of these studies indicate that cognitive capabilities can be reliably measured by games themselves. Subrahmanyam and Greenfield (1994) showed that general spatial capabilities such as anticipating targets and extrapolating spatial paths could be assessed in a computer game (Marble Madness). Greenfield, deWinstanley, Kilpatrick, and Kaye (1994) found that general attention skills such as those dealing with requirements for divided visual attention could be assessed (and improved) by playing video games. Hong and Liu (2003) identified three cognitive strategies (trial and error, heuristic, and analogical thinking) used by computer game players and found that these strategies could be used to assess players' expertise.

In discussing cognitive models in simulations and games, Wulfeck (personal e-mail communication, January 17, 2006) asked, "Is there any indication that attention skills or cognitive strategies transfer to any other tasks?" This is a key question. However, research on the transfer of cognitive skills or strategies acquired in games to real-world tasks remains fragmentary, mixed, and scarce.

For instance, Gopher, Weil, and Bareket (1994) found that groups trained for 10 hours on the Space Fortress II game demonstrated performance in a complex and dynamic aircraft flight environment that was superior to an ability-matched control group not exposed to the game. They attributed the success of the game groups to their learning how to cope with attention demands and high cognitive load. On the other hand, Hart and Battiste (1992) found that assigning trainees to an off-the-shelf game (Apache Strike Force), also dealing with flying, had no transfer effects. Fletcher and Tobias (2006) went so far as to suggest that the physical similarities of game and flight conditions do not affect transfer as much as the similarities in attention and cognitive load demands shared by the game and actual flight.

Clearly, the degree to which basic cognitive capabilities acquired and assessed in games and simulations transfer to the performance of real-world skills and tasks remains to be determined. Fortunately, this chapter avoids this issue by limiting its focus to the representation of cognition in games and simulations in the first place.

The Role of Cognitive Models

Cognitive models concern such processes as human perception, memory, learning, decision making, and, notably, problem solving. They are used to populate games and simulations with synthetic but realistic characters, model the desired end state of learners in instructional applications, and assess the current competencies of users in instructional, decision-aiding, and entertainment applications. Models of current and targeted cognitive end states can help manage users' progress toward achieving instructional objectives, ensure that games and simulations adjust to participant's levels of ability, and provide hints for partial solutions and critiques of completed activities.

In many applications, the performance of participants may be reflected (or overlaid) onto empirically based models of human cognition as the participants interact with games and simulations. This approach has been successfully used in technology-based instruction starting early (e.g., Fletcher, 1975; Sleeman & Brown, 1982) and continuing into the present (Lovett & Anderson, 2005). Use of underlying cognitive models extends ad hoc game and simulation approaches into formal constructs of cognition. Doing so not only yields more comprehensive and generalizable knowledge of players' cognitive processes and abilities but also provides feedback to the models themselves. It will help verify our concepts of human cognition through prediction and exquisitely detailed observation of players' performance. By closing this feedback loop, assessment of cognitive processes and abilities in games and simulations may reveal significant aspects of human cognition that have heretofore been obscured by our limited modalities for assessment. Assessment using games and simulations could transcend its current novelty status by both providing more powerful capabilities for assessing cognitive skills and substantially increasing our understanding of human cognitive processes and their implications for human performance.

Use of games and simulations in assessment is as applicable to teams as to individuals (e.g., Fletcher, 1999; O'Neil, Chung, & Brown, 1997). Members of problem-solving teams must, as Sternberg and Davidson (1992) emphasized, form their own models of the problem that is to be solved. They must also, as Rouse, Cannon-Bowers, and Salas (1992) emphasized, develop a mental model of other participants' knowledge and skill (perhaps by cross training team members in each other's roles and responsibilities) and a shared mental model of the team's goal and subgoal states. In addition, they must develop a shared model of the current situation — a need that has been emphasized by commentators ranging from deGroot (1965) and Chase and Simon (1973) to the current interest in situation awareness (e.g., Endsley, 1995). Finally, teams, and team members, must review the success of their plans, and just as important, they must respond to this feedback by devising new models of the goal, subgoal, and current states. A benefit of using games and simulations to assess team problem solving is that in all these activities mental models and the cognitive processes underlying them are to some extent made visible and explicit through the observable decisions, communications, and actions of team members.

Games and simulations can record all decisions and actions observed from participants' communications, keyboard inputs, and clickstreams. The models of participant knowledge, assumptions, and hypotheses that are inferred from these extensive and detailed records can then be reflected against the "ground truth" known by the system. The outcomes in games and simulations, such as those involving tactics, strategies, and opposing players, may turn out to be unfavorable because of factors over which the participants have no control. If the models are in accord with the true state of the system, then we may be able to assume that participants are taking the right actions for the right reasons, regardless of outcome. By providing a window into the internal cognitive structures and processes a team or team member may be using to solve a problem, cognitive models allow us to distinguish between good problem solving and good luck and between poor problem solving and bad luck.

Modeling Human Behavior

The capabilities of games and simulations to assess cognitive capabilities such as problem solving are embryonic, but the ability to enhance them significantly by using models of human cognition now seems at hand. This work has already begun based on research and development in cognition and efforts to model it, which, in the world of games and simulation, typically comes under the heading of human behavior representation. Modeling is increasingly used in simulations for training and education, analyzing decision alternatives, representing characters and avatars, and designing, developing, and acquiring materiel assets. It appears, implicitly and explicitly, in both military and nonmilitary applications. Its movement into games, multiplayer and otherwise, seems equally at hand.

We are fortunate that a number of systematic reviews and analyses of these models have appeared. Pew and Mavor (1998) reviewed 11 such models, Ritter et al. (2002b) reviewed 7 models not covered by Pew and Mavor, and Morrison (2003) reviewed 19 such models. Morrison's review updated the earlier reports and provided additional analyses.

These models can be implemented in digital form — as computer algorithms. Doing so for any model is a significant demonstration. If the model can be represented in an algorithm, its validity can be tested by comparing its predictions with the observed performance of human participants in games, simulations, and elsewhere. If the model cannot be represented in an effective procedure such as an algorithm, then there is reason to question its adequacy as a model.

Models are especially useful in providing diagnostic as well as summative information. They can provide precise information on individual or team cognitive capabilities for use in devising individually tailored training programs. They can also be used to demonstrate the validity of the model itself, suggesting where it must be modified to account for a more comprehensive range of human cognition. Scientific and technological advances may arise from information of this sort, as well as substantial improvements in our ability to educate, train, and assist learners and users.

Most of these models are systems of if-then, condition-response rules, or *productions*, that simulate cognitive structures and processes. The 19 models Morrison (2003) reviewed are summarized in Table 6.1.

Table 6.2 again summarizes the 19 models by identifying the cognitive functions they cover. Table 6.2 indicates which models, in our judgement, explicitly represent one or more of the following cognitive processes: perception, psychomotor performance, attention, situation awareness, short-term memory, long-term memory, learning, decision making, problem solving, cognitive workload, emotional behavior, and social behavior.

To be indicated in Table 6.2 as present, the documentation and other literature associated with the model had to describe the model's capabilities specifically for that particular function. No inferences were made about the model's potential capabilities to emulate the function with modification. Advocates may reasonably argue that the model could demonstrate additional functions with appropriate modifications. In any case, problem-solving functions are represented in only five of the models. This finding suggests that even though most of these models may be good at reacting to expected situations (i.e., situations for which they are programmed), they may not be so good at adapting to novel, unanticipated situations.

Assessment of Problem Solving

Problem solving and decision making are required when an individual or a group of individuals must achieve a goal, or a combination of competing goals, but are uncertain how to do so (R. E. Mayer & Wittrock, 1996).

Table 6.1 Summary Descriptions of Cognitive Models Reviewed by Morrison (2003)

Model name	Summary description	Reference
Atomic components of thought (ACT) (including atomic components of thought — Rational, ACT-R)	Intended to provide a unified theory of mind and a design basis for instructional environments, intelligent tutors, computer-generated teams and units, and human interfaces. Distinguishes between declarative knowledge (represented with semantic networks) and procedural knowledge (represented using if-then productions). Cognition in ACT-R optimizes choices between environmental demands and computational limitations.	Anderson et al., 2004; Lovett & Anderson, 2005
Adaptive resonance theory (ART)	Family of neural net models designed to explain sensory-cognitive processes (e.g., perception, recognition, attention, reinforcement, recall, and working memory). Postulates bottom-up (e.g., perceptions) and top-down (e.g., expectations, attention control) functions in working memory that interact to produce learning.	Grossberg, 1976a; 1976b Krafft, 2002 http://web.umr.edu/~tauritzd/art
Architecture for procedure execution (APEX)	Intended to reduce time and effort needed to develop models of human performance in complex, dynamic environments such as simulations, explorations of human performance theories, and assessments of equipment design on human performance. Includes goal-directed action selection for tasks and procedures and resource allocation for perceptual (mostly visual), cognitive, and psychomotor functions.	Freed, Dahlman, Dalal, & Harris, 2002 http://www.andrew.cmu.edu/~bj07/apex

Business redesign agent-based holistic modeling system (Brahms)	Models social as well as man-machine interactions. Uses agents to model interactions among physically dispersed groups (e.g., teams) and if-then productions ("detectables" and "beliefs") to model decision making (via "thoughtframes") and behavior within the groups. Emphasizes ethnographic analyses and sociotechnical work practices, activities shaped by sociotechnical environment, and constructivist, situated cognition to model cognition and behavior.	Clancey, Sachs, Sierhuis, & van Hoof, 1998; Acquisti, Clancey, van Hoof, Scott, & Sierhuis, 2001
Cognition and affect project (CogAff) (with associated SimAgent tool kit)	Conceptual space for describing cognitive architectures. Integrates emotional with cognitive processes. Incorporates three layers of cognition (reactive, deliberative, and reflective or meta-cognitive); three layers of information processing (perception, central processing, and action); and three types of emotions (primary based on reaction, secondary based on deliberation, and tertiary based on reflection), all producing different perceptual, memory, and motor functions.	Sloman, 2001, 2003 http://www.cs.bham.ac.uk/~axs/cogaff.html
Cognition as a network of tasks (COGNET) (with associated GINA and iGEN(tool kits)	Intended for cognitive task analysis and description of work domains in multitask environments requiring contemplative, decision-oriented, open-ended responses. Uses three subsystems to represent information processing (sensory/perceptual, mental modeling, action/motor); four forms of if-then, production-based task knowledge (goal-directed task hierarchies, perceptual demons to guide attention, blackboard for organizing declarative information, and possible actions linked to time and resource requirements); and meta-cognitive functions. Allows interfacing with other applications.	Zachary, Campbell, Laughery, Glenn, & Cannon-Bowers, 2001 http://www.chiinc.com/cognethome.shtml

(continued)

Table 6.1 Summary Descriptions of Cognitive Models Reviewed by Morrison (2003) (Continued)

Model name	Summary description	Reference
Cognitive complexity theory (CCT) (with associated GLEAN3 tool kit)	CCT is an elaboration of the goal, operators, methods, and selection (GOMS) and the model human processor develop by (Card, Moran, & Newell, 1973). CCT provides a theoretical basis for GOMS and for natural GOMS language. It is focused on human interface design, human-computer interaction, and sequential task performance. Employs device models (transition networks); user models (sequentially executed if-then productions, the fundamental CCT units of cognition, retrieval from long-term memory); and mental operators to represent covert cognitive processes.	Kieras and Polson, 1985; Kieras, 1999
Cognitive objects within a graphical environment (COGENT)	Intended solely to provide tools (via a visual programming environment that evolves with the model built) for cognitive modeling. Assumes functional modularity (cognition as interaction among semiautonomous subsystems) and uses low-level processing components.	Cooper, Yule, & Sutton, 1998; Yule & Cooper, 2000 http://cogent.psyc.bbk.ac.uk
Concurrent activation-based production system (CAPS)	Hybrid model for central cognitive functions (e.g., reading comprehension). Primary focus is on modeling patterns of brain activation patterns in high-level cognition via if-then productions for specific areas of the brain and associative networks for cognitive subsystems. Total activation in working memory is capped, concerned exclusively with declarative knowledge (facts), but with different limits for different individuals. Long-term memory includes procedural and declarative knowledge.	Just & Carpenter, 1992; Just et al., 1999 http://coglab.psy.cmu.edu

Construction-integration theory (C-I theory)	Uses a symbolic theory of sentence comprehension and propositions (actions and objects of the action), stressing goal formation to provide a general model of cognition. Comprehension progresses from approximations to verified integration through mutually reinforced associations and spreading activation in memory. Extended to cover comprehension of novel computer interfaces (LInked model) and new Web sites (CoLiDeS model) and to incorporate concepts from latent semantic analysis (LSA) used to derive meaning from text.	Kintsch, 1998; Landauer & Dumais, 1997; Kitajima & Polson, 1997; Kitajima, Blackmon, & Polson, 2000 http://psych-www.colorado.edu/ics
Distributed cognition (DCOG)	Intended to model individuals' expert behavior with agents that use multiple strategies to respond to a complex environment (air-traffic control). Based on a two-dimensional space: abstraction with three levels (skill-based responses to signals, production-based responses to signs, and knowledge-based responses to symbols) and decomposition (ranging from individual component to total system processing). Processing within this space depends on level of expertise, workload environment, and an individual's preferred level of engagement.	Eggleston, Young, & McCreight, 2000; Eggleston, Young, & McCreight, 2001
Executive process/ interactive control (EPIC)	Intended to model details of peripheral cognitive processes, input (perception) and output (psychomotor responses) to inform human-system interface design by predicting the order and timing of responses. Includes long-term storage of declarative and procedural knowledge and working memory for assessing their application. Capacity and retrieval limitations arise only from perceptual or psychomotor systems, not from central memory store.	Kieras & Meyer, 1995 http://www.eecs.umich.edu/~kieras/epic.html

(continued)

Table 6.1 Summary Descriptions of Cognitive Models Reviewed by Morrison (2003) (Continued)

Model name	Summary description	Reference
Human operator simulator (HOS)	Intended to inform human-system interface design by modeling human performance based on the sequence and timing of subtasks organized in networks. Uses simulation objects (configuration of displays and controls), task networks (if-then productions selecting verb-object pairs used to manipulate the objects), and micro-models (times to complete required subtasks involving perception, information processing, and psychomotor responses) to determine human response times.	Wherry, 1976; Harris, Iavecchia, & Dick, 1989; Glenn, Schwartz, & Ross, 1992
Man-machine integrated design and analysis system (MIDAS)	Intended to inform human-system interface design by modeling individuals and interactions among individuals in performing multiple, concurrent tasks. Uses sensory input (operators and perceivable — detectable, recognizable, and identifiable — objects); memory (with declarative — beliefs in long-term memory, contexts in working memory — and procedural components); decision making; situation awareness (actual and perceived); and psychomotor output to model attention (with limitations on processing resources); situation awareness (actual and perceived); and psychomotor output to model human operator limitations and capabilities.	Corker & Smith, 1993; Hart, Dahn, Atencio, & Dalal, 2001 http://caffeine. arc.nasa.gov/midas/index.html
Micro systems analysis of integrated network of tasks (Micro Saint)	Simulation tool that uses a detailed task analysis to decompose human performance into a networked hierarchy (with branching logic and sequential dependencies) of discrete tasks and subtasks for which performance estimates can be validated. Network consists of subtask nodes (with launching conditions, time to complete, and effects) and relationships (that may be probabilistic, tactical requiring a threshold value, or multiple initiating more than one subtask). Designed to communicate with other models and applications through middleware.	Laughery & Corker, 1997

Model	Description	Reference
Operator model architecture (OMAR) (uses Developers Interface, a graphics tool kit, for developing performance models)	Models human behavior as interactions among independent computational agents representing interacting individuals or cognitive processes within individuals. Allows both sequentially dependent and parallel task performance with order determined by activation levels of tasks — without an explicit executive process. Allows facile interface with other models.	Deutsch, 1998; Deutsch, MacMillan, & Cramer, 1993
PSI	Attempts to integrate motivation with cognitive processes. Based on three levels of needs that interact to determine motive strength and specific goal behaviors: system needs (water and energy); preservation level (pain avoidance); information level (certainty; competence, affiliation). Action strategies first seek automatized skills, then knowledge-based behavior, then trial and error to satisfy goals.	Bartl & Dörner, 1998; Ritter, Baxter, et al., 2002 http://www.uni-bamberg.de/~ba2dp1/psi.html
Situation awareness model for pilot-in-the-loop evaluation (SAMPLE)	Generalized from original effort to model situation awareness of pilots and air crews in air combat. Uses cognitive task analyses, pattern recognition from Klein's recognition-primed decision-making, Endsley's three levels of awareness (detection, identification, and prediction), and Rasmussen's three tiers of action strategy (skill-based pattern recognition, standardized if-then productions, and knowledge-based problem solving) to provide three stages of processing: information processing (with a continuous state estimator and a discrete event detector); situation assessment (with the information fusion and reasoning required by multitasking); and decision making (with a procedure selector and a procedure executor). Output includes information disparity, situation awareness disparity, and combat advantage index.	Rasmussen, 1983; Klein, 1989; Mulgund, Harper, Zacharias, & Menke, 2000

(continued)

Table 6.1 Summary Descriptions of Cognitive Models Reviewed by Morrison (2003) (Continued)

Model name	Summary description	Reference
State, operator, and result (Soar)	Intended as a comprehensive model of human cognition focused on operational task domains depicting all behavior as goal-driven movement through problem spaces that define states and operators for the tasks at hand. Uses a four-cycle iterative process involving input (via human perception); elaboration (matches if-then, condition-action productions in long-term memory with those in working memory to issue proposals for decision making and direct commands for psychomotor actions); output (psychomotor execution); decision (either selects operators or identifies "impasses" requiring a new subgoal until all impasses are resolved). Uses a single process for long-term memory, learning, task representation, and decision making. All learning occurs through "chunking," which occurs through impasse subgoaling and resolution. Emotions arise from situation awareness clarity and confusion. Integrates individual and team knowledge and allows goals and plans to be shared among team members.	Rosenbloom, et al. 1991; Lewis, 2001 http://ai.eecs.umich.edu/soar http://www-2.cs.cmu.edu/afs/cs/project/soar/public/www/home-page.html http://www.isi.edu/soar/soar-homepage.html http://www.nottingham.ac.uk/pub/soar/ nottingham/soar-faq.html http://phoenix.herts.ac.uk/~rmy/cogarch.seminar/soar.html

Table 6.2 Cognitive and Behavioral Functions Represented in Models Reviewed by Morrison (2003)

Acronym/abbreviation	Perception	Psychomotor performance	Attention	Situation awareness	Working memory	Long-term memory	Learning	Decision making	Problem solving	Cognitive workload	Emotional behavior	Social behavior
ACT	X	X	X		X	X	X	X	X			
ART	X		X		X	X	X	X				
APEX	X	X				X		X				
Brahms	X	X				X		X				X
CogAff	X	X			X	X		X			X	
COGNET	X	X	X	X	X			X	X	X		
CCT	X	X			X	X		X				
COGENT					X	X	X	X				
CAPS			X		X	X		X	X			
C-I theory			X		X	X		X				
DCOG	X		X		X	X		X		X		
EPIC	X	X			X	X		X				
HOS	X	X	X		X			X				
MIDAS	X	X	X	X	X	X		X				X
Micro Saint	X		X			X		X		X		
OMAR	X		X			X		X				X
PSI	X	X	X		X	X	X	X	X		X	
SAMPLE	X		X	X		X		X				X
Soar	X	X	X	X	X	X	X	X	X		X	X

Note. An X indicates that the function is represented by the model.

They require ingenuity and creativity on the part of the problem solvers to understand the current situation, identify the relevant knowledge and skills they need or possess, and transform them into actions that lead to goal achievement. Decision making focuses on the subsidiary step of identifying alternative paths of action and selecting among them, probably through a recognition-primed process as described by Klein (1989), assessing them through a form of mental simulation (Endsley, 1995; Klein, 1989), and choosing the first workable, or "satisficing" (Simon, 1956), path to pursue. The overall process of evaluating the current situation, generating solution paths, choosing a path, acting on it, and modifying it as needed to meet changing circumstances may be described as *problem solving* (e.g., Miller, Galanter, & Pribram, 1960).

Most real-world problem solving is multivariate, complex, and steeped in uncertainty. It is required in everything from designing menus to deploying military personnel. It is a critical component of the skills needed to ensure workforce readiness and viability in the global marketplace (O'Neil, 1999). Assessing problem solving in environments that resemble the real world as much as possible is a significant undertaking that seems to require some degree of simulation combined with adequate underlying models of both the cognitive processes required in general to solve problems and those used by specific human participants.

Five of the models used to represent human behavior listed by Morrison (2003) and in Table 6.2 specifically address problem solving: atomic components of thought (ACT), cognition as a network of tasks (COGNET), concurrent activation-based production system (CAPS), PSI, and state, operator, and result (Soar). As Morrison emphasized, yes/no judgments do not convey the quality and extent to which these models address any particular function, including problem solving. Accordingly, following is a brief discussion of these five models in more detail. These comments are based on Morrison's review, which provides still more detail.

Atomic Components of Thought

ACT evolved from the human associative memory (HAM) model developed by Anderson and Bower (1973). HAM was a connectionist model of semantic memory that represented Anderson's doctoral research at Stanford University. ACT is a synthesis of HAM and a production system theory of memory (Newell, 1973). The first ACT model appeared in fall 1974, and it has been continually updated since that time. The current model, called ACT-R (R for rational), appeared in the work of Anderson (1993). Updated versions of the ACT-R model have appeared since then (e.g., Anderson et al., 2004).

In distinguishing between knowledge types, ACT refers to declarative and procedural knowledge. It views declarative knowledge as stored information concerning facts about the world. In ACT, this knowledge is modeled as a semantic network, not unlike the memory representation in HAM. In contrast, Anderson contends that our knowledge of actions (i.e., how to do something) is quite different. This procedural knowledge is modeled as a production system. Declarative and procedural knowledge are held in long-term memory. These two systems communicate through working memory, which is not a separate memory subsystem but rather the subset of knowledge that is currently active.

Problem solving in ACT is accomplished through analogy and example. It may be represented by changes in activation and strength parameters in the semantic network. Productions may not fire because activations levels are below some threshold. Similarly, incorrect productions may fire because their threshold levels are relatively high with respect to correct productions. Activation and strength parameters also affect the latency of responding. A major contribution of ACT is its ability to provide quantitative predictions of performance time and error rates in problem solving.

ACT was originally developed to address cognitive activity and is good at simulating individual intellectual functions, such as problem solving. ACT-R has had several practical applications, including the development of intelligent tutors for math and computer science aimed at secondary education. It has also been used to model human-computer interaction as design aid, and it has provided a framework for interpreting data from brain imaging. However, the ACT-R architecture does not model collective performance, which may be the next step. Anderson has stated that he wants ACT-R to provide computer-generated forces to inhabit training environments and games.

Cognition as a Network of Tasks

COGNET is a symbolic computational model focused on human competency. It was developed by Wayne Zachary in 1989. Its goal is "to facilitate cognitive task analysis and description of specific work domains" (Zachary, Ryder, & Hicinbotham, 1998, p. 16). A more recent version, COGNET-P, was designed to model performance. It includes mechanisms for incorporating time and accuracy constraints and a metacognitive component for control and self-awareness in carrying out cognitive processes, including problem solving (Zachary, Ryder, & Le Mentec, 2002).

COGNET models begin with the assumption that humans are capable of performing multiple tasks simultaneously. COGNET simulates parallel processing with rapid attention switching by maintaining several tasks in various states of completion but allowing only one of these tasks to execute at a time. It is particularly useful for modeling complex time-constrained, multitask situations that require performers to switch the focus of their attention repeatedly as they do in real-world problem solving and decision making.

The COGNET internal information-processing system is intended to apply to all tasks. It is divided into three subsystems: (a) a sensory/perceptual subsystem that converts incoming physical data into symbolic information for use in information processing; (b) an internal cognitive subsystem that constructs and operates a mental model of the world; and (c) an action/motor subsystem for manipulating the external world.

The perceptual and cognitive subsystems are linked by an information store that subsumes short-term, long-term, and working memory. Zachary et al. (2002) do not deny that different short-term and long-term memory effects exist; rather, they contend that the distinction between the two types of memory stores is unnecessary to model cognitive processes.

The COGNET architecture uses a formal production-based system model to represent all forms of task knowledge needed for problem solving. It consists of (a) a network of tasks expressed as goal hierarchies for representing procedural knowledge; (b) perceptual demons that contend ("shriek" with different amplitude) for the attention of the cognitive processor, like Selfridge's (1959) pandemonium model of attention; (c) a "blackboard" for representing and organizing relevant declarative information relating to the problem; and (d) actions for effecting change in the world.

COGNET seems best suited for contemplative, open-ended tasks that are not strongly perceptual-motor in nature. The metacognitive control functions, together with the ability to model independent cognitive agents, should also give COGNET the capability to model coordination among multiple team members. Production-based task knowledge, attention switching, and the metacognitive components all appear to make COGNET well suited for modeling complex cognitive processes such as problem solving.

Concurrent Activation-Based Production System

CAPS was developed by Marcel Just, Patricia Carpenter, and their colleagues at Carnegie Mellon University. The original version of CAPS was a production system for modeling reading, particularly reading comprehension (Thibadeau, Just, & Carpenter, 1982). A unique aspect of the original model was that it incorporated subsymbolic aspects (spreading activation) into the symbolic production system representation.

Development for CAPS is continuing. A more recent version, 4CAPS, is organized into collaborative modules, which are intended to correspond to the functions of different cortical areas (Just, Carpenter, & Varma, 1999). The primary output of 4CAPS is the location and amount of processing per unit time, which is designed to predict the pattern of brain activity recorded by technologies such as functional magnetic resonance imaging and positron emission tomography.

CAPS makes the following assumptions about human cognition:

- Elements in working memory (facts) have value attributes (activations) that reflect their strength or the degree to which they are believed.

- An element can cause a production to fire if it matches the conditions component of the production and the activation value exceeds a specified threshold.
- Cognitive processing is represented by production firings, which cause activation to be propagated. The flow of propagation proceeds from one working memory element (called the source) multiplied by a factor (called the weight) to another element (called the target).
- Processing is explicitly parallel. No limit exists for the number of productions that can fire on the same cycle, and no explicit mechanism exists to resolve conflicts between productions.
- Long-term memory exists separately from working memory.
- The total amount of activation in working memory is capped at some specified value for each individual. This total activation can be used to keep elements active in working memory or to propagate activation by firing productions (Just & Carpenter, 1992).

CAPS models represent central cognitive functions (e.g., comprehension) and do not include peripheral functions, such as perceptual-motor acts. All knowledge is encoded as productions in long-term storage. No mechanisms to acquire or modify that knowledge (i.e., learning) are included in CAPS.

Memory structures and processes are explicitly defined in CAPS. Long-term memory includes procedural and declarative components. Working memory, in contrast, is exclusively declarative: It contains only facts. Forgetting is modeled by decrementing the activation values of "old" elements that remain in working memory from cycle to cycle without receiving explicit activation.

A feature of CAPS is that it represents processing capacity in a theoretically plausible and empirically valid manner. CAPS uses its capabilities to simulate simple problem solving as a comprehension-like process in which the declarative knowledge in working memory is matched with productions from long-term memory. It has been applied to a problem-solving simulation in which a pilot performing a preflight check is interrupted by critical messages that must be comprehended and then either acted on or ignored.

PSI

PSI is usually presented in all capital letters but has not been defined as an acronym. PSI is unique in focusing on the interaction of cognitive, emotional, and motivational processes. It is currently under development by Dietrich Dörner and his colleagues at the Institut für Theoretische Psychologie der Otto-Friedrich-Universität Bamberg. According to Bartl and Dörner (1998), the PSI project is intended to create an intelligent, motivated, emotional agent that can survive in a variety of domains.

The central psychological construct in PSI is motivation. Motivators are portrayed as analogous to tanks filled with liquids, which must be kept within certain tolerance levels. When the level deviates from the ideal, a motivator is launched to activate behaviors to restore the levels.

Bartl and Dörner (1998) sorted six motivators into three categories of needs: (a) system needs (water and energy), intended to sustain an organism's existence; (b) preservation needs (pain avoidance), designed to maintain an organism's structures; and (c) information needs (certainty, competence, and affiliation) with a cognitive or social basis.

Several needs can be active at once. A problem-solving, motive selection mechanism designates a single need as the actual intention. The mechanism selects the intention with the highest expectancy value, which is defined as the product of the perceived probability of fulfilling the need and the level of need. The resulting product is referred to as motive *strength*.

In PSI, emotions and cognitions are not separate processes. There are three primary mechanisms for shaping or modulating cognition and motivation:

- *Activation Level*: The strengths of various needs lead to specific behaviors and to an increase in general activation level, which speeds information processing and may trigger either or both of the two modulators described next.
- *Resolution Level* (RL): Perceptions are modeled as comparisons among schemata. RL refers to the required precision of those comparisons. At low, general activation levels, RL is high, which results in slow but reliable processing. At high activation levels, RL is low, which leads to fast but inaccurate processing.
- *Selection Level* (SL): SL refers to the ability of PSI to change dynamically the threshold needed to activate a need. This mechanism effectively defends intentions against competing needs, thereby protecting PSI against strong behavioral oscillations.

PSI treats memory as a simple log of perceptions and activities and forgetting as a decay of that record. Elements in short-term memory are transitioned in continuous fashion to an episodic memory, and the remnants of the record (stripped of detail) are eventually transitioned into long-term memory. Emotions interact with memory in that records associated with need satisfaction or with pain have a greater chance of passing to long-term memory than do simple sequences of events.

Output from PSI includes momentary states of motives and the speed and accuracy of simulated behavior. According to Ritter, Shadbolt, et al. (2002), PSI can model a wide variety of learning situations, including associative and perceptual learning, operant conditioning, sensory-motor learning, goal learning (i.e., remembering situations that lead to need satisfaction), and aversions (i.e., remembering situations or needs that cause needs). In addition, Ritter, Shadbolt, et al. (2002) reported that PSI includes several built-in problem-solving strategies, including hill climbing and trial and error.

State, Operator, and Result

According to Ritter, Baxter, Avaramides, and Wood (2002), the Soar developer community stopped regarding Soar as an acronym. Hence, it is not usually written in all caps. Soar is perhaps the most popular model gauged by the number of its proponents. As its name implies, Soar's concept of cognition involves a search through a problem space and application of operators to states to achieve a result.

Part of Soar's popularity can be traced to the fact that it is a multifaceted model that addresses disparate audiences. As described by Ritter, Baxter, et al. (2002), Soar provides both a unified theory of cognition and a set of heuristics for developing theories of cognition. It includes principles and constraints from which one can construct applied models of knowledge-based behavior, including problem solving.

Soar has its roots in work begun in the 1950s by Allen Newell, J. C. Shaw, and Herbert Simon to demonstrate that computers could address complex problem solving. The first model produced by this group was the logic theorist (LT), which was designed to devise proofs of geometry theorems (Newell & Simon, 1956; Newell, Shaw, & Simon, 1957). Those same researchers extended the ideas of the LT to different types of problems in their general problem solver model (Newell, Shaw, & Simon, 1958; Newell & Simon, 1972).

Soar is currently under active development at various sites around the world. Some relevant Web addresses are shown in Table 6.1. Soar development is explicitly constrained by three general assumptions about human cognition and behavior: (a) behavior is flexible and goal driven; (b) learning occurs continuously from experience; and (c) elementary cognitive processes occur well within 1 second (Lewis, 2001).

Another guiding principle of Soar is that it should comprise a small set of independent mechanisms (Rosenbloom, Laird, Newell, & McCarl, 1991). This assumption drives the model not only toward simplicity but also toward uniformity in architecture. For instance, Soar uses a single type of process for modeling long-term memory structure, learning, tasks, and decision making.

Soar depicts all behavior as movement through problem spaces. A problem space defines the states and operators that apply to the task at hand. The knowledge required to execute tasks are modeled as productions (condition-action pairs). The conditions define access paths to knowledge stored in memory, whereas the actions define the memory contents themselves (Lewis, 2001).

The course of information processing in Soar is described by the *decision cycle*. Hill (1999) described the decision cycle as a four-phase iterative process:

1. *Input:* Input productions take information from the external world and place the contents into working memory.
2. *Elaboration:* Productions in long-term memory are matched against the contents of working memory and fire in parallel so that all relevant knowledge is retrieved. Productions that fire create proposals for actions that are evaluated in the decision phase and issue direct commands to the motor system.
3. *Decision:* Proposals for action are examined, and as a result, the system selects appropriate operators. If no such action is called for or several competing actions are indicated, then Soar recognizes an impasse, which automatically sets up a subgoal (creates a new space) for resolving the impasse. If the subgoal recognizes another impasse, then another subgoal is declared for solving it, creating a goal stack. This process proceeds in iterative fashion until all impasses have been resolved.
4. *Output:* Motor commands are executed. Resulting changes in internal and external conditions are considered during the decision phase.

In Soar, perception is represented by encoding productions that take data off of a perceptual buffer (called the *input link*) and place the results into working memory. Sensory models are used to filter what information is potentially perceptible.

All long-term memory (procedural, declarative, episodic) is stored as productions. Productions are used not so much to model behavior but to provide content addressable memory. A production's conditions provide associative pathways to contents contained in its action component. Long-term memory is accessed in parallel: All relevant information is retrieved before Soar's decision cycle is completed. Productions can be added to long-term memory through *chunking*, the acquisition of productions that occur during the process of impasse resolution and subgoaling. No procedures exist for deleting productions from long-term memory.

Working memory provides a store of elements that represent the current situation. This mechanism provides the nexus of information processing in Soar. It integrates inputs from the external world, information in productions stored in long-term memory, and results of Soar's internal decision processes. Working memory is not limited in capacity or time.

Soar posits a third type of memory, preference memory, which stores suggestions or imperatives about current operators (Laird, Congdon, & Coulter, 1999).

Preferences are encoded according to fixed semantics, a process that supports the decision stage in Soar information processing and problem solving.

Soar developers extended its capabilities by devising an explicit model of team goals and plans that are shared among team members. The resulting model, called a shell for teamwork (STEAM), represents an integration of team with individual knowledge (Tambe, 1996). STEAM has been used to model coordination among team members in military units and as the underlying method for improving teamwork in RoboCup '97, an international competition to test multiagent systems using soccer as a simulation test bed (Tambe et al., 1999).

An explicit goal of the Soar research program is that the model demonstrate its ability to represent a variety of intelligent behaviors (e.g., Rosenbloom et al., 1991), including toy tasks (e.g., puzzles and games such as Tower of Hanoi and Cryptarithmetic) and more practical domains, such as knowledge-intensive problems in medical diagnosis (Neomycin-Soar), software design (Designer-Soar), and tactical communications (NL-Soar), and learning in complex expert systems (R1-Soar).

Soar has provided creditable models of performance in a variety of complex simulations. Furthermore, its relatively simple architecture fits an impressive range of task domains. Whereas one might argue that ACT-R is more popular among academic users, Soar is more prevalent in operational applications.

Discussion and Conclusions

Simulation is widely and increasingly used to assess the performance and competence of individuals and teams. Games, viewed here as a subset of simulation, are similarly considered as a source of assessment. The intrinsically motivating characteristics of games make them attractive as means to assess mass audiences, as for example a way to assess the preparation of the national voting public to judge policies, legislation, and regulations concerning technology (National Academy of Engineering, in press). Interest in the use of games and simulations in assessment may well increase as techniques develop for the continuous and unobtrusive modeling of abilities from the communication, keyboard, and clickstream interactions of learners and users with technology-based systems (Fletcher, 1999, 2006).

Problems remain, of course. What are the psychometric properties of games and simulations? Is one pass through a game or simulation sufficient for assessment, or are many needed for reliable, valid, precise measurement? How should we identify critical events and decisions? How should we weigh data obtained from the various modes of interactions used in simulations and games? There are more questions of this sort.

Researchers are making progress in this area (e.g., O'Neil, Allred, & Dennis, 1997). One promising approach is based on Mislevy's evidence-centered design (ECD) (Mislevy, Almond, & Lukas, 2003). In ECD, capabilities are identified for some subject area and organized into a graphical framework. ECD then shows how to connect the responses of test-takers working in a complex simulated environment to this framework. Bennett et al. (2003) provided an example of how ECD might be used to assess scientific inquiry skills in a simulation environment. Readers are enthusiastically referred to more complete discussions of these matters by other authors in this book.

Representing human cognitive processes and capabilities should be a key enabler in developing the techniques for assessing problem solving and other cognitive capabilities through the use of games and simulations. The tools, techniques, and frameworks provided by the 19 models discussed by Morrison (2003) and summarized in this chapter provide substantial capabilities, but work remains to be done.

Both the significance and complexity of representing cognitive processes in a credible and practicable manner have been presented to the modeling and simulation community by their own practitioners as a "grand challenge" (Ciancarini et al., 2002).

Giordano, Reynolds, and Brogan (2004) prepared a list of elements required for human behavior representation and identified those that, in their judgment, "cannot be achieved in a tractable manner ... or there is no known way to accomplish them" (p. 915). Their focus was on the capabilities needed to pass Turing's famous Imitation Game, also known as the Turing test (Turing, 1950). Among the items they identified as unachievable are adapting behavior to dynamic scenarios; pattern recognition coupled with appropriate decision making; and complex cognition, reasoning, and learning.

Assessment of problem-solving ability requires an ability to model human cognition — as suggested in this chapter. A fruitful source of these models, again as suggested, is in the efforts to imbue games and simulations with cognitively realistic participants. But, our cognitive modeling goals need not be as ambitious as those targeted by Giordano et al. (2004) for passing the Turing test. To what degree of completeness, then, and which characteristics must cognitive models possess if we wish to obtain adequate assessments of problem-solving ability from games and simulations?

Assessment is usually and properly performed for a reason, usually to inform a decision, for instance, to select individuals for employment, classify individuals into specific job categories, guide progress of individuals and teams toward achieving instructional objectives, certify the readiness of individuals or teams to perform specific tasks, and so forth. The adequacy of an assessment must depend on its purpose. The same may be said for the adequacy of the underlying model of cognition used in the assessment. There is evidently a rich assortment of models and modeling capabilities to choose from and adopt in developing assessment of all sorts, including, of course, assessment of problem-solving processes and abilities. Principles for making these choices and ways to adopt them are, we suggest, proper topics for research and development on the use of games and simulations for assessment.

References

Acquisti, A., Clancey, W. J., van Hoof, R., Scott, M., & Sierhuis, M. (2001, December). *Brahms tutorial* (Technical Memorandum TM01–0002, Version 0.9.9.4 RFC). Moffett Field, CA: NASA Ames Research Center.

Alluisi, E. A. (1991). The development of technology for collective training: SIM-NET, a case history. *Human Factors, 33,* 343–362.

Anderson, J. R. (1993). *Rules of the mind.* Hillsdale, NJ: Erlbaum.

Anderson, J. R., Bothell, D., Byrne, M. D., Douglass, S., Lebiere, C., & Qin, Y. (2004). An integrated theory of the mind. *Psychological Review, 111,* 1036–1060.

Anderson, J. R., & Bower, G. H. (1973). *Human associative memory.* Washington, DC: Winston.

Bailenson, J. N., Swinth, K. R., Hoyt C. L., Persky, S., Dimov, A., & Blascovich, J. (2005). The independent and interactive effects of embodied agent appearance and behavior on self-report, cognitive, and behavioral markers of copresence in immersive virtual environments. *Presence: Teleoperators and Virtual Environments, 14,* 379–393.

Bartl, C., & Dörner, D. (1998). *Comparing the behaviour of PSI with human behavior in the BioLab game* (Memorandum Number 32). Bamburg, Germany: Universität Bamburg, Lehrstuhl Psychologie II.

Bartle, R. (1990). *Early MUD history.* Retrieved January 25, 2006 from www.mud.co.uk/ richard/mudhist.htm

Bennett, R. E., Jenkins, F., Persky, H., & Weiss, A. (2003). Assessing complex problem solving performances. *Assessment in Education, 10,* 347–359.

Cannon-Bowers, J. A., Salas, E., & Pruitt, J. S. (1996). Establishing the boundaries of a paradigm for decision-making research. *Human Factors, 38,* 193–205.

Card, S. K., Moran, T. P., & Newell, A. (1983). *The psychology of human-computer interaction.* Hillsdale, NJ: Erlbaum.

Chase, W. G., & Simon, H. A. (1973). The mind's eye in chess. In W. G. Chase (Ed.), *Visual information processing.* New York: Academic Press.

Ciancarini, P., Donohue, G., Lorenz, D., Panzarasa, P., Pritchett, A., Swartout, W., et al. (2002). Simulation and agent oriented software engineering: Working group report of the grand challenges Dagstuhl Seminar. In R. Fujimoto, D. Lunceford, E. Page, & A. M. Uhrmacher (Eds.), *Grand challenges for modeling and simulation–Dagstuhl report* (pp. 62–66). Retrieved May 12, 2005 from http:// www.informatik.uni-rostock.de/-lin/GC/report/Dagstuhl_Report.pdf

Clancey, W. J., Sachs, P., Sierhuis, M., & van Hoof, R. (1998). Brahms: Simulating practice for work systems design. *International Journal of Human-Computer Studies, 49,* 831–865.

Cooper, R., Yule, P., & Sutton, D. (1998). COGENT: An environment for the development of cognitive models. In U. Schmid, J. F. Krems, & F. Wysotzki (Eds.), *A cognitive science approach to reasoning, learning, and discovery* (pp. 55–82). Lengerich, Germany: Pabst Science.

Corker, K. M., & Smith, B. R. (1993). An architecture and model for cognitive engineering simulation analysis: Application to advanced aviation automation. In *Proceedings of the AIAA Computing in Aerospace 9 Conference* (pp. 1079–1088). Santa Monica, CA: American Institute of Aeronautics and Astronautics.

deGroot, A. D. (1965). *Thought and choice in chess.* The Hague: Mouton Press.

Deutsch, S. (1998). *Multi-disciplinary foundations for multiple-task human performance modeling in OMAR* (pp. 303–308). Paper presented at the 20th annual meeting of the Cognitive Science Society, Madison, WI.

Deutsch, S. E., MacMillian, J., Cramer, N. L. (1993). *Operator model architecture (OMAR) demonstration final report* (AL/HR-TR-1996-0161). Wright-Patterson Air Forc Base, OH: Armstrong Laboratory, Logistics Research Division.

Drasgow, F., & Mattern, K. (2005). New tests and new items: Opportunities and issues. In D. Bartram & R. Hambelton (Eds.), *Computer-based testing and the Internet: Issues and answers* (pp. 59–76). Chichester, West Sussex, UK: Wiley.

Eggleston, R. G., Young, M. J., & McCreight, K. L. (2000). Distributed cognition: A new type of human performance model. In M. Freed (Ed.), *Simulating human agents: Papers from the 2000 AAAI Fall Symposium* (Technical Report FS-00-03, pp. 8–14). Menlo Park, CA: AAAI Press.

Eggleston, R. G., Young, M. J., & McCreight, K. L. (2001). Modeling human work through distributed cognition. In *Proceedings of the 10th Conference on Computer Generated Forces and Behavioral Representation* (pp. 99–104). Orlando, FL: Simulation Interoperability Standards Organization.

Endsley, M. R. (1995). Toward a theory of situation awareness in dynamic systems. *Human Factors, 37,* 32–64.

Fletcher, J. D. (1975). Models of the learner in computer-assisted instruction. *Journal of Computer-Based Instruction, 3,* 118–126.

Fletcher, J. D. (1999). Using networked simulation to assess problem solving by tactical teams. *Computers in Human Behavior, 15,* 375–402.

Fletcher, J. D. (2002). Is it worth it? Some comments on research and technology in assessment and instruction. In *Technology and Assessment: Thinking Ahead* (pp. 26–39). Washington, DC: National Academy of Science.

Fletcher, J. D. (2006). The ADL vision. In H. F. O'Neill and R. Perez (Eds.), *Web-based learning: Theory, research and practice* (pp. 31–53). Mahwah, NJ: Erlbaum.

Fletcher, J. D., & Rockway, M. R. (1986). Computer-based training in the military. In J. A. Ellis (Ed.), *Military contributions to instructional technology* (pp. 171–222). New York: Praeger.

Freed, M., Dahlman, E., Dalal, M., & Harris, R. (2002). *Apex reference manual for Apex version 2.2.* Moffett Field, CA: NASA ARC.

Garau, M., Slater, M., Bee, S., & Sasse, M. A. (2001). The impact of eye gaze on communication using humanoid avatars. In *Proceedings SIGCHI '01* (pp. 309–316). March 31 to April 4, Seattle, WA.

Garmine, E., & Pearson, G. (Eds). (2006). *Tech tally: Approaches to assessing technological literacy.* Washington, DC: National Academy Press.

Giordano, J. C., Reynolds, P. F., Jr., & Brogan, D. C. (2004). Exploring the constraints of human behavior representation. In R. G. Ingalls, M. D. Rossetti, J. S. Smith, & B. A. Peters (Eds.), *Proceedings of the 2004 Winter Simulation Conference* (pp. 912–920).

Glenn, F., Schwartz, S., & Ross, L. (1992). *Development of a human operator simulator version V (HOS-V): Design and implementation* (Research Note 92-PERI-POX). Alexandria, VA: U.S. Army Research Institute for the Behavioral and Social Sciences.

Gopher, D., Weil, M., & Bareket, T. (1994). Transfer of skill from a computer game trainer to flight. *Human Factors, 36,* 387–405.

Goldstine, H. H. (1972). *The computer from PASCAL to von Neumann.* Princeton, NJ: Princeton University Press.

Green, C. S., & Bavelier, D. (2003). Action video game modifies visual selective attention. *Nature, 423,* 534–537.

Greenfield, P. M., deWinstanley, P., Kilpatrick, H., & Kaye, D. (1994). Action video games and informal education: Effects on strategies for dividing visual attention. *Journal of Applied Developmental Psychology, 15,* 195–223.

Grossberg, S. (1976a). Adaptive pattern classification and universal recoding. I: Parallel development and coding of neural feature detectors. *Biological Cybernetics, 23,* 121–134.

Grossberg, S. (1976b). Adaptive pattern classification and universal recoding. II: Feedback, expectation, olfaction, and illusions. *Biological Cybernetics, 23,* 187–202.

Harris, R., Iavecchia, H. P., & Dick, A. O. (1989). The human operator simulator (HOS-IV). In G. R. McMillan, D. Beevis, E. Salis, M. H. Strub, R. Sutton, & L. Van Breda (Eds.), *Application of human performance models to system design* (pp. 275–280). New York: Plenum Press.

Hart, S. G., & Battiste, V. (1992). Flight test of a video game trainer. In *Proceedings of the Human Factors Society 36th Annual Meeting* (pp. 1291–1295). Santa Monica, CA: Human Factors and Ergonomics Society.

Hart, S. G., Dahn, D., Atencio, A., & Dalal, K. M. (2001). *Evaluation and application of MIDAS v2.0* (SAE Technical Paper 2001-01-2648). Warrendale, PA: Society of Automotive Engineers.

Hayes, R. T. (2005). *The effectiveness of instructional games: A literature review and discussion* (Technical Report 2005-004). Orlando, FL: Training Systems Division, Naval Air Warfare Center.

Hill, R. W., Jr. (1999). Modeling perceptual attention in virtual humans. In *Proceedings of the Eighth Conference on Computer Generated Forces and Behavioral Representation* (pp. 563–573). Orlando, FL: Simulation Interoperability Standards Organization.

Hong, J. C., & Liu, M. C. (2003). A study on thinking strategy between experts and novices of computer games. *Computers in Human Behavior, 19,* 245–258.

Just, M. A., & Carpenter, P. A. (1992). A capacity theory of comprehension: Individual differences in working memory. *Psychological Review, 99,* 122–149.

Just, M. A., Carpenter, P. A., & Varma, S. (1999). Computational modeling of high-level cognition and brain function. *Human Brain Mapping, 8,* 128–136.

Kieras, D. E. (1999). *A guide to GOMS model usability evaluation using GOMSL and GLEAN3.* Retrieved August 27, 2002, from the University of Michigan's Electrical Engineering and Computer Science Department site: http://www.eecs.umich.edu/people/kieras/GOMS/GOMSL_Guide.pdf

Kieras, D. E., & Meyer, D. E. (1995). *An overview of the EPIC architecture for cognition and performance with application to human-computer interaction* (EPIC Report No. 5). Ann Arbor: University of Michigan.

Kieras, D. E., & Polson, P. G. (1985). An approach to the formal analysis of user complexity. *International Journal of Man-Machine Studies, 22,* 365–394.

Kintsch, W. (1998). *Comprehension: A paradigm for cognition.* New York: Cambridge University Press.

Kitajima, M., Blackmon, M. H., & Polson, P. G. (2000). A comprehension-based model of Web navigation and its application to Web usability analysis. In S. McDonald, Y. Waern, & G. Cockton (Eds.), *People and Computers XIV-Usability or Else!* [Proceedings of HCI 2000] (pp. 357–373). Heidelberg, Germany: Springer-Verlag.

Klein, G. A. (1989). Recognition-primed decisions. In W. B. Rouse (Ed.), *Advances in man-machine systems research* (pp. 47–92). Greenwich, CT: JAI Press.

Krafft, M. F. (2002, October). *Adaptive resonance theory.* Retrieved March 5, 2003, from the University of Zurich, Department of Information Technology Web site: http://www.ifi.unizh.ch/staff/krafft/papers/2001/wayfinding/ html/node97.html

Laird, J. E., Congdon, C. B., & Coulter, K. J. (1999). *The Soar user's manual: Version 8.2.* Retrieved June 4, 2000, from http://ai.eecs.umich.edu/soar/docs/manuals/soar8manual.pdf

Laughery, K. R., Jr., & Corker, K. (1997). Computer modeling and simulation. In G. Salvendy (Ed.), *Handbook of human factors and ergonomics* (2nd ed., pp. 1375–1408). New York: Wiley.

Lewis, R. L. (2001). Cognitive theory, Soar. In N. J. Smelser & P. B. Baltes (Eds.), *International encyclopedia of the social and behavioral sciences* (pp. 2178–2183). Amsterdam: Pergamon (Elsevier Science).

Lovett, M. C., & Anderson, J. R. (2005). Thinking as a production system. In K. Holyoak & R. Morrison (Eds.), *Cambridge handbook of thinking and reasoning* (pp. 401–430). New York: Cambridge University Press.

Mayer, R. E., & Wittrock, M. C. (1996). Problem solving transfer. In D. C. Berliner & R. C. Calfee (Eds.), *Handbook of educational psychology* (pp. 47–62). New York: Macmillan.

Mayer, S. R. (1970). Trends in human factors research for military information systems. *Human Factors, 12,* 177–186.

Miller, G. A., Galanter, E. H., & Pribram, K. H. (1960). *The plans and structures of behavior.* New York: Holt, Rinehart, and Winston.

Mislevy, R. J., Almond, R. G., & Lukas, J. F. (2003). *A brief introduction to evidence-centered design* (RR-03-16). Princeton, NJ: Educational Testing Service.

Morrison, J. E. (2003). *A review of computer-based human behavior representations and their relation to military simulations* (IDA Paper P-3845). Alexandria, VA: Institute for Defense Analyses.

Mulgund, S. S., Harper, K. A., Zacharias, G. L., & Menke, T. E. (2000). SAMPLE: Situation awareness model for pilot-in-the-loop evaluation. In *Proceedings of the Ninth Conference on Computer Generated Forces and Behavioral Representation* (pp. 377–378). Orlando, FL: Simulation Interoperability Standards Organization.

Newell, A. (1973). You can't play 20 questions with nature and win: Projective comments on the papers of this symposium. In W. G. Chase (Ed.), *Visual information processing* (pp. 283–310). New York: Academic Press.

Newell, A., Shaw, J. C., & Simon, H. A. (1957). Empirical explorations of the logic theory machine: A case study in heuristics. In *Proceedings of the 1957 Western Joint Computer Conference* (pp. 218–230). Also reprinted in E. A. Feigenbaum and J. Feldman (Eds.), *Computers and thought* (pp. 109–133). New York: McGraw-Hill, 1963.

Newell, A., Shaw, J. C., & Simon, H. A. (1958). Elements of a theory of human problem solving. *Psychological Review, 65,* 151–166.

Newell, A., & Simon, H. A. (1956). The logic theory machine: A complex information processing system. *IRE Transactions in Information Theory, IT-2,* 61–79.

Newell, A., & Simon, H. A. (1972). *Human problem solving.* Englewood Cliffs, NJ: Prentice-Hall.

Olsen, J. R., & Bass, V. B. (1982). The application of performance technology in the military: 1960–1980. *NSPI Journal, 41,* 32–36.

O'Neil, H. F., Jr. (1999). Perspectives on computer-based performance assessment of problem solving. *Computers in Human Behavior, 15,* 255–268.

O'Neil, H. F., Jr., Allred, K., & Dennis, R. A. (1997). Validation of a computer simulation for assessment of interpersonal skill. In H. F. O'Neil (Ed.), *Workplace readiness: Competencies and assessment* (pp. 229–254). Mahwah, NJ: Erlbaum.

O'Neil, H. F., Jr., Chung, G. K., & Brown, R. S. (1997). Use of networked simulations as a context to measure team competencies. In H. F. O'Neil (Ed.), *Workplace readiness: Competencies and assessment* (pp. 411–452). Mahwah, NJ: Erlbaum.

O'Neil, H. F., Jr., Wainess, R., & Baker, E. L. (2005). Classification of learning outcomes: Evidence from the computer games literature. *The Curriculum Journal, 16*, 455–474.

Pew, R. W., & Mavor, A. S. (Eds.). (1998). *Modeling human and organizational behavior: Applications to military simulations.* Washington, DC: National Academy Press.

Rasmussen, J. (1983), Skills, rules and knowledge: Signals, signs and symbols and other distinctions in human performance models. *IEEE Transactions on Systems, Man and Cybernetics, SMC-13*, 257–266.

Ritter, F. E., Baxter, G. D., Avaramides, M., & Wood, A. B. (2002). *Soar: Frequently asked questions list.* Retrieved May 29, 2002, from the Pennsylvania State University's Soar Web site: http://ritter.ist.psu.edu/soar-faq/soar-faq.html

Ritter, F. E., Shadbolt, N. R., Elliman, D., Young, R., Gobet, F., & Baxter, G. D. (2002b). *Techniques for modeling human and organizational behaviour in synthetic environments: A supplementary review.* Wright-Patterson Air Force Base, OH: Human Systems Information Analysis Center.

Robar, J. (2004). Multiplayer technology: A primer. *MS&T Magazine, 6*, 26–29.

Rosenbloom, P. S., Laird, J. E., Newell, A., & McCarl, R. (1991). A preliminary analysis of the Soar architecture as a basis for general intelligence. *Artificial Intelligence, 47*, 289–325.

Rouse, W. B., Cannon-Bowers, J. A., & Salas, E. (1992). The role of mental models in team performance in complex systems. *IEEE Transactions on Systems, Man, and Cybernetics, 22*, 1296–1308.

Rowell, J. T., & Streich, E. R. (1964). The SAGE system training program for the Air Force Defense Command. *Human Factors, 6*, 537–548.

Selfridge, O. (1959). Pandemonium: A paradigm for learning. In *Symposium on the Mechanization of Thought Processes* (pp. 511–529). London: HM Stationary Office.

Simon, H. A. (1956). Rational choice and the structure of the environment. *Psychological Review, 63*, 129–138.

Sleeman, D., & Brown, J. S. (Eds.). (1982). *Intelligent tutoring systems.* New York: Academic Press.

Sloman, A. (2003). How many separately evolved emotional beasties live within us? In R. Trappl, P. Petta, & S. Payr (Eds.), *Emotions in humans and artifacts* (pp. 35–114). Cambridge, MA: MIT Press.

Sternberg, R. J., & Davidson, J. E. (1992). Problem solving. In M. C. Alkin (Ed.), *Encyclopedia of educational research* (Vol. 3, pp. 1037–1045). New York: Macmillan.

Subrahmanyam, K., & Greenfield, P. M. (1994). Effect of video game practice on spatial skills in girls and boys. Special issue: Effects of interactive entertainment technologies on development. *Journal of Applied Developmental Psychology, 15*, 13–32.

Tambe, M. (1996). Teamwork in real-world, dynamic environments. In *Proceedings of the First International Conference on Multi-Agent Systems* (pp. 361–368). Menlo Park, CA: American Association for Artificial Intelligence.

Tambe, M., Adibi, J., Al-Onaizan, Y., Erdem, A., Kaminka, G. A., Marsella, S. C., et al. (1999). Building agent teams using an explicit teamwork model and learning. *Artificial Intelligence, 110*, 215–239.

Thibadeau, R., Just, M. A., & Carpenter, P. A. (1982). A model of the time course and content of reading. *Cognitive Science, 6*, 157–203.

Tobias, S., & Fletcher, J. D. (in press). What research has to say about designing computer games for learning. *Educational Technology*.

Turing, A. M. (1950). Computing machinery and intelligence. *Mind, 236*, 433–460.

Wherry, R. J. (1976). The human operator simulator — HOS. In T. B. Sheridan & G. Johannsen (Eds.), *Monitoring behavior and supervisory control* (pp. 283–293). New York: Plenum Press.

Yule, P., & Cooper, R. (2000, August). *The COGENT tutorial.* Paper presented at the *22nd Annual Conference of the Cognitive Science Society*, Philadelphia, PA.

Zachary, W., Campbell, G. E., Laughery, K. R., Glenn, F., & Cannon-Bowers, J. A. (2001). The application of human modeling technology to the design, evaluation and operation of complex systems. In E. Salas (Ed.), *Advances in human performance and cognitive engineering research* (Vol. 1, pp. 199–247). New York: JAI Press.

Zachary, W. W., Ryder, J. M., & Hicinbothom, J. H. (1998). Cognitive task analysis and modeling of decision-making in complex environments. In J. Cannon-Bowers and E. Salas (Eds.), *Decision-making under stress: Implications for training and simulation* (pp. 315–344). Washington, DC: American Psychological Association.

Zachary, W., Ryder, J., & Le Mentec, J.-C. (2002). *Applied modeling of human competence and performance with COGNET and COGNET-P.* Unpublished manuscript.

7

Problem-Solving Assessment in Games and Simulation Environments

RICHARD E. MAYER

University of California, Santa Barbara

What are the cognitive consequences of interacting with a computer-based simulation or game? In particular, can people improve their problem-solving skills by interacting with a computer-based simulation or game? In addition, what are the features of simulations and games that lead to improved problem-solving transfer? These fundamental questions about the potential educational benefits of games and simulations cannot be addressed without developing appropriate measures of problem-solving skill.

To develop problem-solving measures, it is useful to conduct a cognitive task analysis aimed at pinpointing specific changes in the learner's knowledge — including changes in conceptual knowledge and strategic knowledge (Baker & Mayer, 1999; Mayer, 2002). In this chapter, I describe several projects in which we measured the problem-solving skill of learners who interacted with computer-based games and simulations involving mathematics, science, or technology. My goal is to derive general principles for creating problem-solving assessments of the cognitive consequences of interacting with computer-based games and simulations. In particular, I suggest two forms of assessment: (a) tests of conceptual knowledge, including open-ended verbal questions involving troubleshooting, redesigning, and explaining; and (b) tests of strategic knowledge, including behavioral assessments of learners' strategies in solving transfer problems.

Rationale for Games and Simulations

Considerable effort has gone into developing computer-based simulations and games intended to help people learn scientific and mathematical material (Gredler, 2004; Hettinger & Haas, 2003; Jacobson & Kozma, 2000; Jonassen, 2004; Lajoie, 2000; Linn, Davis, & Bell, 2004; Rieber, 2005; Stanney, 2002; Vosniadou, de Corte, Glaser, & Mandl, 1996), but there is a need for such development efforts to be consistent with research-based principles of multimedia design and grounded in a research-based theory of how people learn. In particular, it is worthwhile to ask what people learn with games and simulations, and whether games and simulations can be used to assess changes in learners' knowledge.

Overall, proponents argue that interactive simulations and games hold potential for improving Web-based training because users find them entertaining and motivating (Gee, 2003; Prensky, 2001; Rieber, 2005; Schank, 1997, 2002). However, research examining this claim is in its infancy (Gredler, 2004; Moreno & Mayer, 2002; Reiber, 2005). In a review of what cognitive science says about how people learn, Bransford, Brown, and Cocking (1999) noted two important features of new instructional technologies that are consistent with the principles of a new science of learning: visual modes of presentation and interactive modes of presentation. First, "technologies can help people visualize difficult-to-understand concepts ... [so] students are able to work with visualization ... software" (p. xix). Second, "new technologies are interactive [so] it is easier to create environments in which students learn by doing" (p. xix). Interactive simulations and games capitalize on both of these features and therefore represent an important venue for rigorous research aimed at improving computer-based training.

There are, of course, many impressive examples of instructional simulations, such as the classic STEAMER simulation (Hollan, Hutchins, & Weitzman, 1987); Lesgold's (Gott & Lesgold, 2000) SHERLOCK troubleshooting simulation; White and Frederiksen's (1998) ThinkerTools simulation; Kozma and Russell's (2005; Kozma, Russell, Jones, Marx, & Davis, 1996) chemistry simulation; and Rieber's (2005) physics simulation. To date, most scholarship on instructional simulations and games has focused on descriptions of development projects or gross comparisons of learning with a particular instructional simulation compared to learning in a conventional environment. However, the next generation of research should pinpoint features of instructional simulations and games that promote learning, and to do this it is necessary to pinpoint the specific types of knowledge that students learn. Thus, the key to this enterprise is the development of sensitive measures of changes in learners' knowledge (Pellegrino, Chudowsky, & Glaser, 2001).

What Are Games and Simulations?

An instructional simulation is a multimedia environment that models the behavior of some system and allows people to interact with it as a way of promoting learning. This definition has three main components: An instructional simulation is a multimedia environment that models a to-be-learned system, an instructional simulation allows for user interaction by responding in rule-based ways to user inputs, and an instructional simulation is intended to promote learner understanding of the to-be-learned system. An instructional simulation can be turned into an instructional game when one or more players compete to achieve some goal, which is accomplished through understanding the subject matter in some way. Instructional simulations are a form of multimedia learning because they are intended to foster learning using words and pictures. The distinguishing feature of an instructional simulation is interactivity, including each of the following forms: a learner gives input and the simulation responds immediately or a learner enters a series of parameters and then "runs" the simulation.

What Is Problem-Solving Assessment in Games and Simulations?

What does someone need to know to be successful in solving problems in a domain? Research in cognitive science suggests that problem-solving performance depends on the coordination of several different kinds of domain-specific knowledge, including facts, concepts, procedures, and strategies (Anderson et al., 2001). *Facts* are basic elements such as knowing that magnets are made of metal. *Concepts* are knowledge of the models or principles that specify the interrelationships among the basic elements within a larger structure. *Procedures* are knowledge of a step-by-step process for how to do something, such as how to add numbers. *Strategies* are general methods for solving a problem. Although most assessment focuses on facts and procedures, problem solving also depends on concepts and strategies (Anderson et al., 2001). In this chapter, I focus mainly in techniques for assessing the learner's conceptual and strategic knowledge.

For the past 20 years, my colleagues and I at the University of California, Santa Barbara (UCSB) have been grappling with how to design assessments of problem-solving knowledge within games and simulations. In this chapter, I share the fruits of our efforts by summarizing some of the ways that we have attempted to measure the learner's knowledge underlying problem-solving performance within seven game or simulation environments: computer programming, educational games, bunny game, design-a-plant game, profile game, Dr. Phyz simulation, and F-16 aircraft simulation. The underlying theme across these seven cases is that each involves interaction between the learner and the computer-based system (interactivity criterion), each involves verbal and nonverbal forms of representations such as graphics (multimedia criterion), and each involves solving problems (problem-solving criterion). The number of items on each test and the time allowed to take the test are based on pilot testing and the logistical constraints of each testing situation. In each case, I report on measures that were successful in distinguishing among groups and thus have earned some modest level of validity.

Assessment of Problem Solving in Computer Programming

Learning to program occurs in a computer-based simulation environment that meets the three criteria of interactivity, including nonverbal forms of representation, and requiring that learners engage in problem solving. During the 1980s and beyond, an important research question was, What are the cognitive consequences of learning computer programming (Mayer, 1988)? A straightforward problem-solving test consists of items in which the learner is given a problem statement in words and is asked to generate a computer program; the score is the number of correct programs produced (or percentage correct). Although this straightforward test gives a general indication of problem-solving performance, it does not tap changes in the underlying knowledge that supports problem solving. In this section, I explore several attempts by my colleagues and I to assess cognitive changes in learners attributable to their learning of computer programming, namely, Logo and BASIC.

First, consider learning of Logo in which students see a turtle on the screen (usually in the form of a triangle) and may give commands to move the turtle such as FD 5 (i.e., move forward 5 turtle steps), RT 90 (i.e., turn right 90°), BK 2 (i.e., move backward 2 turtle steps), and LT 90 (i.e., turn left 90°). By using a small set of commands, students can produce interesting pictures on the screen.

What do students learn from interacting with the Logo machine, that is, from learning how to use Logo to produce programs that generate drawings? The first section in Table 7.1 describes some ways of assessing the cognitive consequences of learning computer programming, including a map test and a command prediction test (Fay & Mayer, 1987, 1994; Mayer & Fay, 1987). In the map test, students are given a map showing several streets (with all intersections at 90° angles) and eight landmarks: home, swimming pool, drug store, pizza parlor, shorts shop, playground, toy store, ice cream shop. Students are given a verbal description of a sequence of landmarks and asked to draw a line within the streets from a designated starting point to home, passing by each of the landmarks in order. Then, students are given the same map with the pathway marked and are asked to write instructions that would lead their friends along the path from the starting point to home. This is repeated for a second map. The score consists of the total number of correct

Table 7.1 Assessing Conceptual and Strategic Knowledge for Problem Solving in Games and Simulation Environments

Test	Knowledge	Source	Description	Score
Purpose: To determine the cognitive consequences of learning Logo or BASIC programming				
Map test	Strategic	Mayer & Fay (1987)	Given a neighborhood map and list of locations draw a path connecting them	Number correct
			Given a neighborhood map showing a path connecting various locations, give verbal directions	Number correct
Command prediction	Conceptual	Fay & Mayer (1987)	Given a Logo command, draw what happens when it is executed	Number correct, misconception type (or bug)
Problem translation	Conceptual	Mayer, Dyck, & Vilberg (1986)	Given a word problem, select a corresponding equation	Number correct
Following procedures	Strategic	Mayer, Dyck, & Vilberg (1986)	Given a list of verbal commands, describe the final output	Number correct

(continued)

Table 7.1 Assessing Conceptual and Strategic Knowledge for Problem Solving in Games and Simulation Environments (Continued)

Test	Knowledge	Source	Description	Source
Purpose: To determine the cognitive consequences of playing educational computer games				
Sentence translation	Conceptual	Mayer et al. (1997)	Given a sentence from a word problem, select the corresponding number sentence	Number correct
Necessary numbers	Conceptual	Mayer et al. (1997)	Given a word problem, select the numbers that are needed to solve the problem	Number correct
Necessary operations	Strategic	Mayer et al. (1997)	Given a word problem, select the arithmetic operations that are needed to solve the problem	Number correct
Game playing	Strategic	Mayer et al. (1999)	Given a new game, make each necessary move	Number of excess moves, type of strategy
Mental rotation	Strategic	Sims & Mayer (2002)	Judge whether two shapes are same or different	Response time, best-fitting model
Form board	Strategic	Sims & Mayer (2002)	Judge whether shapes fit together	Response time

Purpose: To assess knowledge of addition and subtraction of signed numbers in the bunny game

Bunny game	Conceptual	Moreno & Mayer (1999)	Given an arithmetic problem, use virtual joystick to simulate movement of bunny along number line	Number correct, misconception type (bug)
Arithmetic solving	Strategic, conceptual	Moreno & Mayer (1999)	Given an arithmetic problem, type in correct answer	Number correct, misconception type (bug)

Purpose: To assess knowledge of how plants grow in the design-a-plant game

Design-a-plant game	Conceptual	Moreno et al. (2001)	Select roots, stem, and leaves for a plant to grow in a specified environment	Number correct
			Given a plant with specified roots, stem, and leaves, describe the environment for which it is best suited	Number correct

Purpose: To assess knowledge of geology sonar detection in the profile game

Profile game	Strategic	Mayer, Mautone, & Prothero (2002)	Detect geological features in a geology simulation	Number correct, solution time

(continued)

Table 7.1 Assessing Conceptual and Strategic Knowledge for Problem Solving in Games and Simulation Environments (Continued)

Test	Knowledge	Source	Description	Source
Purpose: To access knowledge of how an electric motor works in the Dr. Phyz simulation				
Troubleshooting problem	Conceptual	Mayer et al. (2003)	List possible reasons for motor to not work when turned on	Number of correct answers
Redesign problem	Conceptual	Mayer et al. (2003)	Describe how to change a motor for a certain purpose	Number of correct answers
Principle problem	Conceptual	Mayer et al. (2003)	Explain why an event occurs	Number of correct answers
Prediction problem	Conceptual	Mayer et al. (2003)	Tell what would happen for a specific set of actions	Number of correct answers
Action problem	Conceptual	Mayer et al. (2003)	Tell actions to take to make the motor accomplish a specific goal	Number of correct answers
Purpose: To assess knowledge of an aircraft fuel system in the F-16 aircraft simulation				
Troubleshooting problem	Conceptual	O'Neil et al. (2000)	List possible reasons for fuel system to malfunction	Number correct
Redesign problem	Conceptual	O'Neil et al. (2000)	Describe how to change the fuel system for a certain purpose	Number correct
Prescription problem	Conceptual	O'Neil et al. (2000)	Tell what would happen for a specific set of actions	Number correct

answers (ranging from 0 to 4), that is, correct routes and correct directions. This test is a measure of the learner's strategic knowledge, particularly how to generate and interpret procedural directions.

The command prediction test consists of 24 items, each containing two rectangles printed on a sheet of paper. For each item, the top rectangle shows a turtle (such as the turtle pointing toward the top of the screen) with a command (such as RT 90) printed under the rectangle. The bottom rectangle is blank, and the learner is asked to draw how the turtle will look after the command is carried out. The score consists of the total number of correct predictions (ranging from 0 to 24). This test is a measure of the learner's conceptual knowledge, particularly the meaning of various commands.

A more qualitative way to score the test is to categorize the learner's misconceptions based on error patterns. For example, learners may think RT 90 means to face the right side of the screen (which we call a *face misconception*), move 90 steps to the right (which we call a *move misconception*), or to face the right side of the screen and move forward 90 steps (which we call a *face and move misconception*). The score is the number of each type of misconception (or bug) that the learner displays. This is a measure of the learner's conceptual knowledge, that is, the learner's concept of the meaning of each command.

In the programming test, we tabulate a number of factors related to activity during programming (i.e., program construction), such as number of revision cycles (i.e., the number of times a program is rewritten after it is run) and number of times the program was run, and the quality of the final program (i.e., program quality), such as program modularity (i.e., the number of modules) and program flexibility (i.e., the number of variable inputs). These tests measure strategic knowledge, particularly knowledge of how to modularize a program.

Second, consider the task of learning BASIC as one's first programming language. Is there a connection between "learning to program and learning to think" (Mayer, Dyck, & Vilberg, 1986)? To examine this question, we developed a set of assessment instruments including the word problem translation test and the following procedures test. The word problem translation test consists of 6 items, such as the following:

A car rental service charges $20 a day and 15 cents a mile to rent a car. Find the expression for total cost C, in dollars, of renting a car for D days to travel M miles.

a. $C = 20D + 0.15M$
b. $C = 15D + 0.20M$
c. $C = 20D + 15M$
d. $C = 0.15D + 20M$
e. None of the above

(The correct answer is a.) Each item presents a word problem and asks the learner to select the corresponding equation. The test score consists of the total number correct (ranging from 0 to 6). This is a measure of the learner's conceptual knowledge because it tests the learner's translation from one form of representation to another.

The following procedures test consists of 8 items, such as:

1. Put 5 in Box A.
2. Put 4 in Box B.
3. Add the number in Box A and the number in Box B, put the result in Box C.
4. Add the number in Box A and the number in BOX C and put the result in Box A.
5. Write down the numbers from Box A, B, and C.

What is the output of this program?

a. 5, 4, 9
b. 14, 4, 9
c. 14, 9, 9
d. 9, 4, 9
e. None of the above

(The correct answer is b.) Each item consists of a list of actions concerning numbers in various boxes and asks the learner to select the output of the procedure. This is a test of conceptual knowledge because the learner must understand the meaning of each command.

Overall, our work on assessing the cognitive consequences of learning to program encourages several kinds of assessment measures, including the map test, command prediction test, problem translation test, and following procedures test. Importantly, research on the cognitive consequences of learning computer programming demonstrates that students show growth in knowledge directly related to the target task, such as the ability to generate and comprehend a procedure but not in general cognitive skills such as logical reasoning (Mayer, 1988).

Assessment of Problem Solving in Educational Game Playing

What happens when students regularly attend an after-school computer club in which they learn to play a wide variety of educational computer games? Can we identify any cognitive consequences of learning to play educational computer games? During the 1990s, my colleagues and I at UCSB examined this question within the context of the Fifth Dimension after-school computer club (Mayer, Quilici, & Moreno, 1999; Mayer et al., 1997). We began by performing a cognitive task analysis in which we pinpointed the cognitive skills that students could learn within the computer club, including learning to generate and comprehend instructions. The second section of Table 7.1 summarizes some of the cognitive measures we developed to assess the cognitive consequences of participation in the Fifth Dimension after-school computer club.

The sentence translation test consists of 6 items, such as the following:

Which number sentence is correct? Ann and Rose have 20 books altogether.

a. Ann's books = Rose's books + 20
b. Ann's books + 20 = Rose's books
c. Ann's books + Rose's books = 20
d. Ann's books = Rose's books

(The correct answer is c.) Each item presents a sentence specifying the quantitative relation between two variables and asks the learner to select a number sentence that corresponds. The score is based on the number of correct answers (ranging from 0 to 6). The sentence translation test measures conceptual knowledge because it requires the learner to understand the situation described in the sentence.

The necessary numbers test consists of 6 items, such as the following:

Which numbers are needed to do this problem? A package of 3 toys costs 88 cents. Richie bought 2 packages. How many toys did he buy?

a. 3, 88, 2
b. 3, 88
c. 88, 2
d. 3, 2

(The correct answer is d.) Each item presents a problem that may contain more information than is needed to solve the problem. The learner's task is to select the numbers that are needed to solve the problem. The score is the total number correct (ranging from 0 to 6.) The necessary numbers test assesses the learner's conceptual knowledge, that is, knowledge of types of problem situations.

The necessary operations test consists of 6 items, such as the following:

What should you do for this problem? The 200 children at River View School are going on a bus trip. Each bus holds 50 children. How many buses are needed?

a. Divide, then add
b. Subtract only
c. Multiply only
d. Divide only

(The correct answer is d.) Each item consists of a word problem along with four alternatives for computations to solve the problem. The score is based on the total number correct (ranging from 0 to 6). The necessary operations test is intended to measure an aspect of the learner's strategic knowledge, that is, a strategy for planning a solution procedure.

Another way to assess the cognitive consequences of learning to play educational computer games is to test the learner's strategy for learning a new game. In the puzzle tank game, the learner is given a diagram depicting two water tanks (such as a 7-unit tank and a 2-unit tank) and asked to use the tanks to produce exactly 12 units. The most efficient solution is to fill the 7-unit tank, draw out 2 into the 2-unit tank, deposit the remaining 5 units into the truck, fill the 7-unit tank again and deposit it into the truck, yielding 12 units in the truck. This can be called the subtraction strategy. A less-efficient strategy is to fill the 2-unit tank and deposit its contents into the truck six times. This can be called the addition strategy. The puzzle tank test consists of 3 problems. It is scored by tallying the total number of excess moves across the 3 problems. It is also scored by categorizing the learner's strategy (such as an addition or subtraction strategy). (In this problem, subtraction is the expert strategy.) The puzzle tank test taps the learner's strategic knowledge, that is, the learner's knowledge of how to plan a procedure to win in a computer game.

Finally, in a somewhat-related study, Sims and Mayer (2002) sought to assess the cognitive consequences of learning to play the computer game Tetris. Tetris requires mentally rotating shapes and fitting them together. In the mental rotation test, the learner is shown two shapes; the one on the left is in the upright position, and the one on the right is rotated 0°, 45°, 90°, 135°, 180°, 225°, 270°, or 315° clockwise and is either flipped or not. The learner's task is to press the *same* button if the shapes are the same and the *different* button if the shape on the right is flipped. The score is the mean response time (RT) based on 56 items. Alternatively, the learner can be classified as using a particular strategy based on the pattern of RTs across the 8 possible degrees of rotation. Importantly, the test was most sensitive to Tetris playing experience when it was based on Tetris shapes rather than letters, indicating the domain specificity of Tetris learning.

In the form board test, the learner is shown a graphic containing a Tetris shape above a lower configuration and a graphic showing the result of the Tetris shape moving directly downward into the lower configuration. The learner's task is to press the *yes* button if the second graphic is a correct depiction of the merger and to press the *no* button if it is not. The score is the mean response time across 56 items. Both the mental rotation test and the form board test are assessments of the learner's strategic knowledge concerning how to mentally manipulate Tetris-like shapes.

Assessment of Problem Solving in the Bunny Game

The previous sections show that learning to program and learning to play computer games can have cognitive consequences that are tapped by specific cognitive tests. In this section, I examine the cognitive consequences of learning addition and subtraction of signed numbers in a computer-based multimedia simulation that we call the bunny game (Moreno & Mayer, 1999). In the bunny game, the learner views a screen showing a number line running from −9 on the left to 9 on the right. Sitting on the 0 spot is a bunny facing the learner. Above the bunny are the words, "How would you solve this problem? Try to figure it out by moving the bunny along the number line." Below these instructions is a problem, such as "4 − −5 = ___". At the bottom of the screen is an answer box for the learner to type in an answer. To move the bunny along the number line, there is also a set of four buttons on the screen: JUMP FORWARD, JUMP BACK, FACE LEFT, and FACE RIGHT.

The learner's job is to make the bunny move in a way that corresponds to the problem. After attempting this task and entering an answer, the program then demonstrates the correct set of moves: (a) The bunny moves to the 4 spot and says "FIRST FIND STARTING POINT. 4 means GO TO 4"; (b) the bunny faces left and says "SECOND FIND THE OPERATION. − means FACE LEFT"; (c) the bunny jumps back 5 steps (which is to the right along the number line) while saying "THIRD FIND HOW TO JUMP. −5 means JUMP BACK 5 STEPS"; and (d) the bunny is now at the 9 spot and says "The answer is 9."

The learner learns by solving a series of 16 problems on each of 4 sessions, for a total of 64 problems overall. The third section of Table 7.1 summarizes techniques for assessing what was learned in the bunny game. One useful way to measure learning understanding is to determine the number of correct answers on problems in which one or more of the numbers is negatively signed and the operation is subtraction. Another useful measure is to categorize the learner's misconceptions based on errors in moving the bunny or in the pattern of errors. For example, some students misinterpreted the negative sign in an operand as an operator, as indicated by −8 + −1 = 7. The misconception measure assesses the learner's conceptual knowledge, namely, whether the learner distinguishes between the minus sign as an operator and as an operand. Overall, students who learned with the bunny simulation showed greater reduction in errors and misconceptions than those who learned without the bunny.

Assessment of Problem Solving in the Design-A-Plant Game

The design-a-plant game is a computer-based simulation game in which the learner takes a trip in a spaceship to a distant planet that has specified weather conditions, such as "rainy and windy" and must design a plant that would live there by choosing appropriate roots, stem, and leaves (Moreno & Mayer, 2000, 2004; Moreno, Mayer, Spires, & Lester, 2001). After designing the plant, the learner gets to see whether the plant survives, and an animated pedagogical agent named Herman-the-Bug provides feedback and explanations about plant growth, including narrated animations of plant growth.

As shown in the fourth section of Table 7.1, we assessed problem solving by asking two kinds of questions: (a) asking the learner to design a plant for a new environment (e.g., "Design a plant to live in an environment with low sunlight") and (b) asking the learner to describe an environment that would support the growth of a given plant (e.g., "with thick, small, thin-skinned leaves; thick, long, and bark stem; and branching, shallow, and thin roots"). The score was the number of correct answers. The design-a-plant test assesses the learner's conceptual knowledge of how a plant grows. Overall, this measure distinguished among the cognitive consequences of various instructional methods.

Assessment of Problem Solving in the Profile Game

The profile game is a computer-based geology simulation game in which the goal is to use a sonar-type system to determine the location and type of geological formation (e.g., ridge, trench, basin, island) in a section of a planet (Mayer, Mautone, & Prothero, 2002). The learner can draw lines from one point to another, and the computer will display a profile line showing the elevation in meters along the entire line. By carefully drawing lines and noting the corresponding plot of the profile line, the learner can infer what type of geological formation exists in the area on the screen. When the learner is sure of the answer, he or she enters the answer in a dialogue box.

The fifth section of Table 7.1 shows ways to assess what was learned in the profile game. Problem solving can be assessed by noting the number of correct answers and the mean solution time. In addition, problem solving can be assessed by categorizing the search strategy the learner uses on each problem, such as generating parallel horizontal lines. These measures attempt to tap the learner's strategic knowledge. Overall, students who were given pretraining concerning the shapes of various geological formations performed better in the profile game.

Assessment of Problem Solving in the Dr. Phyz Simulation

The Dr. Phyz simulation is a computer-based simulation environment in which an animated pedagogical agent explains aspects of how an electric motor works in response to learner questions (Mayer, Dow, & Mayer, 2003).

The learner sees a drawing of an electric motor on the screen and can click on any part of it, such as the battery, wires, wire loop, magnets, or commutator. Then, a list of frequently asked questions appears in the upper right portion of the screen, and the learner can click on any of them. For each question, Dr. Phyz flies around the screen in the context of a narrated animation that answers the questions. The learner can click on any parts and any questions for any number of times. When the learner understands how the electric motor works, he or she is given a problem-solving test.

The problem-solving test consists of five main types of problems: troubleshooting, redesign, principle, prediction, and action. These are summarized in the sixth section of Table 7.1. For a troubleshooting problem, the learner lists possible reasons why the motor might not work, such as, "Suppose you switch on an electric motor but nothing happens. What could have gone wrong?" For a design problem, the learner describes how to change a motor for a specific purpose, such as, "What could you do to increase the speed of the electric motor, that is, to make the wire loop rotate more rapidly?" For a principle problem, the learner explains why an event occurs, such as, "Why does the wire loop move?" For a prediction problem, the learner tells what would happen for a specific set of actions, such as, "What happens if you connect the negative terminal to the red wire and the positive terminal to the yellow wire?" For an action problem, the learner tells what actions are needed to accomplish a specific goal, such as, "What can you do to reverse the movement of an electric motor, that is, to make the wire loop rotate in the opposite direction?" The learners had 3 minutes to answer each question. For each question, we generated a set of correct answers that are based on the explanation in the simulation and not simply based on common knowledge. The score on the problem-solving test is the total number of correct answers across all of these types of questions. This test assesses conceptual knowledge of how an electric motor works.

Assessment of Problem Solving an F-16 Aircraft Simulation

Finally, consider a virtual reality simulation of the fuel system of an F-16 aircraft; in this simulation, the learner wears a head-mounted display (O'Neil et al., 2000). In the F-16 aircraft simulation, the learner is asked to move from one section of the fuel system to another in a sort of treasure hunt. Following this training, the learner takes a series of tests, including a problem-solving test (summarized in the final section of Table 7.1) containing a troubleshooting problem ("Suppose you try to transfer fuel from one tank to another, but nothing happens. What could have gone wrong?"); a redesign problem ("What could be done to make fuel transfer more reliable, that is, to minimize the chances of something going wrong when fuel is transferred from one tank to another?"); and prediction problems ("What would happen if the air ejector pump stopped working?" and "What would happen if the fuel flow proportioner stopped working?"). Learners had 2.5 minutes to write their answers. For each problem, we generated a list of correct answers that are based on the simulation and are not just based on common knowledge. The problem-solving test score consisted of the total number of correct answers across all four test problems. This is a test of conceptual knowledge of how the parts of the fuel system are interrelated. Overall, the problem-solving measure was effective in distinguishing among the learning outcomes of people who learned under different instructional methods.

Conclusion

The theme of this chapter is that problem-solving performance in any domain depends on the learner's knowledge, which is measurable. In this chapter, I summarized techniques for assessing two kinds of knowledge that are sometimes neglected in traditional assessments: conceptual knowledge and strategic knowledge.

In our work, we have assessed learners' conceptual knowledge by asking the learner to specify what happens when a command is executed, by translating a word problem into an equation, by telling what numbers are needed to solve a word problem, by asking a learner to role-play what happens for a numerical computation, and by answering open-ended essay questions involving troubleshooting, redesign, predicting, explaining, and prescribing. We have assessed learners' strategic knowledge by asking them to generate or follow directions, describe the output of a procedure, specify the operations needed to solve a word problem, learn to play a new game, make judgments, and solve new problems. Overall, progress in this field depends on the development of ways of assessing what students know (Pellegrino et al., 2001). This chapter offers examples of how effective assessments can take place within games and simulations.

References

Anderson, L. W., Krathwohl, D. R., Airasian, P. W., Cruickshank, K. A., Mayer, R. E., Pintrich, P. R., et al. (2001). *A taxonomy for learning, teaching, and assessing: A revision of Bloom's taxonomy of educational objectives.* New York: Longman.

Baker, E., & Mayer, R. E. (1999). Computer-based assessment of problem solving. *Computers in Human Behavior, 15*, 269–282.

Bransford, J. D., Brown, A. L., & Cocking, R. R. (1999). *How people learn.* Washington, DC: National Academy Press.

Fay, A. L., & Mayer, R. E. (1987). Children's naïve conceptions and confusions about Logo graphics commands. *Journal of Educational Psychology, 79*, 254–268.

Fay, A. L., & Mayer, R. E. (1994). Benefits of teaching design skills before teaching Logo computer programming: Evidence for syntax independent learning. *Journal of Educational Computing Research, 11,* 185–208.

Gee, J. P. (2003). *What video games have to teach us about learning and literacy.* New York: Palgrave Macmillan.

Gott, S. P., & Lesgold, A. M. (2000). Competence in the workplace: How cognitive performance models and situated instruction can accelerate skill acquisition. In R. Glaser (Ed.), *Advances in instructional psychology* (Vol. 5, pp. 239–328). Mahwah, NJ: Erlbaum.

Gredler, M. E. (2004). Games and simulations and their relationships to learning. In D. H. Jonassen (Ed.), *Handbook of research on educational communications and technology* (pp. 571–582). Mahwah, NJ: Erlbaum.

Hettinger, L. J., & Haas, M. W. (Eds.). (2003). *Virtual and adaptive environments.* Mahwah, NJ: Erlbaum.

Hollan, J. D., Hutchins, E. L., & Weitzman, L. W. (1987). *STEAMER: An interactive, inspectable, simulation-based training system.* Boston: Addison-Wesley Longman.

Jacobson, M. J., & Kozma, R. B. (Eds.). (2000). *Innovations in science and mathematics education.* Mahwah, NJ: Erlbaum.

Jonassen, D. H. (Ed.). (2004). *Handbook of research on educational communications and technology* (2nd ed.). Mahwah, NJ: Erlbaum.

Kozma, R., & Russell, J. (2005). Multimedia learning of chemistry. In R. E. Mayer (Ed.), *Cambridge handbook of multimedia learning* (pp. 409–428). New York: Cambridge University Press.

Kozma, R., Russell, J., Jones, T., Marx, N., & Davis, J. (1996). The use of multiple, linked representations to facilitate science understanding. In S. Vosniadou, R. Glaser, E. De Corte, & H. Mandl (Eds.), *International perspectives on the design of technology-supported learning environments* (pp. 41–60). Mawwah, NJ: Erlbaum.

Lajoie, S. P. (Ed.). (2000). *Computers as cognitive tools: No more walls.* Mahwah, NJ: Erlbaum.

Linn, M. C., Davis, E. A., & Bell, P. (Eds.). (2004). *Internet environments for science education.* Mahwah, NJ: Erlbaum.

Mayer, R. E. (Ed.). (1988). *Teaching and learning computer programming.* Hillsdale, NJ: Erlbaum.

Mayer, R. E. (2002). A taxonomy for computer-based assessment of problem solving. *Computers and Human Behavior, 18,* 623–632.

Mayer, R. E., Dow, G. T., & Mayer, S. (2003). Multimedia learning in an interactive self-explaining environment: What works in the design of agent-based microworlds? *Journal of Educational Psychology, 95,* 806–813.

Mayer, R. E., Dyck, J. L., & Vilberg, W. (1986). Learning to program and learning to think: What's the connection? *Communications of the ACM, 29*(7), 605610.

Mayer, R. E., & Fay, A. L. (1987). A chain of cognitive changes with learning to program in Logo. *Journal of Educational Psychology, 79,* 269–279.

Mayer, R. E., Mautone, P., & Prothero, W. (2002). Pictorial aids for learning by doing in a multimedia geology simulation game. *Journal of Educational Psychology, 94,* 171–185.

Mayer, R. E., Quilici, J., & Moreno, R. (1999). What is learned in an after-school computer club? *Journal of Educational Computing Research, 20,* 223–235.

Mayer, R. E., Quilici, J. L., Moreno, R., Duran, R., Woodbridge, S., Simon, R., et al. (1997). Cognitive consequences of participation in a Fifth Dimension after-school computer club. *Journal of Educational Computing Research, 16,* 353–369.

Moreno, R., & Mayer, R. E. (1999). Multimedia-supported metaphors for meaning making in mathematics. *Cognition and Instruction, 17,* 215–248.

Moreno, R., & Mayer, R. E. (2000). Engaging students in active learning: The case for personalized multimedia messages. *Journal of Educational Psychology, 92,* 724–733.

Moreno, R., & Mayer, R. E. (2002). Learning science in virtual reality multimedia environments: Role of methods and media. *Journal of Educational Psychology, 94,* 598–610.

Moreno, R., & Mayer, R. E. (2004). Personalized messages that promote science learning in virtual environments. *Journal of Educational Psychology, 96,* 165–173.

Moreno, R., Mayer, R. E., Spires, H. A., & Lester, J. C. (2001). The case for social agency in computer-based teaching: Do students learn more deeply when they interact with animated pedagogical agents? *Cognition and Instruction, 19,* 177–213.

O'Neil, H. F., Jr., Mayer, R. E., Herl, H. E., Niemi, C., Olin, K., & Thurman, R. A. (2000). Instructional strategies for virtual aviation training environments. In H. F. O'Neil, Jr., & D. H. Andrews (Eds.), *Aircraft training and assessment* (pp. 105–130). Mahwah, NJ: Erlbaum.

Pellegrino, J. W., Chudowsky, N., & Glaser, R. (Eds.). *Knowing what students know: The science and design of educational assessment.* Washington, DC: National Academy Press.

Prensky, M. (2001). *Digital game-based learning.* New York: McGraw-Hill.

Rieber, L. P. (2005). Multimedia learning in games, simulations, and microworlds. In R. E. Mayer (Ed.), *The Cambridge handbook of multimedia learning* (pp. 549–566). New York: Cambridge University Press.

Schank, R. C. (1997). *Virtual learning.* New York: McGraw Hill.

Schank, R. C. (2002). *Designing world-class e-learning.* New York: McGraw-Hill.

Sims, V. K., & Mayer, R. E. (2002). Domain specificity of spatial expertise: The case of video game players. *Applied Cognitive Psychology, 16,* 97–115.

Stanney, K. M. (Ed.). (2002). *Handbook of virtual environments.* Mahwah, NJ: Erlbaum.

Vosniadou, S., De Corte, E., Glaser, R., & Mandl, H. (Ed.), (1996). *International perspectives on the design of technology-supported learning environments.* Mahwah, NJ: Erlbaum.

White, B. Y., & Frederiksen, J. R. (1998). Inquiry, modeling, and metacognition: Making science accessible to all students. *Cognition and Instruction, 10,* 1–100.

8

Assessing Problem Solving in Simulation Games

HAROLD F. O'NEIL, HSIN-HUI CHEN,
RICHARD WAINESS, AND CHUN-YI (DANNY) SHEN

University of Southern California/CRESST

Because of the merits of computer games and simulations, their potential for education and training began to be noticed decades ago (Ruben, 1999), and they have been applied in various fields and settings, for example, in businesses, K–16 education, and the military (e.g., Baker & O'Neil, 2003; O'Neil & Andrews, 2000). However, despite the power of computer games for instruction and training, there are few valid and reliable studies showing the empirical effects of games and simulations on training and learning for adults (O'Neil & Fisher, 2004). Among the critical constraints in such studies are time and expense (e.g., O'Neil, Baker, & Fisher, 2002; Quinn, 1996).

Computer games can provide effective environments for problem solving (Quinn, 1991), which is one of the most critical competencies, whether for lifelong learning or accomplishing specific tasks, in job settings, academic settings (e.g., Dugdale, LeGare, Mathews, & Ju, 1998), or any other setting. Although there is substantial previous research that reveals the utility of problem solving (e.g., Mayer, 2002), the methods to assess it still need to be refined. In response, the National Center for Research on Evaluation, Standards, and Student Testing (CRESST) has developed a problem-solving assessment model to measure content understanding, problem-solving strategies, and self-regulation.

In this chapter, we present a brief review of problem solving and a discussion of games and simulations and their role in teaching problem-solving skills. We then describe three experimental studies conducted to evaluate a computer game (Wainess & O'Neil, 2003) regarding its effectiveness in improving players' problem-solving abilities. We used the problem-solving assessment model developed by CRESST because of its validity and reliability, as indicated in previous studies (Mayer, 2002; Schacter, Herl, Chung, Dennis, & O'Neil, 1999).

Problem Solving

"Problem solving is cognitive processing directed at achieving a goal when no solution method is obvious to the problem solver" (Mayer & Wittrock, 1996, p. 47). In addition, problem-solving strategies can be further categorized into two types: domain independent and domain specific. Self-regulation, a component of problem solving, includes two subcategories, metacognition and motivation; the former further consists of self-checking and self-planning and the latter of effort and self-efficacy.

The components of problem solving can be assessed in different ways. Knowledge mapping, useful for teaching and learning, is also a reliable and efficient measure of content understanding (a component of problem solving). In addition, CRESST has created a simulated Web space to evaluate problem-solving strategies, such as those used in information searches, and a questionnaire to assess self-regulation. Think-aloud protocols are used to assess domain-dependent metacognition.

Although there is substantial previous research that reveals the utility of problem solving (e.g., Mayer, 2002), the methods for assessing problem-solving ability still need to be refined. For example, a test consisting of separate and unconnected multiple-choice questions cannot accurately assess students' problem-solving abilities. Traditional standardized tests do not report to teachers or students which problem-solving processes they should emphasize and why. And, although we can find the greatest number of valid measures for problem-solving competence in the cognitive science literature, these measures (e.g., think-aloud protocols) are inefficient to assess performance for diagnostic purposes because their scoring is laborious and time consuming (O'Neil, 1999).

Games and Simulations

What Are Simulation Games?

As defined by Gredler (1996), "Games consist of rules that describe allowable player moves, game constraints and privileges (such as ways of earning extra turns), and penalties for illegal (nonpermissible) actions" (p. 523). The rules of games do not have to obey those in real-life and can be imaginative. As pointed out by Gredler, games and simulations have differences in both surface structure and deep structure; *surface structure* refers to the observable characteristics, and *deep structure* is defined as the psychological mechanisms operating in the exercise. The surface structure of games, according to Gredler, is like "drawing cards, moving pieces around a board, and so on," and the surface structure of a simulation is "a scenario or a set of data" to be addressed by the participant (p. 522). On the other hand, Gredler pointed out that there are major differences in deep structure: (a) Although a game player intends to compete and win the game, a participant in a simulation of a specific setting is executing serious responsibilities, deliberating feasible job procedures and possible consequences. (b) The event sequence of a game is typically *linear*, which means that once players have completed one step or action, they are not allowed to return and attempt that activity again, and the sequence is the same or repeated for each player at each turn. However, a simulation sequence is *nonlinear* or *branching*, which means that actions and decisions made previously will influence, or result in, the following situations and problems; therefore, the sequence is different/not repeated for each player and depends on the player's steps or decisions made previously. (c) The rules and settings for games are not necessarily realistic or matched in the real world, but those of simulations are authentic and closely related to the real world. (d) Finally, games are usually more fun driven than simulations. Gredler defined a phrase that means the mixture of features from games and simulations, that is, *simulation games* or *gaming simulation*. According to Amory (2001), simulation games are more often applied in educational environments than other types of games because, when playing simulation games, learners can focus on single goals at their own pace and with decreased competition between learners.

Why Are Simulation Games Important?

Researchers began to notice the potential effects of simulations and games in instruction decades ago (Ruben, 1999). The merits of computer games include facilitating learning by doing (e.g., Mayer, Mautone, & Prothero, 2002) and triggering motivation and enjoyment. In addition, some computer simulation games engage learners in a simulated experience of the real world, which makes learning potentially practical (Martin, 2000; Stolk, Alesandrian, Gros, & Paggio, 2001). Based on those merits, games and simulations have been applied in various fields and settings, such as businesses, K–16 organizations, and military organizations (Baker & O'Neil, 2003; O'Neil & Andrews, 2000). Furthermore, as pointed out by

Stolk et al. (2001), for training in some settings where practice and exercises in real situations are expensive and dangerous, computer games and simulations are helpful. For example, instructors in military settings have applied computer-based training tools, such as war games and simulators, for training. The same situation can be found in the field of environmental crisis management; instructional gaming can provide a good training option when live practice in dealing with natural disasters and industrial emergencies is usually expensive and dangerous (Stolk et al., 2001).

Theories Supporting Learning With Games and Simulations

Experiential learning, discovery learning, and deductive learning are three instructional strategies to support training with computer games. *Experiential learning* (Ruben, 1999) is an important approach focusing on increasing the student's control and autonomy, an aspect of constructivism, which relies heavily on student initiative and teachers' availability for guidance. *Inductive/discovery learning* is a method by which learners acquire knowledge by exploring environments by themselves with little or no guidance (Kalyuga, Chandler, & Sweller, 2001; Mayer, 2004; Sweller, 1994). The research literature would indicate that experiential and discovery learning are poor instructional strategies (Kirschner, Sweller, & Clark, 2006). The *deductive* approach to teaching is often an instructional design with worked examples (Kalyuga et al., 2001). A *worked example* is a case of guided instruction that includes a problem statement and explains all solution details. It is a procedure that focuses on problem states and associated operators (i.e., solution steps), enabling students to induce generalized solutions or schemas (Sweller, 1994).

What Does the Literature Say About Adult Learning From Games?

According to O'Neil and Fisher (2004), the effects of computer games and simulations can be generally divided into five categories: promotion of motivation, enhancement of thinking skills, facilitation of metacognition, improvement of knowledge, and evaluating attitudes. However, few studies have shown the empirical effects of games and simulations on training and learning.

Promotion of Motivation

Motivation, one of the elements of problem solving, has been found to have a positive influence on performance. O'Neil and Fisher (2004) pointed out that some computer games provide diversity, interactivity, and importantly, motivation for learning and therefore have been applied in instruction by different sectors, such as business (e.g., Adams, 1998; Washbush & Gosen, 2001); military (e.g., O'Neil & Andrews, 2000); and academic institutions (e.g., Adams, 1998; Amory, 2001; Amory, Naicker, Vincent, & Adams, 1999; Ricci, Salas, & Cannon-Bowers, 1996; Santos, 2002).

Dynamic interaction, competition, and novelty are three characteristics of computer-based gaming that contribute to its motivational appeal, and these three characteristics can produce significant differences in learner attitudes (Ricci et al., 1996). In addition, games possess the characteristics of challenge and elements of fantasy and therefore may trigger players' motivation and interest in the game environment (Malone, 1981). Furthermore, games and simulations may not only combine theoretical concepts and practice but also trigger intrinsic motivation and self-regulated learning (Amory, 2001; Amory et al., 1999; Quinn, 1991; Rieber, 1996a, 1996b) because of their challenge, curiousness, fantasy, and controllability (Rieber, 1996a, 1996b). Despite previous researchers' belief in games' effectiveness for increasing learning motivation, relevant empirical studies with adults and well-designed assessment measures are lacking.

Enhancement of Thinking Skills

According to previous studies, some computer games are assumed to enhance thinking skills. A study conducted by Mayer et al. (2002) is one of the few empirical studies that provided statistical evidence of the effect of games and simulations on the enhancement of thinking skills. The researchers used a transfer test to measure the impact of Profile Game, a computer simulation game on geology learning. The researchers recorded how many of the target problems students had solved correctly and the time each student took to solve the problems. It was found that the computer game helped improve geology students' thinking skills significantly more when they were given some pictorial aid about how to visualize geological features than it did when students received no instructional aids.

In addition, Betz (1995–1996) found that students who learned by both reading a text and playing a computer simulation game about the planning and management of a complex city system scored significantly higher on the examination than those who learned by only reading the text, even though the examination questions were based on the content and application of the text only. Fery and Ponserre (2001) also found that skills learned by playing a golf video game can be transferred to actual golf playing, which is a game of problem-solving strategies. Participants may use the game to improve their knowledge of and skills in playing a real-world golf game by analogizing the knowledge and skills acquired when playing the video game with the situations of a real golf game. The results showed that participants who played the video golf game with an intention to learn golf then played significantly better overall in a live game than did participants who had not played the video game.

Facilitation of Metacognition

O'Neil and Abedi (1996) defined *metacognition*, another element of problem solving, as planning and self-checking and pointed out that it enables people to utilize various strategies to accomplish a goal. In contrast, Woolfolk (2001) defined metacognition as knowledge about one's own thinking processes, which includes three kinds of knowledge. The first is declarative knowledge about strategies for learning, for memorizing, and for performing well. The second is procedural knowledge about how to use the strategies, and the third is conditional knowledge about when and why to apply the former two kinds of knowledge. It has been shown in previous studies that metacognition facilitates knowledge and skills acquisition (e.g., Pirolli & Recker, 1994). Playing computer games may have the potential benefit of enhancing metacognitive skills (O'Neil & Fisher, 2004; Pillay, Brownlee, & Wilss, 1999). For instance, Pillay et al. (1999) found in their qualitative studies that game playing offers players an opportunity to apply metacognitive skills. When playing a game, players checked their own actions, activated their schemata, found relations and made connections, and formed hypotheses. The researchers suggested that the frequent monitoring of thinking by game players is an application of a metacognitive approach. However, there are few quantitative data that support the effectiveness of games' facilitation of metacognition.

Improvement of Knowledge

Moreno and Mayer (2004) pointed out that computer-based science simulation games offer the potential to improve students' understanding of scientific concepts, which are an element of problem solving in science. Several other studies have shown evidence that computer games can enhance learning and retention of knowledge. For instance, Westbrook and Braithwaite (2001) provided evidence that a health care game was an effective tool in improving learning outcomes, such as information-seeking skills and factual knowledge. Ricci et al. (1996) also found that military trainees who were presented information on chemical, biological, and radiological defense in a computer gaming form scored significantly higher on a multiple-choice retention test than those who were presented with the information in a paper-based form.

Another example is found in an empirical study on a computer game used to train cadets at an Israeli Air Force flight school (Gopher, Weil, & Bareket, 1994). Transfer effects of problem-solving strategies from game training to actual flying were tested during several flights, from the transition stage to the high-performance jet trainer. Results showed that, for game-related skills, the training-with-game group performed significantly better than the training-without-game group in test flights. Gopher et al. concluded that the game maintained its relevance and transfer effects even when variables were changed or new tasks with a similar context were encountered, and it therefore was integrated with the regular training program of the Air Force.

Santos (2002) developed a simulation game to help students understand monetary policy. In this study, the researcher gave a survey to participants after they completed an Internet-based, interactive teaching aid game that introduces undergraduate students to the domestic and international consequences of monetary policy. According to the outcome of the survey, 91% of the students believed that their participation in the game improved their understanding of central bank policy and its effects on a global economy.

In Adams's (1998) research on a computer simulation game's educational effectiveness on students' understanding of urban geography, the game did not help students develop computer literacy and knowledge of geographical phenomena and processes.

Evaluating Attitudes

Attitudes are commonly viewed as summary evaluations of objects (e.g., oneself, other people, issues, etc.) along a dimension ranging from positive to negative (e.g., Petty, Priester, & Wegener, 1994). For the evaluation of attitude toward computer games, the Computer Game Attitude Scale (CGAS; Chappell & Taylor, 1997), which evaluates student attitudes toward educational computer games, has been created to assist computer game designers and teachers in the evaluation of educational software games. Chappell and Taylor (1997) further provided evidence of its reliability and validity; the overall reliability estimate for the total scores on the CGAS items was .91 after three of the items were dropped. In two studies, conducted by Westbrook and Braithwaite (2001) and Amory et al. (1999), learner attitudes were measured with questionnaires. Comparing pre- and postquestionnaires, Westbrook and Braithwaite found health administration students' interest in the actual health care system was significantly enhanced after they completed a game that simulated their national health system. A study by Adams (1998) showed that the most important learning associated with using computer games is not the learning of facts but rather the development of certain attitudes acquired through interaction with software (e.g., becoming aware of the complexity of a task, developing respect for decision makers in the real world, and developing humility toward accomplishing the task). In this study using SimCity 2000, participants' attitudes were measured by open-ended questions and were found to have changed positively and significantly. For example, students' answers to the questions revealed that their interest in, appreciation of, and respect for urban planning and planners had grown.

How To Select a Game for Research

In previous studies of games, researchers have argued that playing games affects learning only when the appropriate games are selected and tailored for training (e.g., Amory, 2001; Baird & Silvern, 1990; Dawes & Dumbleton, 2001; O'Neil & Fisher, 2004; Rabbitt, Banerji, & Szymanski, 1989). For example, Rabbitt et al. (1989) claimed that a video game could be tailored to be an efficient training tool for complex industrial and military tasks. Additional research on game selection is found in the empirical study conducted by Dawes and Dumbleton (2001) on game selection to support some aspects of learning in schools. In this study, 11 computer-purchased games were considered based on several factors, such as technical issues, language comprehension, content suitability, teacher's role, time constraints, and types of feedback. It was found that among the 6 intensively studied games, SimCity provided the best learning outcomes. The degree of challenge, task difficulty, teacher interaction, and peer collaboration were reported to trigger learning. Other factors, such as which types and amount of guidance should be given to learners, also need to be considered when applying multimedia resources and gaming as teaching aids (e.g., Mayer et al., 2002).

Often, a game lacks learning objectives because most games are created for fun. Users have to generate any training applications from the game they choose according to their objectives and game specifications and evaluate the effects by themselves. For example, in a three-phase game feasibility study conducted by Wainess and O'Neil (2003), the researchers found only 3 appropriate games among more than 500 commercial off-the-shelf games and chose 1 to use as a platform for research on cognitive and affective issues related to games in education. Wainess and O'Neil managed the selection process based on the research needs and learning objectives of problem solving. Based on those objectives and needs, the three games selected for further consideration had several characteristics, such as adult orientation, for single-user play, and suitability for problem-solving research. The game finally selected was SafeCracker (DreamCatcher Interactive Inc., Toronto, Canada), which was adult oriented and for single-player use. In addition, SafeCracker was suitable for problem-solving research because it required players to use problem-solving strategies when solving the puzzles used to break the safes in the game. Players could be assessed on the problem-solving strategies they had used in the game and on their content understanding of the game.

The following section presents three studies (Chen, 2005; Shen, 2005; Wainess, 2005) conducted on the selected game, SafeCracker.

Assessing Problem Solving in Safecracker

Will simulation games increase players' problem solving? Will adding instructional strategies to game playing improve learning? The following description summarizes three studies (Chen, 2005; Shen, 2005; Wainess, 2005) conducted on the evaluation of a selected computer game, Safe-Cracker, regarding its effectiveness in improving adults' problem solving. All of the studies used the problem-solving assessment model developed by CRESST. In Study 1, players were assessed on their problem-solving ability before and after playing the game without receiving effective instructional strategies. In Studies 2 and 3, assumed effective instructional strategies of worked examples and navigation maps, respectively, were given to the game players.

Methods and Techniques

Formative Evaluation

For the pilot study, the researchers applied the framework of formative evaluation (O'Neil et al., 2002). According to O'Neil et al., the purpose of formative evaluation is to examine the feasibility of a program and improve the program by offering information about its implementation and procedures. The pilot study followed a modified version of the O'Neil et al. methodology to conduct a formative evaluation of a game. The pilot study was conducted first to check the design of assessments for outcome and measurement. Measures were designed and tried out, such as the newly programmed knowledge mapper, the newly designed problem-solving questions, and the computerized trait self-regulation questionnaire. Second, the validity of instructional strategies embedded in the game was checked against the relevant literature. Third, a feasibility review was conducted with students; finally, necessary revisions were implemented.

Participants

Young adults participated in the research for the pilot and main studies. All participants were selected to have no experience in playing SafeCracker.

Puzzle-Solving Game

The selection of SafeCracker was based on a study by Wainess and O'Neil (2003). The researchers had conducted an evaluation of the potential research feasibility of 525 video games of three categories: puzzle games, strategy games, and educational games. The appropriate game was then sought among puzzle games because of their properties and because they provide an appropriate platform for studying games' effectiveness in enhancing problem solving. A participant in a puzzle-solving game is placed in a specific setting or story background and tries to reason out possible task procedures and consequences, and a failure to solve a puzzle previously encountered may result in future problems in the game.

Content Understanding Measure

Knowledge Mapper was used to measure participants' content understanding of SafeCracker. The knowledge mapper used in previous studies (e.g., Chuang, 2004; Hsieh, 2001; Schacter et al., 1999) was reprogrammed to fit the needs of the three studies reported here. Participants were asked to play SafeCracker twice and after each game to create a knowledge map in a computer-based environment. Participants were evaluated, based on their maps, on their content understanding of the game. The maps were scored in real time by comparing the semantic propositions of a participant's knowledge map to those of three expert players' maps. For example, if a participant made a proposition such as "Key is used for safe," this proposition would be then be compared with all of the propositions in the three expert maps. Participants' content understanding scores were computed by comparing the semantic propositions of a participant's knowledge map to those of three maps created by three expert players of SafeCracker. The outcomes were scored as follows: First, the semantic propositions were calculated based on the semantic propositions, two concepts connected by one link, in each of the three expert maps. Every proposition in a participant's knowledge map was compared against each proposition in the three SafeCracker expert maps. One match was scored as 1 point. The average score across all three expert maps would be the semantic score of the participant's map.

Problem-Solving Strategy Measures

In the three studies, domain-specific problem-solving strategies were measured by asking open-ended questions, using modifications of previous researchers' (e.g., Mayer, 2001; Mayer & Moreno, 1998; Mayer, Sobko, & Mautone, 2003; Moreno & Mayer, 2004) assessments of retention and transfer. For example, we adapted Mayer and Moreno's (1998; also Mayer et al., 2003) approach to measure a participant's retention and transfer by counting the number of predefined major idea units correctly stated by the participant regardless of wording.

Self-Regulation Questionnaire

The trait self-regulation questionnaire, designed by O'Neil and Herl (1998), was used to measure participants' degree of self-regulation, one of the components of the problem-solving skill. There was sufficient reliability for the self-regulation questionnaire, ranging from .89 to .94, as reported in a previous study (O'Neil & Herl, 1998). The 32-item questionnaire was composed of 8 items of each for the four factors: planning, self-checking, self-efficacy, and effort. An example of an item to assess planning ability is "I determine how to solve a task before I begin." An example of an item to assess self-checking is "I check how well I am doing when I solve a task." Item response choices ranged from 1 to 4 (1 = *almost never*, 2 = *sometimes*, 3 = *often*, 4 = *almost always*).

Study 1

Study 1 (Chen, 2005) examined the training effectiveness of SafeCracker in increasing players' problem-solving skills. A 40-minute game-playing session was provided to 30 college and graduate students, aged 18 to 35 years. Except for game-playing mechanics such as use of the interface, no game strategy was explained to the participants; that is, the study treatment featured pure discovery and experiential learning. Experimental evidence (Clark, 2001; Mayer, 2004; Sweller, 1994) indicated that those learning strategies may not be effective in instruction; therefore, in the first study, it was predicted that without effective instructional strategies, the game may not facilitate learning (Chen, 2005).

Results

The results showed that participants performed better on the knowledge map after playing SafeCracker. The paired-sample t test (two tailed) on the outcome between pretest and posttest scores showed a significant difference between the means, $t(29) = 4.32$, $p = .01$. Therefore, participants' content understanding was significantly better ($M = 3.44$) after playing SafeCracker than before playing the game ($M = 2.27$). However the performance level was as low as only 2% to 4% of the experts' knowledge.

The results showed also that participants performed better on a problem-solving strategy test of retention after the second round of game playing. Further, according to the paired-sample t test, the difference between pretest and posttest scores was significant, $t(29) = 12.66$, $p = .01$. Therefore, participants' problem-solving strategy of retention was significantly better ($M = 1.52$) after the second round of playing SafeCracker than after the first round of playing the game ($M = 1.13$). In addition, the percentage of agreement between the two raters in the categorization and scoring for the problem-solving retention pretest and posttest was satisfactory (Cohen's $\kappa = .95$).

According to the results, participants performed significantly better on problem-solving strategy test of transfer after the second round of game playing. According to the paired-sample t test, the difference between pretest and posttest scores was significant, $t(29) = 7.05$, $p = .01$. Therefore, participants' problem-solving strategy of transfer was significantly better ($M = 2.76$) after the second round of playing SafeCracker than after the first round of playing the game ($M = 1.70$). In addition, the percentage of agreement between the two raters in the categorization and scoring for the problem-solving transfer pretest and posttest was satisfactory (Cohen's $\kappa = .95$).

Study 2

Study 2 (Shen, 2005) examined the effectiveness of worked examples in a game-based problem-solving task. Previous research indicated that worked examples could effectively facilitate problem solving by reducing cognitive load during learning (e.g., Cooper & Sweller, 1987; Ward & Sweller, 1990). Therefore, in the second study, it was predicted that players who received worked examples would perform better on the problem-solving assessment than those who did not receive worked examples (Shen, 2005). Thirty-five male and 37 female undergraduate or graduate students, aged 18 to 38 years, were randomly assigned into two groups, which were the worked example group and the control group.

Results

First, the participants who received worked examples improved significantly more than those who did not receive worked examples on the knowledge map. The average improvement of knowledge map score for the worked example group was more than that of the control group (i.e., 2.21 vs. 0.62 or 2.73% vs. 0.77%, respectively). Second, the participants who received worked examples improved significantly more than those who did not on the problem-solving retention test. The average improvement of retention score for the worked example group was more than that of the control group (i.e., 1.63 vs. 0.98 or 5.81% vs. 3.52%, respectively). Third, the worked example group improved significantly more than the control group on the problem-solving transfer test. The adjusted average improvement of transfer score for the worked example group was more than that of the control group (i.e., 0.92 vs. 0.52 or 4.19% vs. 2.38%, respectively).

The results obtained in this study provided evidence that worked examples can enhance problem solving in a game-based environment.

Study 3

Study 3 (Wainess, 2005) examined effectiveness of navigational aids in SafeCracker in increasing players' problem solving. According to previous researchers, navigation maps have been shown to be an effective tool for navigating a three-dimensional virtual environment (Cutmore, Hine, Maberly, Langford, & Hawgood, 2000) and provide support for navigating in a problem-solving task in a two-dimensional hypermedia environment (Baylor, 2001; Chou, Lin, & Sun, 2000). Therefore, in our third study, it was predicted that players who received a navigation map of the simulation game would perform better on the problem-solving assessment than those who did not receive the navigation map (Wainess, 2005).

Results

Results of the data analysis indicated that the use of navigation maps did not affect problem solving as measured by performance based on O'Neil's (1999) problem-solving model. Those using the navigation map did not score significantly higher than those who did not use the navigation map in content understanding, problem-solving strategy retention, and problem-solving strategy transfer. In addition, higher levels of self-regulation were unrelated to higher levels of performance regardless of whether a map was used. Last, those who used the navigation map did not exhibit higher continuing motivation than those who did not use the map. The negative results were explained in terms of cognitive load theory.

Discussion and Implications

The results of Study 1 showed consistency with the literature. First, media have little influence on learning without appropriate instructional strategies (Clark, 1994, 2001, 2005). SafeCracker was a commercial, off-the-shelf game, not an educational game, and included no research-based instructional strategies.

Study 1 featured the instructional strategies of discovery and experiential learning, and except for game-playing mechanics such as how the interface worked, no game strategy was explained to the participants. According to previous research (e.g., Clark, 2005; Kalyuga et al., 2001; Kirschner et al., 2006; Mayer, 2004; van Merrienboer, Clark, & de Croock, 2002), without effective instructional strategies, inductive/discovery and experiential learning may not be effective. Furthermore, as pointed out by Mayer (2004), guided discovery learning is more effective than pure discovery learning. In Study 1, learning by playing SafeCracker was pure discovery learning; no guidance about puzzle solving and safe cracking was given to the participants. Also, the learning was inductive/experiential learning; participants were placed in a specific environment (game environment) to play the game and had to figure out the answers and strategies by themselves. Therefore, it may be assumed that the lack of research-based instructional strategies could have contributed to the low extent of learning.

Moreover, for beginners or learners with low background knowledge, research-based instructional strategies, for example, learning with worked examples, are more effective than learning with only problems to be solved (Kalyuga et al., 2001; Touvinen & Sweller, 1999). In Study 1, the learners were beginners, and none of the participants had played SafeCracker before the study. Therefore, lack of worked examples could have contributed to low performance in Study 1.

According to the results of Study 2 (Shen, 2005), worked examples had a significant effect on problem solving in the game-based tasks in Safe-Cracker. That is, after studying worked examples, the participants in Study 2 improved, in both content understanding and problem-solving strategies, more than those who did not receive worked examples. This was consistent with previous research investigating the efficacy of using worked examples in classroom instruction and provided evidence in the effectiveness this strategy (Carroll, 1994; Cooper & Sweller, 1987; Ward & Sweller, 1990; Zhu & Simon, 1987).

However, the learning that occurred in Study 2 was still low compared to experts' performance. The worked examples in Study 2 had the following design characteristics: (a) they were given before the problem; (b) they were complete; (c) they did not include a fading procedure; (d) they used integrated text and diagrams; (e) they used visual-visual instruction; and (f) they were presented in steps (Shen, 2005). The design or structure of worked examples plays an important role in their effectiveness (e.g., Ward & Sweller, 1990; Zhu & Simon, 1987). Therefore, more research needs to be conducted to find out whether using different design characteristics in worked examples may enhance game players' learning of problem solving. For example, worked example formats draw on six instructional principles: before versus after (e.g., Atkinson, Derry, Renkl, & Wortham, 2000); complete versus incomplete (e.g., Renkl, Atkinson, Maier, & Staley, 2002); backward fading versus forward fading (e.g., Renkl et al., 2002); text versus diagrams (e.g., Sweller, 2004; Ward & Sweller, 1990); visual versus verbal (e.g., Mayer & Moreno, 2003); and steps versus subgoals (Catrambone & Holyoak, 1990).

In addition, previous research (e.g., Ginns, Chandler, & Sweller, 2003; Kalyuga et al., 2001; Touvinen & Sweller, 1999) has shown that the most efficient mode of instruction depends on a learner's level of experience. That is, learning from worked examples is superior to learning from problem solving for novices, but the superiority is reversed later. In this study, participants were selected as novice SafeCracker players, so the low degree of learning may be because of inappropriate instructional strategies for their experience level. Therefore, more research needs to be conducted to find out (a) whether previous instruction in game-playing strategies improves learning results, (b) whether an intervention such as giving participants pictorial navigational aids (e.g., Mayer et al., 2002) or worked examples improves the training effectiveness of the game (e.g., Touvinen & Sweller, 1999), and (c) whether effectiveness varies as a function of prior knowledge.

The results of the data analysis for Study 3 indicated that the use of navigation maps did not affect problem solving. These results were surprising because, based on cognitive load theory, an important cognitive goal in design is to control the amount of load placed on working memory, particularly by items not necessary for learning. Navigation maps, a graphical form of scaffolding, would serve such a purpose by distributing the need to retain location and paths from working memory to an external graphical support. It appears from this study, though, that either such support may not have been necessary in this game or the maps did not supply appropriate scaffolding.

The role of navigation maps to reduce the load induced by navigation, and thereby reduce burdens on working memory, is an important issue for enhancing the effectiveness of video games as educational environments. And, as the study showed, not all learning goals or other objectives, such as problem-solving objectives, benefit from the inclusion of navigation maps. This study highlights the need to examine the role of navigation in relation to the overall goal to determine whether sufficient cognitive load is placed on the search process to justify the inclusion of a navigation map.

According to the previous literature, personalized feedback messages are more effective than nonpersonalized feedback (Albertson, 1986; Moreno & Mayer, 2000, 2004; Sales, 1993), and "effective performance feedback must be focused on closing the gap between learning and/or performance goals and the individual's current progress" (Clark, 2005, p. 30). However, the feedback in SafeCracker was not personalized; in fact, the feedback given to every participant in SafeCracker was the same. Therefore, the low performance of participants in this set of studies may indicate the ineffectiveness of nonpersonalized feedback. However, more research needs to be conducted to find out whether personalized feedback designed in a game results in more learning effect than does nonpersonalized feedback or messages.

Scientifically, these three studies were among the few studies to measure problem solving in games and the only ones to use expert-based knowledge maps in this context. Study 2 was the first experimental study with adults using worked examples in a game-based environment. Study 3 was the first to examine the effect of a navigation map on a three-dimensional computer-based video game problem-solving task. These experimental studies increase the knowledge base and provide possible design principles to promote learning from commercial off-the-shelf games.

Acknowledgments

Richard Wainess is now at UCLA/CRESST. Chun-Yi Shen is now at the Department of Educational Technology, TamKang University, Taiwan.

The work reported here was supported under Office of Naval Research Award N00014-04-1-0209 as administered by the Office of Naval Research. The findings and opinions expressed in this report do not necessarily reflect the positions or policies of the Office of Naval Research.

References

Adams, P. C. (1998). Teaching and learning with SimCity 2000 [Electronic version]. *Journal of Geography, 97*(2), 47–55.

Albertson, L. M. (1986). Personalized feedback and cognitive achievement in computer-assisted instruction. *Journal of Instructional Psychology, 13*(2), 55–57.

Amory, A. (2001). Building an educational adventure game: Theory, design, and lessons. *Journal of Interactive Learning Research, 12,* 249–263.

Amory, A., Naicker, K., Vincent, J., & Adams, C. (1999). The use of computer games as an educational tool: Identification of appropriate game types and game elements. *British Journal of Educational Technology, 30,* 311–321.

Atkinson, R. K., Derry, S. J., Renkl, A., & Wortham, D. (2000). Learning from examples: Instructional principles from the worked examples research. *Review of Educational Research, 70,* 181–214.

Baird, W. E., & Silvern, S. B. (1990). Electronic games: Children controlling the cognitive environment. *Early Child Development and Care, 61,* 43–49.

Baker, E. L., & O'Neil, H. F., Jr. (2003). Evaluation and research for technology: Not just playing around. *Evaluation and Program Planning, 26,* 169–176.

Baylor, A. L. (2001). Perceived disorientation and incidental learning in a Web-based environment: Internal and external factors. *Journal of Educational Multimedia and Hypermedia, 10,* 227–251.

Betz, J. A. (1995–1996). Computer games: Increase learning in an interactive multidisciplinary environment. *Journal of Educational Technology Systems, 24,* 195–205.

Carroll, W. M. (1994). Using worked examples as an instructional support in the algebra classroom. *Journal of Educational Psychology, 86,* 360–367.

Catrambone, R., & Holyoak, K. J. (1990). Learning subgoals and methods for solving probability problems. *Memory and Cognition, 18,* 593–603

Chappell, K. K., & Taylor, C. S. (1997). Evidence for the reliability and factorial validity of the Computer Game Attitude Scale. *Journal of Educational Computing Research, 17,* 67–77.

Chen, H.-H. (2005). *A formative evaluation of the training effectiveness of a computer game.* Unpublished doctoral dissertation, University of Southern California, Los Angeles.

Chou, C., Lin, H., & Sun, C.-t. (2000). Navigation maps in hierarchical-structured hypertext courseware [Electronic version]. *International Journal of Instructional Media, 27,* 165–182.

Chuang, S. (2004). *The role of search strategies and feedback on a computer-based collaborative problem-solving task.* Unpublished doctoral dissertation, University of Southern California, Los Angeles.

Clark, R. E. (1994). Media will never influence learning. *Educational Technology Research and Development, 42*(2), 21–30.

Clark, R. E. (Ed.). (2001). *Learning from media: Arguments, analysis, and evidence.* Greenwich, CT: Information Age.

Clark, R. E. (2005). What works in distance learning: Instructional strategies. In H. F. O'Neil (Ed.), *What works in distance learning. Guidelines* (pp. 25–39). Greenwich, CT: Information Age Publishing.

Cooper, G., & Sweller, J. (1987). Effects of schema acquisition and rule automation on mathematical problem-solving transfer. *Journal of Educational Psychology, 79,* 347–362.

Cutmore, T. R. H., Hine, T. J., Maberly, K. J., Langford, N. M., & Hawgood, G. (2000). Cognitive and gender factors influencing navigation in a virtual environment. *International Journal of Human-Computer Studies, 53,* 223–249.

Dawes, L., & Dumbleton, T. (2001). *Computer games in education.* Retrieved June 25, 2004 from BECT Web site: http://www.becta.org.uk/technology/software/curriculum/computergames/docs/report.pdf

Dugdale, S., LeGare, O., Mathews, J. I., & Ju, M. (1998). Mathematical problem-solving and computers: A study of learner-initiated application of technology in a general problem-solving context. *Journal of Research on Computing in Education, 30,* 239–253.

Fery, Y. A., & Ponserre S. (2001). Enhancing the control of force in putting by video game training. *Ergonomics, 44,* 1025–1037.

Ginns, P., Chandler, P., & Sweller, J. (2003). When imagining information is effective. *Contemporary Educational Psychology, 28,* 229–251.

Gopher, D., Weil, M., & Bareket, T. (1994). Transfer of skill from a computer game trainer to flight. *Human Factors, 36,* 387–405.

Gredler, M. E. (1996). Educational games and simulations: A technology in search of a (research) paradigm. In D. Jonassen (Ed.), *Handbook of research for educational communications and technology* (pp. 521–540). New York: Macmillan.

Hsieh, I. (2001). *Types of feedback in a computer-based collaborative problem-solving Group Task.* Unpublished doctoral dissertation, University of Southern California, Los Angeles.

Kalyuga, S., Chandler, P., & Sweller, J. (2001). Learner experience and efficiency of instructional guidance. *Educational Psychology, 21,* 5–23.

Kirschner, P. A., Sweller, J., & Clark, R. E. (2006). Why minimal guidance during instruction does not work: An analysis of the failure of constructivist, discovery, problem-based, experiential, and inquiry-based learning. *Educational Psychologist, 41,* 75–86.

Malone, T. W. (1981). Toward a theory of intrinsically motivating instruction. *Cognitive Science, 4,* 333–369.

Martin, A. (2000). The design and evaluation of a simulation/game for teaching information systems development. *Simulation and Gaming, 31,* 445–463.

Mayer, R. E. (2001). *Multimedia learning.* New York: Cambridge University Press.

Mayer, R. E. (2002). A taxonomy for computer-based assessment of problem-solving. *Computer in Human Behavior, 18,* 623–632.

Mayer, R. E. (2004). Should there be a three-strikes rule against pure discovery learning? *American Psychologist, 59,* 14–19.

Mayer, R. E., Mautone, P., & Prothero, W. (2002). Pictorial aids for learning by doing in a multimedia geology simulation game. *Journal of Educational Psychology, 94,* 171–185.

Mayer, R. E., & Moreno, R. (1998). A split-attention effect in multimedia learning: evidence for dual processing systems in working memory. *Journal of Educational Psychology, 90,* 312–320.

Mayer, R. E., & Moreno, R. (2003). Nine ways to reduce cognitive load in multimedia learning. *Educational Psychologist, 38,* 43–52.

Mayer, R. E., Sobko, K., & Mautone, P. D. (2003). Social cues in multimedia learning: Role of speaker's voice. *Journal of Educational Psychology, 95,* 419–425.

Mayer, R. E., & Wittrock, M. C. (1996). Problem-solving transfer. In D. C. Berliner, & Calfee, R.C. (Eds.), *Handbook of educational psychology* (pp. 47–62). New York: Simon & Schuster Macmillan.

Moreno, R., & Mayer, R. E. (2000). Engaging students in active learning: The case for personalized multimedia messages. *Journal of Educational Psychology, 92,* 724–733.

Moreno, R., & Mayer, R. E. (2004). Personalized messages that promote science learning in virtual environments. *Journal of Educational Psychology, 96,* 165–173.

O'Neil, H. F., Jr. (1999). Perspectives on computer-based performance assessment of problem-solving. *Computers in Human Behavior, 15,* 225–268.

O'Neil, H. F., Jr., & Abedi, J. (1996). Reliability and validity of a state metacognitive inventory: Potential for alternative assessment. *Journal of Educational Research, 89,* 234–245.

O'Neil, H. F., Jr., & Andrews, D. (Eds.). (2000). *Aircrew training and assessment.* Mahwah, NJ: Erlbaum.

O'Neil, H. F., Jr., Baker, E. L., & Fisher, J. Y.-C. (2002). *A formative evaluation of ICT games* (Tech. Rep. to the Institute for Creative Technologies, University of Southern California). Los Angeles: University of Southern California, Rossier School of Education.

O'Neil, H. F., Jr., & Fisher, J. Y.-C. (2004). A technology to support leader development: Computer games. In V. D. Day, S. J. Zaccaro, & S. M. Halpin (Eds.), *Leadership development for transforming organization: Growing leaders for tomorrow* (pp. 99–121). Mahwah, NJ: Erlbaum.

O'Neil, H. F., Jr., & Herl, H. E. (1998, April). *Reliability and validity of a trait measure of self-regulation.* Presented at the annual meeting of the American Educational Research Association, San Diego, CA.

Petty, R. E., Priester, J. R., & Wegener, D. T. (1994). *Handbook of social cognition.* Hillsdale, NJ: Erlbaum.

Pillay, H. K., Brownlee, J., & Wilss, L. (1999). Cognition and recreational computer games: Implications for educational technology. *Journal of Research on Computing in Education, 32,* 203–216.

Pirolli, P., & Recker, M. (1994). Learning strategies and transfer in the domain of programming. *Cognition and Instruction, 12,* 235–275.

Quinn, C. N. (1991). Computers for cognitive research: A HyperCard adventure game. *Behavior Research Methods, Instruments, and Computers, 23,* 237–246.

Quinn, C. N. (1996). Designing an instructional game: Reflections on "Quest for Independence." *Education and Information Technologies, 1,* 251–269.

Rabbitt, P., Banerji, N., & Szymanski, A. (1989). Space fortress as an IQ test? Predictions of learning and of practiced performance in a complex interactive video-game. *ACTA Psychologica, 71,* 243–257.

Renkl, A., Atkinson, R. K., Maier, U. H., & Staley, R. (2002). From example study to problem solving: Smooth transitions help learning. *The Journal of Experimental Education, 70,* 293–315.

Ricci, K. E., Salas, E., & Cannon-Bowers, J. A. (1996). Do computer-based games facilitate knowledge acquisition and retention? *Military Psychology, 8,* 295–307.

Rieber, L. P. (1996a). Animation as feedback in computer simulation: Representation matters. *Educational Technology Research and Development, 44*(1), 5–22.

Rieber, L. P. (1996b). Seriously considering play: Designing interactive learning environments based on the blending of microworlds, simulations, and games. *Educational Technology Research and Development, 44,* 43–58.

Ruben, B. D. (1999). Simulations, games, and experience-based learning: The quest for a new paradigm for teaching and learning. *Simulation and Gaming, 30,* 498–505.

Sales, G. C. (1993). Adapted and adaptive feedback in technology-based instruction. In J. V. Dempsey & G. C. Sales (Eds.), *Interactive instruction and feedback* (pp. 159–176). Englewood, NJ: Educational Technology.

Santos, J. (2002). Developing and implementing an Internet-based financial system simulation game. *Journal of Economic Education, 33,* 31–40.

Schacter, J., Herl, H. E., Chung, G., Dennis, R. A., & O'Neil, H. F., Jr. (1999). Computer-based performance assessments: A solution to the narrow measurement and reporting of problem-solving. *Computers in Human Behavior, 13,* 403–418.

Shen, C.-Y. (2005). *The effectiveness of worked examples in a game-based problem-solving task.* Unpublished doctoral dissertation, University of Southern California, Los Angeles.

Stolk, D., Alesandrian, D., Gros, B., & Paggio, R. (2001). Gaming and multimedia applications for environmental crisis management training. *Computers in Human Behavior, 17,* 627–642.

Sweller, J. (1994). Cognitive load theory, learning difficulty and instructional design. *Learning and Instruction, 4,* 295–312.

Sweller, J. (2004, April). *Why understanding instructional design principles requires an understanding of the evolution of human cognitive architecture.* Paper presented to the National Center for Research on Evaluation, Standards, and Students Testing (CRESST), University of California, Los Angles.

Touvinen, J. E., & Sweller, J. (1999). A comparison of cognitive load associated with discovery learning. *Journal of Educational Psychology, 91,* 334–341.

van Merrienboer, J. J. G., Clark, R. E., & de Croock, M. B. M. (2002). Blueprints for complex learning: The 4C/ID-Model. *Educational Technology Research and Development, 50,* 39–64.

Wainess, R. (2005). *The effect of navigation maps on problem solving tasks instantiated in a computer-based video game.* Unpublished doctoral dissertation, University of Southern California, Los Angeles.

Wainess, R., & O'Neil, H. F., Jr. (2003, August). *Feasibility study: Video game research platform.* Unpublished manuscript, University of Southern California, Los Angeles.

Ward, M., & Sweller, J. (1990). Structuring effective worked examples. *Cognition and Instruction, 7,* 1–39.

Washbush, J., & Gosen, J. (2001). An exploration of game-derived learning in total enterprise simulations. *Simulation and Gaming, 32,* 281–296.

Westbrook, J. I., & Braithwaite, J. (2001). The health care game: An evaluation of heuristic, Web-based simulation. *Journal of Interactive Learning Research, 12,* 89–104.

Woolfolk, A. E. (2001). *Educational psychology* (8th ed.). Needham Heights, MA: Allyn and Bacon.

Zhu, X., & Simon, H. (1987). Learning mathematics from examples and by doing. *Cognition and Instruction, 4,* 137–166.

9

Measuring Collaborative Problem Solving in Low-Stakes Tasks

HAROLD F. O'NEIL

University of Southern California/CRESST

SAN-HUI (SABRINA) CHUANG

CRESST/UCLA

Collaborative problem-solving skills are considered necessary skills for success in today's world of work and school. Many research studies on collaborative problem solving have shown it to have a positive effect on students' cognitive improvement (e.g., Arts, Gijselaers, & Segers, 2002). *Collaborative learning* refers to learning environments in which small groups of people work together to achieve a common goal, and *problem solving* is defined as "cognitive processing directed at achieving a common goal when no solution method is obvious to the problem solver" (Mayer & Wittrock, 1996, p. 47). Thus, *collaborative problem solving* is defined as problem-solving activities that involve interactions among a group of individuals. This chapter addresses several key issues, including theory and measurement of collaborative learning and theory and measurement of problem solving, and presents findings based on three relevant studies in which computers were used for administering, scoring, and reporting collaborative problem-solving skills measures, thus facilitating timely reporting and potentially increasing reliability and validity of collaborative problem solving in low-stakes tasks.

Low-stakes tasks are those in which there are minimal consequences to the individual. A particularly novel feature of our work is that we are defining an approach to measuring and increasing collaborative problem solving by capturing problem-solving processes and providing feedback in real time using networked computers. These studies suggest a promising approach toward increasing collaborative problem-solving ability by providing computerized, real-time feedback.

Importance of Collaborative Problem Solving

In view of the changing needs in the workforce, the National Center for Research on Evaluation, Standards, and Student Testing (CRESST) established a research program to identify and assess workforce skills. They examined the existing literature by reviewing five seminal studies on workforce readiness skills. All five studies identified higher order thinking, interpersonal and teamwork skills, and problem solving as the necessary generic skills needed for success in today's world (O'Neil, Allred, & Baker, 1997). Among these skills, graduates and employees rated thinking, decision making, communications skills, teamwork, and collaborative skills as the most important (Sinclair, 1997).

Many educational assessment programs have also used collaborative small-group tasks, in which students work together to solve problems or to accomplish projects, to evaluate learning results (Barron, 2000; Samaha & De Lisi, 2000; Webb, Nemer, & Chizhik, 1998). In reality, when students enter the workforce, they inevitably have to work in groups. Empirically, collaborative problem solving has been shown in educational research to enhance students' cognitive development (Webb et al., 1998; Zhang, 1998).

Figure 9.1 shows the components of collaborative problem solving and their relationship to each other. As seen in Figure 9.1, collaborative problem solving is first divided into two components: collaborative learning and problem solving. According to O'Neil, Chung, and Brown (1997), collaboration in team skills can be assessed by six skills: adaptability, coordination, decision making, interpersonal skills, leadership, and communication. According to O'Neil (1999), problem solving has three factors: content understanding, problem-solving strategies, and self-regulation. Problem-solving strategies can be domain dependent or domain independent. Self-regulation has two main components — motivation and metacognition — and each has two components. Motivation consists of effort and self-efficacy, and metacognition consists of self-checking and planning.

Assessment of Collaborative Learning Processes

The three studies we review all use the teamwork processes model developed by CRESST researchers for the measurement of collaborative learning processes. The CRESST model consists of six skills: "(a) adaptability — recognizing problems and responding appropriately, (b) coordination — organizing group

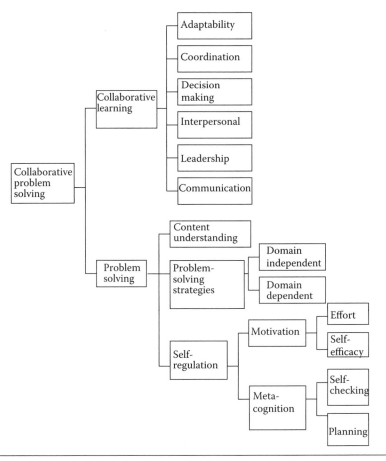

Figure 9.1 Collaborative problem-solving components.

activities to complete a task on time, (c) decision making — using available information to make decisions, (d) interpersonal — interacting cooperatively with other group members, (e) leadership — providing direction for the group, and (f) communication — clear and accurate exchange of information" (O'Neil, Chung, et al., 1997, p. 413).

Adaptability

Adaptability refers to the group's ability to "monitor the source and nature of problems through an awareness of team activities and factors bearing on the task" (O'Neil, Chung, et al., 1997, p. 413). That is, adaptability is mainly used for the detection and correction of problems. In a knowledge-mapping task, adaptable teams should detect problems with their knowledge map at a deep

(semantic) level by identifying inaccuracies as well as the strength and significance of a relationship and at a surface level by recognizing that the given set of
concepts and links should be included in their map.

Coordination

Coordination is defined for a group as the "process by which group
resources, activities, and responses are organized to ensure that tasks are
integrated, synchronized, and completed with established temporal constraints" (O'Neil, Chung, et al., 1997, p. 413). Therefore, in a knowledge-
mapping task, coordinating strategies will include members' use of domain
expertise to determine the relationships between concepts and their con-
sciousness of time constraints and ability to respond appropriately.

Decision Making

Decision making is defined as a group's "ability to integrate information, use
logical and sound judgment, identify possible alternatives, select the best solution, and evaluate the consequences" (O'Neil, Chung, et al., 1997, p. 415). Effective teams employ decision making that takes into consideration available
information, and thus decision making is regarded as playing a significant role
in knowledge map performance (Chung, O'Neil, & Herl, 1999). In addition,
Chung et al. (1999) indicated that compared to group members who lacked
prior knowledge, group members with relevant prior knowledge might be more
likely to engage in substantive discussions concerning the relationships.

In all three studies, participants were expected to have little prior knowledge in the domain of environmental science. However, through seeking
information from the simulated Web space, participants would have the
opportunity to engage in substantive discussion about the concept relationships. Thus, decision making was expected to have a positive effect on
group performance.

Interpersonal Skill

Interpersonal skill is defined as "the ability to improve the quality of team
member interactions through the resolution of team members' dissent,
or the use of cooperative behavior" (O'Neil, Chung, et al., 1997, p. 416).
Interpersonal processes are important because they minimize intergroup
conflict as well as foster team interdependence (Weng, 1999).

Leadership

Leadership is defined as "the ability to direct and coordinate the activities
of other team members, assess group performance, assign tasks, plan and
organize, and establish a positive atmosphere" (O'Neil, Chung, et al., 1997,
p. 417).

Communication

Communication is defined as "the process by which information is clearly and accurately exchanged between two or more team members in the prescribed manner and by using proper terminology, and the ability to clarify or acknowledge the receipt of information" (O'Neil, Chung, et al., 1997, p. 417). According to O'Neil, Chung, et al. (1997), communication (a) promotes the transmission and reception of support behaviors as well as detection and correction of error, (b) helps team members synchronize their activities and affects the quality of decision making, (c) affects the character of team cohesion, and (d) establishes operational norms among team members.

Assessment of Problem Solving

Although the need for problem-solving skills has been well documented, the assessment tools for problem-solving skills can still be improved (O'Neil, 1999). CRESST has developed a problem-solving assessment model with three subelements: (a) content understanding, (b) problem-solving strategies, and (c) self-regulation (O'Neil, 1999). In the following sections, we discuss how these three elements are assessed.

Measurement of Content Understanding

In the cognitive theory of learning, it is stressed that learned knowledge should be organized into long-term memory for later access. In addition, the expertise literature suggests that experts' understanding of domain knowledge is awareness not only of the concepts but also of the connections among the concepts (Schau & Mattern, 1997). Knowledge maps of concepts and their relations have been extensively used in K–12 classrooms, especially in the understanding of science (Schau, Mattern, Zeilik, Teague, & Weber, 2001). Various research studies on knowledge maps have shown them to be effective also for teaching, learning, and assessment purposes (Herl, O'Neil, Chung, & Schacter, 1999; Hurwitz & Abegg, 1999; Ruiz-Primo, Schultz, & Shavelson, 1997; Schau et al., 2001).

A knowledge map is a graphical representation that consists of nodes and links. Each node represents an important term (standing for a concept) in the domain of knowledge. Links are used to represent the relationships of nodes (concepts; Hurwitz & Abegg, 1999). A proposition is the combination of two nodes and a link. It is the basic and the smallest unit in a knowledge map used to express the relationship between two concepts (Dochy, 1996).

Ruiz-Primo et al. (1997) proposed using knowledge maps as an assessment tool in science. For these researchers, knowledge mapping as an assessment tool is further distinguished by three parts: (a) a task in which students use their knowledge in a domain, (b) a response format for students, and (c) a scoring system that accurately evaluates the student's performance. Table 9.1 lists the knowledge map components and variations identified by Ruiz-Primo et al. as modified for use in the current study.

Several researchers have successfully used knowledge maps to measure students' content understanding in science (e.g., Aidman & Egan, 1998; Herl et al., 1999; Schacter, Herl, Chung, Dennis, & O'Neil, 1999; Schau et al., 2001). Schau et al. (2001) used select-and-fill-in knowledge maps to measure secondary students' understanding of science and postsecondary introductory astronomy students' content understanding. In the first study, the students' performance on the knowledge maps correlated significantly with a traditional assessment, which was a standardized, middle school multiple-choice test ($r = .77$ for eighth grade, and $r = .74$ for seventh grade). This correlation provides evidence of the validity of knowledge maps as an assessment tool. In the second study, knowledge maps were compared with both multiple-choice test results and a relatedness ratings assessment. In this study, the knowledge maps had an internal consistency of .83 ($N = 93$). In addition, the map scores showed a significant mean increase from 30% correct at the beginning of the semester ($SD = 11\%$) to 50% correct at the end ($SD = 19\%$). Finally, correlations between knowledge map scores and multiple-choice test scores and the relatedness ratings assessment were large (e.g., for knowledge maps and the multiple-choice test, $r = .51$; for knowledge maps and relatedness ratings, $r = .52$).

CRESST has developed a computer-based knowledge mapping system in which students constructed a group map by collaborating over a network. The system was used in the three studies reported in separate sections of this chapter (Chuang & O'Neil, 2006; Chung et al., 1999; Hsieh & O'Neil 2002).

Measurement of Problem-Solving Strategies

According to O'Neil (1999), problem-solving strategies are either domain independent or domain dependent. Domain-independent strategies can be applied over multiple subject areas, whereas domain-dependent strategies are specific to a particular subject area.

Three examples of domain-independent strategies are discussed here. The first is the use of multiple representations (O'Neil, 1999). Brenner et al. (1997) studied multiple representations strategies in learning algebra. Multiple representations as a problem-solving strategy in math is defined as translating the words of a problem into one or more other modes of representation, for example, using diagrams, pictures, concrete objects, equations, number sentences, verbal summaries, and even the problem solvers' own words. In a study by Cardelle-Elawar (1992), algebra problems were represented in multiple formats, and students learned to solve them in cooperative groups. Students receiving the multiple representations treatment did significantly better on the posttest. They were more successful in

Table 9.1 Knowledge Map Components and Variations Identified

Characteristics	Examples
Assessment component 1: Task	
Task demands	Students are asked to do one of the following: • Fill in a map • Construct a map from scratch • Organize cards • Rate relatedness of concept parts • Write an essay • Respond to an interview
Task constraints	Students may or may not be • Asked to construct a hierarchical map • Provided with the concepts used in the task • Provided with the concept links used in the task • Allowed to use more than one link between nodes • Allowed to physically move the concepts around until a satisfactory structure is arrived at • Asked to define the terms used in the map • Required to justify their responses • Required to construct the map collectively
Content structure	The intersection of the task demands of constraints with the structure of the subject domain to be mapped
Assessment component 2: Response format	
Response mode	• With paper and pencil • Orally • On a computer
Mapper	Map can be drawn by one of the following two: • Student • Teacher or researcher
Assessment component 3: Scoring system	
Components on the map to be scored	Focus is on the following three components: • Propositions • Hierarchy levels • Examples
Use of a criterion map	Compare a student's map with an expert's map; Experts can be the following: • One or more experts in the field • One or more teachers • One or more top students

representing the word problems into different formats and better at solving word problems. Similar effects of a multiple representations strategy on quadratic minimum values in math learning were found by Choi-koh (2000).

The second example of a domain-independent strategy is the use of analogies (O'Neil, 1999). For example, Bernardo (2001) studied high school students learning word problems in basic probability. He found that students who used an analogies strategy were significantly better at (a) transferring problem information between the analogous source and the target problem, (b) retrieving the analogous source problem, and (c) applying the retrieved analogous information.

The third example is search strategies. Electronic information seeking has attracted considerable attention in education and library science. There is no way to avoid it. Cyveillance (Murray, 2000) estimated in 2000 that the World Wide Web contained more than 2 billion publicly accessible information pages, and it will continue to grow. According to National Center for Education Statistics (2005), in 2003 nearly 100% of public schools in the United States had access to the Internet, and 95% of the public schools with Internet access used broadband connections to access it. The National Center for Education Statistics gave the ratio of students to instructional computers with Internet access in public schools as 4.4 to 1. In addition, nationwide, 82% of public schools with Internet access indicated that their school or school district had offered professional development to their teachers on how to integrate the use of the Internet into the curriculum. Overall, by high school, nearly all students (97%) used computers, and a majority (80%) used the Internet. The most popular application involved searching.

However, merely getting online to the World Wide Web does not automatically result in getting the information needed. Information seeking is viewed as a complex problem-solving activity that involves memory, decision making, learning, creativity, and intelligence (Kubeck, Miller-Albrecht, & Murphy, 1999). According to Smith and Broom (2003), students and teachers alike still lack basic information technology knowledge and skills. In addition, the current curriculum, instruction, and assessments do not adequately make use of the capabilities of today's networked information systems (Smith & Broom, 2003). Electronic information seeking is not just a single step, but a process of steps together. It involves determining the information needed, choosing topics to pursue, locating sites, and locating information to increase overall domain understanding, analysis and evaluation of the information found, and finally ending the search and returning to solving the problem (Lazonder, 2000).

To assess information-seeking strategies in a knowledge-mapping task, CRESST created a simulated Internet Web space (Schacter et al., 1999). Schacter et al. (1999) used this simulated Internet Web space to measure individual problem-solving strategies and found that content understanding scores for participants increased significantly with access to a simulated Web space. Information-seeking processes such as browsing, searching, and accessing feedback improved students' performance significantly on the posttest.

The three studies reviewed separately in further sections of this chapter use this close content-controlled, simulated Web space rather than the actual World Wide Web for four reasons. First, with the real World Wide Web, search queries sometimes end with a broken page if there are technical problems. A broken page is defined as a universal resource locator (URL) with contents that cannot be accessed or displayed because of server problems or because it does not exist any more. Second, when real pages are used, there is accessing time, and students often feel frustrated with the World Wide Web if they have to wait a long time for a page to download. For the first two reasons plus the limited time constraint of the task itself, students might become frustrated, and this is a variable that the researchers wished to exclude. Third, scoring would be impossible if the actual World Wide Web were used. In all three studies, part of the search score was determined by the extent of a student's search (number of Web pages retrieved) and by the quality of the search (relevance of the retrieved Web pages). In a real Web environment, it would be impossible to count all the pages or to assign a relevance score to every page. Fourth, use of the simulated Web space made it possible to maintain continuity and comparability between the three studies.

Measurement of Self-Regulation

Self-regulation includes metacognition and motivation (O'Neil, 1999). O'Neil and Herl (1998) and Hong, O'Neil, and Feldon (2005) proposed to examine metacognition in two aspects — planning and self-checking — and motivation in terms of self-efficacy and effort. These four components make up the measurement of self-regulation in problem solving for the CRESST model. Planning is the first step because, to be self-regulated, one must first have a goal and a plan to achieve the goal. Self-monitoring or self-checking is assumed to be an essential mechanism to monitor the processes for goal achievement. Self-efficacy is defined as one's confidence in having the capability to accomplish a particular goal or task, and effort is defined as the extent to which one works hard on a task. Based on their model, O'Neil and Herl (1998) created a questionnaire for self-regulation assessment in problem solving. All four components (planning, self-checking, self-efficacy, and effort) are assessed using eight questions each.

Other Issues in Measuring Collaborative Problem-Solving Processes

Online collaborative problem-solving tasks offer new measurement opportunities when information on what individuals and teams do is synthesized along cognitive dimensions. In the following sections, we describe the interface design features that can support online measurement and then describe three approaches suitable for quantifying online collaborative problem-solving processes. For each approach, we briefly describe the method with examples drawn from our work.

User Interface

The interaction between an individual and the computer interface and the interaction among group members can be rich sources of information when fused with task-related context information. Measures of what students are doing and when they are doing it, synchronized with measures of task-related variables, may provide enough information to draw inferences about learning processes. A key component in achieving this is the user interface. An interface that captures intentional acts that reflect good or poor judgment greatly strengthens the inference about cognition based on online behavior (Chung & Baker, 2003; Chung, de Vries, Cheak, Stevens, & Bewley, 2002). However, a considerable challenge remains: Given a continuous stream of student online behavior and task-related data, how should the data be synthesized to yield useful information about the individual and team? The interface used in our three studies to measure teamwork skills and in our other work developing online assessments offers some guidance.

Figure 9.2 illustrates the user interface for this system. The display is partitioned into three major sections. The lower left part of the screen displays the team members' predefined messages in the order sent. The lower right part of the screen shows 37 numbered buttons. All predefined messages are listed on handouts given to every student (see Figure 9.3). When participants click on a button, the corresponding message is sent to their partners' computer.

Predefined Messages

Existing approaches to measuring group processes rely almost exclusively on observational methods. Behavioral checklists, videotaped and audiotaped observation, and analysis of think-aloud protocols are the most common techniques used to measure group processes. Observations must be transcribed, coded, and analyzed post hoc. These methods are neither practical nor cost-effective in online settings.

One interesting technique we have tested and used to measure group processes is to provide learners with predefined messages that they use to communicate (Chung et al., 1999; Hsieh & O'Neil, 2002; O'Neil, Chung, et al., 1997). O'Neil and colleagues provided participants in their studies with a set of predefined messages. Participants worked in online teams using a custom-developed computer conferencing system. The teams were required jointly to complete a task (a simulated negotiation or a knowledge map). Team members used the predefined messages to communicate with

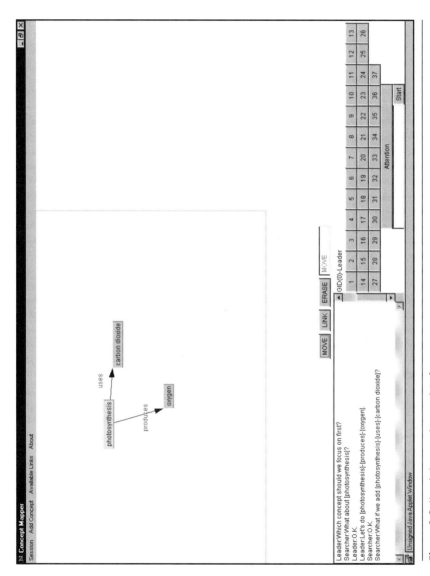

Figure 9.2 Knowledge mapping user interface.

Add Concepts and Links
1. Which concept should we focus on first?
2. What about [C]?
3. Let's [add/erase] [C].
4. Let's link [C] to [C].
5. Let's do [C]-[L]-[C].
6. Let's do [C]-[L1]-[C] instead of [L2].
7. Let's work on [C].
8. What if we [do/add/erase] [C]-[L]-[C]?
9. What if we do [C]-[L1]-[C], not [L2]?

Information From Web
10. Information shows we should do [C]-[L]-[C].
11. Information shows we should do [C]-[L1]-[C], not [L2].
12. Feedback shows we have improved [C].
13. Feedback shows we should work more on [C].
14. Feedback shows [C] in good shape. Don't waste time on it.

Help and Feedback Seeking
15. Help me find the relationship for [C] & [C].
16. Do you want me to check information for [C]?
17. Let's get feedback from computer.
18. What about we get feedback from computer?
19. How does the feedback show?
20. Save the map for feedback.

Keeping Track of Progress...
21. Can you hurry before time runs out?
22. We need to hurry to complete this map.
23. We only have X minutes left.
24. How's your searching?
25. I am trying to search information for [C] & [C].

Messages About the Group...
26. I think you should contribute more.
27. I need to hear from you.
28. You're doing great – keep going.
29. Good idea.
30. Yeah! We have made some progress.
31. We're doing better and better.

Quick Responses...
32. I agree with you.
33. I don't think so.
34. Any ideas?
35. O.K.
36. No.
37. I sent the wrong message. Sorry!

Concepts and Links...

Concepts...[C]
atmosphere
bacteria
carbon dioxide
climate
consumer
decomposition
evaporation
food chain
greenhouse gases
nutrients
oceans
oxygen
photosynthesis
producer
respiration
sunlight
waste
water cycle

Links...[L]
causes
influences
part of
produces
requires
used for
uses

Figure 9.3 Handout of predefined messages used to measure collaborative (team) problem-solving processes.

each other, and measures of teamwork processes were computed from the quantities and types (i.e., each message was coded a priori as representing adaptability, coordination, decision making, interpersonal, or leadership) of messages used. In general, participants were able to communicate using the predefined messages and successfully complete the tasks, and teamwork processes and team outcomes were measurable. The use of messages provided a tractable way of measuring communication and team skills. It allows real-time scoring and reporting of collaborative problem-solving skills.

Simulated World Wide Web Environment

The Web environment designed for our studies contained more than 200 Web pages with text and more than 500 images and diagrams about environmental science. Of the information, 90% was downloaded from the Internet, and 10% of the information was adapted from science textbooks and other science unit materials.

Three Relevant Studies Using the Theoretic Frameworks

Three CRESST studies used both the theory and measures outlined above. In all three studies, the knowledge map construction task included 18 environmental science concepts (i.e., atmosphere, bacteria, carbon dioxide, climate, consumer, decomposition, evaporation, food chain, greenhouse gases, nutrients, oceans, oxygen, photosynthesis, producer, respiration, sunlight, waste, water cycle) and 7 relationships or links (i.e., causes, influences, part of, produces, requires, used for, uses). Students were asked to use these terms and links to construct knowledge maps on the computer.

Study 1: Chung, O'Neil, and Herl (1999)

In the first study, Chung et al. (1999) used a computer-based collaborative knowledge-mapping tool to measure team processes and team outcomes. Team processes were measured through predefined messages, and each message belonged to one of six teamwork skills (e.g., adaptability or coordination) in the CRESST taxonomy of teamwork (O'Neil, Chung, et al., 1997). Prior to Chung et al.'s (1999) work, existing methods of measuring teamwork processes depended on observational methods such as behavioral checklists, videotaped and audiotaped observation, and think-aloud protocols. These methods were labor intensive and time consuming. The observations needed to be transcribed, coded, and analyzed post hoc. These methods were not conducive to fast and reliable analysis.

Chung et al. (1999) provided an alternative to their participants by using a set of predefined messages from which to choose. Using predefined messages had three advantages. First, it eliminated any off-task discussions. Participants were confined to selecting messages, which were completely task focused.

Second, predefined messages prevented ambiguity in the participants' use of language. For example, the message "Vegetation leads to food resources" is potentially ambiguous. Does the participant mean, "Add vegetation leads to food resources," or is the message a response to a question? With predefined messages, message stems could be created to make this situation less ambiguous (e.g., the message stem "Let's add [C]-[L]-[C]," where [C] and [L] are user selected concepts and links).

Third, the use of predefined messages provided the capability to measure team processes in real time. Messages were developed a priori based on a predefined taxonomy of teamwork processes; each message maps to one of these processes (adaptability, communication, coordination, decision making, interpersonal skills, leadership). This taxonomy of teamwork was domain independent and independent of scenarios. By tracking the messages selected and sent (and hence, by definition, the teamwork process category), an index of the kinds of teamwork processes was formed. Each message in a category was assumed equally important, and thus all messages were equally weighed. This technique provided a real-time teamwork assessment system with the potential to be administered, scored, and interpreted in real time. Chung et al.'s (1999) work suggested that this was a feasible and promising approach to assessing teamwork skills.

All participants for Chung et al.'s (1999) study were drawn from the same classes from the same high school. All students spoke English as their first language. For the pretest, 23 groups (69 participants) were drawn from six middle school and high school classes. Technical problems resulted in some computers crashing; thus, usable data for only 15 groups (45 participants) were available. For the posttest, 14 groups (42 participants) were drawn from the same classes 7 months later. Students were randomly assigned to groups in both the pre- and posttest sessions. No attempt was made to maintain intact groups across the pre- and posttest data collections.

Chung et al.'s (1999) study successfully supported the idea that students using a networked knowledge-mapping system could jointly construct a knowledge map. Unfortunately, in the study there were no significant positive relationships found between most team processes and outcome measures; surprisingly, decision making and communication were found to have negative effects on outcome performance.

Chung et al. (1999) provided two explanations for the results of their study. First, they argued that the task they used was highly knowledge dependent, and thus their participants did not have the requisite knowledge to be able to engage each other at a substantive level. The use of predefined messages might focus procedural aspects of constructing the knowledge map rather than any substantive discussion. For example, decision-making messages, which were designed to allow participants to discuss the content, accounted for 6% of the messages used compared to 17–21% for the other categories.

The second explanation was the split-attention effect (Sweller, 1994). Chung et al. (1999) argued that participants not only required attention to examine the message handout to select the appropriate message to send to their partners, but also needed to pay attention to the map and the messages sent to them. If focusing on the knowledge map was the major contributor to constructing good knowledge maps, then it might have been the team leader who engaged others the least who would have contributed the most.

Study 2: Hsieh and O'Neil (2002)

The second study was conducted by Hsieh and O'Neil (2002). They hypothesized that the lack of useful feedback and the type of task involved (not a real group task) may have influenced the results. Therefore, based on these two hypotheses, Hsieh and O'Neil attempted to improve Chung et al.'s (1999) study by changing the nature of the task to a real group task and by providing more extensive feedback. A *group task* is a task for which no single individual possesses all the resources and no single individual is likely to solve the problem or accomplish the task objectives without at least some input from others (Cohen & Arechevala-Vargas, 1987). Therefore, Hsieh and O'Neil modified the original task into a real group task by assigning specific roles (leader vs. searcher) respectively to each group member to meet the requirement of a group task: that no single individual possesses all the resources (information, knowledge, heuristic problem-solving strategies, materials, and skills) and that no single individual is likely to solve the problem or accomplish the task objectives without at least some input from others (Cohen & Arechevala-Vargas, 1987) In addition, to improve group performance, Hsieh and O'Neil implemented two levels of feedback (knowledge of response feedback and adapted knowledge of response feedback) on group map construction processes.

By improving on the methodology in Chung et al.'s (1999) study, Hsieh and O'Neil (2002) successfully demonstrated the use of adapted knowledge of response feedback to be better in group knowledge map performance than knowledge of response feedback. While doing so, like Chung et al., they also evaluated student collaborative problem solving and team processes on a computer-based knowledge-mapping group task with a simulated Web space as an information source. They demonstrated that decision making and leadership were positively related to group knowledge map performance. By assigning students specific roles and their corresponding responsibility to support interdependence between group members, Hsieh and O'Neil raised the level of group outcome performance (i.e., knowledge map score) to almost double that of Chung et al.'s study. Moreover, the positive correlation between decision making and group outcome that was expected in Chung et al.'s study was found among groups who received adapted knowledge of response feedback in Hsieh and O'Neil's study. Furthermore, for the problem-solving process, the request for feedback significantly predicted the group outcome for all groups.

The results of Hsieh and O'Neil's (2002) study showed that the nature of the task was an important determinant for the relationship of group involvement and group productivity. A group task that emphasized task interdependence and equal participation was beneficial for group productivity. In this study, students were assigned to a specific role and a specific responsibility in which no single student could succeed without the help of his or her partner. In general, all groups in this study received higher map scores than students in Chung et al.'s (1999) study. Thus, when the collaboration goal is group productivity, designing a task that includes task interdependency and equal participation can provide important collaborative learning experience.

In addition, students in Hsieh and O'Neil's (2002) study who received adapted knowledge of response outperformed students who received knowledge of response feedback. Consistent with the work of Kalyuga, Chandler, and Sweller (2000), feedback combined with graphical and text-based explanations was beneficial for low-knowledge learners in the computer-based collaborative problem-solving task. Another study in problem solving (Alibali, 1999) has suggested that intervention with feedback plus instruction about a principle, an analogy, or a procedure would be better than intervention with only accuracy feedback. However, these three types of interventions are not equally effective at promoting strategy generation or knowledge transfer (Alibali, 1999). The strategy and improvement information provided in adapted knowledge of response feedback could be regarded as accuracy feedback plus a principle. In Hsieh and O'Neil's study, adapted knowledge of response feedback that provided accuracy feedback with a principle resulted in better performance than knowledge of response feedback that only provided accuracy feedback.

However, in Hsieh and O'Neil's (2002) study, searching was unexpectedly negatively related to group knowledge map performance. In addition, even though feedback provided participants direction regarding which area to improve for search and task performance, the feedback did not provide practical tips on how to improve performance by providing more task-specific feedback on search strategies.

Study 3: Chuang and O'Neil (2006)

Based on the unexpected finding that searching was negatively related to group knowledge map performance, Chuang and O'Neil (2006) designed a third study by modifying Hsieh and O'Neil's (2002) task to provide examples of one specific type of search strategy: use of Boolean operators. In addition to training on searching, Chuang and O'Neil also tested two different feedback situations: task-specific adapted knowledge of response feedback and adapted knowledge of response feedback. These researchers explored the effects of students' teamwork and problem-solving processes on their knowledge-mapping performance. Results showed that task-specific adapted knowledge of response feedback was significantly more beneficial to group outcome than adapted knowledge of response feedback. In addition, as predicted for the problem-solving process, information seeking, including requests for feedback, browsing, searching for information, and searching using Boolean operators, were all significantly related to group outcome for both groups.

The purpose of Chuang and O'Neil's (2006) study was to extend Hsieh and O'Neil's (2002) study both theoretically and empirically. Hsieh and O'Neil's study provided a good model for information seeking as well as feedback access, although in their study searching for information actually was negatively related to outcome performance. Chuang and O'Neil attempted to improve Hsieh and O'Neil's methodology by providing students with training on searching using Boolean operators and by providing more extensive feedback with information on searching using Boolean operators in addition to adapted knowledge of response feedback.

In Chuang and O'Neil's (2006) study, students were randomly assigned to groups of two people. In each group, one person had the role of leader, and the other had the role of searcher. Each group then was assigned to one of the two feedback conditions (task-specific adapted knowledge of response feedback and adapted knowledge of response feedback). Students were considered as low prior knowledge students in environmental sciences and searching using Boolean operators; therefore, a training session on searching with Boolean operators was administered to all groups before the actual knowledge-mapping task. During the actual task, detailed feedback on knowledge map constructions was provided to students who were assigned to be searchers. In other words, the leaders cannot assess the feedback directly; however, they can ask the searcher to request feedback from the computer. The searchers were able to communicate the feedback requested through the predefined messages to the leaders. In addition, feedback on searching using Boolean operators was provided to students assigned to be searchers in the experiment group.

Thus, students could get required knowledge for their map construction through information seeking and could monitor their progress on the task through requesting and receiving feedback from the computer. In other words, even though students might lack the requisite knowledge to do the task, they could get helpful information through information seeking and monitor their performance through feedback.

Combining the methodology of Hsieh and O'Neil's (2002) study with a training session on searching using Boolean operators, Chuang and O'Neil (2006) evaluated student collaborative problem solving and team process on a computer-based knowledge-mapping group task. In addition, the effects of two types of feedback (task-specific adapted knowledge of response feedback and adapted knowledge of response feedback) on group outcomes were also evaluated. Teamwork processes (collaborative process) were measured by predefined messages that were used to evaluate the six scales of teamwork processed (adaptability, coordination, decision making, interpersonal skills, leadership, and communication). Problem solving was measured by content understanding (knowledge map score), problem-solving strategies (information seeking and accessing feedback), and self-regulation (planning, self-checking, effort, and self-efficacy). Teamwork processes, content understanding, and problem-solving strategies were recorded by the computer system. Self-regulation was measured by a paper-and-pencil self-regulation questionnaire.

Participants were 120 college students. They were randomly assigned to a group, a role (leader or searcher), and a type of feedback (task-specific adapted knowledge of response feedback or adapted knowledge of response feedback). Sixty students (30 teams) received the task-specific knowledge of response feedback, and 60 students (30 teams) received the adapted knowledge of response feedback. There were three major findings in this study. First, students who received task-specific adapted knowledge of response feedback performed significantly better in environmental science knowledge mapping than students who received adapted knowledge of response feedback. Second, information seeking had positive effects on group outcome in environmental science knowledge mapping. Browsing and searching were both positively related to group outcome. In addition, request for feedback was positively related to group outcome. Third, searching using Boolean operators had positive effects on problem-solving strategies and group outcome on the knowledge-mapping task. When more Boolean operators were used, the score on the knowledge map was higher. In addition, the task-specific adapted knowledge of response feedback group used more Boolean operators in their searching than the adapted knowledge of response feedback group.

In conclusion, Chuang and O'Neil's (2006) study indicated that task-specific feedback had significant effects on college students' outcome performance in a computer-based knowledge-mapping task. When provided with the more extensive feedback (task-specific adapted knowledge of response feedback), students performed even better than those who received the adapted knowledge of response feedback in Hsieh and O'Neil's (2002) study. Furthermore, in terms of problem-solving processes, all forms of information seeking, including request for feedback, browsing, searching for information, and searching using Boolean operators, were significantly related to group outcome for both groups.

Future Directions

We view our set of studies as an example of dynamic testing. According to Grigorenko and Sternberg (1998), dynamic testing "is a collection of testing procedures designed to quantify not only the products or even the processes of learning but also the potential to learn" (p. 75). To fulfill the claims made for it, dynamic testing involves not only testing end products but also learning processes at the same time. This type of testing is quite different from traditional, static testing that only assesses the learned end products. Another difference between dynamic testing and static testing is the role of feedback (Grigorenko & Sternberg, 1998). According to Grigorenko and Sternberg (1998), in traditional static testing feedback about the performance is usually not given during the test. In dynamic testing, feedback is given during the test to help assess learning. In dynamic testing, an examiner presents a sequence of gradually more difficult tasks. After each performance from the student, the examiner gives the student feedback and continues until the student either solves the problem or chooses to give up. The basic goal of dynamic testing is to see, when feedback is given, whether test takers change and how they change. This is done through provision of feedback. However, there is no agreement about how much information should be included in the feedback. Currently, different approaches in dynamic testing vary in the amount of information contained in the feedback (Grigorenko & Sternberg, 1998). We believe that dynamic testing can provide a theoretical rationale for our future research on the assessment of collaborative problem solving.

Another possible area of research is seen in the relationship of feedback and cognitive load (Kalyuga & Sweller, 2004; Sweller, in press). Cognitive load theory assumes that information should be structured to eliminate any avoidable load on working memory to enhance learning. Kalyuga, Chandler, and Sweller (1999) suggested that because a learner has a limited working memory capacity, any increase in cognitive resources required to process split-attention materials decreases resources available for learning. Their research used computer-based instructional material consisting of diagrams and text and attempted to ameliorate split-attention effects by increasing effective working memory size by presenting the text in auditory form. In their study, the auditory presentation of text proved superior to visual-only presentation. But, when the text was presented simultaneously in both auditory and visual forms, the effect was no better than visual-only representation. Kalyuga et al. (1999) concluded that the visual form was redundant and imposed a cognitive load that interfered with learning. In addition, the frequently assumed idea that presenting the same material in written and spoken form benefits learning and understanding was refuted by their other research (Kalyuga, Chandler, & Sweller, 2004). They concluded that if learners are required to coordinate and simultaneously process redundant material such as written and spoken text, an excessive working memory load is generated. Based on Sweller's cognitive load theory predictions, we plan to investigate the impact of various combinations of visual/auditory treatments in our collaborative problem-solving context.

Acknowledgments

San-hui (Sabrina) Chuang is now at CRESST, University of California, Los Angeles. The work reported here was supported under the Educational Research and Development Centers Program, PR/Award R305B960002, as administered by the Institute of Education Sciences, U.S. Department of Education. The findings and opinions expressed in this report do not reflect the positions or policies of the National Center for Education Research, the Institute of Education Sciences, or the U.S. Department of Education.

References

Aidman, E. V., & Egan, G. (1998). Academic assessment through computerized concept mapping: Validating a method of implicit map reconstruction. *International Journal of Instructional Media, 25*, 277–294.

Alibali, M. W. (1999). How children change their minds: Strategy change can be gradual or abrupt. *Developmental Psychology, 35*, 127–145.

Arts, J. A. R., Gijselaers, W. H., & Segers, M. S. R. (2002). Cognitive effects of an authentic computer-supported, problem-based learning environment. *Instructional Science, 30*, 465–495.

Barron, B. (2000). Problem solving in video-based microworlds: Collaborative and individual outcomes of high-achieving sixth-grade students. *Journal of Educational Psychology, 92*, 391–398.

Bernardo, A. B. (2001). Analogical problem construction and transfer in mathematical problem solving. *Educational Psychology, 21*, 137–150.

Brenner, M. E., Mayer, R. E., Moseley, B., Brar, T., Duran, R., Reed, S., et al. (1997). Learning by understanding: The role of multiple representations in learning algebra. *American Educational Research Journal, 34*, 663–689.

Cardelle-Elawar, M. (1992). Effects of teaching metacognitive skills to students with low mathematics abilities. *Teaching and Teacher Education, 8*, 109–121.

Choi-koh, S. S. (2000). A problem-solving model of quadratic min values using computer. *International Journal of Instructional Media, 27*(1), 73–82.

Chuang, S.-H., & O'Neil, H. F. (2006). Role of task-specific adapted feedback on a computer-based collaborative problem-solving task. In H. F. O'Neil & R. S. Perez (Eds.), *Web-based learning: Theory, research, and practice* (pp. 239–254). Mahwah, NJ: Erlbaum.

Chung, G. K. W. K., & Baker, E. L. (2003). Issues in the reliability and validity of automated scoring of constructed responses. In M. D. Shermis & J. Burstein (Eds.), *Automated essay scoring: A cross-disciplinary perspective* (pp. 23–40). Mahwah, NJ: Erlbaum.

Chung, G. K. W. K., de Vries, L. F., Cheak, A. M., Stevens, R. H., & Bewley, W. L. (2002). Cognitive process validation of an online problem solving assessment. *Computers in Human Behavior, 18*, 669–684.

Chung, G., O'Neil, H. F., Jr., & Herl, H. E. (1999). The use of computer-based collaborative knowledge mapping to measure team processes and team outcomes. *Computers in Human Behaviors, 15,* 463–493.

Cohen, B. P., & Arechevala-Vargas, (1987). *Interdependence, interaction, and productivity* (Working Paper No. 87-3). Stanford, CA: Center for Sociology Research.

Dochy, F. J. R. C. (1996). Assessment of domain-specific and domain-transcending prior knowledge: Entry assessment and the use of profile analysis. In M. Birenbaum & F. J. R. C. Dochy (Eds.), *Alternatives in assessment of achievements, learning process and prior knowledge* (pp. 93–129). Boston: Kluwer Academic.

Grigorenko, E. L., & Sternberg, R. J. (1998). Dynamic testing. *Psychological Bulletin, 124,* 75–111.

Herl, H. E., O'Neil, H. F., Jr., Chung, G., & Schacter, J. (1999). Reliability and validity of a computer-based knowledge mapping system to measure content understanding. *Computer in Human Behavior, 15,* 315–333.

Hong, E., O'Neil, H. F., Jr., & Feldon, D. (2005). Gender effects on mathematics achievement: Mediating role of state and trait self-regulation. In A. M. Gallagher & J. C. Kaufman (Eds.), *Gender differences in mathematics* (pp. 264–293). Cambridge, UK: Cambridge University Press.

Hsieh, I. G., & O'Neil, H. F. (2002). Types of feedback in a computer-based collaborative problem-solving task. *Computers in Human Behavior, 18,* 699–715.

Hurwitz, C. L., & Abegg, G. (1999). A teacher's perspective on technology in the classroom: Computer visualization, concept maps and learning logs. *Journal of Education, 181,* 123–143.

Kalyuga, S., Chandler, P., & Sweller (1999). Managing split-attention and redundancy in multimedia instruction. *Applied Cognitive Psychology 13,* 351–371.

Kalyuga, S., Chandler, P., & Sweller, J. (2000). Incorporating learner experience into the design of multimedia instruction. *Journal of Educational Psychology, 92,* 126–136.

Kalyuga, S., Chandler, P., & Sweller, J. (2004). When redundant on-screen text in multimedia technical instruction can interfere with learning. *Human Factors, 46,* 567–581.

Kalyuga, S., & Sweller, J. (2004). Measuring knowledge to optimize cognitive load factors during instruction. *Journal of Educational Psychology, 96,* 558–568.

Kubeck, J. E., Miller-Albrecht, S. A., & Murphy, M. D. (1999). Finding information on the World Wide Web: Exploring older adults' exploration. *Educational Gerontology, 25,* 167–183.

Lazonder, A. W. (2000). Exploring novice users' training needs in searching information on the WWW. *Journal of Computer Assisted Learning, 16,* 326–335.

Mayer, R. E., & Wittrock, M. C. (1996). Problem-solving transfer. In D. C. Berliner, & R. C. Calfee (Eds.), *Handbook of educational psychology* (pp. 47–62). New York: Macmillan Library Reference USA, Simon and Schuster Macmillan.

Murray, B. H. (2000). *Sizing the Internet.* Arlington, VA: Cyveillance Inc. Retrieved May 24, 2006, from www.cyveillance.com/web/downloads/Sizing_the_Internet.pdf

National Center for Education Statistics. (2005). *Internet access in U.S. public schools and classrooms: 1994–2003* (NCES No. 2005015). Washington, DC: U.S. Department of Education.

O'Neil, H. F., Jr. (1999). Perspectives on computer-based performance assessment of problem solving. *Computers in Human Behavior, 15,* 225–268.

O'Neil, H. F., Jr., Allred, K., & Baker, E. L. (1997). Review of workforce readiness theoretical frameworks. In H. F. O'Neil, Jr. (Ed.), *Workforce readiness: Competencies and assessment* (pp. 3–25). Mahwah, NJ: Erlbaum.

O'Neil, H. F., Jr., Chung, G. K. W. K., & Brown, R. S. (1997). Use of networked simulations as a context to measure team competencies. In H. F. O'Neil, Jr. (Ed.), *Workforce readiness: Competencies and assessment* (pp. 411–452). Mahwah, NJ: Erlbaum.

O'Neil, H. F., Jr., & Herl, H. E. (1998, April). *Reliability and validity of a trait measure of self-regulation.* Paper presented at the annual meeting of the American Educational Research Association, San Diego, CA.

Ruiz-Primo, M. A., Schultz, S. E., and Shavelson, R. J. (1997). *Concept map-based assessment in science: Two exploratory studies* (CSE Tech. Rep. No. 436). Los Angeles: University of California, Center for Research on Evaluation, Standards, and Student Testing (CRESST).

Samaha, N. V., & De Lisi, R. (2000). Peer collaboration on a nonverbal reasoning task by urban, minority students. *The Journal of Experimental Education, 69,* 5–21.

Schacter, J., Herl, H. E., Chung, G. K. W. K., Dennis, R. A., & O'Neil, H. F., Jr. (1999). Computer-based performance assessment: A solution to the narrow measurement and reporting of problem solving. *Computers in Human Behavior, 15,* 403–418.

Schau, C., & Mattern, N. (1997). Use of map techniques in teaching applied statistics courses. *American statistician, 51,* 171–175.

Schau, C., Mattern, N., Zeilik, M., Teague, K., & Weber, R. (2001). Select-and-fill-in concept map scores as a measure of students' connected understanding of science. *Educational and Psychological Measurement, 61,* 136–158.

Sinclair, K. E. (1997). Workforce competencies of college graduates. In H. F. O'Neil, Jr. (Ed.), *Workforce readiness: Competencies and assessment* (pp. 103–120). Mahwah, NJ: Erlbaum.

Smith, M. S., & Broom, M. (2003). The landscape and future of the use of technology in K–12 education. In H. F. O'Neil, Jr., & Perez, R. S. (Eds.), *Technology applications in education: A learning view* (pp. 3–30). Mahwah, NJ: Erlbaum.

Sweller, J. (1994). Cognitive load theory, learning difficulty, and instructional design. *Learning and Instruction, 4,* 295–312.

Sweller, J. (in press). Human cognitive architecture and educational technology. In J. M. Spector, M. D. Merrill, J. J. G. van Merriënboer, & M. P. Driscoll (Eds.), *Handbook of research on educational communications and technology* (3rd ed.).

Webb, N. M., Nemer, K. M., & Chizhik, A. W. (1998). Equity issues in collaborative group assessment: Group composition and performance. *American Educational Research Journal, 35,* 607–651.

Weng, A. L.-B. (1999). *A reliability and validity study of Chinese version of a teamwork skills questionnaire.* Unpublished doctoral dissertation, University of Southern California.

Zhang, J. (1998). A distributed representation approach to group problem solving. *Journal of the American Society for Information Science, 49,* 801–809.

10
Real-Time Diagnostics of Problem-Solving Behavior for Business Simulations

RENÉ MOLKENTHIN AND KLAUS BREUER

Johannes Gutenberg–University of Mainz

ROBERT D. TENNYSON

University of Minnesota

Introduction

Business simulations are based on a computational model that represents the complexity and dynamics of business structures and concepts. Within a simulation, the participants can make decisions to direct the modeled enterprise. A business simulation can make the interdependencies between the different activities within an enterprise transparent to the participants. From an economic perspective, success within a business simulation can be measured by the development of core variables. In the field of business administration, the balanced scorecard is a well-known concept for this purpose.

From an educational perspective, the structure of the cognitive system that is responsible for the economical success is relevant. A related aspect refers to the possibilities to support elaboration of the mental model during the activities within a business simulation. Furthermore, in the context of Web-based learning environments, there is the issue of how to foster self-regulated learning processes.

A prerequisite for effective feedback that supports learning is a continuous diagnosis of the problem-solving process, particularly the diagnosis of the information retrieval and decision-making processes.

This chapter describes the basic concept of the diagnostics within a prototype of a Web-based business simulation labeled solarSYDUS. Besides the model, this simulation contains a component for recording information retrieval and decision-making processes during the simulation for analyzing problem-solving behavior.

Objectives and the Use of Business Simulations

Simulations and games have been used in the context of computer-based learning since the 1960s. They have depicted a specific phenomenon within a model that is executable on a computer. This chapter refers to phenomena in economic contexts, particularly enterprises competing with each other in a simulated market. The model of the enterprises and the market represents the complexity and dynamics of business structures and concepts the participants have to cope with within the simulation. The use of business simulations can target different objectives (Breuer, Molkenthin, & Tennyson, 2006; Lainema & Nurmi, 2006):

- Acquisition of structural knowledge
- Development of domain-specific problem-solving competencies
- Elaboration of holistic views toward complex phenomena
- Fostering meta-cognitive competencies (self-regulation and self-monitoring; O'Neil, 2002)
- Support for the ability of role-taking
- Buildup of the ability for coping with dynamics

The traditional concept of using business simulations can be divided into three phases: briefing, simulation or gaming, and debriefing (Capaul, 2001). The three phases are usually moderated and supported by one or more teachers (= moderator). Within the first phase (briefing), the participants receive an introduction to the structure and the rules within the model. This is necessary to activate prior knowledge, which can be referred to by the participants. Within the briefing, the participants are confronted with a problem they ought to solve within the follow-up simulation, for example, to gain a higher market share within a growing market. Because learning with business simulation refers to the paradigm of problem-based learning, the selection of an appropriate problem is an important aspect (Tennyson & Breuer, 2002). The participants should elaborate their mental model about the concepts represented within the simulation model by solving a given problem; that is, the appropriate knowledge to solve the problem is not available at this point in time. Otherwise, from the perspective of the participants, the presented "problem" would be a task only. In this situation, learning takes place in the sense of automating existing knowledge.

It refers to the distinction between tasks and problems, which Dörner (1976) introduced. In business simulations, the participants are often faced with complex problems. According to the definition of Dörner, these problems have a more general goal that needs to be elaborated before and during the problem-solving process.

Within the simulation phase, the participants solve the given problem. Based on the knowledge about the structure and rules underlying the model and the analysis of the initial state of "their" enterprise, the participants have to make decisions to reach the goal stated in the presentation of the problem. After all decisions are made, the model is simulated for one time step, and the outcomes of the decisions can be analyzed. The participants are expected to analyze the new state of the simulation regarding the expected effects of their decisions. Discrepancies could point out misperceptions about the structure of the model. A perceived discrepancy could initiate a reflection process by the learners to validate and correct their mental model of the simulated enterprise/market and hence the represented economic concepts and their dynamics (Dörner & Wearing, 1995).

During a simulation, the moderator could give additional feedback regarding the problem-solving process itself. Although the feedback during a simulation is more specific to the individual problem-solving process, the phase of debriefing can first be seen as a comprehensive view of the activities during the simulation and second as a way to reflect on and generalize the learning outcomes (Capaul, 2001).

Besides the effort to analyze the individual problem-solving processes to give an individual appropriate feedback, there is a technical issue for using a business simulation. At minimum, there has to be a computer running the simulation model within simulation software, for example, Powersim Studio or Vensim.[1] Furthermore, the participants need to be able to enter decisions and analyze effects. That causes mostly the need for additional computers and a local network. To avoid the technical overlay, the idea of Web-based (business) simulations arose in the late 1990s with the development of e-learning environments (Mandl, Keller, Reiserer, & Geier, 2001).

A second intent was to make business simulations available to a broader audience. By the use of standard technology (i.e., a standard Internet browser), access to a business simulation does not depend on specific software installations. A connection to the Internet is required. Although there is standard technology on the client side to explore the model structure and observe the results of the simulation, the simulation model itself is run on a Web server. Using this Web-based approach has at least two

[1] For the present versions of the modeling software, refer to the Web sites of Powersim Software (www.powersim.com) and Ventana Systems (www.vensim.com).

side effects. A broader audience causes a higher effort to analyze individual problem-solving processes to give appropriate feedback. Second, because of the Web-based setting, participants can access a business simulation from different locations at different times, and direct feedback by a moderator cannot be given to each participant within a simulation. In addition, although Web-based learning is assumed to be more self-directed, instructional support is needed. Especially, novices can be overburdened by the complexity of a business simulation, which could lead to lower learning outcomes (Stark, Gruber, & Mandl, 1998). Hence, besides a simulation model, a Web-based business simulation needs instructional support that supports problem solving. To avoid overextension of the learner, several problems that reflect different levels of difficulty should be integrated within a business simulation. The different problems reflect the chosen didactic strategy (e.g., a gradual increase of complexity). Thus, the cognitive load that is caused by the problem does not lead to an overburdening of the learner but allows further learning processes (Kirschner, 2002).

Another aspect of designing instructional support of Web-based simulations is the transparency of the simulation model. In the context of business simulations, there is an approach based on the idea of a glass box model; that is, the structure and the rules of the simulation model are made transparent to the learner (Alessi, 2000; Berendes, 2002). Because business simulations represent a complex environment with many interconnected variables and different delays of effects, an analysis of the different consequences of decisions would hardly be possible within a black box approach. Therefore, a black box approach could even hinder learning by reducing it to an inefficient and time-consuming trial-and-error process (cp. Kröner, Plass, & Leutner, 2005).

Although the transparency of a model is a prerequisite for efficient learning processes, the learning process itself also has to be supported (Hillen, 2004). This chapter presents an approach to realize continuous feedback for the problem-solving activities during a Web-based business simulation. This approach addresses a microadaptation as proposed by Leutner (1992, 1997). Microadaptation describes a continuous adaptation of the learning environment, referring to the learner in short intervals to improve learning processes.

Success Within Business Simulations

The traditional approach to assess the success of controlling an enterprise in a business simulation is based on the analysis of core variables. A main advantage of this approach is the easy retrieval of the value as a result of the simulation. A main difficulty is to find a set of variables that represent the state of the enterprise in a condensed way. Because this is a typical problem in economics, there are several systems of core variables that are partly oriented at variables from the accounting in enterprises. Thus, one can compare the performance of each learner at the end of the simulation in relation to a given set of core variables. Because these are only end states, the problem-solving process itself is not taken into account. One mistake during the simulation can overlay a successful problem-solving process and distort the comparison between participants. Therefore, a modified (or additional) process-oriented approach of measurement is necessary. Besides the end state of a variable, the relative improvements (or deteriorations) during a simulation could be measured (Hasselmann, 1993).

As mentioned, the core variables often derive from accounting. A more comprehensive and holistic view of the processes within an enterprise is represented by Kaplan and Norton's (1997) concept of the balanced scorecard. In contrast to other sets of variables, this concept integrates explicitly the strategy on an enterprise. In this chapter, the concept cannot be elaborated in detail. Berendes (2002) extended this economical concept with the indicators "goal-orientation," "stability," and "foresight" to measure the competency of controlling a simulated enterprise.

The underlying assumption of the measurement of core variables is that the values of the core variables result from the decisions. The decisions are based on the mental model the learner has of the simulation model. Hence, the better the mental model is, the better the decisions and, at the end, the performance of the learner are (Sterman, 2000).

Besides the problem of the interpretation of the meaning of the core variables, the measurement provides only one part for analyzing and supporting the problem-solving process. The values are easily retrieved from the simulation, but how the learner has accomplished the decision is not taken into account. From that perspective, it could be said that the measurement of core variables can be seen as the economical view in business simulations. Using well-known economic instruments can increase the ecological validity of a business simulation from the learners' view and hence their motivation to cope with the simulation. However, from an educational perspective, the state of the balanced scorecard is "only" a result of a learning process. For an instructional support view, there is the necessity of further analysis of the problem-solving processes to explain how the learner develops decisions.

Analysis of the Problem-Solving Activities

For analyzing problem-solving activities, we can refer to the framework of problem solving given by Dörner (1989; Dörner & Wearing, 1995):

Goal elaboration
Hypothesis formation

Prognosing
Planning and decision making
Monitoring
Reflection

But, as Dörner and Wearing have pointed out: "Neither will these different phases of action regulation always show up in the behavior of subjects, nor is this sequence always sound" (Dörner & Wearing, 1995, p. 70). Thus, how to solve complex problems cannot be seen as a linear sequence but rather as a systematic framework to compare successful and less-successful problem solvers by their activities.

Several research studies by Dörner have revealed typical deficits in solving complex problems (Dörner & Wearing, 1995). He observed that the goal-elaboration and orientation phase of experts lasted longer, and novices tended to start earlier with making decisions. During the simulation, novices showed a muddling-through behavior, whereas experts were more organized. In the phase of hypothesis formation, Dörner distinguished between general orientation, special orientation, and exploration. Although general orientation and special orientation describe the scope of desired information, exploration focuses on the supposed effects of possible actions. Regarding business simulations, exploration could be illustrated, for example, by a question about the possible effect of a higher price on the current market share. Although novices often moved between or within general and special orientation, experts acted more on the level of special orientation and exploration. The forecasting phase takes into account the estimation of possible developments. It has been shown that it is difficult for humans to estimate nonlinear or delayed developments. For this, the argument about the relation between the mental model and the performance of controlling an enterprise mentioned here could be supported. The better the elaboration of mental models is, the better the forecasting of the development of the simulation can be and vice versa. Hence, the discrepancy between forecasted and simulated values could be an indicator of the appropriateness of the mental model.

In the phase of decision making, the experts followed a goal hierarchy in which the main goal becomes divided into subgoals. Decisions become connected to each other. In the scope of business simulations, if an expert wants to gain more market share by lowering the price, then there would be, for example, an increase of the production rate to serve the expected demand. Novices, in contrast, make more isolated decisions. In relation to decision making, another deficit can be observed. The effect of the decisions is not monitored in many cases, and hence deficient decisions are not encountered, and deeper knowledge about the rules within the simulation model is hardly built up. Dörner called this type of decision making *ballistic decisions*, using an analogue of a cannonball: Once fired, the flight path could not be corrected anymore (Dörner & Wearing, 1995). The last phase refers to reflection on the appropriateness of actions. Within a business simulation, this phase can be triggered by effective feedback.

Regarding the problem-solving process, it is not possible to give feedback for a "right" problem-solving schema. The expert-novice comparison has revealed some specific deficits of novices. Hence, a strategy for giving feedback focusing on the deficits could be a promising way to improve problem-solving behavior. From a more general perspective, for the support and improvement, respectively, of the learning problem-solving process, an analysis of the exploration and decision-making processes within a business simulation is necessary.

One instrument to analyze and visualize exploration and decision-making processes can be derived from the research with strategic management simulations (SMSs) by Streufert and coauthors (Breuer & Satish, 2003; Breuer & Streufert, 1995; Streufert & Swezey, 1986). SMSs are quasi-experimental in design, in contrast to business simulations, which are based on a mathematical simulation model. The order of events within an SMS is mostly predefined and cannot be changed by the participants. The participants, however, receive information about the effects of their actions in such a way that they have the impression that their decisions have an effect on the environment. This is done by varying the content of some of the messages by the moderator in their dependency on the prior action of the participant. With that design, each simulation is structurally comparable and hence the environment of performance of the participants. The actions of the participants are recorded. The decision-making process is visualized by the time-event matrix (see Figure 10.1). The matrix shows the action of one participant in different scopes of decision dependent on the simulation time. The time-event matrix can be used as a feedback tool to visualize the behavior of each participant and to point out specific inappropriate patterns of decision making, for example, ballistic decision making. Continuous and individual feedback for each learner based on the analysis of the learner's problem-solving behavior, that is, the exploration and decision-making processes, can be considered as a mode of microadaptation (Leutner, 1992, 1997).

The Business Simulation solarSYDUS

For the development and testing of a microadaptation mode, a prototype of a Web-based business simulation has been developed at the University of Mainz. The business simulation is called solarSYDUS and represents an enterprise that produces and sells solar panels in a simulated market. On the

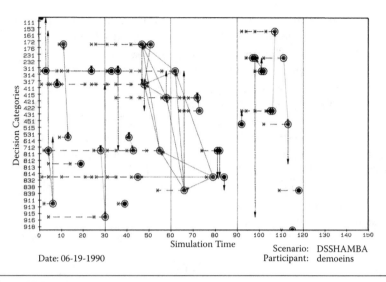

Figure 10.1 SMS graphic representation of the decision-making process of a participant.

market, there are two additional enterprises that represent direct competitors for the enterprise of the learner. The competitive enterprises are controlled by the computer. The structure of the enterprises in solarSYDUS refers to the value chain of Porter (1985). In this regard, a well-known concept within the business administration community is used that divides an enterprise into different activities, for example, inbound logistics, production, and the like. The value chain emphasizes the process perspective of enterprises and hence the systematic interdependencies of the different activities.

The simulation model is based on the previously developed and published SYDUS model by Berendes (2002), which reflects the complexity of business structures. The improved model is now embedded within a Web-based learning environment and is implemented at a Web server. The simulation runs on this server. The learner can access the simulation with a standard Internet browser without any need for additional installation of software. Besides the reduction of technical requirements, the necessary instructional support of a simulation model is addressed to provide individual support for each learner regarding the different cognitive structures and problem-solving processes.

In solarSYDUS, the glass box approach is applied. This means that the structure of the model is transparent to the learner on different levels. Besides the textual information about each activity and the enterprise itself, the learner can access the model structure with definitions of each variable (see Figure 10.2, arrow). For the construction of the model in solarSYDUS, the

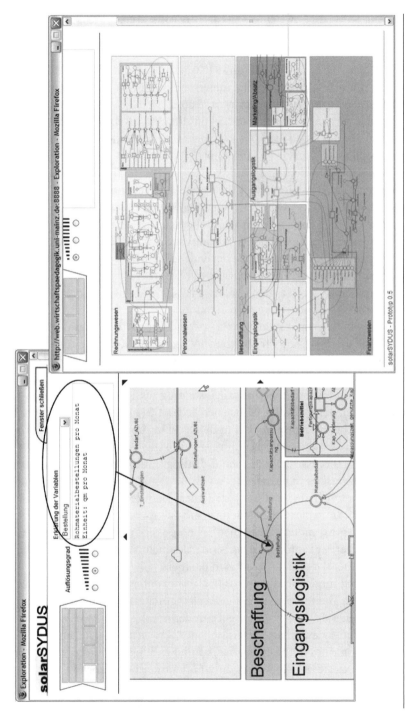

Figure 10.2 Transparency of the model in solarSYDUS.

modeling software Powersim is used. This software supports the modeling technique of system dynamics (SD), which represents reality as stocks and flows, as shown in Figure 10.2 (Forrester, 1968). Stocks, like an inventory, are changed by in- and outflows (e.g., inbound and outbound deliveries). The mathematical equations integrated in the structure quantify the model and make a simulation over time possible.

The learner can explore the model on different levels of resolution (see Figure 10.2). A detailed view of each single activity of the SD model is possible as well as an overview of the whole model.

Besides the information specific to the enterprise, the learner can find more general information about the market and technology of solar cells. Thus, the authenticity of the learning environment is addressed.

For developing tasks to learn with solarSYDUS, the focus is on the distinction between tasks with specific or nonspecific goals. Vollmeyer, Burns, and Holyoak (1996) described the dependence of problem-solving strategy use on goal specificity. Tasks with a specific goal allow the learner to control a variable to reach a given value. Tasks with nonspecific goals focus on exploration of underlying rules in a model (Burns & Vollmeyer, 2002). Learners who are presented with a specific goal at the beginning tend to manipulate the given variable but not learn the structure of a model, whereas learners with a nonspecific goal use strategies to induce the underlying rules of a model (Vollmeyer et al., 1996). Vollmeyer et al. proposed a combination of both types of tasks: starting with a nonspecific goal to explore the structure, followed by specific goal to explore the behavior of the model. The concept of *task* is understood to mean a problem, according to Dörner (see the analysis of problem-solving activities section).

Therefore, there are two modes of dealing with solarSYDUS available for which the tasks can be embedded. The first mode supports the exploration process to get the necessary structural knowledge about the model. The learner can explore the structure and see its behavior by simulating the model. In this mode, the learner has no possibility to make individual decisions. There are automated decision rules included in the model, which represent general decision patterns in business.

The second mode focuses on controlling an enterprise by actively making decisions. Therefore, the learner has to coordinate decisions according to a more general strategy. During a simulation, the other two enterprises are controlled by automated decision rules. The learner also can activate these decision rules in the enterprise, similar to a decision support system, but the automatic decision rules only maintain an equilibrium referring to the current simulation state. To achieve and sustain the externally pregiven objectives, the learners have to make individual decisions.

For the feedback on the effects of the learner's decisions, there are different reports available in each activity. For a more comprehensive view of the state of the enterprise, an adaptation of a balanced scorecard is integrated. In addition to the goal (specific or nonspecific), the tasks provide the possibility to vary complexity for the learner by focusing on specific aspects of the model. The more business concepts are integrated and interact within a simulation, the more complex it could be for the learners, particularly for novices.

Hence, the different tasks should address the different prior knowledge of the business simulation held by different learners by varying the complexity of the nonspecific goal. Thus, the aspect of cognitive overload of the learner is taken into account by not presenting the learner with too much complexity in terms of the learner's current cognitive structure. According to cognitive load theory, cognitive overload can circumvent learning processes and hence the improvement of the mental model (Kirschner, 2002).[2]

If the learner manages the enterprise by making individual decisions during a simulation, then the learner has to make forecasts referring to several direct or indirect connected variables. The forecast comprises the options *no effect, decreasing, steady, increasing*, and setting a concrete value. With the concept of forecast and the development of several variables, the discrepancy between predicted and simulated values is addressed. In this understanding, a higher discrepancy could be interpreted as higher inappropriateness of the mental model in relation to the SD model. An analysis of the discrepancy could result in feedback for the learner regarding specific relations between variables to direct exploring processes and hence the understanding of the structure of the SD model of solarSYDUS.

For analyzing the exploration and decision-making processes, the activities have to be recorded. Therefore, a database server is needed as a second component in addition to the Web server. The database of solarSYDUS contains the values of the different variables for the reports as well as for every decision the learner makes during a simulation run. Furthermore, the database stores the exploration and decision-making activities. Figure 10.3 illustrates the technical architecture of solarSYDUS.

Each relevant request of the learner (e.g., a report) is generated by a Web server and stored in a database server, where it is coded with a specific ID and a time stamp. For integrating the simulation model, there is an additional simulation engine integrated in the Web server. The results of each simulation step also are stored in the database. The decisions of

---

[2] A further elaboration of cognitive load theory could not be provided within this context. An introduction to and reviews of the research within the context of this theory can be found in *Learning and Instruction, 12,* 2002.

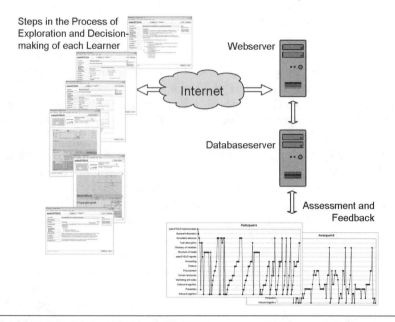

Figure 10.3 Technical architecture of solarSYDUS.

each learner are passed to the simulation engine and stored in the database concurrently. With this architecture, all relevant activities referring to exploration and decision-making processes can be reconstructed and analyzed. The assessment of the exploration and decision-making processes is needed to provide feedback to the learners, which is available for learners as an additional function in solarSYDUS. Assessment is seen in the meaning of intelligent measurement and advice (Bunderson, Inouye, & Olsen, 1993).

The data are available immediately during a simulation run and can be analyzed to find inappropriate patterns of problem-solving behavior (Assessment and Feedback in Figure 10.3). Thus, feedback referring to the activities of a learner could be given with a modified time-event matrix. The matrix could illustrate the behavior of the learner in general and could point out deficient patterns of behavior (e.g., ballistic decisions) to induce self-reflective processes. The effects of this type of feedback can be observed in the behavior of the learner during the follow-up simulation steps. In addition, feedback should improve the performance of the learner. In this way, a link back to the economical perspective within business simulations is drawn.

Exploratory Tests of solarSYDUS

In its current state, the prototype has passed two exploratory tests to ensure stability for a broader audience. Second, the test runs were used to generate real-life data for designing and testing automated algorithms for real-time feedback. The first test run, with students from the University of Mainz/Germany, revealed some technical problems, which were fixed for the second test with 13 apprentices from an enterprise in Mainz, Germany. This test run was organized as a 2-day session with three different tasks each day. Each learner individually had to solve the tasks. Prior knowledge regarding the business concepts integrated in solarSYDUS was little to none. Therefore, the briefing started with a short introduction to the basic business concept of the value chain, the meaning of the symbols used in the structure of the model, and the general handling of solarSYDUS.

The general briefing was followed by a short briefing for the first task, which targeted the exploration of the structure and the underlying rules. Hence, according to the distinction of tasks regarding their goal specificity, this task should contain a nonspecific goal (Burns & Vollmeyer, 2002). The participants were told to identify the important variables of each activity (e.g., inbound logistics or marketing) and how they interact in solarSYDUS. To solve this task, the participants could use the simulation in the first mode; that is, they could simulate the model without individual decisions. The first task lasted about 2 hours. A debriefing followed at the end to explain variables and elements of the structure that remained unclear to the participants.

The second task addressed the ability to control the enterprise with respect to a given goal. Participants were challenged to sustain an increase in sales. Although they had solved the exploration task the day before, achieving this specific goal could involve a large increase in difficulty and thus an increase in cognitive load for learners because of the complexity of the model. Hence, the second task was separated into two parts. Given the goal, participants had to search again to find the important variables and then an appropriate strategy to increase the sales. So, the first part focused on the structure and the rules of the model regarding the goal. In the second part, the learners had to control the model by making their own decisions. The third task had the same structure as the second, but the goal differed. Participants were challenged to increase the profit of their enterprise. Therefore, the costs, that is, the activity "accounting" in solarSYDUS, had to be taken into account as well as the sales, which meant increased difficulty for the learners. The second task took about 2 hours; the third task was accomplished by the participants in about 1 hour. It was observed that most of the participants seemingly became familiar with the simulation, so they needed less time to find information for explaining the actual state of the enterprise and making new decisions. But, the difference also could be explained as an effect of fatigue. To discriminate these two effects, a more detailed analysis of the process-related data is necessary. Some approaches are presented in the next section.

The 2-day session was closed by a debriefing. The core issue was to decontextualize the experience within the business simulation and transfer it to the participants' work environment. Hence, the participants had to identify similarities and dissimilarities of the structure of solarSYDUS and the enterprise where they were doing their apprenticeship.

Exemplary Data Analysis

In this section, some possibilities for assessment and feedback are presented. They are selective and only serve to illustrate the wide range of possibilities for analyzing the process-related data. One orientation is the measurement of managerial competence of Streufert, Pogash, and Piasecki (1988). However, these measurements are related to different experimental conditions; in particular, the simulation model is fixed in its behavior (see "Analysis of the Problem–Solving Activities" on page 205). Hence, these measurements have to be adapted before using them in the context of solarSYDUS.

For assessing the exploration processes, several exploration profiles (e.g., novice and expert profiles) are needed for comparison. These profiles could be derived from the first task, which addresses exploring the structure without individual decision making. One objective of the research with solarSYDUS is to find a measurement to classify the exploration processes.

Although each learner had completed an individual simulation, the initial state of the model (i.e., of each simulation) was identical for all participants. Furthermore, there are only small probabilistic influences on a simulation run, so the automatic decision rules in each simulation produce the same results. Hence, the different simulation runs are comparable. This quasi-experimental condition provides the possibility of comparing the exploration processes of the learner independent of the individual simulation run. Figures 10.4 and 10.5 show the exploration profiles of two participants, A and B, in the first task. Each dot represents one action of a participant in a specific section of the simulation, for example, the request of a report of the activity *Inbound logistics*. The profiles can be analyzed regarding the aspect of a systematic exploration process. The structure of solarSYDUS can be characterized by two main flows: material and financial. An exploration oriented to one of the flows could be interpreted more systematically than an arbitrary "looking around."

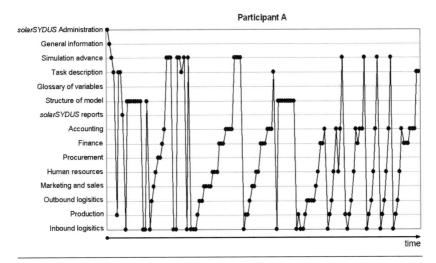

Figure 10.4 Exploration profile of Participant A.

Participant A, for example, started exploring the task description and the structure of the simulation model. After that, the participant explored each activity according to the material flow, from *Inbound logistics* to *Marketing and sales*, and the supporting activities, for example, *Human resources* and *Accounting*. After simulating the model (*Simulation advance*),

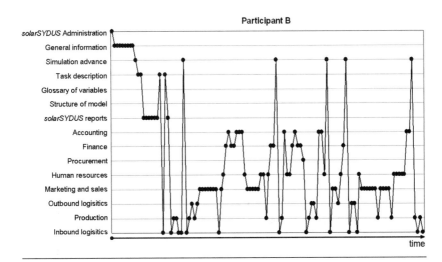

Figure 10.5 Exploration profile of Participant B.

the participant repeated the pattern to see the behavior of the model. This procedure could be described as systematic. But, there are some deficiencies within the exploration process. Participant A only looked once at the global reports of this enterprise and omitted looking at the glossary of variables. Because this is the first task and learners are likely unfamiliar with the model at this point, these functions could be helpful for understanding the structure and hence the behavior of the model. Automatic feedback from solarSYDUS could point out such critical patterns of behavior.

Although Participant A explored systematically, Participant B had a less-structured pattern of behavior. Compared to A, Participant B followed neither the material nor the financial flow. Furthermore, Participant B concentrated action on the activity Marketing and sales. However, this comparative interpretation of behavior is at a qualitative level. To assess and compare profiles, more objective measurements have to be developed. One aspect will be the time dependence of the exploration process. Each learner has an individual speed of exploration that has to be adjusted before the exploration processes can be compared. Furthermore, the figures show that some activities — particularly *Procurement* — are less taken into account than others (e.g., Marketing and sales). That could mean that the breadth of information search is low because the learners do not pay attention to some activities. But, in terms of the whole model of solarSYDUS, the activity Procurement has less meaning and information and fewer reports than Marketing and sales. That means, for qualifying the information search of a learner, the activities in solarSYDUS have to be weighted with their importance relative to the whole enterprise and then by the number of potential actions a learner can do in the specific activity.

Another analysis refers to the time elapsed between actions. Such a measure could be an indication of whether a learner only "clicks through" or processes the presented information because the processing, for example, of a report needs a minimum of time (Winn, 2004). The number of decisions, the elapsed time between decisions, and the number of actions between two decisions could be an indicator of the structuring of the decision-making process. According to Dörner and coauthors (Dörner, Kreuzig, Reither, & Stäudel, 1983), experts in a problem domain will make more decisions than novices. Further, the decisions of experts are attuned to one another and are made as a sequence after an exploration process. Figure 10.6 shows a cutout of such a profile of a participant who solved the task of increasing the profit very well. The figure only shows the actions taken and not the time elapsed between two actions.

In the second task, the learners are able to make individual decisions. The decisions are represented by the bigger, unfilled circles in the profile. The participant first explored the status of his or her enterprise by analyzing

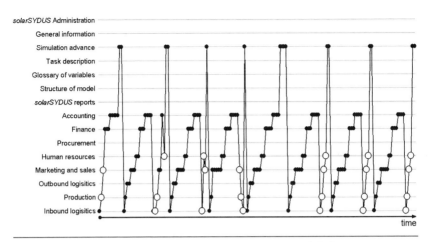

Figure 10.6 Exploration and decision making of a participant in solarSYDUS.

the different reports and then made decisions and advanced the simulation. This pattern repeats several times. Furthermore, the participant explored the consequences of this decision systematically by following the material flow from Inbound logistics to Marketing and sales, and after that, the participant explored the development in the supporting activities (e.g., Accounting). The participant made decisions in all relevant activities but *Finance*, which is in the activities Inbound logistics, *Production*, Marketing and sales, and Human resources. However, the learner did not explore the more holistic reports of *solarSYDUS*, the structure of the model, the glossary of the variables, and the activity Procurement. Because the profile is from the second task, it could be assumed that the learner had become familiar with the structure and the variables; in addition, the activity Procurement is less important than the others. But, the omission of the global reports could be a subject of feedback.

Another pattern of decision making is described as ballistic decisions: Decisions are made, but the consequences are not taken into account. In the context of business simulations, this would mean that the corresponding reports related to a decision are not reviewed after the simulation is advanced one time step. Because the activity of the learner is available immediately in the database, this basic pattern of inappropriate behavior could be identified and returned as feedback to the learner during the simulation.

The database in solarSYDUS stores the simulation data and the data about the related activities of the learner. That enables a more detailed analysis of the actions taken to deal with critical states of the enterprises, such as a lingering loss (cp. Streufert et al., 1988). This could provide insight into how systematically the learner solves such a problem.

This chapter intended to show a variety of possibilities for assessing the problem-solving behavior of the learners in a business simulation only. The target is the development of a measurement to assess problem-solving behavior to give feedback in cases of critical patterns of behavior. At the current state, the analysis is still at an exploratory level to find ways to adapt existing measurements and develop new measurements in the context of Web-based business simulations.

Perspectives

With the use of Web-based business simulation in tandem with a database server, a combination of the traditional measurement of success within business simulations and the measurement of problem-solving behavior becomes possible. This approach can provide more individual feedback to participants within business simulations combining the problem-solving learning processes and outcomes. Therefore, the approach of embedding a huge simulation model within a Web-based learning environment could enhance considerably the potentials of learning with models. Because business simulations represent a complex environment with many interconnected variables, novices could be overextended by this complexity because of the lack of an appropriate structure in their cognitive system to handle the complexity. The additional instructional support could help to reduce the risk of cognitive overload caused by presenting different tasks that reflect different grades of complexity and goal specificity. This ensures that learning processes can take place and that feedback could be regarded as a support for learners' problem solving and not as a source of additional and overextending cognitive load.

Furthermore, the described concept of real-time feedback not only refers to the outcome of the problem-solving process but also takes into account the process itself. This concept augments the traditional (summative) assessment of problem-solving behavior at the end of a simulation with a formative assessment during a simulation. The combination of both behavior and performance analysis could provide more detailed insight into learning processes with simulation models. Because the described concept of real-time feedback refers to problem-solving behavior by identifying inappropriate patterns, it could be applied not only to business simulations but also to simulations in general to train problem-solving behavior within a specific domain represented by the specific simulation model. Therefore, the realization of appropriate algorithms for real-time feedback is the major focus of the ongoing research with solarSYDUS.

Although Web-based business simulations could contain instructional support designed to foster self-directed learning, the business simulation solarSYDUS is still integrated in a classroom context. There are two reasons for this: First, it ensures control over the experimental conditions; second, especially for the debriefing phase, there are additional instructional methods necessary to foster transfer of the principles learned in the simulation. However, the feedback methods could also improve the debriefing phase by providing a differentiated view of the individual learning processes.

The technical concept of the prototype solarSYDUS was tested successfully by students and apprentices. The first look at the data generated for the processes and at participant feedback based on a questionnaire supported the chosen technical approach. The next step will be to analyze the data automatically to find patterns of inappropriate actions in exploration and decision-making behavior and likewise to analyze the effects on learning processes of giving comprehensive feedback to support the learner's problem-solving processes. Therefore, specific measures of aspects of behavior like goal orientation or breadth of information search have to be developed. It is expected that such feedback could improve the performance of learners within business simulations and would be the main aspect of further experiments with the business simulation solarSYDUS.

References

Alessi, S. (2000). Designing educational support in system-dynamics-based interactive learning environments. *Simulation and Gaming, 31*, 178–196.

Berendes, K. (2002). *Lenkungskompetenz in komplexen ökonomischen Systemen*. Wiesbaden: Gabler.

Breuer, K., Molkenthin, R., & Tennyson, R. D. (2006). Role of simulation in Web-based learning. In H. F. O'Neil & R. Perez (Eds.), *Web-based learning: Theory, research, and practice* (pp. 307–326). Mahwah, NJ: Erlbaum.

Breuer, K., & Satish, U. (2003). Emergency management simulations — An approach to the assessment of decision-making processes in complex dynamic crisis environments. In J. J. Gonzaléz (Ed.), *From modeling to managing security — A system dynamics approach* (pp. 145–156). Kristiansand: Norwegian Academic Press.

Breuer, K., & Streufert, S. (1995). Strategic management simulations: The German case. In M. Mulder, W. J. Nijhoff & R. O. Brinkerhoff (Eds.), *Corporate training for effective performance* (pp. 195–208). Norwell, MA: Kluwer Academic.

Bunderson, V. C., Inouye, D. K., & Olsen, J. B. (1993). The four generations of computerized educational measurement. In R. L. Linn (Ed.), *Educational measurement* (Vol. 2, pp. 367–407). Phoenix, AZ: Oryx Press.

Burns, B. D., & Vollmeyer, R. (2002). Goal specificity effects on hypothesis testing in problem solving. *The Quarterly Journal of Experimental Psychology, 55A*, 241–261.

Capaul, R. (2001). *Die Planspielmethode in der Schulleiterausbildung: Theoretische Grundlagen — Praktische Anwendungen*. Bad Heilbrunn/Obb., Germany: Klinkhardt.

Dörner, D. (1976). *Problemlösen als Informationsverarbeitung*. Stuttgart, Germany: Kohlhammer.

Dörner, D. (1989). *Die Logik des Misslingens. Strategisches Denken in komplexen Situationen*. Reinbeck, Germany: Rowohlt.

Dörner, D., Kreuzig, W. H., Reither, F., & Stäudel, T. (Eds.). (1983). *Lohhausen: vom Umgang mit Unbestimmtheit und Komplexität*. Bern, Switzerland: Hans Huber.

Dörner, D., & Wearing, A. J. (1995). Complex problem solving: Towards a theory. In P. A. Frensch & J. Funke (Eds.), *Complex problem solving: The European perspective* (pp. 65–99). Hillsdale, NJ: Erlbaum.

Forrester, J. W. (1968). *Principles of systems*. Cambridge, MA: Wright-Allen.

Hasselmann, D. (1993). *Computersimulierte komplexe Problemstellungen in der Management-Diagnostik: Die Theorie zum Konzept Herausforderung Komplexität*. Hamburg, Germany: Windmühle Verlag.

Hillen, S. (2004). *Systemdynamische Modellbildung und Simulation im kaufmännischen Unterricht* (Vol. 10). Frankfurt/M.: Peter Lang Verlag.

Kaplan, R. S., & Norton, D. P. (1997). *Balanced scorecard: Strategien erfolgreich umsetzen*. Stuttgart, Germany: Schäffer-Pöschel.

Kirschner, P. A. (2002). Cognitive load theory: Implications of cognitive load theory on the design of learning. *Learning and Instruction, 12*, 1–10.

Kröner, S., Plass, J. L., & Leutner, D. (2005). Intelligence assessment with computer simulations. *Intelligence, 33*, 347–368.

Lainema, T., & Nurmi, S. (2006). Applying an authentic, dynamic learning environment in real world business. *Computers and Education, 47*, 94–115.

Leutner, D. (1992). *Adaptive Lehrsysteme: Instruktionspsychologische Grundlagen und experimentelle Analysen*. Weinheim, Germany: Psychologie-Verlags-Union.

Leutner, D. (1997). Adaptivität und Adaptiertheit multimedialer Lehr- und Informationssysteme. In L. Issing & P. Klimsa (Eds.), *Information und Lernen mit Multimedia* (2 ed., pp. 139–149). Weinheim, Germany: Beltz Psychologie Verlags Union.

Mandl, H., Keller, C., Reiserer, M., & Geier, B. (Eds.). (2001). *Planspiele im Internet: Konzepte und Praxisbeispiele für den Einsatz in der Aus- und Weiterbildung* (Vol. 26). Bielefeld, Germany: Bertelsmann.

O'Neil, H. F. (2002). Perspectives on computer-based assessment of problem solving. *Computers in Human Behavior, 18*, 605–607.

Porter, M. (1985). *Competitive advantage*. New York: Free Press.

Stark, R., Gruber, H., & Mandl, H. (1998). Instructional effects in complex learning: Do objective and Subjective learning outcomes converge? *Learning and Instruction, 8*, 117–129.

Sterman, J. D. (2000). *Business dynamics: System thinking and modeling for a complex world*. Boston: McGraw Hill.

Streufert, S., Pogash, R., & Piasecki, M. (1988). Simulation-based assessment of managerial competence: Reliability and validity. *Personnel Psychology, 41*, 537–557.

Streufert, S., & Swezey, R. (1986). *Complexity, managers and organizations.* London: Academic Press.

Tennyson, R. D., & Breuer, K. (2002). Improving problem solving and creativity through use of complex-dynamic simulations. *Computers in Human Behavior, 18,* 650–668.

Vollmeyer, R., Burns, B. D., & Holyoak, K. J. (1996). The impact of goal specificity and systematicity of strategies on the acquisition of problem structure. *Cognitive Science, 20,* 75–100.

Winn, W. D. (2004, April). *The dynamics of learning in artificial environments.* Paper presented at the AERA 2004 annual meeting, San Diego, CA.

11

Use of Visualization Techniques to Improve High-Stakes Problem Solving

WALLACE H. WULFECK

*Space and Naval Warfare Systems Center, San Diego, California,
and Office of Naval Research, Arlington, Virginia*

SANDRA K. WETZEL-SMITH

*Space and Naval Warfare Systems Center, San Diego, California, and Naval
Mine and Antisubmarine Warfare Command, San Diego, California*

Visualization technologies (methods to depict or portray objects or events that are normally observed visually) have been used to investigate difficult tactical, design, and analytic problems for many thousands of years (Bennett, 2001), probably since the beginning of human history. For example, the Lascaux cave paintings in southern France, over 17,000 years old, apparently document hunting techniques. Floor plan drawings and miniature models have been essential for architecture for thousands of years, and the use of mechanical and engineering drawings to describe devices exploded during the industrial revolution. During the last century, the advent of motion picture technologies extended visual depiction into the temporal dimension, and the advent of medical illustration led to improved medical training (cf. Netter, 1990). Methods of scientific visualization have been developed to represent scientific data in graphical or pictorial form. Since about 1960, computer modeling, database, and graphics technologies have enabled a new revolution in the use of visualization that has affected every field of study in science, engineering, medicine, the arts, politics, the military, communications, education, and entertainment.

Visualization techniques are powerful because the human visual-perceptual system is much more than just a biological camera; it has an extraordinary capability to organize and find meaning in the world (Kosslyn, 1994). That is, visual perceptual processes actively construct interpretations of scenes, and they draw on knowledge and experience to make raw visual information comprehensible and meaningful. Carefully designed visualizations therefore can help people understand complex situations and can aid them in analyzing and solving difficult problems. But, this power is a two-edged sword because, conversely, poorly designed visualizations (or intentional illusions) abuse this active construction to mislead, and highly vivid visualizations may actually lead to incorrect recall (Gonsalves et al., 2004).

Since 1990, our research group at the Space and Naval Warfare Systems Center in San Diego, California, and our colleagues at the Naval Surface Warfare Center, Carderock Division (NSWC-CD) in West Bethesda, Maryland, have been applying scientific visualization technologies to provide performance support and training for the incredibly complex tasks involved in naval antisubmarine warfare (ASW). Our effort, called interactive multisensor analysis training (IMAT), has focused on all levels of instruction and performance aiding, from initial apprentice training in formal schools, to team training at sea, to command and staff training for coordinated ASW among multiple ships, to real-world use during at-sea exercises and operations.

In ASW, the main tasks are to search for, locate, identify, and if necessary confront or even attack possible opposing submarines while avoiding counterdetection (detection of own ship by the opposer) or counterattack — clearly "high-stakes" problem solving (O'Neil, 1999, 2002). To do these tasks, teams of people on multiple ships and aircraft choose, configure, place, operate, coordinate, and collect the data from a variety of sensors. They interpret, understand, and determine the tactical implications of this sensor data so they can plan and execute operations to maintain tactical control of the ocean, meaning the ability to conduct operations unrestricted by any threat of attack by an unknown or undetected opposer. Their sensors are typically transducers that capture acoustic energy emitted or reflected from underwater objects and shaped by passage through the undersea environment. (Electromagnetic and electro-optical systems are also used but are outside the scope of this chapter.) The emissions or reflections can vary according to the construction, operating mode, speed, depth, and relative position of the opposing submarine. These variations manifest as temporal changes in frequency, amplitude, and direction of the received energy. To make matters more complicated, the intervening environment affects transmission of the energy from source to sensor depending on ambient or other interfering noise that affects signal-to-noise ratio, ocean terrain absorption and reflection, reverberation, and refractivity of the medium. Refractivity in turn varies nonlinearly with depth due to variation in temperature, pressure, and salinity (the amount of dissolved salts in the water that varies near currents, freshwater outflows, or ice packs). Finally, raw sensor data are manipulated by sophisticated processing systems and displayed in various ways to help detection, classification, and determination of the opposer's position and motion. In addition, actions of our own ships and aircraft can complicate the problem. For example, searching at too slow a speed reduces the efficiency of detection, and going too fast can generate noise that interferes with our own sensors.

All of these factors interact to make ASW incredibly complicated: At all levels from individual sensor operator to senior commander, mission success depends on correctly anticipating the relative merits of position, speed, maneuver, and sensor/weapon employment for each platform in the battle force against the possible range of threat options, within highly variable environmental conditions, in a rapidly changing combat situation in which intelligent opponents try to avoid detection, confuse identification, and gain tactical advantage. All of this is done at the same time as other mission operations, such as air strike or missile defense, which may also have great importance to battle force survival.

Incredibly Complex Tasks

Complex tasks like those involved in ASW are known to be difficult to perform and to learn. For example, Piaget long ago noted that tasks that require coordinating more than one dimension of variation are not learned until late in the school years, if at all (Inhelder & Piaget, 1958). In the early 1970s, the state of Massachusetts noted that many people have difficulty in comparing differently priced and sized portions of products to determine best overall price (a relatively simple two-dimensional task) and imposed a law requiring the price per unit to be posted for most containers. This has the effect of reducing the dimensionality of the problem-space down to one — a comparison among unit prices — and makes the comparison task much simpler. Since then, many other jurisdictions have developed similar statutes.

We use the term *incredibly complex tasks* intentionally, in the sense that such tasks are almost unbelievably complicated. Many people (unfortunately, including many human performance specialists) who are not familiar with extremely complicated tasks do not understand or appreciate this complexity and often apparently believe that task performance can be understood without years of highly contextualized study and experience.

Paul Feltovich and his colleagues (e.g., Feltovich, Spiro, & Coulson, 1991; Feltovich, Hoffman, Woods, & Roesler, 2004) have described several features of tasks or problems that make them difficult. We have added additional criteria in the list below:

Abstract (vs. concrete): In abstract problems, physical phenomena are invisible, and the underlying cause-and-effect relationships cannot be observed. Examples include the propagation of sound in water or the patterns of sensitivity of an acoustic sensor. One reason that abstraction contributes to problem difficulty is that the perceptual/memory system becomes overloaded. The human perceptual system can only hold about four perceptual units in mind (Kosslyn, 1994).

Multivariate (vs. univariate): In multivariate problems, multiple underlying causes can affect an outcome. For example, as noted, the refraction of sound in water results from variations among salinity, pressure, and temperature with depth. Multivariable problems are more difficult because they increase the cognitive load involved in dealing with the problem (Sweller, 2002).

Interactive (vs. separable or additive): Underlying causes may interact with each other, with outcomes dependent on the interaction of variables in addition to each variable acting separately. More generally, the difficulty of problems increases as the dimensionality of salient interactions increases, until people are simply unable to perform them. Halford, Baker, McCredden, and Bain (2005) showed that performance on five-way interactions is essentially at chance level, and that a "four-way interaction is difficult even for experienced adults to process without external aids." (p. 75)

Continuous (vs. discrete): The dimensions of variation are continuous. For example, speed, pressure, and temperature are all continuous variables. Rather than merely memorizing discrete state changes, the learner must understand the effects of continuous change. Both perceptual processes (Massaro & Cowan, 1993) and problem-solving methods (cf. Young, 1992) are qualitatively different for discrete versus continuous problems.

Nonlinear (vs. linear): In nonlinear problems, the relationship of outcome to an underlying dimension is not a simple straight-line function; rather, relationships may be exponential, logarithmic, or even more complex. For example, energy loss in propagation often involves an inverse-square relationship. In general, even mathematically sophisticated people find nonlinear problems more difficult (Kling, 2003)

Dynamic (vs. static): In dynamic problems, the process of variation itself is the subject of analysis, rather than end or intermediate states. A few frozen moments in time are not sufficient to characterize the underlying variation. Another distinction is sometimes made: whether the problem state changes only when there is intervention by the participant versus continual changes in state (Quesada, Kintsch, & Gomez, 2005).

Simultaneous (vs. sequential): Outcomes vary continuously with changes in underlying variables rather than as a succession of states. Quesada et al. (2005) referred to this distinction as "continuous time versus discrete time."

Conditional (vs. universal): Relationships among variables and outcomes may depend on particular boundary conditions or other contextual events. There may be exceptions to general rules, or principles may apply only in certain circumstances and not in others. Reasoning and problem solving under these circumstances require an additional cognitive skill, namely, the capability to reason about alternative conditions or to "mentally undo reality" (Byrne, 2002).

Uncertain (vs. certain): Exact values of underlying variables may not be known precisely. They are subject to measurement imprecision, and some values may be interpolations, estimates, or approximations. These may create risks or opportunities that may require mitigation or exploitation (McManus & Hastings, 2005). A related distinction is stochastic versus deterministic, by which outcomes only sometimes occur when a particular set of conditions is met (Quesada et al., 2005).

Ambiguous (vs. unique): The same combination of circumstances may result in multiple outcomes, or the same outcome may be the result of different combinations of circumstances. For example, in spatial reasoning, the number of alternative mental models that people must keep in mind affects the difficulty of thinking about spatial relationships (Byrne, 1998).

ASW tasks involve all of these attributes. For example, understanding whether detection might occur involves (a) the interaction of the target's radiated signals (which vary in three spatial dimensions around the target by frequency by time); (b) the intervening environment, which may distort or differentially enhance or attenuate signals at particular frequencies; and (c) detectability of signals by a particular shipboard sensor (with directional sensitivity, which also varies in frequency and in three spatial dimensions). This problem is further complicated by (d) radiated noise variation with target speed and depth; (e) own-ship motion effects on directional frequency response of sensors; (f) relative motion between target and sensor; and (g) multipath interactions. There are multiple dimensions of variability. Some are continuous and nonlinear, and others are discrete. Most are interactive. The situation can be highly dynamic, with uncertainty and ambiguity throughout the ASW problem space.

Model-Based Visualization

IMAT takes advantage of decades of development in a large number of university and Navy research laboratories to build computational physics-based models of the sources, sensors, and environment. Additional agencies collect environmental measurements of the variations in physical properties that affect energy propagation and organize them into worldwide databases. These include radiated noise models (computer simulations of the noise produced by, e.g., rotating machinery) and databases that describe characteristics of sound sources; oceanographic models and databases that provide high-resolution bathymetric (depth measurements describing the topography of the ocean bottom) and bathythermographic (variation in water temperature with depth) information, ambient noise, bottom composition, meteorological, and other physical effects on propagation; and sensor performance models of the frequency and direction sensitivity of mobile arrays of sensors. In general, IMAT provides visualization tools that allow the operational and tactical implications of interrelationships among all these interactive variables to become observable rather than invisible. We also build these tools into at-sea performance aids, simulation systems and trainers, as well as training curricula.

Figure 11.1 shows a view from IMAT's interactive modeling facility for transmission loss in the ocean environment. This allows a visual exploration of sound propagation paths caused by reflection and refraction. The top left of the figure gives a loss scale in decibels (a measure of relative power commonly used in engineering), which is color coded (here grayscale coded) for the amount of loss. A sound speed profile (SSP) is displayed on the left of the display. (Sound speed is inversely related to refractivity; as noted, it is a function of pressure, temperature, and salinity variation with depth.) The bottom type, SSP, and bottom contour data can be manually entered or extracted from high-resolution databases. The top right panel shows an example full-field plot of energy loss (using the color code from the top left), with the bottom panel showing transmission loss over range at the sensor depth indicated by the white horizontal line in the top panel. The user can simply drag the depth line to update the transmission loss plot. All the factors that affect transmission loss, such as spreading, absorption by the bottom, and scattering at the bottom and surface, are modeled and contribute to the interactive displays. In this example, it is easy to see several different ways that acoustic energy may propagate from a source, including direct spreading, bottom bounce, and refraction.

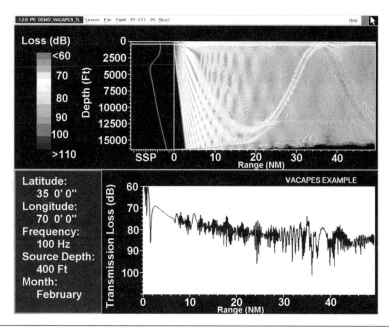

Figure 11.1 Interactive modeling for transmission loss.

IMAT includes extensive range-dependent propagation loss models and databases of environmental data (such as sound speed or bottom absorption) approved by the Oceanographer of the Navy. The term *vacapes* in the figure refers to an area of the ocean off the coast of the Virginia capes corresponding to the latitude and longitude shown. With these modules, a user can select any geographic location and time of year; extract, view, enter, or modify environmental data; specify source and target depths and frequency of interest; and then investigate propagation loss as a function of depth, distance, and azimuth from either a sensor or a sound source.

Early in training, this interactive modeling facility is used by expert instructors to explain the concepts and principles involved. Later, it is used by students in structured exercises in which they learn to make predictions about the likelihood of energy reception under various circumstances. At sea, this facility is used during exercises and operations to plan sensor employment, to monitor environmental circumstances and tactical events, and for later diagnostic analysis to reconstruct what happened and derive lessons learned.

Figure 11.2 shows a screen capture from a series of prediction problems on target motion analysis (TMA) developed for the IMAT program by our colleague Eleanor Holmes. TMA is the process of determining the distance (or range), course, and speed of an opposing ship. TMA is not

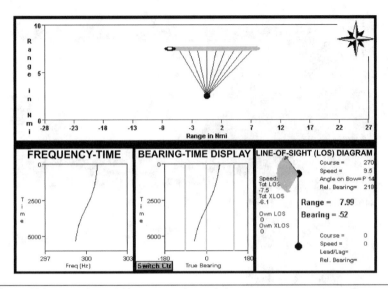

Figure 11.2 Interactive model for target motion analysis.

particularly difficult when used with radar or active sonar because those systems provide range information. But, passive TMA, using only bearing and frequency information (i.e., direction of arrival of a signal from another ship to a sensor and Doppler shift in frequency caused by relative motion) can be extremely difficult.

Visual solutions to the problem of estimating range using bearings-only TMA together with own-ship maneuvering were invented in the early 1950s (Andrews, 1999). (Interestingly, one of the developers of the early technique was Lieutenant Junior Grade Jimmy Carter, later the 39th president of the United States.) These involved plots on navigation charts and overlay templates to help calculations. Although these graphical solution methods are slow by today's standards if done manually, they offer adequate accuracy under some conditions (Nardone & Graham, 1997). They are still taught because it is necessary for practitioners to understand the underlying processes to appreciate the capabilities and limitations of more modern computer-based visualization tools for TMA. Space does not permit a full explanation of the TMA problem, but the interested reader is referred to an unclassified manual for TMA (Naval Education and Training Command, 2004) that includes a detailed description of the graphical techniques involved.

Figure 11.2 shows examples of frequency-time and bearing-time plots and a line-of-sight diagram for predetermined or user-supplied sensor and target behavior. This animated display allows the user to observe the effect of real-world target-sensor relationships on their operational displays. These part-task exercises are intended to build users' understanding of the underlying variables (rate of change of bearing and variation in frequency caused by Doppler effects of relative motion).

The TMA analysis facility can also be run in a "gaming" mode (cf. Figure 11.3). Here, students are asked to correlate target and sensor behavior with one or more of the operational displays used in TMA. In Figure 11.3, a bearing-versus-time display (as appears on some sonar systems) is given in the bottom center. The two top panels represent a geographic view that may or may not correspond to the bearing-time display. The student is asked to judge as quickly as possible whether either of the geographic views, or neither or both, could match the bottom display. During each game, a detailed history of all "player" decisions is kept for diagnostic analysis and review feedback at the end.

Transmission loss and TMA, as difficult as they are, are merely a few of the more fundamental topics in ASW. The concepts and techniques must be well understood and continuously integrated with new knowledge in context before a learner is likely to be successful in real-world ASW. As in many other domains, it is unlikely that a learner will discover the underlying concepts and principles of ASW no matter how rich the practice environment. Further evidence (if any more is needed after hundreds of studies since 1995) that discovery learning is usually inferior to direct instruction was given by Mayer (2004) and Klahr and Nigam (2004).

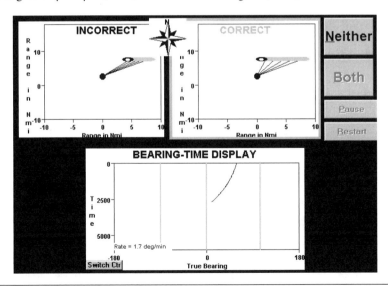

Figure 11.3 The target motion analysis game.

For this reason, and because prior knowledge is so important in the acquisition of new knowledge (Shapiro, 2004; Tobias, 1994), the IMAT program seeks to build on prior knowledge in carefully structured and sequenced problem-solving training in the context of application. According to Shapiro (2004), "In sum, decades of research on prior knowledge effects have made clear that existing knowledge provides an important foundation for new knowledge, and that the level of existing knowledge largely determines the degree to which new knowledge is learned." (p. 166) Just as important, Shapiro also notes that it can be more difficult to acquire knowledge when it conflicts with incorrect prior learning.

Figure 11.4 shows a display from the active acoustic analysis adjunct for IMAT (A4I) developed by the Applied Research Laboratories, University of Texas at Austin. In the left panel (which is too small to read in this printed version), information is provided on the important variables that affect the current problem, such as system setup, and the position, course, and speed for both our own ship and for any contact of interest. The main part of the display provides real-time visualization of moving contacts in a spatial context. It also provides click-through access to overlaid displays such as bathymetry (shown in this case as constant depth curves, like elevation curves on topographic maps) and to other analysis displays. The bottom right corner shows an animated "ping history" display (an animation showing the results of several active sonar events over time) that helps users visualize dynamic change to improve detection and classification.

A4I instruction is provided to journey-level sonar personnel who are already trained and qualified as sonar operators and who have at-sea experience. A4I instruction uses the same process and methods used in earlier IMAT at-sea training research. Interactive laboratory training is given on the operation and employment of active sonar systems, then instructors work at sea during fleet exercises to instruct and assist in system employment and interpretation. Data are collected on exercise events and results and are then used in reconstructions and feedback to participants. Pre- and posttests on problem solving in active sonar employment are given.

Evaluating Simulation-Based Approaches to Improving High-Stakes Problem Solving

Earlier studies on the effectiveness of IMAT approaches have consistently shown effects sizes between experimental and control or pretest-posttest groups ranging from 0.84 to 2.0 standard deviation units (Wetzel–Smith, Ellis, Reynolds, & Wulfeck, 1996; Wulfeck, Wetzel-Smith, & Dickieson, 2004). This compares favorably with typical effects sizes on principle

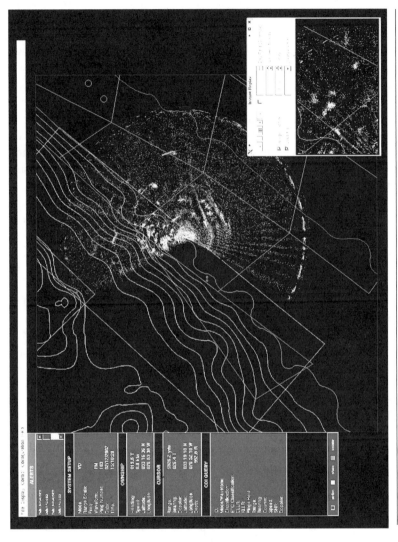

Figure 11.4 Active acoustic analysis adjunct for IMAT (A4I).

and conceptual tasks in problem-based learning of about 0.78 (Gijbels, Dochy, Van den Bossche, & Segers, 2005). In the current A4I study, we have pretest-posttest data on 50 subjects. The effect size is 2.62, and the difference between groups is highly significant (paired $t_{(49)}$ = 15.37, $p < .001$).

There are several ways to evaluate the effectiveness of simulation- and visualization-based training approaches such as those used in IMAT. Kirkpatrick's classic four-level evaluation model (Kirkpatrick, 1998) provides only a partial framework, mainly because it applies mostly to training; performance support systems need special verification and validation. In the U.S. Navy, for example, systems that use computational models and simulations to help make predictions about sensor effectiveness are independently verified by code and algorithm review and are reviewed for proper use of approved databases of input parameters. Computational models are independently validated by comparing their performance on test cases with results obtained from real-world measurements before they can be certified for use as tactical aids. Even for training, simulation-based systems must include all major physical phenomena known to affect sensor/platform performance in real-world operations. Continuing usability studies also are performed with experienced operators and tacticians to provide support through major phases of their tactical tasks and to ensure that training and performance support systems reflect the complexity of real-world operations.

For Kirkpatrick's Level 1, assessing learner reactions to the training, prior studies have shown that IMAT students score significantly higher on attitude scales measuring attention, relevance, confidence, and satisfaction than students in standard Navy classrooms or students in specially designed individualized computer-based training.

As discussed, Level 2 (learning) evaluations show substantial learning gains (Committee on Technology for Future Naval Forces, 1997).

For Kirkpatrick's Level 3 (transfer to real-world performance), IMAT training results in observable improvements in operator and tactician performance during exercises and operations. These show up as improvements in the quality and timeliness of tactical plans and decisions made during tactical execution. Measures include (a) better employment and utilization of sensors, (b) more complete examination of alternative courses of action during planning and execution, and (c) improved availability and processing of information necessary to support planning and execution monitoring.

For Level 4 (organizational results/effectiveness), improved training and performance support systems should result in measurable improvements in military capability. In at-sea observations during exercises and operations, our approach to simulation-based, highly visual, mission-oriented training integrated with the actual systems used to support performance shows (a) increased detection/engagement ranges, (b) increased search rates or area coverage, (c) more rapid localization and classification, (d) reduction in prosecution of false contacts, (e) reduction in counterdetection and counterattack vulnerability, and (f) increased tactical control or advantage. IMAT researchers and training team instructors have provided decision-aiding systems and advanced training to individual ships and to commanders and command staffs for multiplatform ASW. Independent evaluations of performance reveal improvements in all these measures.

A fifth level of evaluation has been termed *return on investment* (Phillips & Stone, 2002). Here, the issue is how the cost of achieving a particular level of performance capability compares with the costs of other approaches to achieving the same level of performance. The appropriate comparison is not only with other training approaches or technologies, but also with hardware improvements to systems or advanced technologies such as automated decision aiding or even completely automated systems. In ASW, IMAT training and performance aiding has been shown to achieve gains equivalent to improvements in sensor performance that cost many times as much (Chatham & Braddock, 2001).

Summary

Visualization technologies are used for training and performance aiding because they greatly aid learning, memory, and performance. In this chapter, we discussed application of visualization to teach the incredibly complex tasks involved in ASW. These tasks are difficult because they are highly dynamic and involve multiple dimensions of variability, discontinuity, nonlinearity, uncertainty, and ambiguity. Our effort on IMAT develops visualization tools based on computational physics-based models and high-resolution oceanographic databases. IMAT aids training and performance by making the operational and tactical implications of interrelationships among interactive variables observable rather than invisible. Results of evaluations show that IMAT training and performance support helps the U.S. Navy achieve important war-fighting capability.

Acknowledgment

The IMAT program is a joint effort of the Space and Naval Warfare Systems Center, San Diego, and the NSWC-CD, supported by several contractor companies. Over 50 people have worked on the IMAT effort, and we particularly thank Bill Beatty and Rich Loeffler (NSWC-CD); Eleanor Holmes (Rite Solutions Inc.); Kent Allen and Jackie Stephens (Anteon Corp.); and Joe Clements (Applied Research Laboratories, University of Texas at Austin) for their contributions to the program. The Capable Manpower

Future Naval Capability program at the Office of Naval Research, Code 34, supports portions of the work described in this chapter. The views and opinions expressed here are those of the authors and should not be construed as official or as reflecting those of the Department of the Navy.

References

Andrews, F. (1999). My view — Submarine development group TWO. Submarine Warfare and tactical development, a look — Past present and future. In B. DeMars (Ed.), *Proceedings of the Submarine Development Group TWO/Submarine Development Squadron TWELVE 50th Anniversary Symposium*. Retrieved May 18, 2007 from http://www.applmath.com/csds50/

Bennett, M. (2001). The crusaders' "Fighting March" revisited. *War in History, 8*, 1–18.

Byrne, R. M. J. (1998). Spatial mental models in counterfactual thinking about what might have been. *Kognitionswissenschaft, 7*, 19–26. Retrieved May 18, 2007 from http://www.tcd.ie/Psychology/Ruth_Byrne/pdf/byrnekognition.pdf

Byrne, R. M. J. (2002). Mental models and counterfactual thoughts about what might have been. *Trends in Cognitive Sciences, 6*, 426–431. Retrieved May 18, 2007 from http://www.tcd.ie/Psychology/Ruth_Byrne/pdf/byrneTICS2002.pdf

Chatham, R., & Braddock, J. (2001). *Training superiority and training surprise* (Report of the Defense Science Board Task Force). Washington DC: Defense Science Board. Retrieved May 18, 2007 from http://www.dtic.mil/ndia/2001testing/chatham.pdf

Feltovich, P. J., Spiro, R. J., & Coulson, R. L. (1991). *Learning, teaching, and testing for complex conceptual understanding* (Conceptual Knowledge Research Project Technical Report No. 6). Springfield: Southern Illinois University School of Medicine. Also published in N. Frederiksen, R. J. Mislevey, & I. I. Bejar (Eds.), *Test theory for a new generation of tests* (pp. 181–217). Hillsdale, NJ: Erlbaum.

Feltovich, P. J., Hoffman, R. R., Woods, D. R., & Roesler, A. (2004). Keeping it too simple: How the reductive tendency affects cognitive engineering. *IEEE Intelligent Systems*, 90–94. Retrieved May 18, 2007 from http://www.ihmc.us/research/projects/EssaysOnHCC/ReductiveExplanation.pdf

Gijbels, D., Dochy, F., Van den Bossche, P., & Segers, M. (2005). Effects of problem-based learning: A meta-analysis from the angle of assessment. *Review of Educational Research, 75*, 27–61.

Gonsalves, B., Reber, P. J., Gitelman, D. R., Parrish, T. B., Mesulam, M., & Paler, K. A. (2004). Neural evidence that vivid imagining can lead to false remembering. *Psychological Science, 15*, 655–660.

Halford, G. S., Baker, R., McCredden, J. E., & Bain, J. D. (2005). How many variables can humans process? *Psychological Science, 16*, 70–76.

Inhelder, B., & Piaget, J. (1958). *The growth of logical thinking from childhood to adolescence*. New York: Norton.

Kirkpatrick, D. L. (1998). *Evaluating training programs*. San Francisco: Berrett-Koehler.

Klahr, D., & Nigam, M. (2004). The equivalence of learning paths in early science instruction. *Psychological Science, 15,* 661–667.

Kling, A. (2003, October 23). Nonlinear thinking. *TCS Daily.* Retrieved May 18, 2007 from http://www.tcsdaily.com/article.aspx?id=102303C

Kosslyn, S. M. (1994). *Elements of graph design.* New York: Freeman.

Massaro, D. W., & Cowan, N. (1993). Information processing models: Microscopes of the mind. *Annual Review of Psychology, 44* [Annual]. Retrieved May 18, 2007 from http://mambo.ucsc.edu/psl/micro.txt

Mayer, R. E. (2004). Should there be a three-strikes rule against pure discovery learning? *American Psychologist, 59,* 14–19.

McManus, H., & Hastings, D. (2005, July 10–15). *A framework for understanding uncertainty and its mitigation and exploitation in complex systems.* Paper presented at the 15th Annual International Symposium of the International Council on Systems Engineering. Retrieved May 18, 2007 from http://web.mit.edu/hmcmanus/Public/INCOSE05noedit.pdf

Nardone S. C., & Graham, M. L. (1997). A closed-form solution to bearings-only target motion analysis. *IEEE Journal of Oceanic Engineering, 22,* 168–178.

National Research Council, Committee on Technology for Future Naval Forces. (1997). *Technology for the United States Navy and Marine Corps, 2000–2035 becoming a 21st-century force: Volume 4: Human resources.* Washington, DC: National Academy Press. Retrieved May 18, 2007 from http://www.nap.edu/catalog/5865.html and http://www.nap.edu/html/tech_21st/hrindex.htm

Naval Education and Training Command. (2004). *Operations Specialist 1* (NAVEDTRA 14308). Pensacola, FL: Naval Education and Training Program Development and Technology Center. Retrieved May 18, 2007 from http://www.globalsecurity.org/military/library/policy/navy/nrtc/14308_ch10.pdf

Netter, F. H. (1990). *The Netter collection of medical illustrations.* Teterboro, NJ: ICON Learning Systems.

O'Neil, H. F., Jr. (1999). Perspectives on computer-based performance assessment of problem solving: Editor's introduction. *Computers in Human Behavior, 15,* 255–268.

O'Neil, H. F., Jr. (2002). Editor's introduction. Perspectives on computer-based assessment of problem solving. *Computers in Human Behavior, 18,* 605–607.

Phillips, J. J., & Stone, R. D. (2002). *How to measure training results.* New York: McGraw-Hill.

Quesada, J., Kintsch, W., & Gomez, E. (2005). Complex problem solving: A field in search of a definition? *Theoretical Issues in Ergonomic Science, 6,* 5–33. Retrieved May 18, 2007 from http://www.andrew.cmu.edu/user/jquesada//pdf/TIESQuesadaKintschGomez2005.pdf

Shapiro, A. M. (2004). How including prior knowledge as a subject variable may change outcomes of learning research. *American Educational Research Journal, 41,* 159–189.

Sweller, J. (2002). Visualization and instructional design. In R. Ploetzner (Ed.), *Proceedings of the International Workshop on Dynamic Visualizations and Learning.* Tübingen, Germany: Knowledge Media Research Center. Retrieved May 18, 2007 from http://www.iwm-kmrc.de/workshops/visualization/sweller.pdf

Tobias, S. (1994). Interest, prior knowledge, and learning. *Review of Educational Research, 64,* 37–54.

Wetzel-Smith, S. K., Ellis, J. A., Reynolds, A. M., & Wulfeck W. H. (1996). *The interactive multisensor analysis training (IMAT) system: An evaluation in operator and tactician training* (Tech. Rep. NPRDC TR 96-3). San Diego, CA: Navy Personnel Research and Development Center.

Wulfeck, W. H., Wetzel-Smith, S. K., and Dickieson, J. L. (2004). *Interactive multisensor analysis training.* Paper presented at the NATO RTO Human Factors and Medicine Panel (HFM) Symposium on Advanced Technologies for Military Training, October 2003, Genoa, Italy. Neuilly-sur-Seine Cedex, France: North Atlantic Treaty Organization Research and Technology Agency.

Young, R. M. (1992). *Calculus, the interplay of the continuous and discrete.* Washington, DC: Mathematical Association of America.

12
Assessing Problem-Solving
Performance in High-Stakes Tasks

ROBERT A. WISHER

U.S. Department of Defense

Military training must ready individuals to enter into harm's way. Each year, the U.S. Department of Defense invests approximately $16 billion to train 1.4 million active duty personnel, and nearly half of this investment is for specialized skill training. This training provides personnel with initial job qualification skills and new or higher levels of skills in military specialties. Training continues in units and during field exercises, enhancing individual and collective performance. Performance for the individual and unit depends on many demanding, high-stake tasks requiring high levels of proficiency (Fletcher & Chatelier, 2000). Training of the underlying facts, concepts, and procedures must ultimately lead to performance that is second nature.

Performance also depends on metacognitive knowledge to understand one's own thinking processes, including "knowing strategies for how to accomplish tasks, knowing about the demands of various tasks, and knowing one's capabilities for accomplishing various tasks" (Mayer, 2002, p. 626). Individuals must be prepared to make decisions, solve problems, and take actions that can have serious consequences. Not all tasks are purely procedural. With a changing threat environment and a shift toward information-rich, net-centric operations, service members must be prepared to think with agility and solve unanticipated problems on the fly (Alberts, Garstka, & Stein, 2000).

This chapter describes an experiment in developing problem-solving skills within a military domain. Specifically, an intelligent tutoring system (ITS) was developed for advanced training of field artillery officers in a crucial planning task for employment of the Multiple Launch Rocket System, hereafter referred to as the rocket system. The task involves creating a solution that proposes where to conceal assets (e.g., ammunition storage), from which points to fire rockets, and how to move within and escape from a 100 square km operations area. Constraining the solution is an operations order that identifies the mission and enemy locations, weather conditions, terrain features, and the need to plan quick exit routes. The training is part of an 18-week career advancement course. The experiment was directed at a culminating exercise at the end of a 2-week block of instruction in which students learned the fundamental doctrine, facts, concepts, and procedures concerning reconnaissance, selection, and occupation of positions. The final exercise is the hands-on development of a plan depicting selection of positions and routes. It is clearly a problem-solving task.

The technical issues in assessing performance in problem solving in this domain concern the development of a performance metric for this particular task, a statistical method for comparing group performance to individual performance, and the effectiveness of an intelligent tutor for coaching individual students during the exercise compared to the practice of having an instructor serve as a coach to a small group during the exercise. Before providing details of the experiment, the framework for problem solving is described, and a quick review of intelligent tutors is presented.

Problem-Solving Framework

The development of a solution for selecting positions and routes follows a common pattern of analysis in the military by dividing the problem solving into seven steps, each with corresponding cognitive processes. The first step is to recognize and define the problem as presented in an operations order. Based on a taxonomy of learning outcomes offered by Anderson et al. (2001), this step involves the process of *understanding*, including classifying elements of the order into categories and interpreting the intent of the order. The second step concerns gathering facts and making assumptions, which depends on the process of *remembering* doctrinal information and enemy capabilities. The third step is to define end states and establish criteria, which involves the process of *analyzing* the overall structure of the solution. Step 4 relates to developing possible solutions, which engages the process of *application*, such as implementing alternative courses of action. Closely related is the fifth step, which is to analyze and compare possible solutions, involving again the process of *application* along with *evaluation*, such as critiquing a proposed route and checking against established criteria. The sixth step is selecting and implementing a solution, which calls on the process of *creation*, or devising the plan and producing the solution. The final step, analyze solution for effectiveness, is performed by an expert, who grades the plan on a set scale.

This analysis is rudimentary and does not capture the deep complexity of the task. (A similar analysis of cognitive processes for learning in after-school computer clubs was offered by Mayer in 2002.) Learner activities such as "mission analyses" force students to process complex information and engage in critical reflection on terrain and weather, enemy forces, facts, assumptions, limitations, implied tasks, and potential changes to the mission. Determining the solution is time sensitive. Several dimensions of problem solving examined here include the influence of prior experience and knowledge on learning in a new situation (Mayer & Wittrock, 1996) and the acts of defining a problem, allocating resources, and tracking progress (Langley, 2006).

Simulation Environment

The exercise of emplacing a rocket system simulates a real environment in which the stakes are high and poor execution can have mortal consequences. The term *simulation* as used here refers to a representation of a real-world phenomenon for the purpose of training, analysis, or experimentation. A simulation does not need to be computer based. Two simulations are examined, one in which a small group of students executes a collaborative plan, under the coaching of a human instructor, on a tabletop representation with miniature objects, described separately. The instructor facilitates problem solving during the small-group training by helping students work through their maneuver plans and other decisions. Students engage in dialogue to create, disclose, and evaluate plans. The second simulation is a computer model of expert behavior, an intelligent tutor, that trains students individually and provides automated coaching as triggered by student actions to the emplacement task.

Intelligent tutoring is a training technology that has matured and is effective if done properly. Fundamental to an intelligent tutor is a body of domain knowledge that is often, but not always, encoded as an expert system of rules (Butz, 2006; Farr & Psotka, 1992). This expertise is imparted to the student, as guided by an instructional strategy, during a problem-solving or other learning exercise. The immediate goal is to have the student construct a mental representation of the domain knowledge — the expert's facts, rules, and procedures — for later application to an unencountered problem.

Origins of Intelligent Tutoring Systems

Early implementations of computer instructional systems presented information in an order that, at best, used simple branching. Academic studies supported learning theories and had reasonable instructional strategies that examined patterns of responses (Atkinson, 1972). However, in ordinary field implementations the learning path was often determined only by a student's previous answer. Student responses during instruction in these simple learning systems were generally regarded as independent events rather than as a pattern reflecting a mental model or a misconception. These practices limit the capability to train skills requiring more complex cognitive processes, such as analysis and synthesis. In many cases, current field implementations continue with the limited analysis of student responses.

The most important aspect of an intelligent tutor is its manner of interaction with learners, teaching or assisting them in processing and understanding complex information (Crowley & Medveda, 2006; Mowlds, Roche, & Mangina, 2005). An ITS can generate and customize hints, help, or problems, in contrast to the fixed feedback of early computer-assisted instruction (CAI) systems. The term *intelligent* refers to the system's algorithmic ability to know what to teach, when to teach it, and how to teach it. It must have the apparent capacity to understand and solve problems posed by the student's imperfect or sometimes-erroneous comprehension of the domain taught.

Evaluations of Early Intelligent Tutoring Systems

SHERLOCK is a computer-based coached practice environment employed by the Air Force to train aviation technicians in a realistic context. A study by Lajoie and Lesgold (1992) compared recent cognitive apprenticeship proposals to coaching via SHERLOCK. The distinction between SHERLOCK and an ITS is that SHERLOCK is not driven by the student model; its focus instead is on responding to student questions rather than active intervention.

Participants consisted of trainees ($N = 63$) at two Air Force bases. The experimental design used a two-group pretest-posttest comparison. The control and experimental groups were considered equivalent because the pretest did not yield any differences. Control group subjects worked on their daily activities in the manual avionics shop; the experimental group spent an average of 20 hours (over 12 days) working with SHERLOCK. Pre- and post-tests were conducted in the form of structured interviews.

Analysis revealed that the two groups were significantly different on several competence factors. The experimental group solved significantly more problems than the control group, with respective means of 30 and 21 [$F(1, N = 62) = 10.29, p < .001$]. The tutored group also displayed significantly more expert-like problem-solving steps than the control group, with respective means of 19.33 and 9.06 [$F(1, 27) = 28.85$, $p < .01$]. The SHERLOCK group also made significantly fewer errors [$F(1, 27) = 7.54$, $p < .01$]. Results demonstrated that subjects who spent 20–25 hours using SHERLOCK were as competent at troubleshooting as technicians with 4 more years of job experience.

Wheeler and Regian (1999) evaluated the effect of the Word Problem Solving (WPS) ITS on the abstract reasoning component of word problem solving. The WPS is an adaptive mathematics tutor. Rather than teaching mathematical calculations, it supplements lecture-style instruction of prealgebra, algebra, and geometry. The WPS contained sample problems, questions, and summaries of the material. It also varied the type of feedback, difficulty level, and number of problems according to the individual skill level of the student.

A sample of ninth-grade students ($N = 632$) was drawn from seven high schools. Students were randomly assigned to one of three groups: a control group ($n = 84$) receiving traditional classroom instruction; a placebo group ($n = 139$) receiving regular instruction except for one session per week with a nonadaptive tutor session; and a treatment group ($n = 409$) receiving classroom instruction, replacing one session per week with the WPS tutor.

All students were administered a pre- and posttest designed to measure each student's ability to solve algebra word problems and to compare abstract and concrete reasoning skills. The average scores on the concrete pretests were 29%, 26%, and 33% for the control, placebo, and treatment groups, respectively, and 51%, 45%, and 65% for the concrete posttest for the same three groups. The average scores on the abstract pretest were 39%, 33%, and 40% and for the posttest 50%, 49%, and 60%, for the same groups, respectively. Differences on the gains were shown to be statistically significant at the .001 level. This study demonstrated that the WPS tutor significantly improved the performance of high school students on both abstract and concrete word problem-solving subtests.

The Intelligent Tutor for Problem Solving

The current experiment involved performance by groups with a conventional "sand table" assisted by instructors compared to performance by individuals assisted by an intelligent tutor. The experiment was conducted during the final 4-hour exercise of a 2-week block on instruction on reconnaissance and positioning. The terminal learning objective of the hands-on exercise is to execute reconnaissance, selection, and occupation of position of a firing platoon operations area and battery headquarters using one form of a simulation along with associated map sheets. The sequence of activities is to receive an operational order, analyze the mission, emplace hiding areas, emplace firing points, establish and move to positions, and organize a battle area. This tracks with the sequence that would be conducted in an actual combat operation. Each step of the sequence involves numerous subactivities, such as ground reconnaissance and movement formations. The cognitive processes that are engaged were described in the section on the problem-solving framework.

The Conventional Approach

The conventional sand table exercise is a low-fidelity technique used to exercise the problem-solving skill during the emplacement task. Soldiers have already completed training on the operation of the rocket system as well as other mission-essential tasks, reload operations, and combat service support needs. The conventional sand table is an actual box of sand about 5 feet high and 4 feet wide resting on a table. Terrain features are molded by hand, and rocket system assets and other cultural features, such as bridges, are portrayed by miniature objects. Such a training device has been used in various forms for centuries.

At the outset, students review the operations order and begin executing the problem-solving steps described. The sand table represents a terrain model of a 100 square km operations area. Students are presented with a unique, unencountered problem. The same problem is presented to all groups. The students discuss proposed plans in a group of five and settle on a consensus plan. The plan is represented as emplacement of miniature objects across the sand table. There are millions of possible combinations for locating different pieces in different positions. Most of the possible combinations on the sand table reflect a poor plan, a few are considered good, and even fewer can be rated excellent. The chances of guessing a good plan are low.

While the group engages in the exercise, an instructor periodically asks the group to explain their logic and offers advice and general guidance. During the process, students consult terrain maps and study the operations order. The students are responsible for the final plan. They have up to 3 hours to complete the task and have an additional hour for the rating and feedback by the instructor, commonly called an *after-action review*. During this time, the final product is rated by an instructor who is well qualified as a subject matter expert. Each member of the group is assigned the same score regardless of how much or how little the member may have contributed. The expert judgments are based on the placement of assets and a description of the routes for movement with considerations for the operations order, terrain features, and doctrinal criteria. One example of a doctrinal criterion is that a hiding area must be at least 500 m from an associated firing point.

Virtual Sand Table

A contract was awarded to Sonalysts Incorporated to develop an intelligent tutor to play the role of the instructor during the exercise. Details of the intelligent tutor, called the Virtual Sand Table (VST), have been reported by Wisher, Macpherson, Abramson, Thornton, and Dees (2001). The rocket system VST is essentially a simulation in which the student's actions are evaluated against a set of expectations that are governed by a set of operational rules. The student receives an operations order in the form of text, graphics, intelligence imagery, and a map display. The task, conditions, and standards are the same for the conventional and VST exercises. The user interface to the VST is presented in Figure 12.1.

The VST provides the ability for the student to define points along reconnaissance routes by pointing the mouse on the two-dimensional map display. The terrain defined by the two-dimensional map is preprocessed for each variable in the mission scenario so that the intelligent tutoring component can rapidly assess the student actions. Preprocessing also determines mobility restrictions, major obstructions, bridge classifications, effective hide areas, and so on. As the student places assets for occupation of position, the simulation component performs calculations of relative equipment positions and line of sight and assesses the student's placement of assets.

The simulation component tracks all of the simulated entities (such as launchers and enemy forces) and their relative positioning with the terrain and each other. The simulation component calculates the line of sight, mobility, and trajectories for the rocket system and other vehicles in real time. The results from the simulation are displayed in the battlefield views and sent to the intelligent tutor component for evaluation.

Two battlefield views are presented to the student: a two-dimensional map and a three-dimensional battlefield terrain view. The two-dimensional map view is used to place assets, plan routes, and mark hide areas and firing points. Figure 12.2 presents the two-dimensional view of one student's partial solution to the problem of emplacing the rocket system in an area of the National Training Center at Fort Irwin, California. The three-dimensional battlefield terrain view is intended for use in the reconnaissance and selection portions of the mission exercise. The student is able to travel through the terrain and observe relevant features and condition indicators from the perspective of riding in a moving vehicle.

The tutoring component is designed to simulate an instructor coaching a student at a conventional sand table. The focus of the coaching is the evaluation of the student's selected positions and routes in accomplishing the problem-solving exercise. Figure 12.3 presents one example of a coaching trigger. Here, the student is advised that a sufficient number of firing points were not included.

Figure 12.1 User interface to Virtual Sand Table (VST).

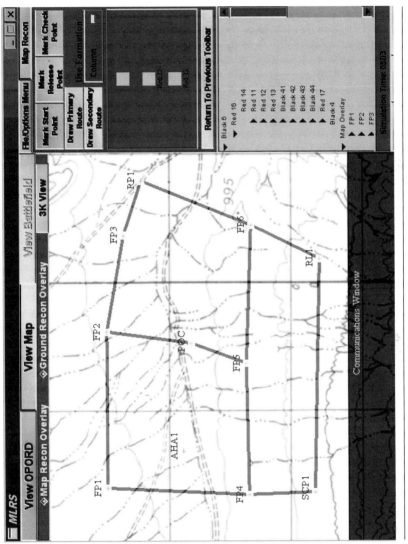

Figure 12.2 Two-dimensional view with one student's solution to the problem of emplacing.

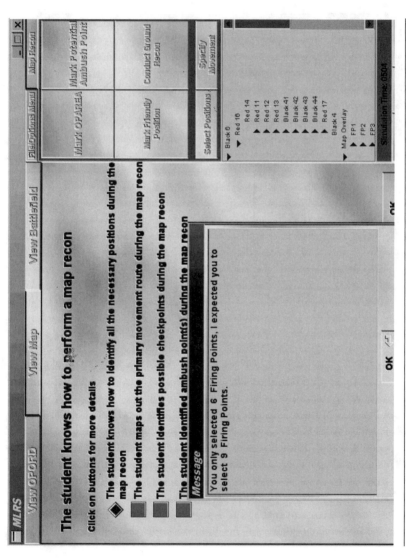

Figure 12.3 Coaching the student during map reconnaissance; the diamond icon identifies the subtask causing the message.

The coaching points are structured to give the student general feedback after the student has performed a certain degree of analysis and application.

Comparison of Effectiveness

The evaluation of the VST was embedded in the normal training schedule for the 18-week career advancement course. The conventional sand table exercise was conducted immediately after students completed the 2-week block related to doctrinal training on the task. Learning outcomes were measured through a hands-on performance test as completed through the sand table or VST exercise.

Participants

Both the VST treatment group (n = 105) and the conventional sand table comparison group (n = 209) were given questionnaires before and after the sand table exercise. For the comparison group, instructors made a point to include in each group at least one soldier who had field experience with a unit equipped with the rocket system (as opposed to experience only with units equipped with cannon). Approximately 20% had such prior knowledge, which could be considered an advantage.

Procedure

For the comparison group, soldiers performed the exercise in groups of five. An operations order was provided, and the group worked together on a solution. Approximately 3 hours were required by the group to complete the plan. Afterward, one student was selected at random (through a drawing of straw lengths) to present the plan. The instructor scored performance on a 10-point scale, with 10 indicating outstanding and 1 indicating poor. Every member of the group was assigned that score. This score served as the learning outcome measure.

For the treatment group, students were directed to a computer laboratory where the VST exercise was installed on a personal computer. The main features of the VST were demonstrated. Also described were the graphical interface procedures for placing rocket assets and marking routes of travel. The students reviewed an operations order displayed on their monitors. They were given 3 hours to complete the exercise. Students worked individually. On completion of the exercise, a copy of the plan (a map showing emplacements and routes) was saved electronically. The same instructor who scored the plans of students in the conventional sand table group applied the same criteria in scoring performance using the same 10-point scale. Scores were recorded individually.

Results

The experimental design for the evaluation was a two-group, posttest design. The results are presented in the following order. First, a comparison of demographic factors between the conventional sand table (comparison) and VST (treatment) groups examines the equivalency between groups as they were not randomly assigned but rather placed into groups based on the particular month they entered the course. Then a description of the technique used to compare the performance scores of the two groups is provided. A statistical test of the performance is presented next. Finally, an effect size is calculated.

Demographic Comparison

The average age of the comparison group was 28.3 years, compared to 28.2 years for the treatment group ($t = 0.34$, ns). Five other comparisons were recorded — rank, branch, rocket experience, cannon experience, and battery experience — but none was statistically significant.

Skill Performance Measure

The comparison group was trained using the conventional sand table approach. The approach consisted of small teams of five students with team assignments that included at least one individual with at least 1 year of rocket experience. Instructor coaching was aperiodic, occurring approximately 15% of the time.

In contrast, the VST acted as a one-on-one tutor, providing hints and informative feedback to the students individually. To compare the VST students with the groups trained with the conventional approach, it was necessary to create post hoc groups of students meeting the specifications for composing the conventional training groups. This in effect would simulate group performance as derived from individual performance scores. The creation of these post hoc groups required the application of resampling theory and procedures (Simon, 1995).

Resampling is one of the Monte Carlo-based computer-intensive statistical techniques. It involves sampling repeatedly, with replacement, from a sample of data. It does not require that the data be drawn from the population at random, but that the sample be representative of the population. The mean of any statistic calculated from the resamples will be the same as that calculated from the data sample. Furthermore, the distribution of the statistic for the resamples themselves will be normal. However, the standard deviation of the statistic will be much narrower. Resampling is different from the usual Monte Carlo approaches in that it employs the original data rather than any summarization of the data.

Of the 105 students who participated in the VST training, 86 were appropriate for analysis. The reasons for exclusion were missing scores for either the rocket experience variable or the performance score. The program Stats.exe

Learning Outcome

Best Fit Normal Curves*

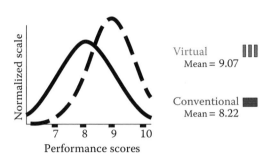

*After Resampling

Figure 12.4 Normalized curves of performance between groups.

from Resampling Stats was used to create 2,000 virtual groups, each with 5 students randomly selected. Each group contained at least 1 student with at least 1 year of rocket experience, thus simulating the basis for group assignment in the conventional training procedure. The highest performance score of each group was then assigned to the group. A critical assumption here is that the group would perform at least as well as the highest-scoring individual. The possible advantages of improvement through group interactions was discounted, and the assumption was considered conservative. These scores were then compared with the group scores from the traditionally trained groups. The results of these are presented in Figure 12.4, in which a best-fit normalized curve was computed for both groups.

Analysis

The null hypothesis, equal performance between groups, was tested using a two-tailed, independent-sample t test. A two-tailed test was employed because there were no preconceptions about an advantage held by either group. Results from our sample indicated that students trained via the VST ($M = 9.07$) significantly outperformed those students trained via the conventional sand table ($M = 8.22$):

$$t = 11.43, \quad p < .001.$$

Effect Size

The computation of effect size is a common method for determining the gain that a particular treatment has over a comparison group. In this particular case, the effect size is the difference of the mean score for the VST group (9.07) and the conventional sand table group (8.22). When this difference is divided by the standard deviation of the conventional group (as a more valid estimate of the population variance when using resampling), the effect size for the VST is 1.05. This translates to a 35% increase in learning (proportion of students surpassing the average performance of the comparison group). The effect size found here is in line with those reported in other studies of intelligent tutors in the military and higher education, which is about 1.0 (Woolf & Regian, 2000).

Final Considerations

The primary conclusion drawn from this experiment is that the VST tutoring system is an effective tool for training soldiers to perform the task for the Multiple Launch Rocket System. The results support the VST as a more effective training program than the conventional sand table. Its service as a coaching device through an intelligent tutor demonstrates how embedded feedback during a problem-solving task can lead to higher performance. This was a case study based on the cost realities and availability of instructors at the field artillery school. Perhaps a full-time, one-on-one instructor for each student in the conventional sand table would have led to superior results. Two secondary implications of implementing the VST are reduced training costs and increased accessibility.

Based on the results reported here, modifications to the VST are under way. The primary modifications consist of enlarging the terrain area and adding capabilities that would allow the role of other command units to appear in the simulation. Some of the additional capabilities would be placing radar units, fire support units, fire direction units, and command post locations on the two-dimensional map. The size of the two-dimensional map would increase from 10 × 10 km to approximately 50 × 50 km allowing for more complex and demanding operation orders. Based on the results of this research, the VST is currently in use as a replacement for the conventional sand table in several courses.

The use of computer technology for teaching and assessing problem solving has been making steady progress. As identified by O'Neil (2002), the present experiment illustrates some benefits of earlier research on hands-on performance assessments. In particular, it demonstrates a possible technique to compare individuals to group performance, comprehensive domain coverage, rapid reporting of results, and the application of intelligent tutoring technology to a problem-solving exercise.

In previous studies of the effectiveness of distance learning media compared to the face-to-face classroom, the "no significant difference" phenomenon (i.e., effect size of 0) has been reported hundreds of times (Russell, 1999). In these studies, the distance learning platform, often video teletraining, replicates the classroom environment. It should come as no surprise, then, that there is not a training advantage for the distance learning media — replicating the classroom replicates the learning outcomes from the classroom. In the present study, the learning conditions of the classroom were not replicated: the training was individualized, feedback during the learning process was customized, the simulation gaming environment was intrinsically motivating, and the training approach was problem based. The large effect size of 1.05 reported here is indicative of the training advantage possible when intelligent tutor technology is applied in a well-designed, learner-centric training environment.

The problem-solving framework presented in this military training domain reflects many of the same cognitive processes identified in educational settings (Mayer, 2002) and video games (O'Neil, Wainess, & Baker, 2005). This should come as no surprise. Learning and memory are the underlying constructs to performance in both educational and training contexts. Understanding content, developing a strategy, and regulating one's mental activities are central to solving a problem in many contexts and for many purposes. The advances in education can be applied to the needs of training and vice versa.

References

Alberts, D. S., Garstka, J. J., & Stein, F. P. (2000). *Network centric warfare: Developing and leveraging information superiority.* Washington, DC: DoD Command and Control Research Program.

Anderson, L. W., Krathwohl, D. R., Airasian, P. W., Cruikshank, K. A., Mayer, R. E., Pintrich, P. R., et al. (2001). *A taxonomy for learning, teaching, and assessing: A revision of Bloom's taxonomy of educational objectives.* New York: Longman.

Atkinson, R. C. (1972). Ingredients for a theory of instruction. *American Psychologist, 27,* 921–931.

Butz, B. (2006). An intelligent tutoring system for circuit analysis. *IEEE Transactions on Education, 49,* 216–223.

Crowley, R. S., & Medveda, O. (2006). An intelligent tutoring system for visual classification problem solving. *Artificial Intelligence in Medicine, 36,* 85–117.

Farr, M. J., & Psotka, J. (Eds.). (1992). *Intelligent instruction by computer: Theory and practice.* Washington, DC: Taylor and Francis.

Fletcher, J. D., & Chatelier, P. R. (2000). Military training. In S. Tobias and J. D. Fletcher (Eds.), *Training and retraining: A handbook for business, industry, government, and the military* (pp. 267–288). New York: Macmillan.

Lajoie, S. P., & Lesgold, A. (1992). Apprenticeship training in the workplace: Computer-coached practice environment as a new form of apprenticeship. In M. J. Farr & J. Psotka (Eds.), *Intelligent instruction by computer: Theory and practice* (pp. 15–36). Washington, DC: Taylor and Francis.

Langley, P. (2006). Cognitive architectures and general intelligent systems. *AI Magazine, 27*(2), 33–44.

Mayer, R. E. (2002). A taxonomy for computer-based assessment of problem solving. *Computers in Human Behavior, 18*, 623–632.

Mayer, R. E., & Wittrock, M. C. (1996). Problem-solving transfer. In D. C. Berliner & R. C. Calfee (Eds.), *Handbook of educational psychology* (pp. 47–62). New York: Simon and Schuster Macmillan.

Mowlds, F., Roche, B., & Mangina, E. (2005). ABITS: Learning more about students through intelligent educational software. *Campus-Wide Information Systems, 22*, 131–139.

O'Neil, H. F. (2002). Perspectives on computer-based assessment of problem solving. *Computers in Human Behavior, 18*, 605–607.

O'Neil, H. F., Wainess, R., & Baker, E. L. (2005). Classification of learning outcomes: Evidence from the computer games literature. *Curriculum Journal, 16*, 455–474.

Russell, T. L. (1999). *The no significant difference phenomenon* (5th ed.). Raleigh, NC: North Carolina State University.

Simon, J. L. (1995). *Resampling: The new statistics.* Arlington, VA: Resampling Stats.

Wheeler, J. L., & Regian, J. W. (1999). The use of a cognitive tutoring system in the improvement of the abstract reasoning component of word problem solving. *Computers in Human Behavior, 15*, 243–254.

Wisher, R. A, Macpherson, D. H., Abramson, L. J., Thornton, D. M., & Dees, J. J. (2001). *The virtual sand table: Intelligent tutoring for field artillery training* (Research Rep. 1768). Alexandria, VA: U.S. Army Research Institute for the Behavioral and Social Sciences.

Woolf, B. P., & Regian, J. W. (2000). Knowledge-based training systems and the engineering of instruction. In S. Tobias and J. Fletcher (Eds.), *Training and retraining: A handbook for business, industry, government, and the military* (pp. 339–356). New York: Macmillan Reference USA.

13

Impact of After-Action Review on Learning in Simulation-Based U.S. Army Training

LARRY L. MELIZA AND STEPHEN L. GOLDBERG

Simulator Systems Research Unit, U.S. Army Research Institute for the Behavioral and Social Sciences

The after-action review (AAR) is a mechanism for providing feedback to military units on their performance of collective tasks. It is an active process that requires unit members to participate to benefit. Much of the work involved in developing and refining the AAR process was accomplished to support the training of U.S. Army units; however, the AAR approach should be relevant to any organization that makes use of collective training methods (e.g., police SWAT [special weapons and tactics] teams). The AAR has been applied to industry (Darling & Parry, 2001) and is under consideration for nonmilitary government applications (Rogers, 2004) as an operational tool.

Simulation-Based Training Environments

U.S. Army units train in live, virtual, constructive, or mixed simulations of battlefield environments. In the live environment, units use operational equipment and actual terrain and perform against an opposition force composed of military personnel (live force on force) or targets (live fire), depending on whether the unit is employing simulated weapon effects or firing live rounds. In virtual environments, units use simulators to represent equipment and weapons. Weapons effects, terrain, and enemy forces are computer generated. In constructive environments, battlefield outcomes (e.g., the unit loses 30% of its personnel) are determined by sophisticated math models to provide battle effects supporting command and staff training. Mixed environments include elements of two or more of the simulation environments. All of these simulation environments are intended to provide individuals with feedback about how their actions contributed to mission success or failure, casualties received, and casualties inflicted on the enemy, the bottom lines of unit performance.

The live and virtual simulation environments available to support training vary greatly from one unit to another. Virtual training environments are available for the Army's mechanized forces. Live simulation training is widely available, but the most highly supported form of live simulation training is generally found at the Army's three maneuver combat training centers (CTCs). CTCs differ from most of the Army's live simulation environments because CTCs provide a cadre of observer/controller/trainers, a dedicated opposing force, instrumented ranges that are capable of collecting position location, firing and status data, and teams of analysts supporting observer/controller/trainers from a data collection and analysis facility. Units will periodically rotate to one of the CTCs for roughly 2 weeks of intensive training.

Intrinsic and Extrinsic Feedback from Realistic Simulations

Collective training exercises can provide intrinsic and extrinsic feedback on soldier and leader performance (Brown, Nordyke, Gerlock, Begley, & Meliza, 1998). *Intrinsic feedback* consists of the cues that exercise participants perceive about their own performance that guide their performance and let them know how well they are performing. For example, a unit may call in artillery fire on a target, observe that artillery rounds are impacting too far from the intended target, and have the supporting artillery unit shift fires. The knowledge of results unit members perceive is intrinsic feedback about how well they are positioned to observe the effects of artillery on the intended target, how well they adjusted fires, and the effectiveness of their actions.

Intrinsic feedback differs as a function of each soldier's job and position on the battlefield. It is also influenced by the fidelity of a specific instance of a simulation environment. If a virtual environment's image generator and display system do not have the resolution to allow observation of artillery rounds out to realistic ranges, then it would not be possible for units to adjust fires as they would in the real world.

There are many events that occur on a battlefield that soldiers and units cannot see because of battlefield obscuration, their position, or what they were doing. Because of the so-called fog of war, when an exercise is over, participants have a limited perspective regarding what happened based on the information available to them and what they saw, heard, and smelled. This limited perspective is referred to as *perceived truth. Ground truth* is the term used to describe the actual situation that occurred. As mentioned, soldiers are often not able to perceive all that is going on around them, so perceived truth is likely to differ from ground truth much of the time. Events may be happening quickly and open to differing interpretations. Perceptions and memories of the occurrence, sequence, and timing of events can be greatly distorted, leading to generation of causal relationships that are not based on the actual facts (Goldberg & Meliza, 1993).

Extrinsic feedback is usually provided by trainers after an exercise ends and is designed to help soldiers and leaders understand the ground truth situation and what caused it. *Extrinsic feedback* consists of information that the exercise participants do not ordinarily have available to them. It can provide insights into how to improve or sustain performance in the future.

A simulation is effective to the extent that exercise participants receive intrinsic feedback regarding their performance, and the actions of individuals can be linked to higher level exercise outcomes. Continuing with the example, if adjusting artillery rounds causes the enemy to sustain casualties, withdraw to another position, or suppress their firing on friendly forces, then the action has had a higher level impact. Sometimes, exercise participants observe the impacts of their actions via intrinsic feedback, but at other times they are not aware of these impacts until they receive extrinsic feedback

Extrinsic Feedback Methods for Collective Training

Formal postexercise feedback sessions are one of the types of extrinsic feedback that can be used to improve unit performance (Brown et al., 1998). Other forms of extrinsic feedback are important because their existence raises issues about the timing and nature of feedback.

Formal Postexercise Feedback Sessions

The AAR is the U.S. Army's doctrinal method for providing extrinsic feedback to units after operational missions or collective training exercises (U.S. Army Combined Arms Center, 1993). The AAR is an interactive discussion guided by a facilitator or trainer known as an AAR leader. During the AAR, unit members discuss what happened, why it happened, and how to improve or sustain performance in similar situations in the future. The AAR includes extrinsic feedback from outside the unit and extrinsic feedback from the sharing of intrinsic feedback among unit member combined with group problem solving (Winquist & Larson, 1998). The AAR process may provide unit members with a view of collective (team, unit, or organizational) performance that was not apparent to, or viewable by, any one participant during an exercise (Meliza, 1999), including trainers who were observing the exercise. The AAR uses a Socratic method in which a series of leading and open-ended questions are used by an AAR leader to help those in the training audience discover what happened and why.

A debriefing or critique conducted by one or more observers of a training exercise is an alternative to the AAR (Hoare, 1996; Scott & Fobes, 1982). The person or persons who provide the critique become the source of ground truth as they see it. They tell the units what they think happened, why they think it happened, and what they think the unit should do about it. Critiques are often taken as criticism by those in training. The opinions expressed may be the undocumented judgments of the person giving the critique. The AAR leader, on the other hand, is someone functioning as a discussion facilitator. Units are expected to discover their performance problems through guided self-evaluation, and they are encouraged to identify possible means of correcting these problems. It is assumed that use of the AAR feedback method results in situations in which units claim ownership of the diagnosis and the corrective actions they identify (Scott & Fobes, 1982).

Other Forms of Extrinsic Feedback

In addition to an AAR, the methods by which extrinsic feedback is provided include coaching and mentoring of key unit leaders during task execution or between exercises and written reviews of unit performance that contain suggestions for specific corrective actions, such as the Take Home Packages prepared by the U.S. Army's maneuver CTCs (Fobes & Meliza, 1989). A Take Home Package describes unit plans, performance strengths, and weaknesses for every mission performed by a unit while it is at a training center. These products describe problems identified through the AAR process or observed by observer/controller/trainers or training analysts that a unit should address when it returns to its home installation.

Automation is enabling some other forms of extrinsic feedback. Software can be used to provide feedback in midexercise in the form of intelligent tutors (Domeshek, 2004) or "during action" review aids (Aiken, Green, Arntz, & Meliza, 2005). These software applications, if used during actual operations to cue and guide performance, become sources of intrinsic feedback. Each of the forms of feedback is likely to explain what happened and why performance problems need to be addressed, but they may differ in terms of whether they provide specific corrective actions or leave it up to units to develop solutions.

Timing and Nature of Feedback

Whether feedback is immediate or delayed has been shown to influence the acquisition and retention of knowledge, skills, and abilities across a wide variety of situations. The impact of the timing of feedback is often influenced by the content of training. For example, the impact of delays in feedback appears to differ between rule-based versus information-integration category learning (Maddox, Ashby, & Bohil, 2003).

Extrinsic feedback regarding unit performance focuses on conceptual knowledge rather than procedural knowledge. Feedback is likely to be more explanatory than directive. The whole process of using interactive discussions to decide what happened, why it happened, and how to improve or sustain performance engenders explanations. Explanatory feedback is superior to directive feedback in terms of conceptual knowledge acquisition (Moreno, 2004). The process a unit goes through in analyzing and identifying its own performance problems and potential corrective actions during an AAR should make this feedback memorable.

Postexercise feedback, by definition, is delayed rather than immediate. It could conceivably be used in conjunction with immediate feedback in the course of an exercise (i.e., through coaching, mentoring, intelligent tutoring, or the application of during-action review aids) so that a unit can take immediate corrective action and perhaps accelerate the training process (Kulik & Kulik, 1988). In the case of collective training, corrective actions in midexercise may help prevent a unit from creating a tactical situation that detracts from the intended training objectives of the exercise. At present, little information is available regarding the integrated use of immediate and delayed feedback to increase the efficiency of collective training, but increasing capabilities for providing immediate feedback to units (i.e., through intelligent tutors and during-action review aids) should increase interest in this research topic.

In relating the AAR process to the feedback literature in general, one should keep in mind that the desired outcomes of unit collective training include conceptual knowledge and defining and implementing solutions to performance problems. A unit may gain a substantial amount of conceptual knowledge from training but not show improved importance in the future unless solutions to performance problems are defined and implemented. A portion of problem solving and solution implementation is likely to take place outside the scope of a formal postexercise feedback session. Opportunities and motivation to design, implement, and refine solutions may be as important as the timing of feedback in determining whether AARs result in improved performance in the future. For example, when a rotation to a CTC is a capstone or culminating event for a unit, there is likely to be a heavy turnover of leadership and soldiers as they return to their home station and move on to assignments in new units as new leaders and soldiers fill the slots they leave behind. In a sense, the unit with training needs that were diagnosed no longer exists (Fobes & Meliza, 1989), and there is a reduced opportunity to implement solutions to performance problems in that unit. However, leaders and soldiers may take the conceptual knowledge they gained at the CTC and use it to assess performance problems and implement solutions in their new units. In this way, many units may benefit from a single unit's rotation to a CTC.

How Realistic Battlefield Simulations Set the Stage for an After-Action Review

The AAR process was first used in actual combat situations to discover what happened by asking questions of those who participated in the action. The process was adapted for training events as the capability to provide realistic simulation of weapons effects occurred during the 1970s and 1980s (Bosley, Onoszko, Knerr, & Sulzen, 1979; Morrison & Meliza, 1999). The AAR was based on the "interview after combat" used in World War II by military historian Samuel Lyman Atwood Marshall and others (Bosley et al., 1979). This interview process requires objective outcomes to function, but in Army collective training exercises, casualty exchanges and mission outcomes were based on the subjective judgments of umpires until the development of tactical engagement simulation (TES) technologies. Such judgments were insufficient to prepare participants for an interview after combat because the participants did not believe that their status as casualties necessarily resulted from their behavior.

TES includes tools and procedures developed in an effort to provide realistic and objective simulation of weapons effects. Perhaps the best-known example of TES is the use of lasers and laser detectors to simulate the effects of line-of-sight weapons, such as rifles and tank main guns. TES opened the door to objective exercise outcomes and application of the AAR as a method for providing extrinsic feedback for training exercises. Field tests demonstrating the effectiveness of early forms of TES, in terms of its impact on unit tactical performance, were actually tests of the combined effectiveness of TES and the AAR process (Banks, Hardy, Scott, Kress, & Word, 1977; Meliza, Scott, &Epstein, 1979; Scott, Meliza, Hardy, Banks, & Word, 1979).

Over time, collective training has included a greater range of battlefield effects than weapons effects. The inclusion of logistics and medical play at the maneuver CTCs allows more soldiers to be trained and to have an impact on exercise outcomes. When soldiers at a CTC become casualties as a result of simulated weapons effects, they are assigned a specific injury, and each wound must be treated according to its severity. If casualties are not evacuated to an aid station within an appropriate time limit for their type of wound, then they are considered to have died of those wounds. This brings medics and other medical personnel into the training exercise. Realistic play in training of a wider range of battlefield effects creates a situation in which every leader and soldier has to contend with more of the variables they would face in actual combat situations.

The general Army principle directing this level of realism is "train as you would fight." The price of attaining high levels of realism includes heavy workloads for trainers supporting battlefield effects in live force-on-force exercises (Brown et al., 1998) and refinements that produce more realism in the behavior of computer-generated forces for exercises in virtual simulation exercises (Meliza & Vaden, 1995). An important result of the principle of train as you would fight is that units accustomed to AARs after training exercises should be better prepared to contribute to AARs in an operational situation.

An example may be useful in illustrating how simulations enable the AAR process. A unit sustains heavy casualties conducting an attack in the context of a battlefield simulation. AAR discussions reveal that the unit sustained most of its casualties when the lead element first made contact with the enemy. The commander and staff may contribute the fact that they planned to protect the lead element by having a forward observer call in artillery on enemy positions when the lead element reached a certain location. The forward observer may contribute to the discussion that he or she was still moving toward his or her position at the time when the lead element was engaged by the enemy. More discussions may lead the unit to discover that the fire support plan was disseminated too late to give the observer time to get into position. The unit learns the negative effect that untimely delivery of a part of the mission plan, such as the fire support component, can have on battlefield synchronization and friendly casualties. A unit can also identify potential methods for making sure that planning products are delivered in a timely manner.

In exercise environments that are realistic and immersive, soldiers may conduct their own informal AAR before the formal AAR begins. An early observation regarding the use of TES in Army collective training was that exercise participants spontaneously began to discuss exercise events with one another (Shriver et al., cited in Sulzen, 1986), providing them with an informal perspective about what happened and why it happened. The probability of spontaneous AARs may have increased since the early 1980s as simulation technology has allowed for more realistic exercises, and soldiers have come to expect, and became comfortable with, the AAR process that in variably follows the exercise conclusion.

The AAR does not require an exhaustive review of all aspects of a unit's performance. Instead, trainers are expected to focus on aspects of performance closely linked to key exercise events and outcomes. Realistic battlefield effects enable objective performance outcomes that can help units and trainers focus on high-payoff activities that went well or poorly.

The Roles of After-Action Review Aids in Supporting Feedback

To be effective, AAR discussions need to be guided by an AAR leader. The leader needs one or more starting points for the discussion and at least a general idea of where the discussion will head. The job of AAR leaders is made easier to the extent that they are already aware of the types of problems the unit has been experiencing. If all an AAR leader knows about a mission is that a unit sustained heavy casualties, then the Socratic method will take a long time to identify the root causes of the problem. If the AAR leader knows that most of the casualties occurred within a few minutes of making contact with the enemy and that few friendly vehicles returned fire on contact, then they are closer to identifying and understanding what happened and why.

At instrumented CTCs and in virtual simulations, AAR aids prepared from electronic data streams can document or illustrate aspects of unit performance that are close to root causes of a unit's weaknesses and strengths. Developments in battlefield simulations technology have provided trainers with a record of electronic data describing position location, firing events, and communications over the course of an exercise. AAR software systems have been developed that allow these data to be converted into a variety of AAR aids demonstrating critical aspects of unit performance (Meliza, 1999). These aids can be used during an AAR to describe or illustrate ground truth. For example, a graph showing the number of rounds fired by each vehicle in a platoon over time may make the point that only one of the vehicles in the platoon fired during the first 5 minutes of an engagement. To gain this information from the AAR process, a unit would have to slowly reconstruct the sequence of events based on their memories. AAR aids also offer the benefit of providing units with ground truth if their recollections are at odds with what actually happened.

AAR aids can be designed to show ground truth as it might have been observed by an exercise participant (e.g., a three-dimensional view of the battle space from the perspective of the commander's location). In other cases, ground truth can be shown using synthetic displays (e.g., a trace of unit movement over time showing that a unit wandered and backtracked).

To the extent that AAR aids illustrate root causes of exercise events, they expedite the AAR process. Consider when a unit does not reach a position in time to perform a task. Possible root causes of the late arrival

Table 13.1 The Role of After-Action Review Aids in Identifying Root Causes of Performing and Guiding Discussions

AAR aid	Root causes of problems that may be illustrated	AAR questions
Battle flow or "snail trail" tracing path taken by unit	The unit wandered or backtracked in its movement	Platoon Leader, when and how did you select your route?
Timeline showing when a unit stopped and the duration of each stop	The unit stopped too many times or for too long during its movement	Platoon Leader, what was the purpose of these halts?

are shown in Table 13.1 along with examples of AAR aids and questions that can help pinpoint the specific cause of the problem. If an AAR aid in the form of a trace of unit movement showed that the unit wandered and backtracked in its movement, then late arrival might be caused by poor navigation or route selection. An AAR leader might address this possibility by asking the unit leader how and when the route was selected. Aids indicating another cause for late arrival, such as a timeline showing a unit halted frequently or for long periods, might lead to a different line of questioning. AAR aid generation capabilities that examine exercise data streams to check specific aspects of unit performance (e.g., generate a trace of movement to look for backtracking and wandering) offer a means of helping AAR leaders and units diagnose unit strengths and weaknesses.

The most frequently used AAR aid is a sequential replay of exercise events. A replay, however, is not necessarily the most efficient or effective way of illustrating key aspects of performance. Sometimes, AAR aids that summarize activity over a period of time can be more effective. For example, keeping track of which portions of the enemy force are engaged can be difficult if watching a moment-by-moment replay of an engagement. A graphic showing shot lines (lines connecting shooter location to impact location) aggregated over a specific period of time can quickly show which potential targets were engaged during the period of interest.

The development of AAR aids that can more effectively and efficiently illustrate key aspects of performance is a continuing goal of AAR system developers. The U.S. Army Center for Army Lessons Learned (CALL) analyzes performance data of units at maneuver CTCs to identify trends across units and over time. CALL findings that identify frequently occurring unit performance problems and their causes are a good source for identifying potential AAR aids.

Past efforts to develop new AAR aids have not always met with success (Shlechter, Bessemer, Rowatt, & Nesselroade, 1994). Although the aids may provide information that would otherwise have to be gleaned from lengthy reviews of replays, poorly received aids tend to be in a form that soldiers cannot readily comprehend (e.g., an exercise timeline). The ideal situation would be one in which exercise participants expect to see certain AAR aids after an exercise and know what to look for in each aid. One factor making it difficult to reach this goal is that each training environment has different capabilities to support AAR aid production. Virtual simulations provide data on the location of round impacts that miss a target, but this information is not available in live force-on-force training events, for example. A graphic that aggregates shot lines over time cannot be implemented in the live force-on-force environment but can be in a virtual simulation.

Shlechter et al. (1994) reported that existing AAR aid development procedures were unable to provide many types of aids in time to support an AAR. In response to this problem, the U.S. Army demonstrated the capability in virtual training environments to use software to automatically create candidate AAR aids during exercises so that they would be available for review by AAR leaders during exercises and ready to support AARs as soon as an exercise ended (Brown et al., 1997).

An important and continuing aspect of AAR aid research concerns the tailoring of AAR aid production to meet the needs of specific environments. For example, urban environments present special challenges in that "buildings and other structures break up the visual field and limit the portion of the battlefield that can be observed by any one person" (Lampton, Clark, & Knerr, 2003, p. 59). The Dismounted Infantry Virtual AAR System (DIVAARS) was developed to support dismounted infantry operations training using a virtual simulation (Knerr & Lampton, 2005). One example of a DIVAARS AAR aid capable of meeting the information needs of dismounted infantry is a trace of unit movement showing which rooms of an office building were entered during a search-and-clear operation. In one instance, a unit that believed it had cleared all of the rooms on a floor found that one room had been missed when it reviewed the movement trace AAR aid (D. R. Lampton, personal communication, April 13, 2005).

Knerr and Lampton (2005) collected data from exercise participants regarding the utility of DIVAARs AAR aids. Participants reported that the AAR system was effective displaying movement inside and outside buildings. They also reported that the system made it easy to decide what happened during a mission, why it happened, and how to do better the next time they had to perform that mission. The DIVAARS also allowed soldiers to keep track of the order in which key events occurred. Participants reported that use of the AAR system was more effective than conducting an AAR without any visual or audio playback system (i.e., the situation to which participants were accustomed).

Comparing the After-Action Review and Critique as Feedback Tools

As mentioned, critiques have been criticized for their subjective nature. The objective outcomes of exercises enabled by TES, and the ability to document unit performance problems with AAR aids, address this problem by providing objective data and a means to present it to a training audience. The provider of a critique can draw on objective outcomes and use AAR aids to document performance problems rather then rely on personal perceptions and opinions. The key remaining difference between the two forms of feedback is the use of input from participants, and this difference greatly favors the AAR process.

One means of demonstrating the value of the AAR method is to consider the types of unit performance problems that need to be diagnosed during a postexercise feedback session and the role of user input in making these diagnoses. Barnett, Meliza, and McCluskey (2001) examined over 200 frequently occurring problems in the performance of units at the U.S. Army's National Training Center and Joint Readiness Training Center and found that they could be categorized under one or more of eight general problem areas, including a lack of awareness of some aspects of the enemy or friendly situation, a lack of awareness of some aspect of the plan, and a lack of understanding of the tactical situation. Diagnosing these problems often requires finding out what leaders knew, when they knew it, what information they were looking for, and what they intended to do with this information. A pure critique method of providing feedback lacks the information provided by the participants that is needed to diagnose a unit's strengths and weaknesses. A unit may move in a formation that is inappropriate to the tactical situation. There are a number of possible causes of this problem. The leader may not know which formation was appropriate to the situation or have had incomplete or inaccurate information about the situation. These differing causes call for different corrective actions, so it is crucial to consider what the leader perceived the situation to be. A large portion of the corrective actions generated during feedback sessions is concerned with improving information flow so that decision makers can maintain awareness and understanding of the tactical situation.

In practice, feedback sessions for simulation-based training will likely use a mix of the AAR and critique methods. Gubler (1997) found this to be the case after reviewing a sample of taped platoon- and company-level AAR sessions from two of the U.S. Army's CTCs. He examined AAR outcomes in terms of the number of performance problems identified and the number of solutions developed as a function of whether the outcome was produced by the AAR leader or the unit. He used a variety of methods to assess the degree to which unit members participated in the AAR. These measures included the ratio of unit members' comments to AAR leader's utterances, percentage of unit members speaking during the AAR, and number of questions asked by unit members. Gubler's goal was to compare recommended versus actual procedures used for conducting AARs. Gubler found that some of the AAR sessions appeared to be closer to critiques than AARs in that the AAR leader did most of the talking and identified most the performance problems and solutions.

Newer Areas of After-Action Review Research

A substantial portion of the research and development accomplished to support the AAR has focused on adapting the AAR process to fit specific training situations and to take advantage of new technologies (Morrison & Meliza, 1999). Described next are feedback issues for four training situations currently demanding the attention of trainers and researcher.

Networked Battle Command

A change in U.S. Army equipment that is having a substantial impact on AAR aids and the AAR process is the introduction of networked command-and-control systems. The newness and complexity of networked command-and-control systems have made their use a prime subject for feedback during the AAR, thereby increasing the number of topics that may need to be addressed. However, networked systems can also solve some of the problems associated with the preparation and application of AAR aids.

Networking allows for continual sharing of evolving mission plans down to the level of individual vehicles or soldiers. The U.S. Army's networked systems convey and display the location of global positioning system-equipped friendly platforms and user reported locations of entities not equipped with a global positioning system, logistical support locations, and threats. Analytic capability has been included that allows platform-based systems to alert leaders when their platforms come within a certain distance of threat situations. Other analytic tools can be applied to gain greater understanding of the tactical situation, such as the capability to calculate circular line of sight from a friendly or enemy position (Dudley et al., 2002). Circular line-of-sight calculations result in displays that show which areas have line of sight in any direction from a specific point on the ground. Such a display may be used to decide which areas can or cannot be observed from a particular battle position. Networked systems provide opportunities to exploit information to gain a tactical advantage, but gaining these advantages requires a lot of work on the part of units to make sure that information is useful and can be applied effectively (Dudley, Johnston, Jones, Strauss, & Meliza, 2001). What a unit does to make sure networked information is useful and exploited to support operations is a new feedback topic.

Networked battle command has the unintended consequence of pulling trainers out of a unit's information loop. A significant amount of information about the tactical situation and performance of the unit used to be gained by listening to radio nets or face-to-face conversations and looking at paper-based plans. Most of this information is now contained in a variety of point-to-point network data streams (Gerlock & Meliza, 1999). Substantial effort is required just to bring the trainer into the network information loop in a way that does not drown trainers in data. User interactions with networked systems also present a class of events that are difficult for trainers to monitor because these systems are distributed down to the level of individual vehicles or even individual soldiers. Information on user interactions important for a collective exercise includes finding out which analytical tools are employed and how filters are set to control the data sent and received for specific nodes within a network (Leibrecht, Lockaby, & Meliza, 2003).

Reconciling the disparity between ground truth and perceived truth has long been an important topic in AARs. This topic becomes much more complex in the network environment because there is a proliferation of perceived truths. Instead of perceived truth simply existing as what leaders believe the situation to be, perceived truth is also what is depicted on situational awareness (SA) display screens throughout a unit. SA displays generally show the locations of friendly elements and assets, enemy elements, and various threat situations over a map background. There may be substantial differences among SA displays because of such factors as variations in the setting of filters that determine whether certain types of information are automatically displayed and updated. There may also be major differences between what a leader perceives to be the truth and the contents of that leader's display because of the way the leader monitors SA displays.

The fact that the AAR process relies on input from exercise participants is of great value in the networked environment. AAR questions can be used to help units evaluate their application of networked systems (e.g., Which strategy did you use for monitoring your SA display?). Guidance developed to help trainers conduct AARs for networked units makes extensive use of questions to help trainers as well as units find out what happened during an exercise (Leibrecht et al., 2003).

Information about a large number of digital activities can be gained during the AAR, but addressing all of these issues in an AAR would result in extremely long sessions. Fortunately, other extrinsic feedback methods (e.g., coaching) may be used to provide feedback. An automated coaching capability has been developed (Aiken et al., 2005) in which software monitors the digital data stream and alerts decision makers when situations occur that require attention, such as when a unit crosses a boundary, entering another unit's sector (i.e., a unit in an area where it is not expected to be is more likely to be mistaken for the enemy and engaged by a friendly unit). The user can call up recommended courses of action and job aids or control the display or redisplay of the alerts. The software captures the alerts and a user's responses to the alerts in an AAR log file that can host a private feedback session for the individual at the decision node where the alerts were triggered.

Networked systems themselves may prove to be a valuable source of AAR aids that can be standardized across simulation environments. Many of the SA displays look like animated plan view replays or snapshots used as AAR aids (i.e., in both cases, vehicles or entities are shown as icons over a graphic map display). Unlike many AAR aids employed in the past, these AAR aids are operational displays that are available across training environments.

Joint and Multinational After-Action Reviews

The AAR process may need to be tailored to support joint operations, multinational operations, and distributed training exercises. Joint exercises include participants from a mix of military services, and multinational operations may involve military and civilians representing a mix of nations or cultures. For both joint and multinational AARs, cultural issues may influence the utility of specific design features of the AAR (e.g., Is it acceptable for a leader from another service or culture to have their mistakes revealed in front of subordinates?). When there are high stakes associated with performance in a simulation-based environment (e.g., if poor performance will reduce the possibility for promotion), it is possible that participants may be more concerned with defending their actions than with learning how to improve their performance in the future. Successful implementation of these AARs will also require designing AAR aids that can help diagnose root causes of the strengths and weaknesses in joint and multinational performance.

Distributed Exercises

In distributed exercises, participants are located at different sites and linked over a simulation network. They perform a mission on a common terrain, but the training audience never gets together at the same location for an AAR (i.e., the AAR also is conducted over a network).

Distributed training will likely bring its own challenges for providing effective AARs. In an early experimental implementation of this method of training, Singer, Grant, Commarford, Kring, and Zavod (2001) found distributed AARs to be slower than face-to-face AARs, and performance did not improve to the same degree. AAR procedures may need to be tailored to address this shortfall. AAR procedures may need to be tailored even further for exercises that involve a mix of joint, multinational, and distributed features.

Summary

Realistic battlefield simulations made it possible for the AAR process to replace the critique as the U.S. Army's primary method of providing extrinsic feedback after collective training exercises. Realistic simulations provide participants with intrinsic feedback that cues and guides their performance and, to some extent, let them know how well they are performing various tasks. The intrinsic feedback received by individuals depends on their job, their location in the battle space, and the quality of the simulation environment. This intrinsic feedback prepares individuals to participate in interactive discussions that can help a unit decide what happened, how it happened, and how to improve performance. A significant part of the extrinsic feedback process is to bring perceived truth regarding exercise events in line with ground truth (e.g., what actually happened), and the sharing of intrinsic feedback enables a view of the situation that is closer to ground truth than is the view of a single individual. In realistic battlefield simulations, a wide variety of participants is able to see, through intrinsic or extrinsic feedback, how their actions contributed to the bottom lines of unit performance.

A major advantage of the AAR relative to the critique is that the AAR makes use of input from exercise participants. This source of input increases in importance as changes in equipment and missions create more situations in which critical exercise events cannot be observed by trainers.

The AAR process makes use of the Socratic method of asking leading and open-ended questions to guide unit discussions. The AAR process can be expedited through the use of aids that use electronic data streams from exercises to document key aspects of performance that are close to the root causes of unit strengths and weaknesses. Designing these aids and implementing their production is a continuing activity.

The AAR process or AAR aids have been tailored many times to fit specific instances of the live, virtual, and constructive training environments and to fit changes in unit equipment and missions. Tailoring efforts at various stages are under way to reflect networked battle command, joint operations, multinational operations, urban operations, and distributed networked training.

Growth in the number of topics that may need to be addressed during AAR sessions makes it necessary to consider greater application of other forms of extrinsic feedback, such as coaching, in association with AARs. The development of automated coaching methods is expected to motivate research on how to better integrate coaching with postexercise feedback sessions.

Acknowledgment

Opinions expressed are those of the authors and do not represent an official position of the U.S. Army or the Army Research Institute.

References

Aiken, D. S., Green, G. E., Arntz, S. J., & Meliza, L. L. (2005). *Real time decision alert, aid and after action review system for combat and training* (ARI Tech. Rep. 1165). Alexandria, VA: U.S. Army Research Institute for the Behavioral and Social Sciences.

Banks, J. H., Hardy, G. D., Scott, T. D., Kress, G., & Word, L. E. (1977). *REAL-TRAIN validation for rifle squads: Mission accomplishment* (ARI Research Rep. 1192). Alexandria, VA: U.S. Army Research Institute for the Behavioral and Social Sciences.

Barnett, J. S., Meliza, L. L., & McCluskey, M. R. (2001). *Defining digital proficiency measurement targets for U.S. Army units* (ARI Tech. Rep. 1117). Alexandria, VA: U.S. Army Research Institute for the Behavioral and Social Sciences.

Bosley, J. J., Onoszko, P. W. J., Knerr, C. S., & Sulzen, R. H. (1979). *Tactical engagement simulation training techniques: Two training programs for the conduct of after action review* (ARI Research Product 79-2). Alexandria, VA: U.S. Army Research Institute for the Behavioral and Social Sciences.

Brown, B., Nordyke, J., Gerlock, D., Begley I. J., II, & Meliza, L. L. (1998). *Training analysis and feedback aids (TAAF Aids) study for live training support* (ARI Study Rep. 98-04). Alexandria, VA: U.S. Army Research Institute for the Behavioral and Social Sciences.

Brown, B., Wilkinson, S., Nordyke, J., Riede, D., Huyssoon, S., Aguilar, D., et al. (1997). *Developing an automated training analysis and feedback system for tank platoons* (ARI Research Rep. 1708). Alexandria, VA: U.S. Army Research Institute for the Behavioral and Social Sciences.

Darling, M. J., & Parry, C. S. (2001). After action reviews: Linking reflection and planning in a learning practice. *Reflections, 3, 2,* 64–72.

Domeshek, E. A. (2004). *Phase II. Final report on an intelligent tutoring system for teaching battle command reasoning skills* (ARI Tech. Rep. 1143). Alexandria, VA: U.S. Army Research Institute for the Behavioral and Social Sciences.

Dudley, M. G., Hill, R., Johnston, J. C., Jones, W. S., LeGare, M., Leibrecht, B. C., et al. (2002). *Measuring digital proficiency: Assessment approaches and echelon considerations* (ARI Research Rep. 1791). Alexandria, VA: U.S. Army Research Institute for the Behavioral and Social Sciences.

Dudley, M. G., Johnston, J. C., Jones, W. S., Strauss, C. P., & Meliza, L. L. (2001). *Making the transition from analog to digital warfighting: Changes in unit behavior and knowledge* (ARI Research Rep. 1785). Alexandria, VA: U.S. Army Research Institute for the Behavioral and Social Sciences.

Fobes, J. L., & Meliza, L. L. (1989). *Integrating National Training Center feedback into home station training management* (ARI Research Rep. 1523). Alexandria, VA: U.S. Army Research Institute for the Behavioral and Social Sciences.

Gerlock, D., & Meliza, L. (1999). Supporting exercise control and feedback in the digital domain for virtual simulations. *Proceedings of the Interservice/Industry Training Systems and Education Conference*, Orlando, FL.

Goldberg, S. L., & Meliza, L. L. (1993). Assessing unit performance in distributive interactive simulations: The Unit Performance Assessment System (UPAS). In *Proceedings of NATO Defence Research Group Meeting, Panel 8 (Defence Applications of Human and Bio-Medical Sciences). Training Strategies for Networked Simulation and Gaming). Technical Proceedings AC/243 (Panel 8) TN/5*, 173–182, Munich, Germany.

Gubler, J. C. (1997). *Unit simulation training system after action reviews (AAR): A novel approach to achieve effectiveness.* Unpublished master's thesis, University of Central Florida, Orlando, FL.

Hoare, R. (1996). From debrief to after action review (AAR). *Modern Simulation and Training, 6,* 13–17.

Knerr, B. W., & Lampton, D. R. (2005). *An assessment of the Virtual-Integrated MOUT Training System (V-IMTS)* (ARI Research Rep. 1163). Alexandria, VA: U.S. Army Research Institute for the Behavioral and Social Sciences.

Kulik, J. A., & Kulik, C.-L. C. (1988). Timing of feedback and verbal learning. *Review of Educational Research, 58,* 79–97.

Lampton, D. R., Clark, B. R., & Knerr, B. W. (2003). Urban combat: The ultimate extreme environment. *Journal of Performance in Extreme Environments, 7,* 57–62.

Leibrecht, B. C., Lockaby, K. J., & Meliza, L. L. (2003). *A practical guide for exploiting FBCB2 capabilities* (ARI Research Product 2003-05). Alexandria, VA: U.S. Army Research Institute for the Behavioral and Social Sciences.

Maddox, W. T., Ashby, F. B., & Bohil, C. J. (2003). Delayed feedback effects on rule-based and information-integration category learning. *Journal of Experimental Psychology: Learning, Memory, and Cognition, 29,* 650–662.

Meliza, L. L. (1999*). A guide to standardizing after action review (AAR) aids* (ARI Research Product 99-01). Alexandria, VA: U.S. Army Research Institute for the Behavioral and Social Sciences.

Meliza, L. L., Scott, T. D., & Epstein, K. (1979). *REALTRAIN validation for rifle squads: Tactical performance* (ARI Research Rep. 1203). Alexandria, VA: U.S. Army Research Institute for the Behavioral and Social Sciences.

Meliza, L. L., & Vaden, E. A. (1995). Measuring entity and group behaviors of semi-automated forces. *Proceedings of the Fifth Conference on Computer Generated Forces and Behavioral Representation*, 181–192.

Moreno, R. (2004). Decreasing cognitive load for novice students: Effects of explanatory versus corrective feedback in discovery-based multimedia. *Instructional Science, 32*, 99–103.

Morrison, J. E., & Meliza, L. L. (1999). *Foundations of the after action review process* (ARI Special Rep. 42). Alexandria, VA: U.S. Army Research Institute for the Behavioral and Social Sciences.

Rogers, E. (2004). *Pausing for learning: Adapting the Army after action review process to the NASA Project World*. NASA White Paper. Retrieved August 18, 2005, from http://smo.gsfc.nasa.gov/knowman/documents/whitepapers/Pausing_for_Learning.pdf

Scott, T. D., & Fobes, J. L. (1982). *After action review guidebook I. National Training Center* (ARI Research Product 83-11). Alexandria, VA: U.S. Army Research Institute for the Behavioral and Social Sciences,

Scott, T. D., Meliza, L. L., Hardy, G. D., Banks, J. H., & Word, L. E. (1979). *REALTRAIN validation for armor/anti-armor teams* (ARI Research Rep. 1204). Alexandria, VA: U.S. Army Research Institute for the Behavioral and Social Sciences.

Shlechter, T. M., Bessemer, D. W., Rowatt, W. C., & Nesselroade, K. P., Jr. (1994). *Evaluating the Unit Performance Assessment System's after action review displays* (ARI Technical Rep. 997). Alexandria, VA: U.S. Army Research Institute for the Behavioral and Social Sciences.

Singer, J. J., Grant, S., Commarford, P. M., Kring, J. P., & Zavod, M. (2001). *Team performance in distributed virtual environments* (ARI Tech. Rep. 1118). Alexandria, VA: U.S. Army Research Institute for the Behavioral and Social Sciences.

Sulzen, R. H. (1986). *Annotated bibliography of tactical engagement simulation 1966–1984* (ARI Tech. Rep. 725). Alexandria, VA: U.S. Army Research Institute for the Behavioral and Social Sciences.

U.S. Army Combined Arms Center. (1993). *A leader's guide to after-action reviews* (Training Circular 25-20). Fort Leavenworth, KS.

Winquist, J. R., & Larson, J. R., Jr. (1998). Information pooling: When it impacts group decision making. *Journal of Personality and Social Psychology, 74*, 371–377.

14
Measurement of Learning Processes in Pilot Simulation

DEE H. ANDREWS, ROBERT T. NULLMEYER,
JUSTINE GOOD, AND PATRICIA C. FITZGERALD

Air Force Research Laboratory

Introduction

There are few human activities as complex as safely piloting an aircraft. All human capabilities and resources are put to the test on a frequent basis in flight, and there are multiple examples of accidents and incidents that have been caused when those capabilities and resources were not sufficient to the task. Examples of capabilities and resources include cognitive, visual, psychoperceptual, kinesthetic, proprioceptive, psychomotor, and social skills. Flight situations call for the pilot to use many of these capabilities and resources simultaneously. Measurement of the performance of pilots requires approaches that take into account all of the complex interactions that occur when so many different human capabilities are used at the same time. As this chapter shows, decades of research and experience have yielded significant advances in the area of pilot performance measurement. Yet, there is still much to be learned about how to measure and analyze this dynamic realm of human behavior.

Researchers and practitioners in the aviation field have a variety of reasons why they need to measure pilot performance accurately and reliably. Key functions for which quality measurements are required include pilot selection, cockpit design, testing, cost estimation, and many others. Much of what we know about pilot measurement has come from functions other than training, yet training has greatly benefited. In turn, pilot training performance measurement work has produced concepts, methods, and tools that have been beneficial to the other functions. This chapter concentrates on measurement for the training function mainly in simulators.

A Brief Historical Overview of Flight Simulation

The use of flight simulation in pilot training is nearly as old as manned flight itself. The first flight simulator was developed around 1910. This low-technology device, a barrel with short wings that was physically manipulated by the instructor, offered students the opportunity to practice basic flight control (Moroney & Moroney, 1999). During the following two decades, other attempts were made to design flight training devices; the usefulness of these simulators, however, was limited. In 1929, the modern flight simulator was born with the development of the Link trainer, which allowed movement around all three axes of roll, pitch, and yaw (*Link Simulation*, n.d.). Following World War I, the primary focus of performance measurement was on the medical and physiological effects of flight (Moroney & Moroney, 1999). In 1934, the Army Air Corps and the Navy began using flight trainers to assess student pilot performance.

During World War II, the use of the devices for pilot training and selection increased dramatically (*Link Simulation*, n.d). From the end of World War II through the late 1950s, the increasing number and types of aircraft in service and under development prompted the design and deployment of simulators that replicated the characteristics of specific aircraft. During this period, the airlines began using the devices for pilot training. Furthermore, measurement research in simulators expanded to include the development of methods to improve flying safety. In the late 1960s and early 1970s, the advanced processing power of computers led to the development of more sophisticated, high-fidelity devices and the ability to obtain objective performance measures from the simulator (Dickman, 1982). Today, flight simulation is widely used in every aspect of pilot training, from private pilot certification through advanced military distributed mission operations. A number of issues that may affect measurement and performance, however, must be considered.

Issues in the Measurement of Pilot Performance

Several factors may affect the accuracy of performance measurement in simulators, as well as in the operational environment. The evaluation process is complex and depends a great deal on the instructor's judgments of the student's competency. The extent to which the assessment is objective or subjective is a critical issue. Furthermore, performance in the simulator versus the actual flight environment is qualitatively different, a fact that must also be considered in measurement. Finally, the effects the instructor has on the person evaluated may influence performance, either negatively or positively. These factors are discussed in greater detail.

Subjective versus Objective Measures

The measurement of human performance in aircraft began shortly after the advent of manned flight (Meister, 1999). Performance evaluation occurs on two basic levels. Subjective measures are generally provided by instructors or subject matter experts and assess the performance of the trainee on multiple elements. These data may be qualitative (e.g., comments) or quantitative (e.g., items on a Likert-type scale); however, the metrics often depend on human judgment. Objective measures, on the other hand, consist of specific and well-defined data collected during the training exercise, typically by means of digital computers. The parameters that indicate acceptable performance are empirically based. Although objective data are most desirable, subjective information has been shown to offer rich data that provide a great deal of insight regarding many of the factors that influence human performance (e.g., Nullmeyer, Spiker, Wilson, & Deen, 2003; Spiker & Willis, 2003).

Objective Measures

The development of effective training programs is an iterative process that requires the best performance data available (Vreuls et al., 1975). Although the options for obtaining objective measures of pilot performance in field settings are currently often cost prohibitive, technologies are available to capture this critical information. In actual flight, the military collect objective data through the use of instrument pods (i.e., measurement equipment attached to the wings) that record flight characteristics, weapons information, and flight maneuvers over the course of the mission (Panarisi, 2000).

Because of the costs associated with acquiring the technology required to collect objective performance data in the operational environment, it is more affordable to obtain such data in flight simulators. The current generation of flight simulators affords the collection of a tremendous amount of flight and performance data. Accordingly, training objectives and systematic design principles should be used to ensure that the most appropriate variables are targeted for the performance measurement process (Salas, Milham, & Bowers, 2003).

Subjective Measures

Although objective measures are required for the accurate assessment of performance, the overall picture is incomplete when objective performance data are relied on exclusively for pilot evaluations. Many of the traditional measures used in the evaluation of pilot performance in operational and simulated environments are subjective, typically including proficiency ratings and instructor comments. Furthermore, in the simulated flight environment, subjective assessments of the students' behavior or performance help to identify the conditions that the instructor selects for subsequent training (Dickman, 1982; Fowlkes, Lane, Salas, Franz, & Oser, 1994; Williams & Thomas, 1984). In efforts to make subjective evaluation more objective, methods have been developed to assess behavior systematically. Event-based methods identify expected behaviors and acceptable responses a priori, and rating scales are designed with specific criteria for all possible levels (Fowlkes et al., 1994; O'Connor, Hormann, Flin, Lodge, & Goeters, 2002). These measures, in conjunction with typical subjective and objective measures, contribute to the accuracy of the overall assessment.

Pilot Behavioral Differences

Of additional interest are pilot behavior differences in the simulator as opposed to actual flight conditions and potential effects on performance. Specifically, the social psychological literature documents instances when performance is altered in the presence of others (e.g., Diaper, 1990; Shivers, 1998; Staal, 2004). Diaper (1990) stated that research participants who were unaware that they were involved in a study performed better than their aware counterparts. In his review of the literature on performance and stress, Staal (2004) reported that performance is enhanced when performing familiar tasks in the presence of others. When engaging in complex tasks that have not yet been well learned, however, performance tends to suffer. Likewise, in his study of employee evaluation and performance, Shivers (1998) concluded that assessment appears to increase apprehension, resulting in negative effects on performance. In operational and simulated environments, the presence of an experimenter or instructor pilot may similarly influence the behavior or performance of the pilot assessed. Accordingly, these factors need to be considered in terms of performance measurement in each environment.

Furthermore, the level of stress experienced by the pilot and the ways in which stressful situations are handled differ in each environment (Staal, 2004). For instance, Wilson, Skelly, and Purvis (1999) reported student pilot heart rates 50% higher in actual flight emergencies in comparison to simulated flight emergencies, suggesting a higher stress level in the actual flight environment. Although studies of this nature suggest the need to be cautious about generalizing simulator study research findings to actual flight, the clear benefits of training in flight simulators are evident in the discussion that follows.

Reliability and Validity Issues in Pilot Training Performance Measurement

To understand reliability and validity challenges in pilot training, it is necessary to understand that such training takes place in different phases and with a range of training media. Initial training, also called ab initio, is conducted with the goal of obtaining a pilot's wings. They are then certified to fly solo. In the military, they then move to training in the actual aircraft they will fly in operational duties (e.g., F-16 fighter, B-1 bomber, C-130 transport). During ab initio and advanced training, they will train using a variety of media. These may consist of paper diagrams, computer-based training, part task training devices with low-to-moderate physical and functional fidelity, sophisticated flight simulators, and finally actual training aircraft. *Physical fidelity* refers to whether the cockpit controls, displays, and out-the-widow scene "look" like the actual aircraft's, and *functional fidelity* refers to whether those items provide the pilot trainee with a "feel" like that of the actual aircraft.

Depending on the phase of pilot training, both reliability and validity of measurement range from fairly straightforward to very complex. For example, if in the initial stages of training we are concerned about a trainee's ability to locate and operate the correct controls in the cockpit, it is not difficult to measure the trainee's performance consistently and validly. Assuming high physical and functional fidelity in the training medium, proper operation of the controls always results in the same functional outcome whether in a training device, a simulator, or an aircraft. In the case of learning the controls and displays and their effect on the aircraft, both reliability and validity can be very high.

However, as pilots move on to more advanced training objectives, such as operating the aircraft in extreme situations (e.g., poor flying conditions or combat flying), it becomes much more difficult to measure and guarantee high reliability and validity. Part of the reason for this difficulty is that, despite some significant advances in the training community's capability to accurately simulate flying events, cues, and sensations (Hawkins, 2002), there are still a variety of areas in which we fall short of attaining complete fidelity with the actual flying environment. For example, although there are promising advances under way in simulating visual out-of-the-cockpit scenes for the pilot, the current state of the art only provides visual fidelity that is less than half the resolution that a pilot can see when flying in the real world. Such decrements in fidelity have a profound effect on our ability to replicate real-world cues validly in a simulated aircraft and to measure reliably a pilot's reaction in a complex setting. In the case of visual cues, it is possible that the pilot might do something differently in the actual aircraft because there is not a full range of visual cues.

The reliability and validity issue is particularly pronounced in training combat skills. For example, take the case of fighter pilots training to fight against other fighter pilots in air-to-air engagements. The various standard fighter combat maneuvers (e.g., barrel rolls, Immelman turn, low yo-yo, drag) can be taught and practiced with fairly well-defined measures of performance in a training setting. It is difficult to judge how well the maneuvers were performed in actual combat because the recording of the maneuvers either in the aircraft or from a ground monitoring station can be difficult in combat situations and because pilots may have to perform the maneuver much differently from the accepted standard maneuver because of the conditions of the engagement.

Combat also presents the most difficult cognitive performance tasks because of the great novelty and variety a pilot faces in various combat settings. It is difficult to establish standards for reliability in such situations because of the need for flexibility in the way a combat pilot assesses the situation and develops a solution. In turn, the validity of various measures of combat performance is difficult to establish because the training goal is to provide the trainee with a reasonable sampling of combat situations. Because of the subjective nature of the "goodness" of a particular solution to an actual combat setting, the validity may or may not be high when transfer from the training setting to the real-world setting is considered. Indeed, much of pilot performance measurement is derived from expert judgments of that performance so that even in relatively straightforward areas like cockpit procedures training each expert might have variations in how consistently and validly those subjective measurements are made compared to their fellow experts and even with themselves over time.

The remainder of the chapter explores pilot performance measurement issues in two related but different flight domains: ab initio training (i.e., beginning undergraduate pilot training) and wide-body aircraft flight training.

Performance Measurement In Simulation-Based Undergraduate Pilot Training

The U.S. Air Force (USAF) trains officers to become pilots through a 52-week program currently known as Joint (meaning shared with the U.S. Navy and U.S. Army) Specialized Undergraduate Pilot Training. The course objectives throughout the phases of Joint Specialized Undergraduate Pilot Training remain the same: to qualify graduates for the aeronautical rating of pilot and for follow-on phases of training and for future responsibilities as military officers and leaders. This training includes flying training to teach the principles and techniques used in operating high-speed jet aircraft; ground training to supplement and reinforce flying training; and officer development training to strengthen the graduate's leadership skills, officer qualities, and understanding of the role of the military pilot as an officer and supervisor.

The basic methodology for USAF training is first to instruct the concepts in an academic training environment, demonstrate the concept to the student in a training medium either on the ground or in the air, then provide the student an opportunity to practice the concept. Phase I training begins with academic training. Once the students have a sufficient amount of "book knowledge," they are introduced to some basic flying concepts in the simulator. Measurement of their academic learning is typically straightforward and possesses both high reliability and high validity. When the students complete Phase I, they continue to the next phase of training in a specific aircraft.

Newer simulator systems for undergraduate pilot training, such as for the T-6 (a single-engine, tandem-cockpit propeller aircraft), offer ways to record and measure student performance electronically during a simulator sortie (a *sortie* is one flight regardless of whether it is in the simulator or the actual aircraft). However, the majority of the grading and evaluation is done by instructor observation. In the older training devices, such as the T-1 (a jet engine, business jet-like trainer) and T-38A (a twin-engine, high-performance jet trainer) simulators, it is possible to record and even sometimes document the aircraft's flight path and performance electronically during certain maneuvers (e.g., an instrument approach). Although the system is not readily used by instructors for evaluation because they do not find the performance measurement system user friendly, it may be used to debrief the particular maneuver or the overall sortie if necessary. One of the more commonly used capacities of the simulator is the ability to have the student perform a maneuver, and if the student incorrectly performs the maneuver, the simulator can be stopped, instruction can be offered to the student, and the student can be given another opportunity to perform the maneuver. In many cases, some simulators have the ability to record the performance parameters and replay the exact student performance so the student can watch what he or she was doing to the aircraft during the maneuver. This helps the student recognize errors and learn from them. It also provides an excellent opportunity for the instructor to show the student exactly what was going on at the time and have the students' full attention during the instruction.

For undergraduate pilot training, the grading standards for both flying and simulator training are defined as follows:

No grade: The maneuver is demonstrated by the instructor pilot but not practiced by the student.

Unable to accomplish: The student is unsafe or lacks sufficient knowledge, skill, or ability to perform the operation, maneuver, or task.

Fair: The student performs the operation, maneuver, or task safely but has limited proficiency. Deviations occur that detract from performance.
Good: The student performs the operation, maneuver, or task satisfactorily. Deviations occur that are recognized and corrected in a timely manner.
Excellent: The student performs the operation, maneuver, or task correctly, efficiently, and skillfully.

Although there are relatively clear descriptions of the standards used to judge which of the rating categories should be assigned, considerable latitude is given to the instructor in making the subjective evaluations.

By the nature of flying, during every sortie the students are presented with a number of variables and problems they must solve to complete the mission safely and successfully. Sometimes, these issues are known and anticipated; however, many times they are unexpected. Some of the most critical areas of instruction and most difficult tasks/concepts for the students to develop and grasp involve a significant amount of problem solving: risk management/decision making, task management, and situational awareness (SA). For example, in the T-1 undergraduate syllabus, for risk management/decision making (T-1, 2003, p. 16), students are expected to:

a. Identify probable contingencies and alternatives
b. Gather available data before arriving at final decision
c. Encourage crew participation in the decision making process
d. Clearly state decisions to the crew
e. Provide rationale for decisions

Similar to this is task management, for which the student is expected to prioritize multiple tasks correctly and use all available resources to manage workload. Clearly, measuring and evaluating proficiency in all these skills is difficult.

SA is the skill area students typically have the most difficulty developing. These difficulties often lead to a large percentage of unsatisfactory performances on evaluation sorties. Although each aircraft may necessitate a somewhat different definition of SA, essentially the SA concept can be defined as it is in the T-1 syllabus (Joint Specialized Undergraduate Pilot Training, 2003, p. 16):

a. *Awareness:* Keep track of what is happening on the ground, in the air, and with other crew members. Cope with any subsequent mission impact as a result of these happenings.
b. *Flexibility:* Cope with rapidly changing situations or conditions, inflight or on the ground, and adjust mission as needed to obtain desired objectives.
c. *Capacity:* Cognizant of the awareness level of self and other crew members and acts to maintain a high level of SA for all.

The students are expected to demonstrate the ability to maintain awareness and minimize the effects of adverse factors on the crew. These skills are required in the student pilot, who must maintain and recognize the SA of the other members of the flight. The bottom line of SA is that the pilot never allows the crew to exceed their capability to fly safely. Again, for an instructor to measure and evaluate such a complex cognitive function as SA in a simulator or in the aircraft takes a gifted instructor because of the task's subjectivity.

Crew Performance Measurement in Wide-Body Flight Simulators

Wide-body aircraft are generally considered to be any aircraft that have multiple crew members. The wide-body aircraft is larger than a small training aircraft or fighter aircraft. Examples of wide-body aircraft are commercial jet liners, civilian and military transport aircraft, bombers, and military tankers. Pilot measurement issues in wide-body aircraft can be more complex than in non-wide-body aircraft because of the multiple-person crew.

The backbone of student performance measurement in military wide-body simulator training programs is instructor observation of student behaviors, including associated impacts on the simulated training environment. Automated performance measurement capabilities may augment these observations, serving at least two purposes: (a) to enhance the instructor's awareness of student behavior in the instructional environment and (b) to improve the quality of feedback given to students. There is long-standing interest in using performance measurement capabilities for a third purpose: to support competency-based progression through simulator training experiences. However, students are given fairly fixed sequences of experiences in most simulator training programs today. Limited availability of simulators (with the simulator sometimes a one-of-a-kind device) often results in limited scheduling flexibility. In addition, tailoring instruction to the needs of one individual in a multiperson crew is complicated by impacts on the other crew positions.

Instructor-Based Performance Measurement

Instructor observations remain the primary inputs both for posttraining mission debriefing and for documenting the adequacy of student progress in student records. Observations are recorded in several ways. Using C-130 training as an example, instructors fill out an Aircrew Training Progress

Record after each simulator mission. This form provides a set of required proficiency levels for task-based training events such as airdrop checklist, simulated engine failure, night vision device operations, and so forth. Performance and knowledge are rated using 4-point knowledge and skill scales. The second method for documenting student performance is instructor comments provided for each simulator mission on a separate Training Comments Record. The comments are unstructured and are not necessarily tied to the required items covered in the Progress Record. Instructors may laud exemplary performance or describe deficiencies and can use the Training Comments Record as a teaching or debriefing aid. Instructor comments have proven to be good sources of insight concerning student strengths and weaknesses in both Navy and Air Force applications.

Spiker, Berkman, and Hunt (2002) analyzed S-3B aircraft student training records (two-person crews) from Navy familiarization training. Each instructor comment was assigned to a category and subcategory within a comprehensive Aircrew Proficiency Classification Framework. Example categories (and subcategories) included perception (cue detection, perceptual illusion); knowledge (of systems, operating limits); procedural (checklist, standard operating procedures); and so forth. The remaining categories were aircraft handling, task management, communication, crew coordination, attitude, decision making, situation awareness, thinking patterns, mission assessment, and emergency procedures. Frequencies of positive and negative comments proved an effective way to pinpoint strong areas of S-3B training effectiveness (crew backup) and weak areas that represent opportunities to improve instruction (communication discipline, attitude awareness).

Spiker and Willis (2003) applied the S-3B taxonomy to review C-130 instructor comments. Of some note, decision making and risk assessment were virtually never mentioned in C-130 student records, yet they were two of the leading factors in C-130 mishaps (Nullmeyer et al., 2003). Subsequent discussions with instructors revealed that these skill areas were no longer emphasized in simulator and flight training, which may explain their prominence in mishap reports. For both S-3 and C-130 instruction, instructor comments helped identify friction points in the training process that had gone undetected. We view instructor comments to be powerful but typically untapped data that can be used to gauge both student proficiency and training effectiveness.

The nature of comments recorded by C-130 simulator instructors may have implications for automated performance measurement. Comments from C-130 mission qualification simulator training were divided into two groups: (a) task-related skills such as task execution, procedures, checklist accomplishment, and aircraft handling; and (b) more cognitive skills such as crew coordination, SA, and mission planning. Overall, 39% of comments were task oriented, and 61% pertained to more cognitive aspects of student performance such as crew coordination, communication, SA, and mission planning/evaluation (data obtained from Spiker & Willis, 2003). These proportions varied across crew positions. For student aircraft commanders, most simulator instructor comments pertained to procedures and tasks or aircraft handling. For loadmasters, comments were evenly distributed across procedures and more cognitive skills. For the remaining crew positions, the largest proportions of comments addressed cognitive skills. These data are summarized in Table 14.1. It is clear that a comprehensive performance measurement system must address cognitive skills.

The skills included in the bottom row of Table 14.1 overlap considerably with traditional crew resource management (CRM) skills. For Air Force aviators, CRM is defined in terms of six skill areas: mission planning, SA, communication, risk assessment/decision making, task management, and crew coordination/flight integrity. Researchers in all military services have successfully used behaviorally anchored rating scales to capture and quantify CRM skills. Using this measurement approach, CRM skill ratings have been strong predictors of mission performance. In several studies, CRM skill levels for experienced crews were measured during annual simulator refresher training using 5-point behaviorally anchored rating scales. These scales addressed specific aspects of each CRM skill category. Both the specific aspects to be measured and the behavioral anchors that exemplify the points were populated with inputs from platform-specific subject matter experts. Thompson, Tourville, Spiker, and Nullmeyer (1999) and Nullmeyer and Spiker (2003) reported equally strong CRM/mission performance correlations in simulator training for MH-53J and MC-130P crews, respectively. In each of these research studies, subject matter experts used paper-based forms to capture CRM skills. This measurement approach has now been modified to support continuing CRM data collection during operational simulator training for MC-130P student crews to

Table 14.1 Frequency (Percentage) of C-130 Simulator Instructor Comments by Crew Position

Skill area	Aircraft Commander	Copilot	Navigator	Flight Engineer	Loadmaster
Task-related skills	164 (58%)	72 (38%)	42 (20%)	85 (32%)	110 (52%)
Cognitive skills	124 (43%)	118 (62%)	170 (80%)	179 (68%)	103 (48%)

guide subsequent training to address areas of greatest need (Thompson et al., 1999).

Automated Performance Measurement

Performance monitoring and reporting capabilities are included as instructional features in most high-fidelity simulators. Many early systems (delivered in the 1980s) captured aircraft system status data and flight parameters like air speed and altitude. Polzella, Hubbard, Brown, and McLean (1987) surveyed over 100 Air Force C-130, H-53, E-3A, and B-52 simulator instructors concerning frequency of use and value of parameter/procedure monitoring tools designed to enhance instructor awareness in simulators. Instructors who were located at an external instructor/operator station (IOS) reported that performance and procedure monitoring capabilities were frequently used and had moderate-to-high training value. Instructors who were colocated with students could observe targeted behaviors "over the shoulder" directly. These instructors expressed a strong preference for direct monitoring of student performance to include cockpit displays, crew interactions, and the out-the-window scene. Utility and utilization ratings for monitoring tools by these instructors were significantly lower but still moderately positive.

Polzella and his colleagues (1987) also addressed the utility and utilization of enhanced student feedback capabilities. Features corresponding to this function included record/playback and hard copy printouts of flight parameters, which were available on the majority of devices. VHS recorders were also common to capture crew interactions. Training value and utilization ratings for these capabilities were both generally low. Many instructors reported that performance retrieval with these features was time consuming, unreliable, and difficult. In addition, products were often difficult to interpret.

MH-53J helicopter simulator instructors were surveyed to identify opportunities for improving instructor/simulator interfaces (Nullmeyer, Cicero, Spiker, Tourville, & Thompson, 1998). These instructors are colocated in the simulator with their students and yet indicated a high level of interest in monitoring capabilities that added to their awareness of specific aspects of the training environment, especially displays that provided knowledge of the electronic combat environment and accurate position information relative to salient objects such as terrain, threats, cultural features, and planned routes and way points. Instructors viewed performance-capturing capabilities to improve feedback as "nice to have," but they consistently gave a higher priority to increased awareness. This may have been influenced by their experience with automated performance measurement capabilities that they described as not providing the information they would use to enhance debriefings.

Automated simulator performance measurement technology is advancing along at least two fronts. The first involves the technology itself. Much of the limited enthusiasm in early simulator instructor surveys may have been the product of equipment such as VHS recorders that made data retrieval so cumbersome and time consuming that instructors often viewed such features as more disruptive than beneficial. Again using the C-130 community as an example, automated data visualization and analysis capabilities have been added to the C-130 full-mission simulators. Flight data are digitally recorded and can be displayed in several forms, ranging from graphs and navigational charts to synchronized video and detailed three-dimensional graphic animations of the flight. Event markers and other retrieval tools resolve many of the problems reported with earlier technologies. Event markers are digital time stamps that the instructor can make in the simulator's data archiving system so that, after the simulator sortie, the instructor can quickly return the student to a critical part of the sortie for replay and remediation if necessary.

The second area of advancement is broadening the types of data that are captured. Military training researchers are finding that aircraft system status and aircraft position data, although important, do not suffice as stand-alone measures of crew performance; other factors are emerging as essential elements. One major emerging factor is mission preparation. Bergondy, Fowlkes, Gualtieri, and Salas (1988) found that well over half of debriefing items in Navy Air Wing Integration Training addressed mission planning and briefing, and only 42% addressed execution issues. Spiker, Nullmeyer, and Tourville (2001) found that MC-130P crew interactions during planning and briefing for a simulator mission accounted for over 60% of variance ($r = .78$) in independent expert ratings of mission performance, a relationship that was also reported by Thompson et al. (1999) for rotary wing crews (76%, $r = .87$). Consistent with these data, the capability to add crew plan information into the performance monitoring capability of MH-53 simulators emerged as a highly desirable feature. Clearly, crew interaction skills like communication and crew coordination will also need to be addressed.

These needs are reflected in common simulator IOS requirements that were established as part of the Navy Aviation Simulation Master Plan (Walwanis Nelson, Smith, Owens, & Bergondy-Wilhelm, 2003). An IOS provides the instructor and simulator's operator with a variety of methods for controlling the simulator sortie and for recording the trainee's performance. In the Navy Aviation Simulator Master Plan, performance measurement is reaffirmed as a major function of the IOS. The Navy vision incorporates both automatic and manual measurement. Automatic recording capabilities would be based on trigger events and give instructors more references to support the debriefing. Manual measurement would be supported by the capability to insert event markers that allow instructors to highlight particular moments in the scenario and retrieve the desired information quickly and easily. Of 26 possible IOS requirements, only data-recording capabilities and bird's-eye view playback were identified by all platforms, indicating strong instructor support for these functions. In simulator terms, a bird's-eye view allows the instructor and trainee to look at a map of the simulated terrain over which the trainee has flown the training sortie.

Conclusion

As shown in this chapter, the aviation community's ability to measure the performance of pilot trainees accurately and validly has grown tremendously since the early days of flight. The use of advanced simulators for undergraduate and advanced pilots has opened many doors to better performance measurement. The days of requiring an instructor pilot to make all of the judgments about trainee pilots based solely on their own subjective observations are now finished. However, even with all of the automated simulation-based performance measurement tools described in this chapter, it will always be up to an experienced instructor pilot to make the final instructional and evaluative decisions about the trainees.

Acknowledgment

The opinions expressed in this chapter are those of the authors and do not necessarily represent the official views or policies of the Department of Defense or the Department of the Air Force.

References

Bergondy, M., Fowlkes, J., Gualtieri, J. & Salas, E. (1998, November). Key team competencies for Navy air wings: A case study. In *Proceedings of the 19th Interservice/Industry Training Systems and Education Conference*. Arlington, VA: National Training Systems Association.

Diaper, G. (1990). The Hawthorne effect: A fresh examination. *Educational Studies, 16*, 261–267.

Dickman, J. L. (1982, November). Automated performance measurement: An overview. In *Proceedings of the 4th Interservice/Industry Training Equipment Conference* (pp. 153–165). Arlington, VA: National Security and Industrial Association.

Fowlkes, J. E., Lane, N. E., Salas, E., Franz, T., & Oser, R. (1994). Improving the measurement of team performance: The TARGETs methodology. *Military Psychology, 6,* 47–61.

Hawkins, F. H. (2002). *Human factors in flight.* Aldershot, UK: Ashgate.

Link simulation and training setting the standard for over 75 years. (n.d.) Retrieved January 6, 2006, from http://www.link.com/history.html

Meister, D. (1999). Measurement in aviation systems. In D. J. Garland, J. A. Wise, and V. D. Hopkin (Eds.), *Handbook of aviation human factors* (pp. 34–49). Mahwah, NJ: Erlbaum.

Moroney, W. F., & Moroney, B. W. (1999). Flight simulation. In D. J. Garland, J. A. Wise, and V. D. Hopkin (Eds.), *Handbook of aviation human factors* (pp. 355–388). Mahwah, NJ: Erlbaum.

Nullmeyer, R. T., Cicero, G. D., Spiker, V. A., Tourville, S. J., and Thompson, J. S. (1998, November). Improving instructor operator stations to enhance electronic warfare training. In *Proceedings of the 20th Interservice/Industry Training Systems and Education Conference.* Arlington, VA: National Training Systems Association.

Nullmeyer, R. T., & Spiker, V. A. (2003). The importance of crew resource management in MC-130P mission performance: Implications for training evaluation. *Military Psychology, 15,* 77–96.

Nullmeyer, R., Spiker, V. A., Wilson, D., and Deen, G. (2003, November). Key crew resource management behaviors underlying C-130 aircrew performance. In *Proceedings of the Interservice/Industry Training Systems and Education Conference.* Arlington, VA: National Training Systems Association.

O'Connor, P., Hormann, H. J., Flin, R., Lodge, M., &Goeters, K. M. (2002). Developing a method for evaluating crew resource management skills: A European perspective. *International Journal of Aviation Psychology, 12,* 263–285.

Panarisi, M. T. (2000). A comparative analysis of internal and external solutions to provide air combat maneuvering instrumentation (ACMI) functionality. School of Advanced Air Power Studies, Air University, Maxwell Air Force Base, AL. Retrieved January 6, 2006 from Defense Technical Information Center Scientific and Technical Information Network Web site: http://stinet.dtic.mil/

Polzella, D. J., Hubbard, D. C., Brown, J. E., and McLean, H. C. (1987). *Aircrew training devices: Utility and utilization of advanced instructional features (phase IV summary report)* (AFHRL-TR-87-21, AD-A188 418). Williams AFB, AZ: Operations Training Division. Project 1123, Contract F3315-84-C-0066, University of Dayton Research Institute.

Salas, E., Milham, L. M., & Bowers, C. A. (2003). Training evaluation in the military: Misconceptions, opportunities, and challenges. *Military Psychology, 15,* 3–16.

Shivers, C. H. (1998). Halos, horns and Hawthorne: Potential flaws in the evaluation process. *Professional Safety, 43*(3), 38–41.

Spiker, V. A., Berkman, A. A., & Hunt, S. (2002, November). *Identifying human factors trends in VS-41 training records* (ASI Tech. Rep. 1450-1). Santa Barbara, CA: Anacapa Sciences.

Spiker, V. A., Nullmeyer, R. T., and Tourville, S. J. (2001, November). Relationship between mission preparation and performance during combat mission training. *Proceedings of the 23nd Interservice/Industry Training Systems and Education Conference*. Arlington, VA: National Training Systems Association.

Spiker, V. A., & Willis, P. (2003). *Analysis of C-130 training records to identify critical CRM behaviors* (ASI Tech. Rep. 1392-2). Santa Barbara, CA: Anacapa Sciences.

Staal, M. A. (2004). *Stress, cognition, and human performance: A literature review and conceptual framework* (NASA Tech. Rep. NASA/TM-2004-212824). Ames Research Center, Moffat Field, CA. Retrieved January 5, 2006, from http://humanfactors.arc.nasa.gov/web/publications/20051028105746_IH-054%20Staal.pdf

T-1 Joint Specialized Undergraduate Pilot Training/Fixed-Wing Transition Syllabus P-V4A-G. (2003, December). Randolph AFB, TX: Headquarters Air Education and Training Command.

Thompson, J. S., Tourville, S. J., Spiker, V. A., and Nullmeyer, R. T. (1999, November). Crew resource management and mission performance during MH-53J combat mission training. *Proceedings of the 21st Interservice/Industry Training Systems and Education Conference*. Arlington, VA: National Training Systems Association.

Vreuls, D., Wooldridge, A. L., Obermeyer, R. W., Johnson, R. M., Norman, D. A., & Goldstein, I. (1975). *Development and evaluation of trainee performance measures in an automated instrument flight maneuvers trainer* (NAVTRAEQUIPCEN 74-C-0063-1). Naval Training Equipment Center, Orlando, FL: Human Factors Laboratory. Retrieved January 6, 2006 from Defense Technical Information Center Scientific and Technical Information Network Web site: http://stinet.dtic.mil/

Walwanis Nelson, M. M., Smith, D. G., Owens, J. M., & Bergondy-Wilhelm, M. L. (2003, November). A common instructor operator station framework: Enhanced usability and instructional capabilities. *Proceedings of the Interservice/Industry Training Systems and Education Conference*. Arlington, VA: National Training Systems Association.

Williams, A. M., & Thomas, G. S. (1984, November). A research tool to improve the effectiveness of performance measurement within the IOS. In *Proceedings of the Sixth Interservice/Industry Training Equipment Conference* (pp. 117–120). Washington, DC: National Security and Industrial Association.

Wilson, G. F., Skelly, J., & Purvis, B. (1999). Reactions to emergency situations in actual and simulated flight. *Human Performance in Extreme Environments, 4*(2), 34–45.

15

A Computational Approach to Authoring Problem-Solving Assessments

GREGORY K. W. K. CHUNG, EVA L. BAKER, GIRLIE C. DELACRUZ,
WILLIAM L. BEWLEY, JESSE J. ELMORE, AND BRUCE SEELY

CRESST/UCLA

Authoring Systems for Assessment

In this chapter, we describe an approach to the design of an authoring system intended to support nonassessment experts in the design of problem-solving assessments. Our approach is based on an explicit representation of how the interactions among problem-solving variables modulate task complexity. We capture this interaction in a constraint network (Montanari, 1974), which allows the specification of important problem-solving variables, the states the variables can assume, and the set of permissible variable and state combinations. An important capability that constraint processing affords is simultaneous evaluation of all the constraints making up the network — implying a "good" design when all constraints are satisfied.

This work is related to the current effort to automate the test design and assembly process. We are addressing the lack of tools and technologies to support rapid development of assessments that conform to good design, particularly for tests that require complex performance. In his reflection on the current state of testing, van der Linden (in press) observed, "Any outsider entering the testing industry would expect to find a spin-off in the form of a well-developed technology that enables us to engineer tests rigorously to our specifications. … To draw a parallel with the natural sciences, it seems as if testing has led to the development of a new science but the spin-off in the form of a technology for engineering the test has not yet been realized."

Van der Linden's (2005, p. xi) observation highlights the current state of assessment development. What is needed is a method to explicitly represent the variables bearing on the design of an assessment such that actual assessments or their specifications can be derived. Establishing the design model as a constraint network will provide traceability between the assessment (instantiated in a particular content area for a particular purpose and population) and the assessment model. By *traceability*, we mean the capability to link the final product (i.e., the assessment itself or its specification) and its particular features (e.g., the prompt explicitness) to a particular set of constraints in the assessment model. Traceability is important because it exposes the underlying logic behind the assessment model and provides a means to evaluate the relation among the assessment model, the assessment specifications, and performance on the derived assessments. Such transparency is a prerequisite for demystifying the test development process and is central to moving toward a "technology for engineering the test."

One of the most important capabilities of an assessment authoring system would be shortening the time required to gather validity evidence for different purposes (Baker, 2002; O'Neil & Baker, 1997). Historically, the development life cycle of assessments, particularly for measuring complex learning (e.g., performance assessments), requires significant amounts of time and resources (O'Neil & Baker, 1997). Thus, an authoring system should have the capability to rapidly generate tasks appropriate for different assessment purposes.

When authoring is applied to the field of testing, additional requirements come into play. With assessment and testing, the key requirement is *validity*, that is, the extent to which inferences drawn from the result of the test or assessment are warranted (Messick, 1995). Linn, Baker, and Dunbar (1991) have described essential elements of validity applied to open-ended assessment tasks. These validity criteria include cognitive complexity, linguistic appropriateness, transfer and generalizability, content quality, reliability, and instructional sensitivity. Moreover, when designing an authoring system (rather than a test, for example), one is interested in the utility of the system for its users (teachers or test developers) in addition to the value of the data yielded by administering tests to students.

In testing, it is often the case that instructors who need to use tests and assessments routinely in their classrooms have little time and expertise to create high-quality assessments of student learning. They may use a craft approach, creating each test one at a time with a wholly new format, scoring approach, and set of cognitive requirements. This approach generally produces tests of low quality with inferences that may be suspect. As instructors attempt to bring all students up to high challenging standards, there is a concomitant desire to test performance in such a way that it stimulates complex cognitive processing (McDonnell & Choisser, 1997; Stecher, Barron, Chun, & Ross, 2000; Wolf & McIver, 1999). Usually, instructors use essays or other extended written examinations to elicit such performance. These types of tests are difficult to calibrate, take considerable time and cost to evaluate, and frequently result in low reliability in scoring. Instructors need a straightforward way to create assessments that require students to demonstrate complex knowledge representations, including declarative, procedural, and systemic knowledge.

Finally, in many training and education situations, a highly desired outcome is a student who can use the knowledge and skills appropriately in novel and complex situations — problem solving and transfer. However, practical constraints and limitations in expertise suggest that testing students for problem-solving skill and transfer will not become common practice without a support structure that simultaneously makes the development and testing process more feasible (i.e., to fit within the practical constraints of the classroom) and provides useful information to the instructor that can be acted on to improve instruction immediately. Baker (2002) elaborated further on issues related to authoring systems for assessment.

Current Assessment Authoring Systems

Prior work related to assessment authoring systems is anchored at three points. At one end are numerous resource Web sites that house existing assessments with unknown quality. Performance Assessment Links in Science (PALS; Quellmalz, Hinojosa, Hinojosa, & Schank, 2000) has been one of the few efforts to adopt a systematic vetting procedure to ensure that the assessments housed at the site meet a set of standards related to validity and reliability. More commonly, assessment sites are primarily warehouses for tasks with undefined technical properties (e.g., Eisenhower National Clearinghouse, 2001). Search and filter capabilities are usually provided to make it possible to retrieve assessments by different criteria (e.g., grade, task type, domain, standard). At the second point are systems that provide the means to build (but not design) assessments. These systems typically exist within learning management systems that have the infrastructure to deliver multiple test formats (e.g., multiple choice, true-false, short answer, and essay). However, the assessments are essentially forms that need to be filled in (e.g., Learning Manager, 2005; LON-CAPA, 2005; QuestionMark, 2005; TRIADS (Tripartite Interactive Assessment Delivery System), 2005;

WebCT, 2005). At the third point are authoring systems that are targeted to assessment developers and teachers (Chung, Baker, & Cheak, 2001; Chung, Klein, Herl, & Bewley, 2001; Chung et al., 2004; Educational Testing Service, 2000; Mislevy, Steinberg, Breyer, & Almond, 1999; O'Neil, Slawson, & Baker, 1991; Osmundson, Jeffries, & Herman, 1998). These systems build in some underlying knowledge about good assessment design (e.g., concepts of validity and reliability) by structuring the interaction with the user using wizards or templates.

More recent efforts by CRESST and others (e.g., the Principled Assessment Designs for Inquiry (PADI) project; Mislevy, 2005) have continued focusing on improving support for assessment design. For example, CRESST developed an authoring system intended to support teachers' creation of assessment mapping to standards, cognitive demands, and subject matter content (Niemi, Baker, & Wang, 2005). Wizard interfaces guide teachers in the specification or selection of critical assessment criteria and enable teachers to design their own assessments by graphical composition. In this chapter, we present an approach that can extend authoring to include evaluation of task designs.

Research Questions

Consistent with the desire to develop methods to support nonassessment experts, we assume the authoring system should provide support that maximizes the likelihood of the assessments conforming to modern assessment practices. We also focus on problem solving because of the difficulty in designing complex tasks. Thus, the set of research questions guiding this work are as follows: (a) To what extent can a problem-solving assessment framework be codified in computational form? and (b) To what extent can a user's design of a problem-solving assessment be evaluated computationally?

In the following sections, we first present our problem-solving assessment framework. This framework defines our view of the major variables involved in problem-solving tasks. Next, we describe how the design of problem-solving tasks can be represented with constraint networks and present a preliminary list of constraints. We then present an example using a simple assessment task and show how our interpretation of the quality of the task maps on to the constraints, show which constraints are violated, and show how changes to the task would lead to a better task (and satisfy constraints).

Problem-Solving Assessment Framework

The assessment framework used in this work is based on Baker and O'Neil's (2002) approach to designing problem-solving assessments using computer technology. This approach first characterizes three types of problem-solving tasks: (a) a task in which an appropriate solution is known in advance, (b) a task in which there is no known solution to the problem, and (c) a task that requires an application of a given tool set to a broadly ranging set of topics. Baker and O'Neil highlight the relevant variables that characterize these types of problems while focusing on complex, scenario-based problem-solving tasks.

Identifying the problem is often one of the most difficult aspects of problem solving (see Vendlinski & Baker, Chapter 16, this volume). The ambiguity of problem identification may be dependent on the prior knowledge that is required of the examinee as well as the purpose of the assessment. An assessment author could adjust its difficulty by either stating the problem explicitly or obscuring it in an embedded setting. Likewise, the information sources that make up the scenario can vary in quality from their accuracy to their credibility.

The problem to be solved can also be multiply masked, in which the solution to one part of the task determines the nature of the next part of the task. An examinee may be required mentally to test various hypotheses for solving the problem under extreme time constraints and demonstrate proficiency in contingency planning to recover from an error.

Baker and O'Neil (2002) emphasized the advantage of problems that are sequential and conditional in nature both because of their fidelity to real-life situations and their potential utility in the measurement of competence. Computer-based assessments can measure an examinee's proficiency using only the task outcome or using process and performance on different parts of the task. In this environment, an examinee can execute an action and be allowed to continue, be given the opportunity to correct an invalid procedure, or be provided with a partial solution to proceed with the rest of the task. By doing this, evidence of an examinee's competence on the relevant skills can be gathered throughout the task.

In the following section, we list and define the major variables and allowable states (in parentheses) that those variables may assume. As will be seen, these variables and states will play a central role in an authoring system and be the basis on which problem-solving tasks are designed. Note that the values for the variables are not intended to be exhaustive; rather, we assume that they are preliminary and subject to modification as we continue the research.

Definitions

Assessment Purpose (certification, diagnosis): The intended purpose for the assessment.

Cognitive Demand (factual, content understanding, reasoning): The type of cognitive processing required of the student to complete the problem-solving task successfully.

Problem Identification

Explicitness (stated, partially identified, embedded, multiply masked): Describes the ambiguity of the problem to be identified. Explicitness can be (a) stated, with no ambiguity, the problem has been identified for student; (b) partially identified, with the problem slightly ambiguous, but problem statement still provides some guidance regarding where to look to identify the problem; (c) embedded, with no guidance regarding which information sources would help identify the problem, and the student needs to look at all information sources for problem identification, and information presented at one time; and (d) multiply masked, for which, like an embedded problem, the student needs to look at all information sources for problem identification, but the problem is revealed as the student progresses through the task, and information changes based on what the student does.

Barriers to getting information (none, allow for barriers): Describes whether the task will make it hard to get information. Barriers can be (a) none, with all of the information sources that are needed to identify the problem made easily available to the student; and (b) allowed, with information needed to solve the problem difficult to access.

Time constraints (external, self-paced): Time demands of the problem itself. Time constraints can be (a) external, with something in the problem space determining the time demand; and (b) self-paced, with completion of the task not constrained by time.

Consistency among information sources (consistent among information sources, allow for inconsistency among information sources): Describes whether different information sources contradict each other. Consistency among information sources can (a) be consistent, with the information from different sources internally consistent; and (b) allow for inconsistency, by which the information from one source may contradict information from another source.

Consistency within information sources (consistent within information sources, allow inconsistency within information sources): Describes whether information from one information source is changing over time (reflecting, e.g., faulty instrumentation, the degree of reliability, or an information source intentionally trying to mislead). Consistency within information sources can (a) be consistent, with the information within a source consistent; and (b) allow inconsistency, by which the information within a source may be changing.

Accuracy of information sources (accurate information sources, allow inaccurate information sources): Describes whether information is correct. *Accuracy* can (a) be accurate, with the information within the information source accurate; and (b) allow inaccuracy, by which the information within an information source may be inaccurate.

Completeness of information sources (complete, allow for partial, allow for incomplete): Describes the degree to which all information sources are provided to student—even those sources that are not useful for solving the problem. Note that this does not address whether the information is inaccurate. Completeness can (a) be complete, with all of the information sources made available; (b) allow for partial information, with some of the information sources made available, and information that is missing may be inferred from available sources; and (c) allow for incomplete information, with information that is missing and cannot be inferred from an available source.

Credibility of information sources (not credible, low credibility, high credibility): The trustworthiness of the information from the source. Credibility can be (a) not credible, for which information should be dismissed or ignored; (b) low, with the information highly subjective and probably needing additional information for corroboration; (c) medium, with information fairly credible, and for the most part there is no reason to question information from this source; and (d) high, with no reason to question the credibility of the information.

Relevancy of information sources (allow for no relevancy, low relevancy, medium relevancy, high relevancy of information source): Whether an information source is relevant to identifying the problem. Relevancy can (a) allow for no relevancy, with information provided that is irrelevant to identifying the problem; (b) be low, with information tangentially related to identifying the problem and the problem could be identified without this information; (c) be medium, with information helpful with identifying the problem but not absolutely necessary; and (d) be high, without the information, identifying the problem would be impossible.

Number of information sources (zero, single, multiple): The number of information sources that make up the problem space. Number of information sources can be (a) zero, with no information sources available; (b) single, with the problem information contained in one source (e.g., a diagram); and (c) multiple, with the problem information contained in multiple sources (e.g., a diagram, graph, text, audio, etc.).

Prior knowledge (low prior knowledge, high prior knowledge): The amount of domain knowledge required to identify the problem. Prior knowledge can be (a) low, with little knowledge of the domain required to identify the problem; and (b) high, with much knowledge of the domain required to identify the problem.

Problem Characteristics

Type of task (execute, fix, change usual sequence, improvise steps, combination of tasks): Describes the type of problem solving required of the student once the problem is identified. Type of task can be to (a) execute, by which the student needs to execute a known algorithm; (b) fix, for which the student needs to carry out the solution; (c) change usual sequence, for which the student needs to use a set of steps that is other than the most common one available; (d) improvise steps, by which the student needs to use a novel solution to a problem; and (e) use a combination of tasks, for which the student needs to use a combination of the other techniques to solve the problem.

Solution Strategy

Steps (explicit course of action, nonspecified course of action): Whether the solution to the problem follows a prescribed sequence of actions. Steps can be (a) explicit, for which there is a prescribed sequence of actions to solve the problem, and typically this is for tasks of type *fix*; and (b) nonspecified, for which there is no prescribed sequence of actions, and typically this is for tasks of type *improvise steps.*

Problem subdivision (required, not required): Describes the degree to which the problem needs to be decomposed into smaller parts to solve it. Problem subdivision can be (a) required, for which solving the problem requires breaking it up into smaller parts; and (b) not required, for which solving the problem does not require that it be decomposed into smaller parts.

Contingency planning (required, not required): Describes whether the solution requires student to have a backup plan. Contingency can be (a) required, for which the solution to the problem may not work because of a faulty assumption or incorrect hypothesis, and the student will need to be able to recover from the error; and (b) not required, for which once a solution is identified, it is guaranteed to work.

Help seeking (required, not required): Describes whether the student needs to ask for help to solve the problem. Help seeking can be (a) required, for which the task creates conditions in which help seeking is necessary (e.g., information is withheld); and (b) not required, for which, if the student needs help to solve the problem, it is because of a lack of knowledge rather than a function of the task.

Cognitive strategies (domain independent, domain dependent): Describes whether a problem can be solved with a general algorithm or domain-specific techniques. Cognitive strategies can be (a) domain independent, for which the problem can be solved with a general algorithm independent of domain knowledge (e.g., trial and error); and (b) domain dependent, for which the solution to the problem requires domain-specific techniques.

Solution Characteristics

Solution space (convergent, divergent). Describes open-endedness of the problem. Solution space can be (a) convergent, with a single right answer; and (b) divergent, for which it is open ended, with scoring criteria (typically judgmentally scored).

Solution correctness (multiple acceptable solutions, partially acceptable solution): Solution correctness can be (a) multiple, with the problem having more than one correct answer; and (b) partially acceptable, for which partially correct performance is used as a measure of competence.

Subsolution contingencies (sequential, nonsequential): Describes how the task unfolds. Subsolution contingencies can be (a) sequential, with the performance on one step of the task determining what is presented in the next step, and information is dynamic and contingent on what the student does; and (b) nonsequential, for which performance does not determine the path the problem takes, and the problem can be solved in one step with the information static and not based on user actions.

Supporting the Design of Problem-Solving Tasks

A basic assumption underlying an authoring system is that the assessment model is kept independent of the domain model at the software level. The separation promotes generalizability across domains by providing a framework from which to derive the task or their specifications. A set of common design criteria increases the likelihood that particular assessment tasks will inherit properties of the assessment model (providing traceability to a model). Presumably, the existence of such a structure (and guidance based on the structure) will result in an increase in the overall quality of tasks for authors with little knowledge of assessment design.

Key technical challenges for developing a domain-independent representation for the assessment of problem solving are (a) identifying the key variables that represent the domain of problem solving with respect to assessment, (b) identifying the set of states the variables can assume, and (c) codifying the relationships among variables. Key technical challenges for developing a domain-dependent representation are (a) instantiating, in a particular domain, the domain-dependent correlates of the assessment variables; and (b) ensuring adequate domain coverage to provide content and context rich enough to exercise examinees' problem-solving skills.

The key technology that underlies our authoring system approach is a constraint network. In a constraint network, nodes are variables that can assume a range of values, and the topology specifies how the variables and values are related (Montanari, 1974). To support assessment design, the constraint network codifies the major concepts and relations that underlie high-quality assessments (e.g., Linn et al., 1991). A constraint-processing engine then evaluates the user's design (i.e., detects constraint violations).

Assessment Design as Constraint Satisfaction

For the purpose of assessment design, a constraint network can be used to represent an assessment model explicitly, providing a description of assessment parameters, the constraints governing relationships among the parameters, and computational access to the parameters and constraints. This representation can be used, for example, to provide guidance to assessment authors as they design assessments for particular purposes under particular constraints. That is, the explicit structure is of high utility because it allows the enforcement of a common and consistent framework. This structure can be leveraged to assist assessment authors (particularly nonexperts) in designing assessments. Assessment authoring support could be in the form of (a) eliciting from assessment authors the problem-solving values specific to the users' purposes, (b) constraint checking that would alert the authors of incompatible relations, and (c) presenting allowable alternatives from which the author could choose.

We have defined the top-level variables and allowable states related to problem-solving tasks and 18 constraints that capture the problem-solving model described by Baker and O'Neil (2002). These constraints specify the allowable conditions of problem-solving task design. For each constraint, the variable and value(s) are listed in the following format:

<category>::<category variable>::(possible values)

A constraint is satisfied if all variables are set to the specified values. A design is acceptable if all constraints are satisfied. Note that the model in Table 15.1 represents one point of view of a problem-solving assessment model. Other perspectives will have different representations and constraints. Although this idea is not new (e.g., see Baker, 1997; van der Linden,

Table 15.1 Constraints Associated With Designing a Problem-Solving Task

Set No.	Constraint
1	COGNITIVE DEMAND::-::(reasoning)
	PROBLEM IDENTIFICATION::explicitness::(partially identified, embedded, multiply masked)
	PROBLEM IDENTIFICATION::barriers to getting information::(allow for barriers)
	PROBLEM IDENTIFICATION::prior knowledge::(low prior knowledge, high prior knowledge)
2	COGNITIVE DEMAND::-::(content understanding)
	PROBLEM IDENTIFICATION::explicitness::(partially identified, embedded, multiply masked)
	PROBLEM IDENTIFICATION::barriers to getting information::(none)
	PROBLEM IDENTIFICATION::prior knowledge::(high prior knowledge)
3	COGNITIVE DEMAND::-::(factual knowledge)
	PROBLEM IDENTIFICATION::explicitness::(stated)
	PROBLEM IDENTIFICATION::prior knowledge::(high prior knowledge)
4	PROBLEM IDENTIFICATION::explicitness::(stated, embedded)
	PROBLEM IDENTIFICATION::prior knowledge::(low prior knowledge)
5	PROBLEM IDENTIFICATION::explicitness::(stated, embedded)
	SOLUTION CHARACTERISTICS::subsolution contingencies::(nonsequential)
6	PROBLEM CHARACTERIZATION::type of task::(improvise steps, combination of tasks)
	SOLUTION STRATEGY::steps::(nonspecified course of action)
7	SOLUTION STRATEGY::contingency planning::(not required)
	SOLUTION CHARACTERISTICS::solution space::(convergent)
	SOLUTION CHARACTERISTICS::subsolution contingencies::(nonsequential)
8	SOLUTION STRATEGY::contingency planning::(required)
	SOLUTION CHARACTERISTICS::subsolution contingencies::(sequential)
9	PROBLEM CHARACTERIZATION::type of task::(execute, fix)
	SOLUTION STRATEGY::steps::(explicit course of action)
10	PROBLEM CHARACTERIZATION::type of task::(execute, fix)
	SOLUTION CHARACTERISTICS::solution space::(convergent)
	SOLUTION CHARACTERISTICS::solution correctness::(single acceptable solution)

(continued)

Table 15.1 Continued

Set No.	Constraint
11	PROBLEM IDENTIFICATION::prior knowledge::(low prior knowledge)
	SOLUTION STRATEGY::cognitive strategies::(domain independent)
12	PROBLEM IDENTIFICATION::prior knowledge::(high prior knowledge)
	PROBLEM CHARACTERIZATION::type of task::(execute)
	SOLUTION STRATEGY::cognitive strategies::(domain dependent)
13	PROBLEM IDENTIFICATION::time constraints::(self-paced)
	SOLUTION STRATEGY::cognitive strategies::(domain dependent)
14	PROBLEM IDENTIFICATION::time constraints::(external)
	SOLUTION STRATEGY::cognitive strategies::(domain independent)
15	PROBLEM IDENTIFICATION::explicitness::(stated)
	PROBLEM IDENTIFICATION::number of information sources::(zero)
16	PROBLEM IDENTIFICATION::explicitness::(partially identified, embedded, multiply masked)
	PROBLEM IDENTIFICATION::number of information sources::(single, multiple)
17	PROBLEM IDENTIFICATION::explicitness::(stated, partially identified)
	SOLUTION STRATEGY::problem subdivision::(not required)
18	PROBLEM IDENTIFICATION::explicitness::(embedded, multiply masked)
	SOLUTION STRATEGY::problem subdivision::(required)

in press), what has changed is the availability of computational tools that make feasible the capturing and processing of the model computationally.

Example Applications of the Framework

In an ideal assessment design, the specifications of the task would be determined by how the information from the assessment would be used. The purpose of the assessment would drive the complexity of the problem as well as define the strategies necessary for students to solve the problem. We present two examples that demonstrate this notion of matching the task specifications with the assessment purpose. The first example is based on an assessment in use from a classroom research study, and we describe potential unintended consequences from the assessment. We describe the assessment task in terms of the variables and values in the problem-solving framework and describe which constraints are violated. In the second example we describe how slight adjustments to the task would improve the task design and satisfy the constraint rules.

Example 1. Mismatch Between Assessment Purpose and Assessment Design

This example comes from an assessment used in a mathematics lesson (reported in Koency, 2000). This example illustrates how the intended purpose of the assessment can be undermined by the interaction between prompt and information source. The teacher's objectives for the unit included students demonstrating understanding of percentages and the relationships among percentages, fractions, and decimals. In this case, the teacher administered the task at the end of the unit to gather information on whether students had mastered percentages.

The Task

At the end of the unit, the teacher gave students a worksheet that showed an advertisement for two different brands of luggage (Brand A and Brand B), which are both on sale. Brand A's sale prices are 25% off the regular price, and Brand B's sale prices are 50% off the regular price. The advertisement showed pictures of the two different brands of luggage, a column that described the type of luggage (e.g., wheeled garment bag or 26-inch upright), warranty information, and the regular prices of each brand. The students were given the prompt (which was written by the teacher), "Which one is the better sale (A or B)?" and were asked to provide a written explanation justifying their choice. Using the variables in Table 15.1, the task can be described as shown in Table 15.2. The major aspects of the task are: (a) assessment purpose (*certification*), (b) cognitive demand (*content understanding*), (c) explicitness of problem identification (*embedded*), and (d) relevancy of information sources (*allow for no relevancy of information sources*).

Comments

The teacher's purpose was to assess whether the students understood the meaning of percentages (*certification* and *content understanding*) by using percentage arithmetic to calculate the savings and make a quantity comparison between two values. The problem asked students to determine which one is the better sale, but the assessment scenario contained a number of irrelevant information sources (e.g., warranty information, luggage features, wheels) that were not needed to solve the problem. These additional features could contribute to determining a better value that went beyond considering the sale prices. For instance, if two pieces of luggage only differed in prices by $10 but the more expensive one was bigger and had a longer warranty, it could be concluded that

Table 15.2 Task Specifications of a Diagnostic Assessment (Examples 1 and 2)

Variable	Value	Comments
COGNITIVE DEMAND	Content understanding	Example 1: Problem requires the student to use content knowledge; incompatible with the vague problem statement prompt (embedded)
	Content understanding	Example 2: Problem requires the student to use content knowledge
PROBLEM IDENTIFICATION Explicitness	Embedded	Example 1: Student asked to identify which is the better sale in the luggage sale worksheet; given the information sources contained in the scenario, a student may use the irrelevant information (e.g., warranty details, luggage features) to determine which is the better sale
	Stated	Example 2: Problem statement prompt asks the student to calculate the savings and use the results to identify which is the better sale in the luggage sale worksheet
Relevancy of information sources	Allow for no relevancy	Example 1: Information such as the warranty information and luggage descriptions (e.g., wheels) is included but is not necessary to solve the problem; having irrelevant information might cause confusion about how to solve the problem and possibly cause a mismatch between a student's performance and the student's actual knowledge
	Allow for no relevancy	Example 2: Information such as the warranty information and luggage descriptions (e.g., wheels) is included but is not necessary to solve the problem; because the problem statement is explicit, allowing for irrelevant information should not cause confusion

the more expensive one was actually the better sale. A prompt that simply asks which is the better sale leaves open what should be considered in determining the better sale beyond computing prices.

In its current form, the task has an *embedded* problem identification and contains information sources that *allowed for no relevancy* given that the prompt could be interpreted to mean the student should consider all of the additional information (e.g., warranty and luggage features) with cost — a reasonable approach given the "authentic" context of the task. An *embedded* problem is appropriate for tasks requiring the cognitive demand of *reasoning*, not for *content understanding*. This is an instance for which the teacher had precise objectives in mind (to calculate savings using percentage arithmetic), which were not clear in the prompt given to the students ("which one is the better sale"). Poor performance on the task could result from misinterpreting what the problem is asking for rather than not knowing the material. This source of construct-irrelevant variance subverts the intended purpose of the assessment, to provide information on whether students have attained the objectives.

Example 2. Correcting the Mismatch Between Teacher's Assessment Purpose and Assessment Design in Example 1

The problem in Example 1 lies in the four incompatible values of the assessment design: purpose (*certification*), cognitive demand (*content understanding*), explicitness (*embedded*), and relevancy of information sources (*allow for no relevancy of information source*). To fix the task design in Example 1, the explicitness of the problem to be identified should be *stated*. An example of an explicit prompt is, "Based on the calculated savings, determine which offer is the better sale." The prompt makes explicit that the decision should be based only on the calculated savings. Presumably, students will apply only their knowledge of percentages (*content understanding*) to carry out the task rather than considering the extraneous information contained in the scenario (*reasoning*). The slight adjustment to the prompt aligns the assessment purpose with cognitive demand (*content understanding*) and problem identification explicitness (*stated*). The revised common task specifications are listed next, and the differences between Example 1 and Example 2 are shown in Table 15.2.

Assessment purpose (certification): Assessment is given at the end of the lesson. Teacher wants to assess mastery of using percentages.

Barriers to getting information (none): Student can access all information sources.

Time constraints (self-paced): Students are not given a time constraint other than the class period.

Consistency among information sources (consistent): Information from sources is not dependent on each other.

Consistency within information sources (consistent): There are no changing values within an information source.

Accuracy of information sources (accurate): All of the information is accurate.

Completeness of information sources (complete): Everything is presented in the scenario, including less-useful information.

Credibility of information sources (high credibility): All of the information in the scenario is credible.

Number of information sources (multiple): Prices, percentages off, warranty information, luggage descriptions, and so on.

Prior knowledge (high): Assessment is taken at the end of the unit, so it is assumed that the student fully understands percentages.

Type of task (execute): Problem requires that the student execute known algorithms to solve the problem.

Steps (explicit course of action): There is a known solution to the problem.

Problem subdivision (required): Student must first calculate the savings and then, given the results, must make a comparison to determine which sale is the better sale.

Contingency planning, help seeking: Does not apply.

Cognitive strategies (domain dependent): Use knowledge of percentages to solve the problem, which cannot be solved using weak methods such as trial and error or means-ends analysis.

Solution space (convergent): The problem has a known solution: to calculate the savings using percentages.

Solution correctness (multiple acceptable solutions): Does not apply.

Subsolution contingencies (nonsequential). Data in the scenario are not presented sequentially; the problem space does not change based on performance on the task.

Discussion and Next Steps

In this chapter, we outlined an approach to the design of an authoring system for problem-solving tasks. A key feature to support evaluation of assessment designs is the use of a constraint network to capture the allowable relations among the assessment model variables. The basic idea is that major assessment and task variables can assume a fixed set of values, and that constraints among the variables define allowable relations or conditions. A task design can then be validated by checking for constraint violations.

Technologies that can support the assessment authoring design process seem particularly promising because of the nature of the anticipated users: nonexperts who lack breadth and depth of knowledge of assessment. A constraint-based authoring system can impose both structure on the authoring process, focusing users' attention on the important variables underlying the assessment task, and verify that user-specified values are consistent with the underlying assessment model. The advantage of a constraint-based approach is a tighter coupling between the assessment model and the instantiated task. Presumably, the more the task design adheres to the assessment model, the higher the task quality will be, which is particularly useful for novice assessment authors.

Although we are confident that the technology component (i.e., constraint processing) exists, the larger assessment issues are whether the domain can be captured in terms of variables and states and whether such technology-enabled solutions result in higher-quality assessments (Baker, 2003). We have attempted to illustrate how problem-solving tasks could be represented with constraints and how constraints could "catch" design flaws, but more work is needed to test the notion of constraints applied to assessment design, the variety of constraints, their interactions, and the implications for designing tasks.

Next steps for this work include gathering evidence on the degree to which our framework yields judgments similar to those of experts for good and poor assessments. Constraint violations should be detected for poor tasks and be absent for good assessments. Such evidence would support the interpretation that the framework was capturing meaningful aspects of the assessment design. A second test is to examine how the authoring system would work for authors of differing backgrounds. For example, one set of comparisons is between novice test designers with and without the authoring framework (e.g., typical classroom instructors). Effectiveness of our system would be evidenced by higher quality assessments created by novices using our system compared to those not using our system.

As assessment design moves from craft knowledge to an engineering discipline, models and tools will be needed to facilitate the systematic development of assessments. We have presented one approach that could be implemented using constraint networks to support the assessment design process.

Acknowledgments

The work reported here was supported under Office of Naval Research Award N00014-02-1-0179, as administered by the Office of Naval Research, and under the Educational Research and Development Centers Program PR/Award R305B960002, as administered by the Office of Educational Research and Improvement, U.S. Department of Education. The findings and opinions expressed in this report do not reflect the positions or policies of the Office of Naval Research or the U.S. Department of Education. We would also like to thank Joanne Michiuye of the University of California, National Center for Research on Evaluation, Standards, and Student Testing, for review and editorial help with the manuscript.

References

Baker, E. L. (1997). Model-based performance assessment. *Theory Into Practice, 36*, 247–254.

Baker, E. L. (2002). Design of automated authoring systems for tests. In National Research Council, Board on Testing and Assessment, Center for Education, Division of Behavioral and Social Sciences and Education (Eds.), *Technology and assessment: Thinking ahead: Proceedings from a workshop* (pp. 79–89). Washington, DC: National Academy Press.

Baker, E. L. (2003). Reflections on technology-enhanced assessment. *Assessment in Education, 10*, 421–425.

Baker, E. L., & O'Neil, H. F., Jr. (2002). Measuring problem solving in computer environments: Current and future states. *Computers in Human Behavior, 18*, 609–622.

Chung, G. K. W. K., Baker, E. L., & Cheak, A. M. (2001). *Knowledge mapper authoring system prototype* (CSE Tech. Rep. 572). Los Angeles: University of California, National Center for Research on Evaluation, Standards, and Student Testing (CRESST).

Chung, G. K. W. K., Klein, D. C. D., Herl, H. E., & Bewley, W. (2001). *System specifications for the design of a knowledge map authoring system* (Deliverable to OERI). Los Angeles: University of California, National Center for Research on Evaluation, Standards, and Student Testing (CRESST).

Chung, G. K. W. K., Sinha, R., de Souza e Silva, A. A., Michiuye, J. K., Cheak, A. M., Saadat, F., et al. (2004). *CRESST Human Performance Knowledge Mapping Tool Authoring System* (Deliverable to Office of Naval Research). Los Angeles: University of California, National Center for Research on Evaluation, Standards, and Student Testing (CRESST).

Educational Testing Service. (2000). Assessment Wizard: Software for designing and sharing student assessments [Computer software]. Princeton, NJ: Author.

Eisenhower National Clearinghouse. (2001). *The Eisenhower national clearinghouse for mathematics and science education.* Retrieved March 1, 2006 from http://www.enc.org/topics/assessment/selections/

Koency, G. (2000). *Reliability and validity of rational number problem-solving assessments.* Unpublished doctoral dissertation, University of California, Los Angeles.

Learning Manager. (2005). *The learning manager.* Retrieved August 23, 2005 from http://www.thelearningmanager.com/

Linn, R. L., Baker, E. L., & Dunbar, S. B. (1991). Complex, performance-based assessment: Expectations and validation criteria. *Educational Researcher, 20*(8), 15–21.

LON-CAPA. (2005). *Computer-assisted personalized approach (CAPA)*. Retrieved September 14, 2005 from http://www.lon-capa.org/

McDonnell, L. M., & Choisser, C. (1997). *Testing and teaching: Local implementation of new state assessments* (CSE Tech. Rep. No. 442). Los Angeles: University of California, Center for the Study of Evaluation.

Messick, S. (1995). Validity of psychological assessment. *American Psychologist, 50,* 741–749.

Mislevy, R. J. (2005, April). *Overview of the PADI design system.* Paper presented at the annual meeting of the American Educational Research Association, Montreal, Canada.

Mislevy, R. J., Steinberg, L. S., Breyer, F. J., & Almond, R. G. (1999). A cognitive task analysis with implications for designing simulation-based performance assessment. *Computers in Human Behavior, 15,* 335–374.

Montanari, U. (1974). Networks of constraints: Fundamental properties and applications to picture processing. *Information Sciences, 7,* 95–132.

Niemi, D., Baker, E. L., & Wang, J. (2005, April). *Moving technology up: Computer-aided formative assessment.* Paper presented at the annual meeting of the American Educational Research Association, Montreal, Canada.

O'Neil, H. F., Jr., & Baker, E. L. (1997). A technology-based authoring system for assessment. In S. Dijkstra, N. M. Seel, F. Schott, & R. D. Tennyson (Eds.), *Instructional design: International perspectives* (pp. 113–133). Mahwah, NJ: Erlbaum.

O'Neil, H. F., Jr., Slawson, D. A., & Baker, E. L. (1991). Design of a domain-independent problem-solving instructional strategy for intelligent computer-assisted instruction. In H. Burns, J. W. Parlett, & C. L. Redfield (Eds.), *Intelligent tutoring systems: Evolutions in design* (pp. 69–103). Hillsdale, NJ: Erlbaum.

Osmundson, E., Jeffries, C., & Herman, J. (1998, April). *DEEMS: A Web-based tool for science and math program evaluations.* Demonstration presented at the annual meeting of the American Educational Research Association, San Diego, CA.

Quellmalz, E., Hinojosa, T., Hinojosa, L., & Schank, P. (2000). *Performance Assessment Links in Science (PALS): An on-line resource library* (Final Rep. to NSF). Menlo Park, CA: SRI, Center for Technology in Learning.

QuestionMark. (2005). *QuestionMark.* Retrieved September 14, 2005 from http://www.questionmark.com/us/home.htm

Stecher, B., Barron, S. L., Chun, T., & Ross, K. (2000). *The effects of the Washington State education reform on schools and classroom* (CSE Tech. Rep. No. 525). Los Angeles: University of California, National Center for Research on Evaluation, Standards, and Student Testing (CRESST).

TRIADS. (2005). *Tripartite Interactive Assessment Delivery System (TRIADS).* Retrieved September 14, 2005 from http://www.derby.ac.uk/assess/newdemo/mainmenu.html

van der Linden, W. J. (2005). *Linear models for optimal test design.* New York: Springer.

WebCT. (2005). *WebCT.* Retrieved September 14, 2005 from http://www.webct.com/

Wolf, S. A., & McIver, M. C. (1999). When process becomes policy: The paradox of Kentucky state reform for exemplary teachers of writing. *Phi Delta Kappan, 80,* 401–406.

16
Templates and Objects in Authoring Problem-Solving Assessments

TERRY P. VENDLINSKI, EVA L. BAKER, AND DAVID NIEMI

CRESST/UCLA

Introduction

The idea that students should understand the concepts they are learning well enough to actually apply them in an appropriate context has been a central theme in both teaching and educational assessment for more than a century (Gould, 1996). Although achieving this ideal has remained elusive for most of that century, the growing presence of computers in U.S. classrooms seems to offer us an opportunity now to make applied problem solving the norm in many educational domains and to change how such exercises are evaluated and used by educators and policymakers (Baker, 2004; Edelstein, Reid, Usatine, & Wilkes, 2000). In fact, educational stakeholders are increasingly asking that students not only demonstrate that they can re-present a corpus of learned knowledge but also demonstrate the reasoning necessary to apply that knowledge to solve problems likely to be faced in future educational or other life pursuits (Herman, 1992; Quellmalz & Hartel, 2004). To exploit these new opportunities fully and satisfy the demands of these stakeholders requires new ways of thinking about what we assess, how we author such assessments, and how we interpret assessment results.

What has not seemed to change in this discussion is what we mean by the terms *problem* and *problem solving*. In this chapter, we take as our definition of a problem the one proffered by Newell and Simon (1972): A person recognizes they have a problem when they desire a goal but do not immediately know the series of actions necessary to achieve the goal. Problem solving, then, is the series of mental or physical actions a solver takes to transform the present state (desiring to achieve the goal) to the final state (achieving the goal). For now, we make the assumption that the problem solver's goal is identical to the one intended by the problem (assessment) designer, but we relax this assumption when inferring goals from the actual solution strategies used by a problem solver.

Although the physical actions of a problem solver are observable, in most educational settings we must usually infer the mental activity either from the physical activity itself, from the problem solver self-reports, or from some combination of the two. Previously, evaluations of student problem solving relied almost exclusively on self-reports provided by the student. Evaluating such written or oral reports of activity not only imposed a time burden on evaluators but also often introduced variables such as student writing ability and self-filtering into our inferences (Mayer, 2003). An additional difficulty in inferring mental action from physical activity was our inability to provide a rich enough problem-solving space to accommodate the support (scaffolding) or tools that a problem solver needed. Because such limitations can have dramatic effects on how students solve problems, they can lead to faulty inferences about student understanding (Gobert, Buckley, & Clarke, 2004; Norman, 1993; Rogoff, 1998). Our challenge, then, is to provide sufficiently rich environments and necessary tools that will allow us to infer accurately how well a student's individual mental model of the world can accommodate, integrate, and be used to explain concepts from the domain of interest (Buckley & Boulter, 2000; Seel & Schenk, 2003).

Modern computer-based simulations offer an opportunity to meet this challenge. First, they allow us to offer test takers a large, but finite, problem-solving space with a given amount of complexity. Second, they allow us to record every interaction a student has with tools in the problem space and how (or if) the student uses each tool. When used in a controlled environment (such as a classroom or under observation), we can further control or account for the external tools and artifacts to which problem solvers have access when they attempt to solve the problem. The actions a student takes to solve a particular problem should allow us to make valid inferences about how a student couples available tools with extant understanding and the depth of that understanding (Vendlinski, 2001; Vendlinski & Stevens, 2000). Consequently, assessment designers can both focus on specific solution strategies, if desired, and limit the complexity of the problem space.

It is these limitations in problem space complexity that give rise to simulations of reality. As an imitation of reality, simulations are designed to replicate the real world or have the appearance of reality without the same complexity, cost, danger, or inaccessibility. Simulations are to reality what the small-scale map is to a 1:1 scale map of the world. As in the real world, however, we would also require that simulations have some capacity for problem solvers to formulate and test various hypotheses or to follow various paths to reach a conclusion and that there be feedback to the problem solver as the solver makes perturbations in the system. Because well-tailored feedback has been consistently shown to improve educational outcomes (Black & Wiliam, 2004), simulations might logically promote the same outcomes.

We view simulations as a subset of problem-solving assessment environments; others include, but are not limited to, written or verbal applications of knowledge to a given situation (Baker, Freeman, & Clayton, 1991); explanations of a problem and proposed solution (Schworm & Renkl, 2006); and symbolic or written explanations of problem solutions, including worked examples (see, e.g., Halabi, Tuovinen, & Farley, 2005; Paas, Renkl, & Sweller, 2003; Renkl, 2002; Sweller & Cooper, 1985). In each case, students are presented a particular problem context, and they apply their extant knowledge to reach a solution or desired goal. Collectively, we refer to such problem contexts as *information sources*, and we see simulations as a special category of information source because they allow students to interact with dynamic information that, through feedback, allows users to formulate or even reformulate problem solutions.

This conceptualization of simulations integrates well with the vision that learning is a transformation that allows someone capable of certain performances to become capable of performing additional ones (usually better) without losing preexisting ability and usually integrated with other capabilities so they can be evoked when appropriate (Newell & Simon, 1972). This presupposes, however, that simulations be used *properly*, namely, that they "help people of all ages make connections among different aspects of their knowledge" (Bransford, Brown, & Cocking, 1999, p. 92) by building on what they know and how we scaffold the task (Vygotsky, 1962). Among other activities, Bransford and colleagues (1999) suggested that this scaffolding includes interesting and motivating the child, adapting the task to the cognitive ability of the learner, and providing feedback. Although motivation is an important piece of this mix (Quinn, 2005), cognitive ability seems to be as important, and knowledge (organized domain-specific knowledge, self-regulation, and problem-solving strategies), in at least one study, has been found to explain almost four times as much of the variance in student learning as motivation (Schraw, Brooks, & Crippen, 2005). The multimedia tools made possible by computer technology now make it possible to design intriguing situations that involve the learner in an inquiry process in which facts are gathered from data sources, similarities and differences among facts noted, and concepts developed.

Although simulations need not necessarily be digital and provide immediate feedback (e.g., actual wind tunnels in aerodynamics or multiyear plant propagation studies in horticultural genetics), one of the benefits of computerized simulations is that tools delivered on a computer can offer students immediate feedback as well as an opportunity for assessors to collect, organize, and analyze the voluminous amounts of data that often result from simulations. The computerized analytical tools this technology provides can also minimize evaluation time. Clearly, however, all computer-based information sources or problem spaces are not created equal.

Our experience suggests that educators search for and select learning and assessment experiences for a wide variety of reasons. For example, in a study (Vendlinski, Niemi, & Wang, 2005), we asked teachers to share the problem spaces they use to teach and assess the concepts of force and motion. Among the various ideas shared was a simulation task that required students to design a roller coaster from the cardboard tubes inside bathroom tissue. After a brief explanation, the teacher confided that she only required students to design a roller coaster that physically constrained a marble through a minimum number of turns. Although the activity was reportedly motivational and engaging for students, the teacher could identify no specific force and motion concepts, standards, or ideas that students needed to master or explain to complete this task successfully.

The overriding requirement that learning experiences be fun and motivational, regardless of their ability to stimulate or assess understanding of core concepts or "big ideas," is a consistent theme in the pedagogical situations we encounter. Although we concur that the motivation (desire) to reach a goal is necessary for problem solving and learning to occur (Caine, McClintic, & Klimek, 2005; Dweck, 2002; Zull, 2002), it alone is not sufficient and ultimately, as suggested, may not be as important as how concepts are organized or how a problem solver reflects on his or her solution strategies. This suggests that it was not the information source (a simulation in the case of the marble roller coaster) that was faulty, but a mismatch between educational goals and a deficiency in the inferences made about student understanding based on the data provided by the simulation. The fact that students could design a track that constrained a rolling marble may have had little to do with the student's understanding of force and motion. As is the case with any type of assessment, data do not equal valid inference. The purpose of the assessment and the inferences that will be drawn must be considered when selecting or designing assessments, including problem-solving simulations.

We have also been involved with educators who have developed learning experiences that both stimulated learning and provided valuable data on which to base summative and formative inferences of how well students had learned and could actually apply concepts. In one instance, for example, civil engineering students were asked to carry out an investigation of a hazardous waste site at an abandoned airfield. The Integrated Site Investigation Software (ISIS) simulation allowed students to develop links between classroom theory and real-world situations and to apply and test these theories. The simulation was embedded within instruction and was comprehensive in terms of both subject matter and the broader context of engineering. Results from the ISIS study suggested not only that student content understanding improved, but also that the students learned concepts at a deeper level. In addition, the students felt ISIS was effective at improving their ability to handle complex projects, allowed them to link classroom theory with real-world applications, and improved their problem-solving performance (Chung, Harmon, & Baker, 2001). We have also investigated the effective use of simulations in middle school and high school science, mathematics, and postgraduate instruction on decision analysis.

These experiences suggest to us a way to assess learning effectively and a method to mediate design through the use of templates and manage inference validity by employing objects. In the remainder of this chapter, we first identify the characteristics of simulations that our experience suggests are necessary to make them appropriate for pedagogical and assessment purposes. Next, we discuss the models and frameworks (templates) we have used to ensure these characteristics are considered. Finally, we describe two computerized instantiations (objects) of these frameworks and implications for the follow-on design of simulations.

Important Characteristics of Good Simulations

There is growing evidence that students learn best when they are presented with academically challenging work that focuses on individual sense making and building the necessary strategies (skills) to solve problems within a domain (Chung & Baker, 2003; Fuchs et al., 2004). In particular, simulations have been shown to improve learning and to provide important insights into student learning if properly implemented (Gredler, 2004; Leemkuil, Jong, & Ootes, 2000; Randel, Morris, Wetzel, & Whitehill, 1992; Rieber, 2005). Unfortunately, as discussed here and in other chapters in the current volume, merely engaging student interest is insufficient to motivate or assess deep conceptual understanding of a knowledge domain or to help students develop rich schema.

Good simulations (like other instructional materials and assessments) have proven difficult to integrate effectively with instruction for a number of reasons. Our experience suggests that effective use of problem-solving simulations and assessments require they:

Support a clearly stated learning goal that is aligned with the overall instructional goal and must be reasonably expected to produce results suitable to both developing and assessing the attainment of this goal. Validity of inference must be considered when designing and using any assessment, including simulation-based assessment (Gearhart et al., in press). For example, we are aware of a simulation that was designed to increase and test student understanding of dissolved gases in the blood. The goal was clear and aligned with overall goals. The students, however, were able to complete the simulation by repeated guessing and checking their solution until they solved the problem. An e-mail to the students' instructor only required students to fill in the parameters they used to complete the simulation — parameters they could obtain directly from the simulation itself. Although a guess-and-check (generate-and-test) strategy might be an appropriate problem-solving methodology, one must be clear that the type of problem solving is clearly identified and can be validly inferred from simulation data. In this case, the instructor inferred that students who successfully completed the simulation had a deep understanding of blood gas chemistry, which was often an incorrect conclusion. Implicit in this requirement is that the content of the simulation or assessment is accurate.

Specify the degree of understanding necessary to solve the problem and allow assessors to accurately differentiate levels of understanding among problem solvers. We refer to this as the *cognitive demand* of the information source or assessment (Baker, 1998). Often, students with a wealth of prior knowledge or those who have been exposed to an identical (or nearly identical) problem before may be merely recalling a solution algorithm instead of developing a solution. This does not mean that simulations and assessments should never address recall, just that they must allow us to accurately discriminate deeper understanding from recall when such inferences are desired or required. A student may have to complete multiple (similar and dissimilar) cases of a simulation or assessment, and assessors might need to evaluate student solution strategies to make these types of inferences (Newell & Simon, 1972). As suggested by the expert-knowledge literature (see, e.g., Anderson & Leinhardt, 2002; Chi, Feltovich, & Glaser, 1981;

Ericsson, 2003; Hmelo-Silver & Pfeffer, 2004; Jacobson, 2001), solution strategies should be indicative of the degree of student understanding represented. In fact, the Modeling Across the Curriculum project has reported (Buckley, Gobert, Gerlits, Goldberg, & Swiniarski, 2004) an ability to interpret student interactions with various simulations as evidence of specific student mental models and complex learning (or lack thereof). Implicit in this feature of simulation, however, is that it engage the student sufficiently to ensure that we are measuring a student's cognitive ability and not the lack of motivation (Quinn, 2005).

Allow for alternative solution strategies indicative of understanding in the domain taught or assessed (Gredler, 2004). It is often assumed that students engaging in problem solving in a specific simulation or problem space will use a single, expected solution method. But, such a constrained process can hide alternative conceptions (including misconceptions) that more accurately represent a student's mental model, inform pedagogical interventions, and improve the accuracy of our inferences about student understanding (Glaser & Baxter, 2000; Stiggins, 1994). The key to identifying important deficiencies in student understanding, however, rests on our knowledge of the features of the performance that are most salient or indicative of the learning about which we want to make inferences (Bransford & Schwartz, 1999; Mayer, 2003). By targeting specific attributes of various solution strategies, we can infer a student's understanding of the concepts necessary to perform that task, including similarities to how experts organize the domain and the common misconceptions novices in that domain are likely to have (Cromley & Mislevy, 2004). If a simulation does not allow problem solvers to use various problem-solving strategies (both domain dependent and domain independent), then inferences about student understanding may be erroneous. Designers must consider these alternative strategies when developing simulation-based assessments and the evaluation methods they will use to draw inferences from the data these simulations generate. We have seen, for example, students correctly solve simulations because they were able to rule out all other answers based on the solutions to previous instantiations of the problem or students who used knowledge other than that provided in the simulation to narrow possible answers down to a meaningful few and then guess at an answer. Unfortunately, neither solution strategy was anticipated, and this led to the even more egregious inference that student understanding was improving as students accomplished each succeeding case of the simulation.

Have a level of complexity that corresponds to the learning goal. As problem spaces and assessments become more complex (either because the problem is virtually unbounded or because the number of items that the problem solver must consider is large), students may change the way they approach a problem (Kirschner, Sweller, & Clark, 2006). In particular, when the complexity of a problem space or a solution far exceeds student ability, students often change solution strategies or even give up on a solution (Vendlinski, 2001). This becomes a serious threat to the validity of our inferences about student understanding, especially when aspects of the simulation are irrelevant to the instructional goal (Mayer & Moreno, 2003). In such cases, an assessor may lose the ability to discern accurately what a student understands and may even discourage learning (Steffe & Thompson, 2000). We may also be unable to distinguish a lack of motivation to continue and an inability to continue that results from a lack of understanding. On the other hand, if the simulation is too easy, the simulation may not discern more sophisticated degrees of student understanding. Our experience, and that of others (Mayer, 2003; Sweller, 2003), suggests that problem space complexity is partly related to the tools available to the problem solver and the number of items a student must remember. A related issue is that an overly constrained problem space may inaccurately represent the content domain and encourage the development of misunderstandings (VanLehn, 1990). Greer (1992), for example, noted that when children learn multiplication using only repeated integer addition, they often mistakenly conclude that the product of any multiplication must be larger than either the multiplier or the multiplicand. This raises consequential validity issues (Messick, 1989). An accurate task analysis should identify the constraints necessary to achieve the desired learning goal (Mislevy, Steinberg, Breyer, Almond, & Johnson, 1999; Steffe & Thompson, 2000).

Satisfy other practical constraints. The time necessary to administer and evaluate student performances on the simulation or assessment must be reasonable, and the differential impacts of time on subpopulations must be considered. Moreover, as solutions become more complex (involving many concepts) or if the steps to a solution can be ordered in many ways, the time required to make accurate evaluations of the ability of a test taker is further increased. As the complexity of the problem space increases, the resulting inferences about student understanding can become so nuanced and complex that they become unusable by teachers or policymakers. In addition to simulation attributes that detail how the simulation will interact with users, there are environmental considerations. Among these considerations are operating platform, software dependencies (including support applications such as Internet browsers, Adobe Acrobat™ or RealPlayer™), central processing unit speed, computer memory, fast interconnectivity, and technical support.

Using the Characteristics to Design Simulations and Assessments for Educational Use

A long history of research briefly recounted by DeCorte, Greer, and Vershaffel (1996) suggested educators have difficulty helping their students develop a deep understanding of concepts because prevalent instruction and assessment methods focus on the "recall of facts, computation, and standard procedures … [and] cannot yield useful information on problem solving, modeling of complex situations, or ability to communicate. … Nor can they provide the detailed diagnostic feedback for the teacher appropriate to the view of the learner as an individual constructor of knowledge" (p. 530). If our vision of education is for learners to problem solve, model, communicate, and develop higher-order thinking (National Council of Teachers of Mathematics [NCTM], 2000; Pellegrino, Chudowsky, & Glaser, 2001), then Glaser (2001) argued that, "Achievement measurement should be designed to emphasize not only content considerations, but also knowledge structures and process considerations that are involved in facilitating competence" (p. 19).

Along these lines, our current research (Vendlinski, Niemi, & Wang, 2005; Vendlinski, Niemi, Wang, & Monempour, 2005) suggests that we can scaffold instructional and assessment task design in a way that will encourage designers (a) to focus their assessment design on student understanding of the key concepts or principles that govern a domain (big ideas) rather than the recall of decontextualized facts; and (b) to develop scoring rubrics and methods as part of their assessment design and refinement that encourages reflection on the purpose of the assessment.

Various researchers have developed additional frameworks for assessment design using simulated tasks. One of the most researched of these models is Mislevy's idea of evidence-centered design (ECD). The research of Mislevy, Almond, and Lukas (2004) suggested an assessment framework that combines task and student models and so allows different classes of student responses to be aggregated with various statistical models to inform both instruction and learning theory. Mislevy and colleagues used ECD to examine real-world situations in which people engage in the behaviors and utilize the knowledge emblematic of a domain. They then determined the types of tasks appropriate for assessment, as well as performance features (including misconceptions) that may be important to capture in assessment. These tasks can then be modeled using templates.

Furthermore, models of student cognition can be interpreted with probabilities of latent trait analysis and probabilistic (Bayesian) networks to determine student proficiency.

Tatsuoka, Corter, and Tatsuoka (2004) focused on the rule-space method (RSM) to discover and measure important attributes of performance involved in domain competence. RSM develops "a one-to-one correspondence between subject item response patterns and the corresponding ideal item score patterns" (p. 905). For some years, brain and cognitive scientists have been investigating similar categorization schemes to explain how humans make meaning from a sensory input space (e.g., Bobick, 1987; Richards, Feldman, & Jepson, 1992).

Finally, Stevens and Palacio-Cayetano (2003) also developed a method for investigating student problem-solving strategies during scientific problem solving; the method is organized around the notions that (a) individuals select what they consider to be their best strategy; (b) people adapt strategies based on changing rates of success; (c) paths of development emerge as students gain experience; and (d) performance improvements are accompanied by increases in speed and a reduction in the data processed. Although each of these models contributes to a generalized framework for the development of problem-solving simulations and assessments, none alone completely satisfies the requirements outlined earlier.

Over 15 years of research in model-based, cognitively sensitive assessments (e.g., Baker, 2002, 2004, 2005) suggests that we must first focus on desired student cognition and learning, then focus on the specific subject matter (content) to develop simulations and assessments that will produce useful and usable information. Assessments that focus on student cognition and learning must address (a) content understanding; (b) problem solving; (c) metacognition; (d) communications; and (e) teamwork and collaboration. Each of these "families of cognitive demands" can be further refined. For example, content understanding can be distilled into the elements of (a) student understanding of the big ideas in a domain; (b) seeing the relationships between these big ideas; (c) avoiding misconceptions about or when using these big ideas; and (d) integrating these big ideas with prior knowledge. This framework has been used to develop performance-based assessments for the Hawaii State Assessment (Baker et al., 1996), the Los Angeles Unified School District assessment program, and the Chicago Public Schools. More germane to this volume, we have also used these models to design and make prototypes for simulation-based assessments for the U.S. Navy and to develop an online assessment design system for classroom teachers (Vendlinski et al., 2004). Others have adopted similar basic frameworks as well (e.g., Accreditation Board for Engineering and Technology, http://www.abet.org).

Typically, measurement experts have argued that accountability and diagnosis should be conducted with separate types of assessments, but for practical, economic, and conceptual reasons, we argue that they can be merged into a single measure with different methods of reporting the data for different purposes (Baker, Aschbacher, Niemi, & Sato, 1992). Findings in recent studies supported this hypothesis. So, instead of building assessments that evaluate if students have "all the facts," we are evaluating both the facts they have and how those facts are organized while realizing that the organizing principles of learners and experts are likely to be different (Chung & Baker, 2003; Doerr, 2003; Hmelo-Silver & Pfeffer, 2004; Mestre, 2000).

Building Simulations

We have used these models to construct a number of simulation information sources that are associated with a key big idea in a knowledge domain of interest. For example, working with associates at the University of Southern California, we designed a rocket ship docking simulation that requires problem solvers to dock a rocket in a number of different bays. Users can set thrust levels (amount of force) for specific amounts of time and can immediately see the resulting motion of the rocket. The simulation designer, course instructor, or the simulation itself can change the mass of the rocket either randomly for each simulated "case" or on a specified schedule, depending on pedagogical needs. The simulation is applicable to many concepts in the knowledge domain of Newtonian force and motion, given a frictionless environment (space), but it focuses on the single organizing principle of Newton's laws in a straightforward manner. The simulation allows problem solvers an almost limitless number of solution strategies while supporting simple (manual) to complex (programmed) thrust schedules. Finally, the simulation interface records the interaction between the problem solver and the simulation for later analysis using artificial neural and Bayesian networks. The simulation allows assessors to determine student understanding of a number of concepts, ranging from accurately predicting resultant motion (vectors) to calculating and applying correct amounts of force given changes in mass or desired changes in speed and acceleration. At its heart, however, the simulation provides data to make inferences of student understanding about Newton's laws.

Based on a number of similar successes with designing assessments around information sources, we piloted an assessment template that scaffolds the integrated framework described here (Vendlinski & Niemi, 2006). The resulting system allows users the ability to intelligently design and deliver a wide range of assessments, including problem-solving simulations to students.

The Assessment Design and Delivery System Template

The Assessment Design and Delivery System (ADDS) is a powerful set of computerized tools that (a) provide utilities for individual teachers, teams of teachers, or other assessment builders to become designers and users of assessments that yield usable information to guide their pedagogy and student learning; and (b) allow designers to embed content, assessment, and pedagogical knowledge to assist teachers in both developing assessments and interpreting student progress. The ADDS is composed of four tools: the Designer, the Assembler, the Scheduler, and the Gradebook, but we only discuss the Designer in this chapter; the other tools are explained elsewhere (Vendlinski, Niemi, & Wang, 2005; Vendlinski, Niemi, Wang, & Monempour 2005).

The Designer acts as an assessment design template and is essential to both assessment and information source development. It instantiates the National Center for Research on Evaluation, Standards, and Student Testing models (see "Using the Characteristics in Design Simulations and Assessments for Educational Use"). Although the ADDS is useful for anyone designing an assessment, its primary intent was to infuse assessment development research directly into the classroom in a format educators found easy to use. The Designer scaffolds a teacher-user's thinking about the assessment that will be most applicable in a particular situation. Although not specifically designed for simulation implementation, the ADDS allows designers to focus on and specify the attributes of simulation design that will make the resulting simulations both useful and usable as assessments. Scaffolding, in the form of a development template, serves both to focus the user on the essential attributes of high-quality assessment and as an aid in searching for exiting assessments. Some of the assessment attributes designers must consider are commonplace. For example, it is essential that the grade-level and linguistic complexity of the assessment item match the general ability level of the target population. This is just as true for information sources that provide the context for the assessment (such as simulations) as it is for the assessment questions that prompt the student response. Even though information sources can be useful in a number of contexts, the question prompt is designed to elicit specific student responses or to focus student attention. Nevertheless, the two must work together. The ADDS asks assessment designers to specify these attributes at the beginning of the assessment design process.

It is, however, the consideration of more atypical attributes of an assessment and the information source that the research cited here and our experiences suggest are key to developing a teacher-user's assessment acumen. Again, this is just as true in designing an information source like a simulation as it is for assessment design in general. For example, one of the most critical attributes in developing a good simulation and a good assessment is the need to specify the depth and type of knowledge a student will need to complete a task successfully. The cognitive difficulty of recalling previously presented data differs greatly from the cognitive demands of explaining an idea or constructing a more novel solution strategy. An information source that allows students an opportunity to explore a problem space and then solve a problem or generalize a solution to a set of similar problems is much more cognitively demanding than one that merely provides formulas students can use to find an answer algorithmically. Although the ADDS accommodates both types of cognitive demands, it pushes assessment designers to distinguish them and then to design assessments to fit that need by asking designers to provide this information as an assessment attribute for each assessment and information source the designer creates. Another key requirement is specification of the standard or topic (big idea) to be assessed. Although some (e.g., Stiggins, 1994) have argued the need for assessment designers to state explicitly the standard or topic to be assessed for some time, such a requirement is only becoming ubiquitous since the No Child Left Behind Act (2001).

Given the importance of the relationship between an information source and a problem space, the ADDS encourages assessment designers to consider exactly how the information sources (such as simulations) will support the inferences about student learning they wish to make from the assessment that is under design. Information sources can be textual, images, animation/video/audio files, or simulations. The design process for the simulations used in the ADDS follows the process used for any other information source and assessment. Initially, the grade level of the student-user is considered, followed by a determination of the domain or topic (or content standard) of interest. It should be noted that, although we have focused on state educational standards here, what is important is that there be a pedagogical goal driving the design and use of the simulation whether it is set by the state, educator, designer, or student-user, and that this goal be explicitly stated rather than remaining an implicit or ill-defined notion (Gearhart et al., in press). Next, the designer or design team must consider the cognitive demands that the simulation will place on the student. In the ADDS, simulations could place varying demands on students. At certain times, the simulation might require students to supply recalled information; at other times, students might be asked to predict the outcomes of activities.

By asking assessment designers to supply key attributes of an assessment item or information source, the ADDS template scaffolds design and focus development on the objective of the assessment from the inception of an assessment. We use the simulation of Newtonian ramps as an example of how this process works in actual practice.

In California, middle school science students explore key concepts of Newtonian mechanics such as the relationship between unbalanced forces and motion and the relationship between force and acceleration. They also are required to understand velocity, know how to find average speed, and be conversant with graphs of both position and speed versus time. These standards, then, form the general objective of an assessment, provide an idea of the developmental level of the student, and help a test developer focus on the cognitive demands an assessment will require. In thinking about what would be required of students in this particular case, the test developer wanted various assessments that would allow the students to experiment, hypothesize, and make conclusions about force, mass, and acceleration in the Newtonian frame (the big idea). The developer also wanted a context that would allow students to collect data, present the data graphically, and interpret the data to find position and average speed at various times in the experiment.

The variety of these needs suggested that a problem-solving simulation would provide an appropriate assessment context. The test designer felt that the simulation information source could be useful for students from 4th to 10th grade because students in all those grades should find it easy to interact with the simulation, and standards in each grade deal with topics addressed by such a simulation. This is not to imply that each grade deals with force and motion. The standards in Grades 8 and 10 deal with force and motion, but the standards in Grade 4, for example, deal with constructing graphs from measurement. We find that encouraging test developers to think about where information sources might be useful encourages them to think more about how big ideas develop over time and are interconnected rather than just testing isolated facts at a single point in students' educational careers. In fact, we have found that, unlike their peers, teachers who design assessments using the ADDS are much more likely to begin the assessment development process by noting the broad idea that they were trying to assess, and their assessments were more likely to have the students address these big ideas rather than merely recalling specific facts from a particular unit of study (Vendlinski, Niemi, & Wang, 2005).

Although we have used simulations with embedded assessment questions, we have found that embedding questions directly in the simulation (or any information source), rather than posing them outside the simulation, can limit the simulation's adaptability as a learning-and-assessment instrument and can often dramatically change the solution strategies of students. In the case of the Newtonian ramps simulation, for example, embedded assessment items not only focused the simulation on a specific standard but also tended to make the assessment less adaptable to various assessment needs (the student was prompted to find the solution antici- pated by a specific question rather than explore and explain the student's understanding of the problem space). Azevedo and colleagues (Azevedo, Cromley, & Seibert, 2004), however, sought to foster student metacogni- tion and improve learning through questions generated in response to stu- dent interactions with the system (adaptive scaffolding). They found that this type of scaffolding not only improved important student cognitive processes (planning to use and activating prior knowledge, monitoring the progress of their solution, and using multiple appropriate problem- solving strategies) more than fixed scaffolding (hard-coded questions or prompts), but also students exposed to adaptive scaffolding learned more declarative knowledge than did their counterparts using a system of fixed scaffolds. Even more surprising, the no-scaffolding condition was more effective than fixed scaffolding in promoting student metacognitive devel- opment (Azevedo, Cromley, Winters, Moos, & Greene, 2005). Moreno and Mayer (2005) also investigated adaptive scaffolding and discovered greater learning gains when they asked students to justify correct answers but not incorrect choices.

Obviously, designing simulations and assessments in this way also meant that our analytical methods needed to adapt to the nature of the assessment, and that all simulations were not equally useful in supporting all types of inferences. For example, although the clickstream data from simulations allowed us to look at the problem-solving strategies used by the students, assessments that required explanation provided more detail on student understanding of particular facts or concepts. Again, the learn- ing and instructional goals of the teacher and the reason for the assessment should determine the type of scaffolding or questioning present within the simulation and the analytical methods employed to make valid inferences. The assessment methods must align with educational goals and objectives (Baker, 2005; Gearhart et al., in press).

The ADDS template guides thinking about the development of infor- mation sources and assessments, but it does not mandate that designers or developers supply every attribute of the assessment. However, what seems to be most critical is not that designers check the attribute boxes in the ADDS when designing a particular assessment item, but that designers consider these attributes when they are selecting or creating information sources (such as simulations) and designing assessments. Moreover, as the assessment or information source is used for more varied populations, to cover other topics or standards, or to assess different cognitive demands, attributes can be changed or new attributes added. As an assessment is used, details of how the assessment and the information source function in practice can be recorded in the Notes section of each ADDS assessment item. In this way, the template serves not only to scaffold the development and selection of information sources and assessments, but also to allow developers and users to organize the information sources and assessments so they can be reused from year to year or across classrooms, schools, districts, and states.

Another aspect of information source selection and assessment design we have found critical to the development of good assessment is that teachers specify or select a scoring criterion or method and have some expectation of likely student responses. This is roughly akin to a task analysis in ECD (Mislevy et al., 2004). Our experience suggests that the very process of developing these criteria encourages test writers to clarify or refine the test question. Rubrics can also be aids for instructional development and content building for teachers because teachers can now clearly see not only what their students are expected to know, but also how they will be expected to use that knowledge. Unfortunately, most teachers seldom keep their rubrics from one year to the next, and so the possibility of long-term assessment "polishing" is lost (National Research Council [NRC], 1999). In our studies with the ADDS system, we found that the system encouraged teachers to construct rubrics, and that when working without the scaffolding supplied by ADDS, teachers seldom did that on their own (Vendlinski, Niemi, & Wang, 2005).

Objects

Teachers need to have not only a deep understanding of the content knowledge and skills they are teaching and knowledge of how students develop that knowledge but also usable materials and strategies for diagnosing student learning and modifying the course of instruction when students are having difficulty (Ball, Lubienshi, & Mewborn, 2001). To address this need, we plan to provide the ADDS with an ability to make "intelligent" assessment recommendations. We will embed two objects in the ADDS to facilitate such a capability. We have borrowed the term *object* from computer science. In that field, an object is seen as a data structure and methods to operate on the data contained within that structure. In most cases, objects can be used by any program that complies with their input and output specifications (reusable); can inherit common data structures and methods for processing data from one or more other related objects (inheritance); accomplish a task in a way concealed from the user (encapsulation); and have clearly stated input parameters, output parameters, and ways of interacting with other objects (interaction). *Learning objects* are similar in that they can be reused in different contexts, interact with different applications, be used for different purposes, and have defined input and output parameters, such as a common data model associated with competency definitions, hierarchies, and maps (e.g., see http://ieeeltsc.org); however, the objects we describe for the ADDS are more properly seen as imbuing the ADDS with the ability to deliver targeted assessment objects. The first object described next manages student responses to tracked assessment items (the input), computes various psychometric parameters based on this input (a method), and passes those data to another object (interaction). This second object then uses its own data to suggest that a student has either mastered a topic or should be delivered another specific assessment item (output). Each of these objects is described in more detail next.

The first object in the sequence is a "gradebook" object. In a sense, this object is similar to Mislevy's (Mislevy, Steinberg, & Almond, 2003) student model. As is suggested by its name, this object keeps a record of available student demographic data, the tasks each student has completed, and an evaluation of how a student did on each of those tasks. This data structure currently exists in the ADDS. We plan to add methods to this object that will give it the ability to update performance records and to report various characteristics of student ability (including Item Response Theory (IRT) estimates of student ability). The object will also have methods to apply the analytical power of artificial neural networks and lag sequential analysis to classify the strategies that a student uses to solve specific types of problems.

The second object that will be added to the ADDS is an ontological object. This object builds on the ECD (Mislevy et al., 2004), RSM (Tatsuoka et al., 2004), and strategic (Stevens & Palacio-Cayetano, 2003) models by situating each problem-solving and assessment task in the context of a domain of knowledge. Based on our work and the work of our colleagues (Chung & Baker, 2003), we have developed mappings (called *ontologies*) of the relationships between big ideas within domains of knowledge as organized by experts. Each assessment task is then mapped onto this ontology based on how well the task predicts that a student understands the given concept. Although the assessment developer can make this mapping manually, we have exploited the power of Bayesian network analysis to determine the relationship between a task and a concept.

In a manner similar to that described by Mislevy et al. (2003), the ontological object uses historical data about the task and students who have accomplished the task to determine the probability that a subject who correctly or incorrectly accomplishes the task understands the concept. By using this method, the ontological object can quickly update the relationship between every assessment task and every concept in the ontology. By communicating with one another and the ADDS template interface, the two objects are able to isolate the concepts an educator wants to assess, the ability of a student or of a student group given responses to other tasks, and the likelihood that the individual or group understands that particular concept. Based on this analysis, the ADDS can then recommend the most appropriate next assessment task to the teacher.

As currently envisioned, the system will recommend the task that most dramatically improves our estimate that a student (or student group) understands a specific concept.[1] Because the Bayesian net calculates the probability of understanding a concept based both on the results of individual tasks and the likelihood that other concepts are understood, the system may recommend assessing a different, more fundamental concept than initially identified by the teacher. We suspect that more accurate inferences of student understanding and ability might be possible by exploiting a number of different indicators (item technical parameters such as reliability and generalizability measures [Shavelson & Webb, 1991]; neural network analysis [Principe, Euliano, & Lefebvre, 2000]; Markov models [Rabiner, 1989]; and lag sequential analysis [Bakeman & Gottman, 1997]).

Summary and Discussion

Our experience developing problem-solving simulations and assessments suggests that the following must be specified at the start of the assessment or simulation design process and be considered throughout that process:

- The simulation or assessment has a specific goal or learning outcome. In the ADDS template, this goal is represented by a state standard and an ontological representation of how knowledge (a big idea) develops in the domain of interest.
- The cognitive level required to complete the task (or each subtask) successfully is clearly stated, and the problem allows the differentiation of levels of understanding. Problem-solving simulations in the ADDS template can have multiple levels of cognitive demand (recall, explain, problem-solving application, make connections to other knowledge, transfer) depending on the questions that wrap the simulation. We have created simulations in which a user could solve the simulation by merely recalling the oxidation states of two elements or memorize what occurs next in an algorithmic problem-solving context. The user's ability to do this was closely linked to limited types of problem-solving strategies. Ultimately, then, "whatever task a teacher poses, its cognitive demand is shaped by the way [they have]

---

[1] For each task associated with a concept, the ontological object will calculate the difference between the probability that a student understands the concept given successful task completion and the probability that a student understands the concept given unsuccessful task completion. The object then returns the task with the maximum difference.

students use it" (Kilpatrick, Swafford, & Findell, 2001, p. 335). As we have suggested, one can make tasks more cognitively demanding by varying the context (information source) and assessment demands (questions prompts) of a task, and these variations seem essential not only to ameliorating misconceptions, but also to preventing them from forming in the first place.

- The problem has associated criteria or methods that an evaluator can use to accurately evaluate the problem-solving performances generated by users. Our work and the work of colleagues repeatedly concluded that specifying criteria as part of the development process is correlated with improved assessment tasks. For the Newtonian ramp problem, there was a single correct solution but no single way to arrive at the solution, and a user's ability to solve such a problem seemed more tied to deep understanding than mere recall of fact. Detailed scoring criteria provide users a metric to discern various levels of performance. Moreover, when educators consider the evaluation criteria associated with an assessment task as part of their choice of an assessment, instruction is improved. It must also be remembered that research suggests that a mix of various assessment formats (selected response, explanation, application, computer based, pencil and paper, real world, or "wet labs") provides the most accurate indication of student ability.

- The complexity of the assessment or simulation should correspond to the learning and instructional goals of the educator or course of instruction.

- Finally, users must consider the impact of external constraints. Timed conditions, connectivity, and hardware (including variables such as the speed of connectivity to the World Wide Web, the computer [and network] operating system [especially Mac/PC], available memory, and support software) can have detrimental effects on the usefulness of computer-based assessments.

Acknowledgments

We would like to thank Drs. William Bewley and Greg Chung for their feedback during the preparation of this chapter and Joanne Michiuye and Bryan Hemberg for editing our work. The Inter-agency Educational Research Initiative supported work described in this chapter (Award 0129406). The findings and opinions expressed in this report are those of the authors and do not necessarily reflect the positions or policies of the National Science Foundation, U.S. Department of Education, or National Institutes of Health.

References

Anderson, K. C., & Leinhardt, G. (2002). Maps as representations: Expert novice comparison of projection understanding. *Cognition and Instruction, 20,* 283–321.

Azevedo, R., Cromley, J. G., & Seibert, D. (2004). Does adaptive scaffolding facilitate students' ability to regulate their learning with hypermedia? *Contemporary Educational Psychology, 29,* 344–370.

Azevedo, R., Cromley, J. G., Winters, F. I., Moos, D. C., & Greene, J. A. (2005). Adaptive human scaffolding facilitates adolescents' self-regulated learning with hypermedia. *Instructional Science, 33,* 381–412.

Bakeman, R., & Gottman, J. M. (1997). *Observing interaction: An introduction to sequential analysis.* Cambridge, UK: Cambridge University Press.

Baker, E. L. (1998). *Model-based performance assessment* (CSE Tech. Rep. No. 465). Los Angeles: University of California, National Center for Research on Evaluation, Standards, and Student Testing (CRESST).

Baker, E. L. (2002). Design of automated authoring systems for tests. In N. R. Council (Ed.), *Technology and assessment: Thinking ahead* (pp. 79–89). Washington, DC: National Academy Press.

Baker, E. L. (2004, March). *Assessing and monitoring performance across time and place.* Paper presented at the U.S. Department of Education Secretary's No Child Left Behind Leadership Summits "Empowering Accountability and Assessment Using Technology," St. Louis, MO.

Baker, E. L. (2005). Technology and effective assessment systems. In J. L. Herman & E. H. Haertel (Eds.), *Uses and misuses of data for educational accountability and improvement.* NSSE Yearbook (Vol. 104, pp. 358–378). Chicago: National Society for the Study of Education.

Baker, E. L., Aschbacher, P. R., Niemi, D., & Sato, E. (1992). *CRESST performance assessment models: Assessing content area explanations* (No. 652). Los Angeles: University of California, National Center for Research on Evaluation, Standards and Student Testing (CRESST).

Baker, E. L., Freeman, M., & Clayton, S. (1991). Cognitive assessment of history for large-scale testing. In M. C. Wittrock & E. L. Baker (Eds.), *Testing and cognition* (pp. 131–153). Englewood Cliffs, NJ: Prentice-Hall.

Baker, E. L., Niemi, D., Herl, H., Aguirre-Muñoz, Z., Staley, L., & Linn, R. L. (1996). *Report on the content area performance assessments (CAPA): A collaboration among the Hawaii Department of Education, the Center for Research on Evaluation, Standards, and Student Testing (CRESST) and the teachers and children of Hawaii* (Final Deliverable). Los Angeles: University of California, National Center for Research on Evaluation, Standards, and Student Testing (CRESST).

Ball, D. L., Lubienski, S. T., & Mewborn, D. S. (2001). Research on teaching mathematics: The unsolved problem of teachers mathematical knowledge. In V. Richardson (Ed.), *Handbook of research on teaching* (4th ed., pp. 433–456). Washington, DC: American Educational Research Association.

Black, P., & Wiliam, D. (2004). The formative purpose: Assessment must first promote learning. In M. Wilson (Ed.), *Towards coherence between classroom assessment and accountability* (Vol. 2, pp. 20–50). Chicago: University of Chicago Press.

Bobick, A. F. (1987). *Natural object categorization.* Unpublished doctoral dissertation, Massachusetts Institute of Technology, Cambridge.

Bransford, J. D., Brown, A. L., & Cocking, R. R. (Eds.). (1999). *How people learn: Brain, mind, experience, and school.* Washington, DC: National Academy Press.

Bransford, J. D., & Schwartz, D. L. (Eds.). (1999). *Rethinking transfer: A simple proposal with multiple implications* (Vol. 24). Washington, DC: American Educational Research Association.

Buckley, B. C., & Boulter, C. J. (2000). Investigating the role of representations and expressed models in building mental models. In J. K. Gilbert & C. J. Boulter (Eds.), *Developing models in science education* (pp. 105–122). Dordrecht, The Netherlands: Kluwer.

Buckley, B. C., Gobert, J. D., Gerlits, B., Goldberg, A., & Swiniarski, M. J. (2004, April). *Assessing model-based learning in BiloLogica.* Paper presented at the annual meeting of the American Educational Research Association, San Diego, CA.

Caine, R. N., Caine, G., McClintic, C., & Klimek, K. (2005). *Twelve brain/mind learning principles in action: The fieldbook for making connections, teaching, and the human brain.* Thousand Oaks, CA: Corwin Press.

Chi, M. T. H., Feltovich, P. J., & Glaser, R. (1981). Categorization and representation of physics problems by experts and novices. *Cognitive Science, 5,* 121–152.

Chung, G. K. W. K., & Baker, E. L. (2003). An exploratory study to examine the feasibility of measuring problem-solving processes using a click-through interface. *Journal of Technology, Learning, and Assessment, 2*(2), 1–30.

Chung, G. K. W. K., Harmon, T. C., & Baker, E. L. (2001). The impact of a simulation-based learning design project on student learning. *IEEE Transactions on Education, 44,* 390–398.

Cromley, J. G., & Mislevy, R. J. (2004). *Task templates based on misconception research* (CSE Tech. Rep. No. 646). Los Angeles: University of California, National Center for Research on Evaluation, Standards, and Student Testing (CRESST).

DeCorte, D., Greer, B., & Vershaffel, L. (1996). Mathematics teaching and learning. In D. Berliner & R. Calfee (Eds.), *Handbook of educational psychology* (pp. 491–549). New York: Simon and Schuster Macmillan.

Doerr, M. (2003). The CIDOC conceptual reference module: An ontological approach to semantic interoperability of metadata. *AI Magazine, 24,* 75–92.

Dweck, C. S. (2002). The development of ability conceptions. In A. Wigfield & J. Eccles (Eds.), *The development of achievement motivation* (pp. 57–88). New York: Academic Press.

Edelstein, R. A., Reid, H. M., Usatine, R., & Wilkes, M. S. (2000). A comparative study of measures to evaluate medical students' performances. *Academic Medicine, 75,* 825–833.

Ericsson, K. A. (2003). The search for general abilities and basic capacities: Theoretical implications from the modifiability and complexity of mechanisms mediating expert performance. In R. J. Sternberg & E. L. Grigorenko (Eds.), *Perspectives on the psychology of abilities, competencies, and expertise* (pp. 93–125). Cambridge, UK: Cambridge University Press.

Fuchs, L. S., Fuchs, D., Prentice, K., Hamlett, C. L., Finelli, R., & Courey, S. J. (2004). Enhancing mathematical problem solving among third-grade students with schema-based instruction. *Journal of Educational Psychology, 96,* 635–647.

Gearhart, M., Nagashima, S., Pfotenhauer, J., Clark, S., Schwab, C., Vendlinski, T., et al. (in press). Developing expertise with classroom assessment in K-12 science: Learning to interpret student work interim findings from a 2-year study. *Educational Assessment.*

Glaser, R. (2001). Conflicts, engagements, skirmishes, and attempts at Peace. *Educational Assessment, 7,* 13–20.

Glaser, R., & Baxter, G. P. (2000). *Assessing active knowledge* (CSE Tech. Rep. No. 516). Los Angeles: University of California, National Center for Research on Evaluation, Standards, and Student Testing (CRESST).

Gobert, J., Buckley, B., & Clarke, J. E. (2004, April). *Scaffolding model-based reasoning: Representation, cognitive affordances, and learning outcomes.* Paper presented at the annual meeting of the American Educational Research Association, San Diego, CA.

Gould, S. J. (1996). *The mismeasure of man.* New York: Norton.

Gredler, M. E. (2004). Games and simulations and their relationships to learning. In D. H. Jonassen (Ed.), *Handbook of research on educational communications and technology* (pp. 571–582). Mahwah, NJ: Erlbaum.

Greer, B. (1992). Multiplication and division as models of situations. In D. A. Grouws (Ed.), *Handbook of research on mathematics teaching and learning* (pp. 276–295). New York: Macmillan.

Halabi, A. K., Tuovinen, J. E., & Farley, A. (2005). Empirical evidence on the relative efficiency of worked examples versus problem-solving exercises in accounting principles instruction. *Issues in Accounting Education, 20,* 21–32.

Herman, J. (1992). *Accountability and alternative assessment: research and development issues* (CSE Tech. Rep. No. 348). Los Angeles: University of California, National Center for Research on Evaluation, Standards, and Student Testing (CRESST).

Hmelo-Silver, C. E., & Pfeffer, M. G. (2004). Comparing expert and novice understanding of a complex system from the perspective of structures, behaviors, and functions. *Cognitive Science, 28,* 127–138.

Jacobson, M. J. (2001). Problem solving, cognition, and complex systems: Differences between experts and novices. *Complexity, 6*(2), 1–9.

Kilpatrick, J., Swafford, J., & Findell, B. (Eds.). (2001). *Adding it up: Helping children learn mathematics.* Washington, DC: National Academy Press.

Kirschner, P. A., Sweller, J., & Clark, R. E. (2006). Why minimal guidance during instruction does not work: An analysis of the failure of constructivist, discovery, problem-based, experiential, and inquiry-based teaching. *Educational Psychologist, 41,* 275–286.

Leemkuil, H., Jong, T. D., & Ootes, S. (2000). *Review of educational use of games and simulations.* Ae Enschede, The Netherlands: University of Twente.

Mayer, R. E. (2003). *Learning and instruction.* Upper Saddle River, NJ: Merrill Prentice-Hall.

Mayer, R. E., & Moreno, R. (2003). Nine ways to reduce cognitive load in multimedia learning. *Educational Psychologist, 38,* 43–52.

Messick, S. (1989). Validity. In R. L. Linn (Ed.), *Educational measurement* (pp. 13–103). New York: Macmillan.

Mestre, J. P. (2000). Progress in research: The interplay among theory, research questions and measurement techniques. In A. E. Kelly & R. A. Lesh (Eds.), *Handbook of research design in mathematics and science education* (pp. 151–168). Mahwah, NJ: Erlbaum.

Mislevy, R. J., Almond, R. G., & Lukas, J. F. (2004). *A brief introduction to evidence-centered design* (CSE Tech. Rep. No. 632). Los Angeles: UCLA/National Center for Research on Evaluation, Standards, and Student Testing (CRESST).

Mislevy, R. J., Steinberg, L. S., & Almond, R. G. (2003). On the structure of educational assessments. *Measurement: Interdisciplinary Research and Perspectives, 1,* 3–66.

Mislevy, R. J., Steinberg, L. S., Breyer, F. J., Almond, R. G., & Johnson, L. (1999). A cognitive task analysis with implications for designing simulation based performance assessment. *Computers in Human Behavior, 15,* 335–374.

Moreno, R., & Mayer, R. (2005). Role of guidance, reflection, and interactivity in an agent-based multimedia game. *Journal of Educational Psychology, 97,* 117–128.

National Council of Teachers of Mathematics (NCTM). (2000). *Principles and standards for school mathematics: An overview.* Washington, DC: NCTM.

National Research Council (NRC). (1999). *Global perspectives for local action: Using TIMSS to improve U.S. mathematics and science education.* Washington, DC: National Academies Press.

Newell, A., & Simon, H. (1972). *Human problem solving.* Englewood Cliffs, NJ: Prentice-Hall.

No Child Left Behind Act. 20 u.s.c. 6301 (2002).

Norman, D. A. (1993). *Things that make us smart: Defending human attributes in the age of the machine.* New York: Addison-Wesley.

Paas, F., Renkl, A., & Sweller, J. (2003). Cognitive load theory and instructional design: Recent developments. *Educational Psychologist, 38,* 1–4.

Pellegrino, J., Chudowsky, N., & Glaser, R. (Eds.). (2001). *Knowing what students know: The science and design of educational assessment.* Washington, DC: National Academy Press.

Principe, J. C., Euliano, N. R., & Lefebvre, W. C. (2000). *Neural and adaptive systems.* New York: Wiley.

Quellmalz, E. S., & Hartel, G. (2004). *Technology supports for state science assessment systems.* Washington, DC: National Research Committee on Test Design for K–12 Science Achievement.

Quinn, C. N. (2005). *Engaging learning: Designing e-learning simulation games.* San Francisco: Jossey-Bass.

Rabiner, L. (1989). A tutorial on hidden Markov models and selected application in speech recognition. *Proceedings of the IEEE, 77*, 257–286.

Randel, J. M., Morris, B. A., Wetzel, C. D., & Whitehill., B. V. (1992). The effectiveness of games for educational purposes: A review of recent research. *Simulation and Gaming, 23*, 261–276.

Renkl, A. (2002). Worked-out examples: Instructional explanations support learning by self-explanation. *Learning and Instruction, 12*, 529–556.

Richards, W., Feldman, J., & Jepson, A. (1992). From features to perceptual categories. In D. Hogg & R. Boyle (Eds.), *British Machine Vision Conference 1992* (pp. 99–108). Berlin: Springer-Verlag.

Rieber, L. P. (2005). Multimedia learning in games, simulations, and microworlds. In R. E. Mayer (Ed.), *The Cambridge handbook of multimedia learning* (pp. 549–567). Cambridge, UK: Cambridge University Press.

Rogoff, B. (1998). Cognition as a collaborative process. In D. Kuhn & R. S. Siegler (Eds.), *Handbook of child psychology: Cognition, perception and language* (Vol. 2, pp. 679–744). New York: Wiley.

Schraw, G., Brooks, D., & Crippen, K. J. (2005). Using an interactive, compensatory model of learning to improve chemistry teaching. *Journal of Chemical Education, 82*(4), 637–640.

Schworm, S., & Renkl, A. (2006). Computer-supported example-based learning: When instructional explanations reduce self-explanations. *Computers and Education, 46*, 426–445.

Seel, N. M., & Schenk, K. (2003). An evaluation report of multimedia environments as cognitive learning tools. *Evaluation and Program Planning, 26*, 215–224.

Shavelson, R., & Webb, N. (1991). *Generalizability theory: A primer.* Thousand Oaks, CA: Sage.

Steffe, L. P., & Thompson, P. W. (2000). Teaching experiment methodology: Underlying principles and essential elements. In A. E. Kelly & R. A. Lesh (Eds.), *Handbook of research design in mathematics and science education* (pp. 267–306). Mahwah, NJ: Erlbaum.

Stevens, R., & Palacio-Cayetano, J. (2003). Design and performance frameworks for constructing problem-solving simulations. *Cell Biology Education, 2*, 162–179.

Stiggins, R. J. (1994). *Student-centered classroom assessment.* New York: Macmillan College.

Sweller, J. (2003). Evolution of human cognitive architecture. In B. Ross (Ed.), *The psychology of learning and motivation* (Vol. 43, pp. 215–266). San Diego, CA: Academic Press.

Sweller, J., & Cooper, G. A. (1985). The use of worked examples as a substitute for problem solving in learning algebra. *Cognition and Instruction, 2*, 59–89.

Tatsuoka, K. K., Corter, J. E., & Tatsuoka, C. (2004). Patterns of diagnosed mathematical content and process skills in TIMMS-R across a sample of 20 countries. *American Educational Research Journal, 41*, 901–926.

VanLehn, K. (1990). *Mind bugs.* Cambridge, MA: MIT Press.

Vendlinski, T. P. (2001). *Affecting U.S. education through assessment: New tools to discover student understanding.* Unpublished doctoral dissertation, Massachusetts Institute of Technology, Cambridge.

Vendlinski, T. P., Munro, A., Bewley, W. L., Chung, G. K. W. K., Pizzini, Q., Stuart, G., et al. (2004, December 6–9). *Proceedings of the Interservice/Industry Training, Simulation, and Education Conference (I/ITSEC) 2004. Learning complex cognitive skills with an interactive job aid.* Orlando, FL: National Training Systems Association.

Vendlinski, T. P., & Niemi, D. (2006, April). *Making simulations educationally beneficial.* Paper presented at the annual meeting of the American Educational Research Association, San Francisco.

Vendlinski, T., Niemi, D., & Wang, J. (2005, March). *Learning assessment by designing assessments.* Paper presented at the Society for Information Technology and Teacher Education (SITE) 16th International Conference, Phoenix, AZ.

Vendlinski, T., Niemi, D., Wang, J., & Monempour, S. (2005, July). *Improving formative assessment practice with educational information technology.* Paper presented at the Third International Conference on Education and Information Systems, Technologies and Applications (EISTA 2005), Orlando, FL.

Vendlinski, T., & Stevens, R. (2000). The use of artificial neural nets (ANN) to help evaluate student problem solving strategies. In B. Fishman & S. O'Connor–Divelbiss (Eds.). *International Conference of the Learning Sciences: Facing the Challenges of Complex Real-World Settings* (pp. 108–114). Mahwah, NJ: Lawrence Erlbaum Associates.

Vygotsky, L. S. (1962). *Thought and language* (C. M. V. John-Steiner, S. Scribner & E. Souberman, Trans.). Cambridge, MA: MIT Press.

Zull, J. (2002). *The art of changing the brain: Enriching the practice of teaching by exploring the biology of learning.* Sterling, VA: Stylus.

Index